GUIDE TO FASHION CAREER PLANNING

Job Search, Résumés, and Strategies for Success

SECOND EDITION

V. ANN PAULINS

Ohio University

JULIE L. HILLERY

The University of New Mexico

Fairchild Books
An imprint of Bloomsbury Publishing Inc

BLOOMSBURY
NEW YORK · LONDON · OXFORD · NEW DELHI · SYDNEY

For my students past, present, and future. My opportunity to work with you has fed my soul. Each of you continuously teaches me; collectively you have become my most valuable career network.
—VAMP

For the past students whose wisdom made this a better resource, and me a wiser person.

To the students for whom this book is written. May you find a career that is as rewarding to you, as teaching is for me.
—JLJH

Fairchild Books
An imprint of Bloomsbury Publishing Inc

1385 Broadway
New York
NY 10018
USA

50 Bedford Square
London
WC1B 3DP
UK

www.bloomsbury.com

**FAIRCHILD BOOKS, BLOOMSBURY and the Diana logo
are trademarks of Bloomsbury Publishing Plc**

First edition *Careers! Professional Development for Retailing
and Apparel Merchandising* published in 2005

This edition published 2016

© Bloomsbury Publishing Inc, 2016

Library of Congress Cataloging-in-Publication Data
Names: Paulins, V. Ann, author. | Hillery, Julie L., author.
Title: Guide to fashion career planning : job search, résumés,
and strategies for success / V. Ann Paulins, Julie L. Hillery.
Description: New York, NY : Fairchild Books, an imprint of Bloomsbury Publishing, Inc., [2016]
Identifiers: LCCN 2015038205 | ISBN 9781501314643
Subjects: LCSH: Fashion design—Vocational guidance.
Classification: LCC TT507 .P357 2016 | DDC 746.9/2023–dc23
LC record available at http://lccn.loc.gov/2015038205

ISBN: PBK: 978-1-5013-1464-3
ISBN: ePDF: 978-1-5013-1465-0

Typeset by Lachina
Printed and bound in the United States of America.

CONTENTS

PREFACE

We are grateful to have enjoyable and rewarding faculty teaching careers with students who have studied fashion and who have then progressed into dynamic and varied leadership positions in the industry. Together, we have worked with thousands of students in the processes of selecting their majors, identifying career goals, seeking work experiences, completing course requirements, and entering their careers. We share a sense of great pride and accomplishment as we watch our former students, who are now graduates, find success in their careers. Similarly, we are enriched by the many industry professionals with whom we have built friendships as a result of networking opportunities.

The enthusiasm, curiosity, and dedication—true professionalism—that our students exhibit have motivated us to compile the information and materials presented in this book. This book contains *their* stories and advice. We hope that our presentation of their experiences will motivate the readers to envision and "write" their own career success stories.

We have observed that the path to a successful career is often tedious. Endless questions abound regarding the "right" way to embark on the career-planning and search process. Our goal in writing this book is to provide a reference guide for (1) students as they initiate career plans, (2) graduates and entry-level employees as they negotiate the transition from student to professional, and (3) mid-career professionals who seek to re-evaluate their current positions and embark on new paths toward their ultimate career goals.

ORGANIZATION OF THE TEXT

Guide to Fashion Career Planning: Job Search, Résumés, and Strategies for Success, 2nd Edition, a thoroughly revised and updated edition of the text *Careers! Professional Development for Retailing and Apparel Merchandising,* offers several features that we want to emphasize. We have updated and expanded the career profiles, which highlight career positions and offer advice from the professionals who are showcased. Each chapter includes boxes that contain newsworthy short articles, step-by-step guidelines, and quick references for relevant topics. A glossary is provided as a helpful resource to aspiring and new professionals in the fashion industry.

Throughout the book, we emphasize the theme of career and professional development. Each chapter contains learning objectives and questions for discussion. Readers should find Chapter 1 helpful in identifying career opportunities. We believe that awareness of a variety of workplace environments and job categories within the fashion industry can provide insight into realistic career planning. In Chapter 2, we encourage readers to assess their own personal characteristics, strengths, and interests while considering the myriad of career paths presented in the first chapter in order to find a fit between the two. Chapter 3 contains information about what it means to be a professional, emphasizing the difference between the terms *job* and *career*. The concept of self-promotion is key to this chapter and new to this edition of the text; this section highlights how to develop your own professional brand. In today's highly technical world, use of social media is a given. We share insights about the ways social media can work for (and against) you. Chapter 4 introduces the professional portfolio—an instrument that readers are encouraged to continually develop and maintain as a complement to career search activities. As readers progress through the professional development process, subsequent chapters focus on professional networking and job searching (Chapter 5), interviewing (Chapter 6), and résumé and cover letter writing (Chapter 7) to provide practical guidance for these activities.

The expectation that fashion students will embark on work experiences (e.g., internships) as part of their studies is key to the well-rounded academic program. Chapter 8 provides a discussion of the value of these experiences and offers advice on seeking high-quality, appropriate positions.

Moreso than ever, ethics plays a key role in career success. We provide an exploration of ethics—in both personal and professional contexts in Chapter 9. In this chapter, readers are encouraged to explore their own ethical constructs and create both a personal mission statement and a personal code of ethics. We believe that it is essential for all professionals to develop an awareness of the importance of ethics in the professional arena—particularly before they enter the working world full-time. Moreover, we urge young professionals to use personal mission statements and ethics codes as supplementary tools in the career search process.

Chapter 10 provides information to readers as they embark on the transition from student to full-time professional. This transition, we have observed, is often difficult for students; it can be a time of uncertainty, apprehension, and fear. By presenting this material for aspiring professionals to read and to consider, we hope to allay those fears and uncertainties and to make success more likely for young men and women entering their first career experiences. Furthermore, we provide insights for mid-career professionals as they consider re-entering a job search and address work-life balance issues. Strategies to achieve continual career success are also presented.

We realize that the order of topics presented in this book may differ from the order in which these topics are covered in academic courses. This book is designed so that the chapters "stand alone" and do not need to be read in progression. Our intention is for this book to be read, shared, and reread as career opportunities present themselves. Thus, we encourage you to keep this book as a reference for the multiple stages and decisions you can anticipate in your career. We believe that readers will find complete information on the given topic in each chapter and in the accompanying STUDIO. Likewise, we anticipate that instructors will find the questions for discussion and suggested activities helpful in developing course assignments that are meaningful for students in their career search endeavors.

GUIDE TO FASHION CAREER PLANNING STUDIO

Fairchild Books has a long history of excellence in textbook publishing for fashion education. Our new online STUDIOs are specially developed to complement this book with rich media ancillaries that students can adapt to their visual learning styles.

The STUDIO Activities that accompany each chapter of *Guide to Fashion Career Planning* are designed to reinforce the information presented in the book and to actively engage students in career development activities. We seek to provide students with a sound foundation as they prepare for careers in the fashion industry. Our *Guide to Fashion Career Planning* STUDIO contains "study smarter" self-quizzes featuring scored results and personalized study tips, and flashcards that draw from the glossary and help support your understanding of key fashion industry terms. We have developed videos that depict best practices and examples of communication interactions in career search settings, such as career fairs and workplace assessment meetings. The STUDIO also contains downloadable templates to get you started with résumés, cover letters, and other professional documents referenced throughout the book.

STUDIO access cards are offered free with new book purchases and also sold separately through Bloomsbury Fashion Central (www.BloomsburyFashionCentral.com).

ACKNOWLEDGMENTS

We are deeply grateful to the people who have enthusiastically cooperated with us to develop this book. We acknowledge the students, alumni, industry professionals, and new members of our network who blog and publish the textbox materials contained here. Without their contributions, this book would not have been completed. We owe a deep debt of gratitude to everyone who took the time to discuss their careers with us. To those who shared examples of their work, we are particularly grateful. Special thanks are due to the Fairchild Books / Bloomsbury Publishing team, whose thoughtful insights and suggestions have helped make this textbook the best possible—particular recognition is due to Amy Butler, development editor, and Edie Weinberg, art development editor; your guidance and support throughout this process have been truly invaluable.

We would also like to thank Amanda Breccia, senior acquisitions editor (Fashion & Textiles), who shepherded our foray into this second edition of the *Careers!* book; your patience and willingness to move the process forward are recognized and appreciated. Additionally, we thank Kiley Kudrna, editorial assistant, for her facilitation of the STUDIO components of the book. We also appreciate the work of all the experts who served as reviewers for our book: Chantel Bryant, Long Beach City College (US); Shawn Carter, Fashion Institute of Technology (US); Kelly De Melo, Art Institute of Dallas (US); Naomi Ellis, Phoenix College (US); Hasan Gilani, Brighton University (UK); Crystal D. Green, Art Institute of Charlotte (US); Katherine Schaefer, Columbia College Chicago (US); and Aaron Sturgill, Ohio University (US). Your advice and direction have made this a better product. Additionally, we are grateful to Cierra Boyd, who assisted with the compilation of the Glossary, execution of the video scripts, and acquisition of the video talent.

We authors also each want to recognize the contributions of the other. It is a joy to be part of a writing team that "works like one." We appreciate and value our uncanny abilities in reading each other's minds! Our strong partnership is something that we hope to model for students and other colleagues—it enables a cohesive final product.

CHAPTER 1
INTRODUCTION TO THE INDUSTRY

I decided to have a career.

—DIANE VON FURSTENBURG

OBJECTIVES

- To provide a brief introduction to the fashion industry.
- To provide an overview of the fashion industry and its breadth of career choices.
- To identify select entry-level fashion and retail merchandising career opportunities in the areas of sales, management, buying, product development, design, visual merchandising, styling, and promotional activities.
- To identify personal characteristics and qualities necessary for success in entry-level fashion career positions.
- To identify prospects for career growth beyond entry-level, and to understand the way foundational career choices lead to later career opportunities.
- To become familiar with typical fashion career paths, and the interrelatedness of discrete jobs within the industry.
- To provide insight from real-world examples of both young and experienced professionals who are engaged in fashion careers.

INTRODUCTION TO THE FASHION INDUSTRY

Fashion is a diverse and exciting career choice—one that is full of endless opportunities for career development. Contrary to popular belief, careers in fashion, which often grow from retail sales experiences, can entail many more options than working in a store. In the United States alone, it takes *millions* of sales associates, store managers, buyers, product developers, merchandisers, wholesalers, marketers, promotional specialists, and designers to sustain this multibillion-dollar industry. In fact, retailing—where fashion meets the consumer—is one of the largest industries in the world. Careers in fashion, retail, apparel, and home furnishings manufacturing provide opportunities for global reach in a myriad of career positions.

Additionally, employment needs are expected to grow at a healthy rate in future years despite the somewhat uncertain economic environment. It is projected that between 2012 and 2022, almost a half million new retail sales positions will emerge (US Bureau of Labor Statistics, 2014). There are over one million retail companies in the United States selling items such as building materials, garden supplies, food, automobiles, apparel and accessories, furniture and home furnishings, pharmaceuticals, sporting goods, books, jewelry, and more. In addition to traditional retail stores, merchandise is available from formats such as catalogs, television, and the Internet. Online retail sales projections call for continued increases. From $7.8 billion in 1998's early days of the Internet, online sales are projected to exceed $262 billion in 2015 (US Department of Commerce, 2013). Long lists of career options continue to emerge as retail formats are expanded in the marketplace, particularly with the emergence of social media. In addition to the employment opportunities with retail firms, professionals are needed to support the design and manufacture, wholesale supply, and promotional requirements of retailers.

Even in an age of corporate downsizing, successful retailers such as Kohl's®, Walmart, and Target continue with vigorous plans for expansion. Retailers continue to develop innovative new avenues to reach customers, as well as implement improved technologies that enhance methods of production, distribution, inventory, and acquisition of merchandise. Internet retailing has become a preferred channel for many shoppers, with catalog, television, email, and social media apps remaining strong supplemental ways to shop. With these consumer trends, exciting new employment opportunities related to retail and fashion are abundant. As long as consumers keep buying, retailers and product manufacturers will have a market and will be looking for quality people to help satisfy those markets.

IS THIS A CAREER FOR YOU?

Whether you are creative-minded, aspiring to work in design, trend forecasting, or visual promotions, or you are business-minded and analytical, there is a fashion career for you. On the retail side of the industry, team-oriented and people-focused positions in sales (both wholesale and consumer) and management are excellent entryways to the industry, as well as lucrative career paths in their own right. Regardless of your specific product interest, preference for a specialty store or mass merchandiser, or curiosity for e-commerce retail formats, there are career opportunities in sales, buying and merchandising, product development and design, trend forecasting and fashion direction, PR, social media, marketing, and advertising. In addition to these major career choices, the fashion industry provides opportunities in related areas, including distribution, loss prevention, construction and store design, and human resources.

Early career experiences lay the groundwork for future positions in executive leadership, entrepreneurship, college teaching, and research. Top-performing, ambitious, and goal-oriented employees are afforded numerous opportunities for advancement. Furthermore, because fashion is such a fast-paced and rapidly expanding industry, the pace of advancement can be quite quick. Although some entry-level positions may pay slightly less than the average in other fields, it is common in the retail industry for successful individuals to double their salaries within the first five years. Keep in mind that because of the diverse and dynamic nature of fashion-oriented careers, many professionals gain experience in multiple paths and experience smooth transitions from one prosperous career specialty to another.

The field of fashion, with its product design, manufacturing, merchandising, selling, and analytics components, offers diverse opportunities for career exploration and growth. Another appealing aspect of the industry is that many times it allows individuals to merge a hobby or interest with a career. For example, many apparel-product–development professionals became interested in their field through sewing and designing their own clothing as teenagers. Successful stylists have long had a knack for "dressing" themselves and others. Just as automobile enthusiasts are apt to find great reward in selling automobiles, parts, and services, and musicians have insight into musical instruments and can therefore be skilled at sharing their insights and expertise with customers, an interest in fashion can springboard into a lucrative and satisfying career. You may have an interest in design or product development, social media, buying, merchandising, sales, manufacturing, visual display, promotion, management, or store planning. Often, experience in one area of retailing, merchandising, design, or product development leads to opportunities in others.

Few career choices lend themselves so well to adaptability, allowing individuals to shift from one facet of the industry to another, as fashion does. Many industry buyers began their careers as retail managers, while account executives often have experience as buyers. Designers often become business owners and leaders of companies. Careers in human resources are a natural progression from merchandising and management positions. The retail industry is composed of countless interrelated career paths, as you will see illustrated throughout this chapter. You may wish to develop a niche in some particular area, or to continue to explore options in several career paths.

Due to the special nature of fashion, an industry that largely employs part-time retail employees seasonally, entry into the retailing industry is relatively simple. Most people in retail management positions today—as well as many in high-level fashion careers—likely gained valuable experience working part-time retail while still students. In fact, Matthew Shay, president and CEO of the National Retail Federation, notes that a retail job is the place many people learn the "crucial basics" of work—how to arrive on time, work productively with customers and coworkers, and pitch in with a team (Shay, 2015). Such experience affords you the opportunity to explore exciting careers in areas such as apparel merchandising, buying, promotion, product development, and design.

As a student, making good use of your weekend, holiday, and summer breaks can gain you a competitive edge that will prove beneficial to you as you plan your career goals and seek internships and entry-level career positions. In fact, one of the most common items that retail managers look for when seeking entry-level management candidates is prior retail experience. This is because a person with prior experience will have some understanding of what a retailing position entails. From a management perspective, this means that you are more likely to be committed to retailing as a career choice. Many people without prior retailing experience do not have realistic expectations of what this field involves and therefore are more of a "risk" for management to hire, especially given the costs associated with an executive training program. For those with prior retail experience, the attrition rate is much lower, training is easier, and advancement is generally faster (Poloian, 2013).

At the 2004 National Retail Federation convention in New York City, H. Lee Scott, Jr., former president and chief executive officer (CEO) of Walmart, included a statement in his keynote address about "what makes retailing fun." He professed that retailing is fun because of the people with whom you work and interact, the great relationships you form with suppliers and customers, and the interesting assortment of merchandise to select and sell. He also mentioned that he is proud that working in the retail industry provides a great foundation for any other career path. He went on to say that about 70 percent of Walmart's management team began as hourly workers—proving that experience in entry-level positions with a company really does pay off in terms of career advancement.

Likewise, recruiters for entry-level fashion and merchandising careers recognize the valuable contributions retail experience provides. For example, Aaron Sturgill drew from his early experience in food retailing as a foundation for his post-graduation management position with Kohl's—which, in turn, was essential work that informs him in his current position as a college leadership center career coach. Kelly Burt Deasy, Director of Trend and Design for Cost Plus World Market, encourages aspiring fashion professionals to recognize the interrelatedness of departments and divisions within fashion companies, noting that retail activities enlighten buyers, allocators, financiers, and designers with essential information they need to do their jobs. (See Chapter 6, Careers Up Close 6.1 to read about Kelly Burt Deasy; turn to Chapter 2 to read more about Aaron Sturgill in Careers Up Close 2.2.)

WHAT'S IN A JOB?

All fashion positions are customer centered. That is, ultimately fashions must be sold—so market forces and customer behaviors inform the professionals who deliver fashion. Many fashion positions fit into the areas of sales, management, buying, product development, promotion, and marketing. With this in mind, this chapter presents many common entry-level positions within fashion, and provides insight into some of the employment possibilities that accompany career growth.

Sales

At the heart of all of retail job opportunities is the common goal that customers must be satisfied. Although not all positions involve interaction with retail customers, the success of each one depends on the customer's ultimate satisfaction with the product. For this reason, it is important for buyers, designers, and promoters to have a sophisticated understanding of the dynamics of customer service at the retail level.

Retail Sales Associate

Retail selling is an essential function of all facets of the retail and apparel merchandising complex. Although retail sales positions are often viewed as a starting point to gaining valuable experience, for those individuals who are people-oriented and enjoy the challenges, retail sales can be quite rewarding. In fact, commissioned sales can provide an exciting and lucrative career.

Regardless of your particular career aspirations, you will benefit from some experience in sales at the store level. After all, the retail transaction between a salesperson and customer is the driving force behind the trillion-dollar retail industry. As a future buyer, manager, or merchandiser, you will gain valuable insight into the retailing complex through store sales. In fact, most companies will require prior retail experience for those seeking entry-level management or merchandising positions. Entry-level store management positions, which generally involve a good deal of sales, can be opportunities leading to merchandising, buying, and wholesaling positions. Robin Forsythe, a graduate of Ohio University, recognized upon searching for an internship the need to have store experience. She felt that to succeed in buying or merchandising at a corporate level she needed to better understand and experience the selling environment. As she interviewed with several larger retailers, she stated her request to be placed in a store and explained why. Robin's insight into her skills, and the fit between her skills and the needs of the retailer, made her stand out in a competitive job market.

Amy Beymer Fulton, now sales representative and product development specialist for Triniti Designs, recognized early on that solid retail experience could give her necessary insight to pursue a corporate merchandising position. She set her sights on a position with The Limited, and sought a retail management position at a store located in their corporate office region in Columbus, Ohio. "The store at Easton was a key 'laboratory' for the merchants," reflected Amy. "I positioned myself there so that I had the opportunity to network with buyers and regional managers when they visited the store." Amy capitalized upon her expanding network in the company and made sure that people knew she wanted to make a move to the corporate office. Her sound understanding of the retail operations positioned her for a promotion to store management in Tuttle Mall, then a transition to senior merchant for Express men's shirts, which she achieved within a short time. Her early work in sales provided a foundation to advance in the fashion industry. Now with a dual role as sales representative and product development specialist, she draws from a broad depth of experiences as her career continues to evolve.

Customer service is the primary responsibility of every salesperson. Customers have come to expect friendly salespeople, and most want to be acknowledged when they enter a store. Customers also expect sales associates to provide product information and to assist them in coordinating merchandise. Many customers desire more personalized service than what they often receive. Successful salespeople recognize the needs and desires of customers, respond appropriately to customer comments and demands, and intuitively offer suggestions that are appreciated by customers. An outgoing personality, good communication skills, and the ability to interact with a variety of people are must-haves for those looking to succeed in retail sales. Of course, a love for the product you are selling always helps, too.

Generally, the training for an entry-level sales position is best done through on-the-job experiences. An effective store management team will provide guidance and suggestions to help their sales staff develop customer service skills. Most retailers will provide written guidelines or manuals on ways to approach customers, tips for suggestive selling, and other general customer service expectations. Additionally, learning about the store product and the target customer will also be included in your training. Successful retailers realize the important role that the sales personnel play because often customers form their impressions of stores based on how the sales personnel treat them. In fact, most times the sales personnel are the customer's only link to the store. All of the planning, merchandising, and product development that the retailer does ahead of time may only be as effective as the sales personnel.

Employees who prove themselves valuable to retailers may quickly enjoy the benefits of wage increases and possibly a promotion to commission sales. Sales of certain merchandise categories, such as shoes, cosmetics, appliances, and technology, typically involve commissions. Increasingly, apparel retailers are offering commissions as an effort to enhance customer service, motivate employees, and increase sales. Successful commissioned sales personnel working at upscale stores can earn an impressive salary and sometimes earn substantially more than those in a more "prestigious" career position, such as a buyer or a visual merchandiser. A *Forbes* article (Wong, 2011) presented Nordstrom, The Container Store, and Sephora USA as companies with the highest paid sales associates. Compensation in sales is directly related to the level of customer service; commissioned salespeople can earn six figures annually.

Manufacturer Sales Representative/ Brand Representative

A wholesaler, or sales representative (sales rep), is responsible for obtaining orders from retail stores for the manufacturing company. Sales reps generally work with store buyers to provide merchandise for the store's customers. Some manufacturer sales representatives are referred to as *road reps* because they are assigned geographic territories and usually travel a great deal to their clients—the stores and buying offices—in that territory. A typical territory in the Midwest may include stores in Ohio, Indiana, Illinois, and Michigan. However, sales reps in the garment district in New York City work from a showroom where their clients (e.g., buyers and entrepreneurs) come to them. All manufacturer sales reps also attend numerous trade shows each year in regional or national markets to sell their merchandise. The International Boutique Show, which is held biannually in New York City, is an example of such a show, as is the *MAGIC* show held biannually in Las Vegas.

The position of sales representative is usually not an entry-level one; however, entry-level experience can be gained in a manufacturer's showroom as a showroom assistant or through an opportune internship. Many wholesalers seek to hire retail managers or buyers when filling a position because those with retail store experience have a better understanding of the buyers with whom they will be working. A wholesale representative with a retailing perspective can be invaluable to both the manufacturer he or she represents and also to the buyers who are the rep's customers.

As a showroom assistant, or entry-level sales rep, your duties usually include general office organization, including reception; scheduling appointments for the sales staff; keeping records; maintaining files; faxing; communicating with buyers in person, on the phone, and through email; and organizing each season's product lines to ready them for showing and selling to buyers (e.g., receiving, hanging, ironing, and ticketing). Occasionally the showroom assistant may even be asked to model garments for clients. Some of these tasks may seem mundane to the recent college graduate, but keep in mind that many employers want you to learn the business "from the ground up." This is especially true in the manufacturer's showroom. The more positive your attitude and willingness to learn, the more quickly you will be given additional responsibility. As this happens, tasks with increased accountability will likely include writing up orders, reordering goods for retail stores, following up on deliveries, and analyzing inventory reports. During market week, when the showroom is extremely busy, you may even be asked to "show the line" (or sell) as needed.

As would be expected, a person wishing to pursue a career as a manufacturer's sales rep should have strong interpersonal and communication skills, sales skills, a high energy level, and an aptitude for math. Sales reps should also be highly flexible and well organized. As mentioned previously, retail experience, and an understanding of retail store assortment planning, is also a definite plus. Generally training for manufacturer sales rep positions occurs on the job. Salaries of brand reps range dramatically, depending on the sales volume generated. Successful and ambitious sales reps earn upwards of six figures once clients are established and accounts are efficiently and successfully maintained. Read the Careers Up Close 6.2 profile, featuring Molly Doyle and Katie Cawley, in Chapter 6 for a real-world look at the manufacturer sales rep position and the key account position (an upper-level sales position).

Retail Management

If you thrive in the retail environment and are successful in retail selling, store management may be just the job for you. Store managers are responsible for intra- and inter-store operations. They must ensure that merchandise is properly stocked and displayed within their stores, and that employees are efficiently assigned and adequately informed to assist customers. Managers organize and supervise people, as well as products, and are responsible for enforcement of policies and expectations of the store or business. The smooth operation of any type of store or business depends largely on the effectiveness of the manager. Although entry-level management positions will vary by type of retail store, they generally include management trainee, department or area manager, and assistant store manager.

Manager in Training (MIT)

Most department stores and many specialty stores require managers to complete a training program, typically called an MIT, that lasts from three to twelve months. Trainees are most often recent college graduates and are viewed by the company as potential buyers, managers, or merchants. Because the competition for department and big-box store training programs is stiff, a bachelor's degree is necessary, as is a high grade point average and prior retail experience.

During their training period, management trainees are exposed to all aspects of the retail business, including merchandising, advertising, human resources, distribution and logistics, marketing, budgeting, and sales. Training usually consists of a combination of formal classroom instruction and in-store training. As an example, the 16-week training program at Saks Incorporated includes the classroom topics of retail math, inventory management, merchandise processing systems, assortment planning, pricing, and leadership. The "hands-on," in-store training covers operations of the store, staffing, visual merchandising, business analysis, and customer service. By the completion of training, the Executive Trainees at Saks Incorporated are provided experience with systems' operations, the buying office, corporate support, and time in the stores (Saks Incorporated, n.d.). Connor Goddard (see Careers Up Close 1.1) completed the Big Lots® Stores MIT program, which launched his career as a Visual Merchandiser. The MIT program included in-depth learning about all aspects of store operations as well as work projects that required team participation and leadership—projects that positioned Connor with both the opportunity to highlight his creative merchandising skills and the experience to learn how to apply those in the context of his company's store operations.

CAREERS UP CLOSE 1.1
CONNOR GODDARD
Visual Merchandiser
Big Lots Stores

Attention to detail and visual expression have long been strengths for Connor Goddard. He has drawn from his strong skill set, his exceptional creative energy, and his natural enthusiasm for learning to launch a career in visual merchandising.

As an undergraduate majoring in organizational communication at Ohio University, Connor ventured toward a career in event planning. After dabbling in areas such as architecture and photography, Connor declared a minor in retail merchandising. In order to further develop his knowledge and interest in the retail industry, Connor continued his education as a graduate student in the apparel, textiles, and merchandising program at Ohio University. Connor held retail jobs and positions within the university in a range of areas. From learning community peer mentor to kitchen specialist at the Ohio University child development center, and from undergraduate teaching assistant to graduate assistant, he developed a strong reputation for his high quality work and dedication to responsibility. He took on leadership roles such as Creative Directing Assistant for the campus-based fashion publication, *Thread Magazine*; Special Events & Concerts Executive Chair for the campus University Program Council; and president of the honor society Phi Upsilon Omicron. During his time as a graduate student, Connor taught, facilitated, and designed retail merchandising and customer service courses. Connor wrote his thesis on the efficacy of consumer education with regard to luxury counterfeit consumption. His study focused on how consumer education affects students' knowledge, attitudes, and behavior. All of these experiences enabled Connor to develop his professional profile in a manner that supported his bid for a corporate merchandising position.

Upon graduation, Connor was accepted into the prestigious Merchant in Training (MIT) program with Big Lots Stores. In that nine-month training program, he rotated through roles in merchandise planning, buying, and allocation. This program afforded him the opportunity to learn about merchandising for a variety of departments—including seasonal, food, and hard home domestics. Connor reflects that his early academic and work experiences prepared him to apply his knowledge to real-world problem solving. Additionally, he developed a work ethic that included careful fact checking, thorough review and revision, and execution of highly refined presentations. These essential skills have enabled him to succeed in his current position. In the typical sense, this program is designed to train candidates to embark in a career as a buyer, merchandise planner, or allocation analyst. However, after presenting four development projects to the Big Lots senior management, Connor was identified as a candidate whose creative intellect would serve well in the marketing department.

As the first MIT graduate at Big Lots to join the marketing team, Connor began his journey in corporate retail as a visual merchandiser. Connor is now a member of the Big Lots' marketing team, where he works closely with merchants to define and understand their core customer base. Connor's responsibility is to interpret customer characteristics so that all visual communications "speak" to that customer. His responsibilities include setting the merchandise in the mock store and reviewing the presentations with the merchandising team. He then uses Adobe Photoshop and InDesign to build planoguides that give the stores a visual representation of what each presentation should look like and how it should be completed. He then communicates these strategies to the stores to ensure proper execution of the visual presentation. He emphasizes, "It is important that these merchandising strategies are executed and communicated well, because every decision we make at the general office directly affects all of our stores."

As aspiring students consider visual merchandising careers, Connor advises them to begin researching where they want to work. Upon graduation, Connor used LinkedIn to connect with recruiters across various channels of the retail industry. After participating in countless conversations and interviews, he knew that Big Lots had the friendly and team-based corporate environment that he sought. Students should be open-minded to the possibilities of growth within any company. Connor's career path has taken many turns even in the first year, and it is crucial to sit tight and not be afraid of a challenge. Sometimes you have no idea how much you'll love a role until you're given a glimpse of how it all works. If you think you're ready for a career in visual merchandising, start reaching out to recruiters and just get a feel for what you could be expected to do. Visual merchandising is extremely hands-on, and that's what Connor loves about his career—you are unpacking samples, setting the presentations, completing tasks upon request of the merchandising team, all while having to digitally photograph, edit, and create the planogram. Then, you're in charge of notifying the stores of what tasks they should be prioritizing. Connor says that it is probably the busiest he's ever been in his life, but if you find that kind of fast-paced environment enjoyable, you'll never have a dull moment in visual merchandising! While his job is hectic at times, Connor loves being a part of a team where everyone truly cares about one another and where they consistently practice the Big Lots motto: one team, one goal!

In general, training periods not only give the company a chance to evaluate the trainee, but can also help the trainee identify his or her particular area of interest within the retail store or the company. Once the training program is complete, some companies may offer trainees options for their particular placement within the company. However, it is more typical for the trainee to be placed in a department or store, depending on the needs of the retailer and the potential that supervisors see in the trainee based on his or her performance during the training period. A promotion to department manager, or an entry-level buying position, is typical upon completion of the training program. For example, at most

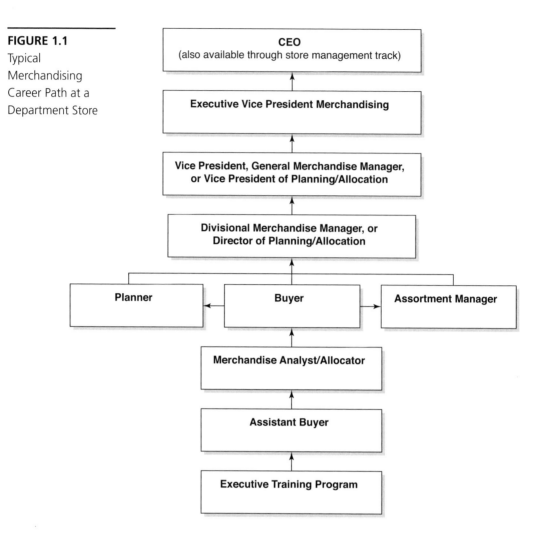

FIGURE 1.1

Typical Merchandising Career Path at a Department Store

CEO
(also available through store management track)

Executive Vice President Merchandising

Vice President, General Merchandise Manager, or Vice President of Planning/Allocation

Divisional Merchandise Manager, or Director of Planning/Allocation

Planner

Buyer

Assortment Manager

Merchandise Analyst/Allocator

Assistant Buyer

Executive Training Program

major department stores, the executive trainee may choose one of two career paths. A typical merchandising (buying/planning) career path is illustrated in Figure 1.1, and a store management career path is illustrated in Figure 1.2.

To be successful, manager trainees will possess strong organizational and analytical skills, good communication skills, leadership ability, computer proficiency, and a high level of energy and motivation. Because of the varying demands of the job, a manager trainee must also be extremely flexible, thrive on some level of stress, and operate daily with a "sense of urgency."

Department or Area Manager (Department Store)

In addition to having a store manager, department stores and big-box retailers such as Target also have managers for each department or area

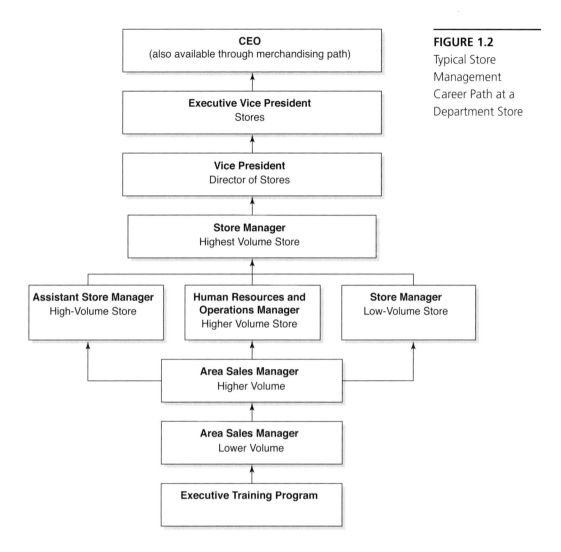

FIGURE 1.2
Typical Store Management Career Path at a Department Store

within the store. The department/area manager position is generally the first position available after completing the management trainee program. However, some companies fill these positions directly by hiring recent college graduates or other individuals with prior retail experience. Like entrepreneurs, each day these managers are responsible for a diverse collection of duties within their particular departments or areas. Varied responsibilities include selling, visual merchandising, opening and closing the registers, receiving, stocking, inventory control, loss prevention, public or customer relations, and the training, supervision, and retention of all associates. Department managers also often communicate with the buyers concerning sales and inventory.

On a store management track, as illustrated in Figure 1.2, the department or area manager is typically promoted to an increasingly higher volume department or area, after which he or she becomes an assistant store manager, then the store manager. However, some department stores give department managers the opportunity to follow a merchandising career path that eventually leads to a buying position. Skills needed for a department or area manager are essentially the same as those for the management trainee position.

At the store manager level, in addition to a base salary, compensation is also given in relation to the volume of business the store produces. Effective store managers can earn attractive bonuses—sometimes as much as 30 percent of their annual salary. In fact, many successful department or big-box store managers earn six-figure incomes.

Assistant Store Manager (Specialty Store)

This entry-level position is offered by stores such as The Limited and Gap. Responsibilities in this position vary somewhat by company but generally involve assisting the store manager in all aspects of store operations. The duties are generally the same as those of the department or area manager; however, the assistant store manager is responsible for an entire store rather than one specific area.

Although the responsibilities of a specialty store manager are similar to those of a department or area store manager, their career paths are somewhat different. Figure 1.3 shows a typical specialty store management career path. Note that this career path does not lead to a buying position, which may be an option in department stores. As shown, a

FIGURE 1.3

Typical Specialty Store Management Career Path

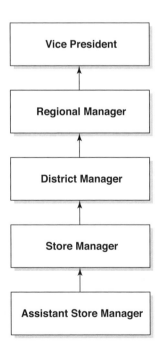

typical promotion for a specialty store manager would be to that of district or regional manager, which would involve overseeing the growth operations for several stores in a given area.

Store Manager

Once you have some experience leading in store environments and have demonstrated your ability to lead people, multi-task store operations activities effectively, and understand inventory management, you may want to seek a store manager's job, or your company may seek to promote you to a store manager. The scope of a store management job can vary widely. In a specialty store located within a shopping mall, the store manager may oversee just one general product category and 20–30 part- and full-time employees. Alternately, the store manager of a big-box or department store oversees multiple departments, with product categories ranging from apparel to grocery, hardlines and softlines, and hundreds of employees.

District and Regional Management

The promotional path in store management expands to district (DM) and regional levels (RM), where the DM or RM oversees a group of stores that include a territory within a given geographical area. The specific roles of the DM and RM depend on the number of stores within the company. For a company with a large number of stores, a district manager might report to a regional manager; with fewer stores, the two roles could be interchangeable. A DM is the direct supervisor of the store managers. Usually, the district or regional office is housed within a centrally located store in the division. DM's are facilitators between the corporate offices and the individual store managers. For both DM and RM positions, strong leadership skills, a breadth of retail management experience, good knowledge of budgeting and math, and an understanding of employee supervision are necessary. DM and RM positions require travel and flexible working hours to ensure adequate coverage of the region.

Corporate Headquarters

Human Resources

Many in-store retail management positions lend themselves to career growth in Human Resources (HR). Some large store retailers have HR divisions within the store itself; other companies have HR units that operate within the corporate office. Virtually all store management positions include human resources components—on- and off-boarding, training, and employee evaluation. Human resources operations typically go hand in hand with collegiate recruiting—attending career fairs and reaching out to Career Centers and college instructors who can connect their students with prospective jobs. Comprehensive HR divisions ensure compliance with the company values and legal hiring practices. Diversity and inclusion activities generally fall under the HR umbrella—and are important components for building strong employment teams as well as ensuring that retail companies effectively serve consumers across demographic groups. Target has long been recognized for its strong support of diversity and inclusion; its website contains the following statement: *When we put our unique talents and perspectives together, we build a better experience for every guest.* See Beth Bonarrigo's Careers Up Close 5.1 profile in Chapter 5 to read more about the work of an HR specialist.

Buying Office

Many merchandising students aspire to become buyers. This rewarding, yet demanding, career choice is not an entry-level position. The role of a buyer is key to the success of a retailer, and the buyer's judgment is constantly scrutinized as each season progresses. The buyer uses forecasting ability and analyzes trends to produce an assortment of merchandise that appeals to the targeted market of the store. With advances in technology and an increased emphasis on private label merchandise, the buyer's responsibilities continue to evolve. Although many buyers today still buy merchandise from well-recognized name-brand manufacturers, many also find themselves involved in the product design and development of the retailer's exclusive private label merchandise. Professional skills that are absolutely essential for buyers include negotiation, organization, analysis, and a strong math aptitude. Two of the more traditional and common entry-level opportunities that lead to a career as a buyer are those of an allocation analyst or planner or an assistant buyer. MacKenzie King's Careers Up Close 8.3 profile in Chapter 8 presents insight into work in a buying office.

Allocation Analyst or Planner

This position is commonly the starting point for a career in buying. The primary purpose of an allocation analyst—or a planner, as this position may also be titled—is to control inventories and allocations for a particular department or classification of products. The goal of the allocation analyst is to ensure that inventory at the retail level meets customer demands in order for the company to meet sales and profit plans. Primary responsibilities for the allocator include developing and reviewing actual and forecasted sales to determine distribution models, timing and quantities of purchases, and initial inventory demand quantities.

The allocation analyst or planner continually reviews data generated at the retail level to identify specific market segments and store needs, which will drive distribution orders. It is the analyst who ensures that items are shipped at the right time, in the right quantity, and in the right assortment. Related responsibilities include analyzing and reporting on test merchandise and promotional activities, preparing store assortment plans based on trends, reviewing sales projections to determine merchandise flow through the company distribution center, and moving merchandise between stores as needed to meet customer demand. The allocation analyst must possess strong organizational and communication skills because he or she maintains effective documented communication among many areas of the company, including planning, allocation, distribution, buying, and the stores.

At the basic level, the allocation analyst's goal is to prevent any out-of-stock situations at the retail level, which is a primary cause of customer dissatisfaction. Chances are that if you have ever gone shopping for a particular item and found that the item you wanted was out of stock, the company's allocator or planner is to blame. Typically, an allocation analyst can follow one of two career paths: one that leads to store planning, the other that leads to buying. See Colleen Clemans' profile in Careers Up Close 1.2 for one successful path through allocation.

CAREERS UP CLOSE 1.2
COLLEEN CLEMANS
E-commerce Site Merchandiser
JCPenney®

Years in merchandise planning and allocation prepared Colleen Clemans with the experience she needed to move into her current position as E-commerce Site Merchandiser with JCPenney®. In fact, Colleen has steadily progressed through her fifteen-year career, capitalizing on opportunities for growth and new responsibilities.

Upon graduation from Ohio University, where she earned a bachelor's degree in retail merchandising with a minor in business administration, Colleen joined Lane Bryant's corporate headquarters as a Production Assistant. Her product knowledge, retail math skills, and strong commitment to customer service acquired during college, along with her time as a store sales associate during summer and winter breaks, prepared her for an entry-level corporate office position. As a Production Assistant, she was responsible for item set-up and purchase order creation for Lane Bryant's stores. In this position, Colleen was able to draw on her customer service experience and work with various internal and external customers, including marketing, supply chain, vendors, and product development. Early in her career, Colleen's interest in the ways fashion products moved from idea conception through production and transportation to reach the consumer fueled her goal to work in corporate environments. Colleen reflects, "I was fascinated by all the moving parts and the number of people behind the scenes necessary to create great product."

Within a year, Colleen's strong analytical, organization, and communication skills positioned her for the role of Store Allocator in women's apparel at JCPenney®. This career move also enabled her geographic move from Ohio to Texas, where she worked at the Plano corporate headquarters. Colleen quickly demonstrated her capacity for leadership, gaining promotions and considerable experience in planning and allocation, with increasing responsibilities.

Three years later, when a job as Merchandise Planner and Allocator became available within the Zale Corporation, Colleen was well positioned to expand her experiences in that position, which was located in Irving, Texas. Colleen's professionalism and strong established relationships within JCPenney® supported ongoing networking and enabled her to be rehired a few years later.

When she returned to the JCPenney® headquarters, Colleen quickly demonstrated her capacity for leadership, gaining promotions from Senior Allocator in tabletop and innovative gifts to Project Manager for the home division. With each promotion, Colleen took on additional responsibilities with financial management, employee training and development, and project leadership. Throughout the first ten years that Colleen spent with JCPenney®, retailing's evolution with technology was stunning, with tremendous growth in consumer use of the Internet for shopping and information

gathering. The new retail technologies forged career opportunities, such as Colleen's position from 2010–2013 as E-commerce Business Analyst for window coverings. As E-commerce Business Analyst, Colleen was responsible for establishing sales plans and receipt flow by program in order to maintain stock levels for customer fulfillment and achieve sales and profit goals. Colleen notes that her early training in apparel product development, merchandising, and allocation provided a foundation for understanding forecasting and production of merchandise. In addition to managing product assortments, Colleen oversaw training and development of new employees and trainees. This motivated her toward creative problem solving and continuous quality improvement strategies.

Currently, Colleen holds the position of E-commerce Site Merchandiser for bedding and bath. In this job, she draws from previous experiences and also faces new challenges on a daily basis. "This position allows me to utilize my analytical, creative problem solving, organizational and communication skills. I am able to directly impact the online customer shopping experience." As a Site Merchandiser, Colleen is responsible for improving the customer experience by updating site content, analyzing customer shopping behavior, and modifying navigation to enhance the customer experience. This position enables her to understand the customers better and support their needs, which change on a daily basis. In this position she interacts with many cross-functional teams, including Marketing, Buyers, Planning, Allocation, Vendors, Copy, Site Operations, and SEO (search engine optimization).

"Learning as much as I can, getting a mentor, shadowing other associates, asking a lot of questions and learning how my job impacts everyone in the product lifecycle has helped me be successful throughout my career."

Assistant/Associate Buyer

Assistant buyers are directly responsible to the buyer, and therefore must be familiar with the buyer's role in a given organization. Sometimes the entry-level buying position is actually the associate buyer role; in larger organizations, the associate buyer position is a promotion from assistant buyer and reports to the buyer in much the same way an assistant buyer does. As the title suggests, the primary purpose is to provide assistance to the buyer. Responsibilities of the assistant buyer will most likely include analyzing weekly business reports with the buying team, preparing and expediting purchase orders, competitive shopping, inspecting merchandise for quality, assisting allocators with new merchandise distribution, and sourcing new products. Identification of top-selling items and items that are not moving is another important task. An assistant buyer communicates with vendors as well as with the buyer and often must serve as mediator between the two. In this capacity, the assistant buyer may be required to place reorders of merchandise, negotiate with vendors for price and delivery, confirm orders with vendors, and advise the buyer of any potential problems with the orders. Organization of the buyer's files and knowledge of the buyer's goals are other essential duties required of an assistant buyer. If the development of private label merchandise is involved, the buyer's duties may become more closely aligned with those of a technical designer, which are explained later in this chapter.

When asked about the skills necessary for success in this position, an assistant buyer for a nationwide specialty store chain replied that first and foremost an assistant buyer must possess patience. This is, he claims, because assistant buyers must often calmly communicate with angry or frustrated vendors and buyers. Furthermore, assistant buyers must be able to take criticism well and keep calm when things seem to be in crisis. It is important to be adaptable, because one minute you may be assigned one task and two minutes later asked to do something else. Personal qualities that are helpful for assistant buyers include self-confidence, creativity, and an ability to look at problems objectively. Buyers, he continued, must be able to see the needs of the target market and not be swayed by their own taste in apparel: "It might not be your style, but it may suit thousands of people just right!"

Buyer

The buyer is typically the highest-ranking merchant, and is responsible for a staff of people who contribute to the buying operation. Career advancement through buying ranks is typically directly related to the dollar volume of the buyer's responsibility. For example, an associate buyer in the juniors fashion division who is a candidate for a promotion to buyer would likely be assigned a lower-volume category such as boys. Promotions occur as buyers move to positions with greater monetary responsibilities.

Design and Product Development

With the emergence of private label merchandise in most department and specialty stores, design and product development career opportunities have grown. Merchandise that traditionally had been designed and then produced exclusively by manufacturing companies is now often influenced and developed for the specific needs of retailers. Although designing in the traditional sense is a popular and feasible career option, many retailers offer opportunities for design-oriented employees to work directly with manufacturers to produce unique and cost-effective private label merchandise. Typical entry-level positions in design and product development include those of technical designer and quality assurance assistant.

Design Assistant

A good entry-level position in the design field is as a design assistant. While the direction of the line is led by the designer—and informed by the trend team—it truly takes a team effort to pull a season of fashions together. Design assistants do a lot of research of fabrics, styles, and current trends so that they are equipped to contribute to the development of product samples. Traveling to tradeshows and factories creates opportunities for the design assistant to serve as a liaison between the designer and the production and distribution processes. Design assistants are integral to showing the lines—working to produce fashion shows and participate in fashion week activities promoting the lines.

Technical Designer

The technical designer is the person who takes the designer's idea and translates it into the actual product. A primary responsibility in doing so is ensuring that the product can be manufactured efficiently and within a particular budget. Because the cost of making the product determines the retail price, technical designers need to know how much their particular customers are willing to pay, and whether that price will be enough for the retailer to make a profit. The technical designer helps develop a prototype from which subsequent products are made; at the entry-level position as an assistant to the technical designer, your training will be multifaceted. For example, in the apparel industry, this would involve learning about fabrics and findings, fitting techniques, pattern making, garment construction, sizing, specification writing, and computer applications. Once promoted to a technical designer, your primary responsibility would be the development of a particular category of clothing, such as ladies' knit shirts or men's sport jackets. Technical designers are found at recognized brand-name manufacturers (e.g., Levi's®) as well as major retailers, where they develop private label merchandise (e.g., Sonoma for Kohl's®). According to the website www.wetfeet.com, buyers who have product development and private label experience will be in a position for which demand will grow.

Corporate Designer

Creative direction is ultimately the responsibility of the designer, who coordinates the ideas of design assistants and trend specialists to refine and finalize the fashion products to be developed for a given season or line.

Product Development Specialist

Many fashion retailers and brands rely on product development teams to get designs to the development and retail stages of distribution. Rather than design unique patterns, professionals in product development work closely with manufacturers to replicate or modify existing design concepts so that the merchandise lines can be produced. Product development specialists work very similarly to designers in terms of conception and vision for the fashions that will be created; their role is focused primarily on detailed specifications of the garments so that consistent mass production of the designs is coordinated with one or more factories. The production of fashion garments for the purpose of getting the merchandise to the market (retailer) is the key goal. Typically, private label and mass merchandisers employ product development teams who follow fashion trends and ensure garment production of merchandise that will fit the needs and desires of their customers.

Quality Assurance

Quality Assurance Assistant

With the vast assortment of merchandise being produced for retailers all over the world, quality assurance is an important issue. Customers expect that merchandise they purchase will hold up to normal use and will perform as expected. Retailers and product developers, therefore, must implement quality assurance programs to reduce the chances of having large amounts of merchandise returned due to shoddy manufacture. Quality assurance personnel work to guarantee the quality of the goods their firms produce. Working in a laboratory setting, their responsibilities include verifying dimensions, color, weight, texture, strength, or other physical characteristics of their products. Soft goods must be tested to determine whether they will shrink or fall apart in the wash, and whether they are colorfast. Depending on the product being produced, other tests may include those for flammability, moisture resistance, seam strength, and wrinkle resistance. Often, in addition to the material used for clothing products, a variety of findings—zippers, thread, and buttons—must also be tested. For example, quality assurance may conduct tests to determine what happens to the buttons on a garment after repeated washing and ironing.

One student recalled a quality assurance problem that arose during her internship as a merchandise coordinator. A flannel sleepwear item had been designed with pant legs each of a different fabric. A customer, she noted, returned a pair because one leg had shrunk more than the other. This is a typical quality assurance matter. The challenge for employees of the quality assurance department is to identify and solve problems before the merchandise is distributed for sale in the stores.

The person seeking to work in a quality assurance position should possess knowledge of the performance properties of various fibers and textiles and also have an understanding of garment construction techniques. Attention to detail and good communication skills are of utmost importance, especially when conducting and reporting on product testing.

Social Compliance Manager/Auditor

The complexity of fashion product production—with factories concentrated in places such as China, Bangladesh, India, and Sri Lanka—presents a need for brand owners and retailers to ensure that their fashions are produced in factories that uphold global standards. Brand owners must invest in personnel who monitor working conditions of their factories to protect their reputations. Social compliance managers work as auditors and liaisons between the retailers and the factories where the merchandise is produced. These are not entry-level employees; however, their experiences in product development, as buyer's assistants, and as brand representatives fuel the networking and knowledge needed to succeed in the role. Global awareness and multi-language skills are needed in this position. (See Figure 1.4 for a typical job position description.)

Promotion

Promotion includes display, store layout, event planning, coordination of merchandise, trend analysis and presentation, and marketing. The goal of the promotional department is to create an environment in which

Manager of Compliance and Global Social Responsibility

Company X has over 1,000 stores with buying offices in China, Hong Kong, India, and Bangladesh and seeks a manager for the China headquarters to work in three chidrenswear divisions—infants, young girls, and young boys.

Responsibilities:

- Monitor and evaluate the social compliance activities; conduct factory visits and investigations.
- Develop and enhance key reporting protocols and performance analysis tools to support management of compliance programs and to provide visibility to compliance activities for senior leadership team
- Perform risk analyses in terms of social compliance.
- Support implementation of social monitoring program in collaboration with HQ
- Ensure all internal controls, policies and procedures to improve the quality of work and transparency.
- Provide assistance on concerning corporate responsibility topics.
- Ensure communication are timely, accurate, and comprehensive.
- Maintain records (factory profile, recent social compliance audit reports, recent social compliance certificates) for each factory that is being used for production
- Work with all agents and factories to make sure documents are up to date

- Work with production managers to ensure all factories being used for production are following our social compliance standards
- Work with individual retailers to ensure each factory that is approved for production
- Register, request audits, follow-up with all corrective action plans accordingly and deactivate factories that are not in use
- Request social compliance audits for new factories that cannot provide necessary documents
- Work with factories to achieve and maintain a high standard of compliance that is acceptable by industry standards and by each retailer
- Adhering to Company policies, procedures, and directives regarding standards of workplace behavior in completing job duties and assignments.
- Accounts include but are not limited to: Macy's, Wal-Mart, Sears Holding Company, Spalding, Jockey, Nike, Target, Kohl's Department Stores, ShopKo, JCPenney
- Frequent travel required

Qualifications:

- Minimum 5 years of experience managing a CSR program or related; ideally, within a retail buying office environment
- Strong understanding of the global CSR landscape, key issues and best practices, along with knowledge of the roles in the private, non-profit and public sectors.
- Knowledge of fashion product development.
- Excellent written communication and verbal skills, including public speaking, meeting facilitation and presentations. Excellent project management and administration skills.
- Must have strong English communication skills; ability to converse and correspond in Chinese strongly preferred.

- Must be computer literate with strong working knowledge in Microsoft Access and Excel.
- Able to bring new ideas and perspective to existing practices and processes. Ability to manage multiple tasks simultaneously to completion. Proven ability to work effectively with all levels of management, across sectors, and across cultures.
- Must reside in China.
- Minimum of Bachelor Degree. Strong business and financial acumen; strong familiarity with the global fashion industry.

FIGURE 1.4

Sample Social Compliance Position Description

the merchandise is appealing to the customer. Knowledge of the store environment, channels of distribution, and current trends, as well as an ability to construct displays and create interesting space, are all important components of effective promotion. A thorough understanding of the store's target market is also essential. Common positions in the promotion area include display and visual merchandising assistant, merchandise coordinator or merchandiser, marketing coordinator, fashion coordinator or director, and stylist. See Olivia Hosler's profile in Careers Up Close 1.3 to read about her marketing trajectory.

CAREERS UP CLOSE 1.3
OLIVIA HOSLER
Marketing Specialist
Victoria's Secret

The role of social media in marketing promotions was of special interest to Olivia Hosler when she searched for an internship with a fashion company during college. Fortunately, her strong preparation in communications, coupled with her ability to demonstrate knowledge of platforms such as Facebook, Twitter, Instagram, and Yelp, positioned Olivia for a summer internship with DSW—in which she was so successful that the company retained her until graduation over a year and a half later. Olivia's background of retail working experiences—as a barista and cashier—gave her the insight necessary to combine social media skills with retailing. Additionally, an earlier marketing internship with Granville Fellowship gave her experience managing a corporate Facebook page, designing promotional items such as pamphlets and flyers, and handling client contact lists.

Overall, Olivia credits strong organizational skills along with tangible examples of work outcomes among the key strong points of her career search. Now as marketing specialist at Victoria's Secret, Olivia oversees the Facebook, Twitter, and Instagram accounts for Victoria's Secret Sport. She drives content strategy and framework for the copywriter and creative director to ensure voice and creative perspectives that are brand-right and consistent. She creates and maintains content calendars, performs platform and content assessment, and optimization. She generates social KPI (key performance indicators) reports that show sales, engagements, follower growth, and insights on a weekly basis—and analyzes those to determine changes and new opportunities in social media. Finally, Olivia supports on-site, real-time event coverage for model and sponsored events.

Being responsible for a company's social media presence requires diligence with respect to awareness of competitors' marketing programs as well as cutting edge knowledge of the latest applications and platforms. Keeping a finger on the pulse of communication media for customers—in the current target market as well as in markets her company seeks to reach—is an essential career activity. Additionally, Olivia notes that the team-oriented projects in which she participated as a college student have strong relevance to her current work. She leads and participates in cross-functional teams that oversee merchandising strategies. Olivia emphasizes the importance of understanding the people who comprise your team with the following advice: When working with a team you need to be able to recognize the type of people you are working with and adjust your communication strategy to accommodate the way their brains think. For example, you will want to approach your creative partner in a different way than you address your legal team. Always be willing to offer assistance to your partners and work to make sure they are not feeling overwhelmed. Not only does that make you a great partner, but it will also make them more willing to help you out in the future. Lastly, remember, "if there is a will, there is a way." At times you may not be given the assets that you need, or your copy team may be too busy to write a post. At that point, you need to roll up your sleeves and do it yourself. That is, go into a store and take a picture of the product on the shelves or take a picture of the creative inspiration board at the office, and write your own copy. Then you can pull everything you need for a post and run it by your team. It will show them your resourcefulness, as well as take some of the weight off their shoulders.

Olivia reflects that the degree you graduate with does not always determine your job. In retail, employers are looking for people who are resourceful, hard working, and passionate. She states, "You don't have to plan your next step in life to a "t"; most of the time, it doesn't work out how you planned. Take every opportunity you are given in life to learn something. I started out website coding and tweaking partner deadlines for store handouts, but these experiences ended up being helpful in social [media] when working with partners because I could understand their jobs, and I knew how to make their jobs easier on them. Just work hard, show your passion, and get scrappy."

Display and Visual Merchandising

Most department stores and specialty stores have a display and visual merchandising division whose employees are responsible for creating the stores' floor plans as well as eye-catching displays that highlight the merchandise. Visual merchandising specialists not only set the entire store image, but they also are responsible for the physical placement of merchandise. How the racks and fixtures in a store are placed has a huge impact on customer traffic flow and the resulting sales. An effective visual merchandiser knows how to place the merchandise to positively influence sales and promotions. Additionally, the merchandising must be done with adherence to regulations such as fire codes and the Americans with Disabilities Act (ADA).

Specialty stores, particularly large chains, typically house their visual merchandising departments within the corporate headquarters. For example, at Claire's Accessories, the visual team plans the merchandising of their stores through the use of a model store replicated at their corporate office. Visual teams are responsible for communicating the stores' merchandising plans via promotional manuals, or planograms, which are distributed to the stores and implemented by the managers and sales associates. A planogram, which can be computer generated or hand drawn, is a visual plan detailing where merchandise is to be placed in each store. Most times it will also outline instructions for building in-store and window displays. Most chain stores implement a uniform planogram in every store to ensure that the store image is maintained and consistent in all stores.

Although creativity is important to this position, there is much more to a visual merchandising job than making the store look nice. As the visual merchandiser, your primary goal is to create appealing displays that will generate sales. To be effective, you should have an understanding of consumer behavior, be familiar with the different floor layouts and traffic patterns, know about various store fixtures and display items, be comfortable working with technology (most planograms are computer generated), and realize the importance of attention to detail. An understanding of the principles and elements of design is also essential.

Social Media

One of the most exciting new opportunities since the emergence of the Internet is the job of social media specialist. Generally part of the marketing division, the role of social media assistant is typically an internship or entry-level position. Clearly, customers represent broad ranges of demographics and use social media in very different ways. Therefore, the new, "cutting edge" nature of social media lends job opportunities to young professionals who are familiar with and regularly use social media themselves. The ability to interpret uses for social media that will promote and enhance company performance—and reach out to new markets—can position you to use those skills on the job. Interestingly, social media is creating jobs (think Uber employees) as well as job categories within marketing and management divisions.

Public Relations

Both brand owners and fashion publications need to promote the latest fashion trends and product. Therefore, public relations (PR) positions exist within design firms and with fashion magazines and other publications—including online. Additionally, people in the public eye, from celebrities to newscasters, rely on publicists to promote the fashions that they wear—particularly at high profile events such as the Oscars. In fact, PR representatives for fashion brands work closely with magazines and personal publicists to provide clothing and accessories for public viewing.

Advertising

As with PR positions, advertising is generated by the brand, and by the publications that rely on consumer interest to generate magazine sales or blog views. Advertising can work hand in hand with social media and PR. Advertising sales is an important component of print and online media—sales professionals seek companies to pay for advertisements in their publications to offset costs to consumers. Advertising professionals who work directly for retailers or brand owners are sometimes in-house and sometimes freelance. In the case of freelance, advertising companies retain retailers and brands as clients.

Merchandise Coordinator or Merchandiser

A merchandise coordinator, sometimes known as a merchandiser or sales coordinator, is responsible to a particular manufacturing company for ensuring that appropriate merchandising is occurring at the stores where the products are offered. Therefore, this is a somewhat unique position because it provides the opportunity to work with both the retailing and the wholesaling aspects of the industry.

Typically a merchandiser services one chain of stores within a particular area (e.g., Macy's® East located in the New York City region). Brands such as Polo Ralph Lauren®, Lilly Pulitzer®, Nike®, and Guess® are offered by retailers who have agreed to contract conditions regarding the manner in which the merchandise will be displayed, priced, and promoted. The merchandise coordinator is the liaison between the manufacturing company and the retailer.

Merchandise coordinators spend most of their work weeks traveling among the various retailers who sell their products, communicating the needs and goals of the manufacturer, recruiting sales associates for the designated product areas, instructing them regarding selling strategies and product knowledge, displaying and merchandising the products according to manufacturer's policy, putting stock on the floor, taking inventory, delegating projects and assignments, trouble-shooting, and problem solving as conflicts are anticipated or become apparent. The merchandise coordinator also provides extra sales help when special promotions occur at the store. One of the merchandise coordinator's most important jobs is to make sure the allotted number of square feet assigned to a product is maintained. Competitors are always more than willing to take away floor space if the opportunity presents itself.

Training for this position usually takes place on the job and is provided by a regional merchandise coordinator or the brand representative for the particular store. The entry-level merchandise coordinator may also obtain some product-knowledge training from the manufacturer's showroom or other brand resources, including its website. Skills that are particularly important include sales and negotiation, creativity for merchandising and promotion of the merchandise, attention to detail, strong interpersonal and communication skills, self-motivation, and a high level of energy. Typical promotions from this position would be to that of a regional merchandise coordinator or a manufacturer's sales representative.

Marketing Coordinator

The marketing coordinator ensures that the retailers' advertising and promotion program is developed and implemented at the local and national level. Generally, the marketing coordinator develops advertising campaigns by selecting the media through which the advertising is done, determining the copy, and indicating the frequency of the message. Overall, it is the marketing coordinator's job to create an image for the store that will stimulate business with new and existing customers. Of course, this all has to be done within the department's budget. Thus, the marketing coordinator has to be both creative and analytical.

This position also requires a great deal of organization, considering what is involved in implementing the comprehensive marketing strategy. The marketing coordinator may be supervising magazine, newspaper, and television advertising; direct-mail promotions; website design and development; and in-store events—all at the same time. Although the marketing coordinator position is not an entry-level job, all retailers, usually at the corporate level, have entry-level marketing positions such as a marketing coordinator assistant or advertising assistant. Other titles for entry-level positions in a marketing department may include assistant copywriter and layout assistant. In addition to a retailing or apparel merchandising degree, those interested in this area may consider a minor or a double major in one of the following fields: marketing, advertising, or journalism.

Fashion Director

Large companies with a fashion-forward image often have a fashion office that is overseen by the fashion director. Merchandise marts and many consumer magazines also have fashion offices run by a director. Buyers look to the fashion office for advice on product trends. Store image is shaped and tweaked in the fashion office. Fashion information is collected, compiled, and disseminated through the fashion office. The fashion director oversees the entire process of trend identification and promotion. It is the responsibility of the fashion director to coordinate store presentation, advertising, catalogs, and website messages so that the company is effectively promoting its image and communicating a consistent fashion message. Knowledge of world events, factors that affect the economy and fashion trends, and a willingness to travel the world to identify emerging fashion trends, as well as an understanding of the history of fashion and its influences on the future, are essential for success as a fashion director.

Although this is not an entry-level position, individuals with a keen interest in fashion trends, strong leadership, superb communication skills, and an ability to multitask may aspire to the position of fashion director. The assistant fashion director and others who report to the fashion director are responsible for analyzing and presenting trends that will be promoted within their companies. Fashion directors typically have among their career duties coordinating and producing all fashion-related events such as market fashion shows and trunk shows. They often serve as booking agents for runway and showroom models. In addition, many fashion directors work with colleges and universities in regard to internship programs and experience-related opportunities at markets.

Stylist

Did you ever wonder who dresses the actors on your favorite television show or the characters in commercials? Have you thought it might be exciting to select clothing for a movie star—or perhaps the news anchor at a local television station? The role of a stylist is to do just that.

Typically a stylist is self-employed as a freelance agent. Producers in the movie, television, or advertising industries hire stylists to select clothing—and in some cases build costumes—for the characters in their productions. Good listening skills are essential as stylists work with producers and directors to create the right "look" for each part in the production. Knowledge of fashion trends, both current and historic, is important so that the look that is created fits the setting. Stylists and their assistants put in long days and must demonstrate high energy levels, excellent customer service and communication skills, and extraordinary patience as directors make changes and production plans evolve. Successful stylists have regular clients and impressive networks of industry contacts. They also have a lot of work and are generally looking to hire assistants who are interested in learning the business and contributing to the projects at hand. The best way for aspiring stylists to break into the industry is to seek an internship or work experience with an established stylist.

While studying at the American Intercontinental University in London, a recent student reflected upon her opportunity to work with stylist Robin Dutt. Dutt has been featured in magazines and on television, and has authored *Gilbert and George: Obsessions and Compulsions*, published by Wilson Philip Publishers, Limited. To prepare the students in his class for work as stylists, Dutt divided them into teams that prepared models for photo shoots focused on particular topics and themes. To prepare for the photo shoots, the student teams brought "tear sheets," or magazine cut-outs, with ideas for a shoot and they discussed the "look" they wanted to play on or achieve while in the studio. In addition, they visited museums and art galleries for inspiration. They brought items they owned or purchased suitable items at vintage markets such as the Portabello market. At the studio, they brought everything they had collected together and set up the entire shot, including the selection of lighting and props. These activities reflect the procedures that stylists follow as they work with clients. As a result of their experiences with Robin Dutt, the students were able to compile portfolios portraying their photo shoots. Armed with that experience and industry contacts, they are set to pursue careers as stylists.

Successful stylists typically begin their careers in this manner. Contacts within the advertising, television, movie, and fashion industries are essential for stylists to secure work. Referrals from professionals already active in the industry who are familiar with your abilities and work ethic are equally important for securing projects. Creative problem solving and strong communication skills will enhance your probability of success as a stylist. See Chapter 4, Career Profile 4.1 to read about Jeromy Coleman's career as a stylist.

Historic Preservation and Display

Fashion Curator

Museums and costume collections need curators to inventory, promote, expand, cull, and display their fashion holdings. A curator has opportunities to work with the public—often in settings tantamount to retailers—and to engage in research and education about historic trends and cultures. Students who particularly enjoy historic aspects of textiles and apparel should be aware of the opportunities to launch careers using those interests. In fact, the Smithsonian offers an excellent internship program, and the Metropolitan Museum of Art regularly stages outstanding historic designer collections. See Adam MacPharlain's profile in Careers Up Close 1.4 to learn more about the career of a curator.

CAREERS UP CLOSE 1.4
ADAM MACPHARLAIN
Curatorial Assistant,
Fashion Arts and Textiles
Cincinnati Art Museum

A project in a historic costume course, setting up an exhibition of dresses at a regional historic house, fueled Adam MacPharlain's love for fashion history, though it took a few more years and two internships to confirm that he could make a career of it. During his undergraduate program in apparel design and merchandising at Eastern Kentucky University, he was given several opportunities to gain insight into historic costume. An independent study allowed Adam to work alongside the department chair (one of several mentors) with the department's historic costume collection; she encouraged him to seek out a museum internship in addition to the internship he had already completed in the contemporary fashion industry. Adam used his two internships—one with Kasper Knitwear in New York City, the other with the Kentucky Historical Society in Frankfort, Kentucky—to thoroughly explore his interests and to confirm his need for a career that enabled his creative skills to shine. Both internships were highly successful, with respective supervisors offering encouraging support for career growth.

Ultimately, Adam attended the master's program in Museum Studies at the University of Leicester, solidifying his academic foundation for a career in the museum field. Like the fashion industry, museum work has provided many projects that are visually tangible, such as exhibitions and research presentations; therefore, he keeps detailed records of the activities he completes, which can be presented in physical or digital formats as examples of his professional accomplishments.

During his museum internship and early career, Adam worked in museum registration, which oversees the physical and legal control of the collections. His internship supervisor at the Historical Society served as a mentor, continuing to guide him toward developing a museum career, encouraging him to contribute to the field through participation in professional organizations and conferences. Likewise, Adam urges students to participate in networking activities—even though it may feel awkward. Adam emphasizes the importance of staying connected with the networks you develop, stating, "After the internship is over, continue to follow up with your former supervisors and maintain professional relationships." He advises, "Don't just meet people and leave it at that; make connections and follow up."

Adam's other advice: There are more careers in fashion than the traditional design and merchandising route. The role of the fashion historian can lead down several rewarding paths. To look into this field, he recommends seeking internships, which are available in a variety of formats and can be accessed in multiple ways, and suggests that academic advisors and university career centers are good places to start. Also, look into organizations such as the Costume Society of America, American Alliance of Museums, and other regional and national groups.

Entrepreneurship

Savvy retailers, buyers, and designers often find success in debuting their own businesses. According to Barbara O'Neill (2014), there is a strong trend among employers to hire independent contractors (freelancers)—a practice that diminishes administrative complications such as on-boarding activities, training, potential layoffs, payroll taxes, paying for health insurance, and offering fringe benefits such as retirement contributions. As your skill set and networks increase, you may be in a position to work independently as a consultant. Some examples of consulting fields include trend forecasting, representing fashion lines (independent line rep), social compliance, advertising, and display or visual merchandising. The avenues for entrepreneurial ventures into fashion-oriented careers are virtually endless.

With the advent of new technologies, continued concerns about fashion design copyrights, and global issues related to human rights for manufacturers, a relatively new career area is fashion law. Rosemary Feitelberg (2015) reports in *Women's Wear Daily* that Fordham Law School and the Fashion Law Institute offer degrees in fashion law.

In addition to focused entrepreneurial endeavors such as these, we present some of the typical career paths for fashion entrepreneurs.

Store Owner

If you are looking to fill a niche in a marketplace, passionate about seeing projects through from incubation to execution, well skilled in the myriad of roles that go into fashion retailing, and up to the challenge of hard work and high levels of responsibility, store ownership may be for you. Store owners are afforded the ability to set their own goals and create their own visions. The risks of launching your own store are certainly present, but the rewards can be very satisfying and lucrative. Sarah Snyder shares her journey to store ownership in Careers Up Close 1.5.

CAREERS UP CLOSE 1.5
SARAH SNYDER
Entrepreneur and Store Manager
Blue Bridal Boutique,
Denver, Colorado

Retail management experience and expertise prepared Sarah Snyder for her 2009 launch of Blue Bridal Boutique in Denver, Colorado. Sarah's desire to lead her own business grew from her love of retail operations and her keen awareness of the importance of customer service in high-end and personalized fashion sales. Sarah pulled from her sales and management experience with Neiman Marcus and her beauty industry training as a licensed esthetician to create the "full package" of services for Denver area brides.

Sarah's goal to become an entrepreneur emerged early; as she grew up in her mother's quilt shop, she knew that she wanted to have her own business someday too. Sarah's father and most of her aunts and uncles were entrepreneurs too, so she had several examples of successful business owners to look up to. Although she always had a love of fashion and knew she wanted to have her own businesses, she did not realize her love of bridal fashion until working at Neiman Marcus in Las Vegas after graduating from Ohio University. Sarah knew that she would need to have a lot of knowledge about running a business, managing inventory, effective sales strategies, and good networks to draw from for advice and moral support.

With her long-term goal in mind, Sarah earned a bachelor's degree in retail merchandising and a minor in business administration from Ohio University. She completed an internship with Neiman Marcus, where she implemented sales and management activities and found that she was good at communicating with buyers, vendors, and customers. Through working at Neiman Marcus, Sarah realized she had a knack for merchandising and enjoyed analyzing the numbers and sales trends in the business.

In addition to the merchandising aspects of store ownership and management, Sarah wanted to find a way to distinguish herself as a business woman, particularly in the bridal business. She pursued experiences as a makeup artist and esthetician, first at Neiman Marcus, then at various spas, before starting her own freelance makeup company, Sarah Betsy. When she was ready to establish her own storefront, Blue Bridal Boutique, Sarah was prepared to offer a full service bridal experience, incorporating both apparel and beauty aspects in preparation for her clients' "big days."

Sarah notes that there is never a dull moment as a business owner, and she has learned many things. For example, "you have to find a way to differentiate yourself, whether that is through competitive pricing, merchandise assortment, or customer service. For Blue Bridal, we are known for our unique assortment of dresses and our impeccable customer service. There are always new stores opening and closing around us, and keeping our customer as our top priority and knowing our company culture are the main things that set us apart."

Sarah emphasizes, "Our online presence is *very* important. We did almost NO advertising for the first four years and relied strictly on PR and word of mouth by providing excellent customer service to everyone that entered our doors or called the business. SEO has been and still is one of the most important aspects of my business." Sarah explains, "Twitter, Facebook, Instagram, and blogging were integral parts of the Blue Bridal online marketing effort to grow the business without relying on spending money on marketing. I had only $2,000 when I opened the business, so being thrifty and creative were extremely important in getting the business up and running."

Designer

No fashion entrepreneurs are better recognized than fashion designers. While most fashion design professionals work within company structures, launching your own design business is a realistic goal. As an entrepreneurial designer, you will want to be sure that you have strong business knowledge (and advisors) as well as a sound plan for marketing your designs to a well-defined customer group. Joy Teiken shares her insights about her design company Joynoelle in Chapter 3 in the Careers Up Close 3.3.

Blogging

Today's technologies and popularity of the Internet have made blogging a popular hobby. Business-minded bloggers can capitalize on the consumer interests that make blogging so lucrative. The ShopStyle Collective, formerly called ShopSense, is a search engine that connects bloggers and their posts to interested readers of Shopstyle.com. According to Rachel Strugatz (2015), bloggers generate a million dollar industry. She reports that top bloggers such as Chiara Ferragni (The Blonde Salad) and Aimee Song (Song of Style) can earn six figures per month though brand partnerships and advertising. Stephanie Clark's Careers Up Close 4.2, Chapter 4, provides insight about a blogger's career.

Researcher

Market Research

Smaller companies can benefit tremendously from research conducted for hire by professional firms. Similarly, non-profits or other groups who want to promote their brand or products often seek researchers to conduct surveys, analyze marketplace performance, and conduct specific research to inform their decisions. Experience working within the industry and acumen with statistics and trend forecasting position aspiring entrepreneurs for work in market research. Market research positions are also available within corporate offices—sometimes as an arm of the retailer and other times as stand-alone firms.

Academic Research

Many of the college and university professor positions require advancing the scholarship that supports a global understanding of the textile, apparel, and design industry. Therefore, a faculty position may provide an extended opportunity to engage in academic research—a skill that is generally learned as a master's or doctoral student. Different from marketing research, academic research is typically conducted independently of proprietary (corporate) support, and is published in accessible peer-reviewed journals rather than held by corporate sponsors as private information.

Journals such as *Clothing and Textiles Research Journal*, the *Family and Consumer Sciences Research Journal*, the *Journal of Fashion Marketing and Management*, and the *Journal of Retailing* are examples of outlets for academic research. As a student, you may find the published results of academic research to be helpful as you complete projects and conduct your career search. In fact, you may see the names of your professors listed as authors in these journals. As a practicing professional, the information generated through academic research may support or inform your decisions as a manager or buyer.

Instructor

Industry professionals who possess strong knowledge of retail, design, buying, visual merchandising, and so on have skills that need to be passed along to the next generation of fashion professionals. In addition to mentoring on the job, there are opportunities to be a formal teacher.

Part-Time College Teacher

Many colleges and universities local to your area have fashion programs. It is quite possible that part-time teaching opportunities exist. If you have an interest in teaching, we encourage you to reach out to your local college or university to inquire about the qualifications necessary to teach, and also to find out whether any courses now or in the future might need an instructor. Generally, a master's degree is the preferred qualification for college level instructors, but substantial industry experience along with a bachelor's degree may qualify you for this role. Strong organization, knowledge of teaching pedagogy, excellent communication skills, and a genuine interest in working with students are key skills necessary for teaching.

Full-Time Lecturer or Professor

Clearly, the fashion programs preparing you to earn associate, bachelor's, and master's degrees offer courses and advising delivered primarily by full-time faculty members. Ideally, these faculty hold experience in one or more facets of the fashion industry, as well as the academic degree required for their appointments. Many full-time lecturer positions require a master's degree along with industry experience. Professors, who teach and also conduct scholarly research that advances the body of knowledge regarding such topics as retailing, fashion and design theory, consumer behavior, and customer service, generally must possess a doctoral degree. For those of you with a passion for learning, consider advancing your education—and with career experience in the industry you could be well positioned to transition to an academic career as a professor. Halimat (Hali) Ipaye's journey to her teaching position is presented in Careers Up Close 1.6.

CAREERS UP CLOSE 1.6
HALIMAT (HALI) IPAYE
Lecturer, Retail Merchandising
and Fashion Product Development
Ohio University

A strong background in the business of fashion enabled Halimat (Hali) Ipaye to land a career position as a university teacher. Early in life, Hali's father's native—and very colorful—Nigerian textiles and clothing made an impression and provided a context for her interest in the aesthetics of dress. Hali pursued a degree in marketing, where she focused on business and financial aspects of the fashion industry. She landed a position as an account executive with a marketing firm, but decided that she really wanted to focus more on fashion products and processes within the industry. Her study abroad endeavors to Northern Ireland and China, coupled with her desire for a global view of fashion, prompted Hali to return to college for more education.

With a master's degree in textile and apparel management in hand, and supporting academic experiences that included teaching and peer mentoring, Hali was equipped to take on her current position as a Lecturer in a merchandising program. Hali's enthusiasm for working with people and advancing their knowledge of and appreciation for fashion fuels her success as a teacher. Her opportunity to participate as a Ronald E. McNair Post-Baccalaureate Achievement Program Scholar solidified her understanding of the importance of collaboration and broad input and influences when facilitating learning—particularly with respect to the global world of fashion. She articulates her value of an inclusive approach to teaching by explaining, "While teaching, I strive to create a learning environment that seeks to honor the diversity and experiences of all students in the classroom."

Hali draws from her breadth of knowledge and from her growing network of industry professionals and continues to incorporate contemporary research into her teaching activities. She uses service-learning and experiential class-based activities to address course competencies such as sustainability, cultural aspects of clothing, design techniques, and merchandising management. Hali credits academic and career mentors, as well as family, as key people who have provided support and direction. She observes, "The people who really care about you also know a lot about you, and can help you make important decisions. Relationships are key during your career."

Getting Started

Although the entry-level job opportunities and the career paths described in this chapter are the more common ones, they are by no means all-inclusive. Rather, they are meant to spark your interest so that you will be motivated to learn more about these and other opportunities that are available. You can get started by working through the activities in this textbook, which include speaking with professionals, networking at career fairs, résumé writing, and exploring internship and work opportunities. In completing these activities, regardless of your particular career interests at present, remember to keep an open mind to the professional opportunities that await you. Soon you will find your niche and be headed toward an exciting and rewarding retail merchandising career!

Projects

1. You want to find a career that is best suited to you. Toward that end, you are trying to find out what each career feels like and what each job entails. One way to go about it is by doing what's known as an informational interview. Here's how it works:

   a. Identify at least two people in your locality who actually do the work in which you are interested. If you do not know of anyone, ask your friends, neighbors, fellow classmates, parents, and professors for their help in identifying someone.

   b. Call or email the persons you identify to ask for an appointment with them. Ask for only ten minutes of their time and be sure to stick to that time limit once you meet.

c. At your meeting, ask the following questions:

- How did you get started in this work?
- What do you like the most about it?
- What do you like the least about it?
- Where else can I find people who do this kind of work? (You should always ask them for more than one name, so that if you run into a dead end at any point, you can easily visit the other people they suggested.) If it becomes apparent to you, during the course of this ten-minute visit, that this career, occupation, or job definitely *doesn't* fit you, then the last question can be turned into a slightly different query: Do you know anyone else I could meet with to discuss my skills and interests (favorite subjects), so I can find out what other careers they might point to? If they can't think of anyone, ask them if they know anyone who *might* know. Then go visit the people whose names they give you.

d. Write a thank-you note or letter to the persons you interviewed.

e. Upon completion of your informational interviews, prepare a separate report for each. Include the following information: name of person interviewed, position, company or organization, and his or her responses to the interview questions. Also provide a summary of your reaction to the information you collected in each of the interviews, including why this does or does not sound like a position suited to you.

2. Identify an entry-level position that you find interesting and would perhaps like to pursue. Prepare a three- to five-page report about the position, including a summary of the responsibilities of the position, specific companies offering such a position, the skills needed for success, and your qualifications for such a position. If you currently do not have the needed skills or qualifications, provide a brief discussion as to what you can do while a student to develop these skills prior to graduation. You should also include in the report a flowchart illustrating the typical career path based on the entry-level position.

Questions for Discussion

1. What positions do you find especially interesting? Why? How could you find out more information about them?

2. Are there particular positions that you would not like? Explain why.

3. Pick three of the entry-level positions discussed in the chapter. What are five skills, or personal characteristics, that you think would be especially important for those positions? Why would they be important?

4. What are five required courses in your major, and how will they be important to a fashion career?

5. Based on the career paths, can you identify particular advantages of working for a department store rather than a specialty store and vice versa?

6. What are some other areas in fashion that you would like to know more about? How could you find out about them?

7. What are some specific stores, companies, or brands that you would like to work for? Why are you interested in them?

STUDIO Activities

Visit the *Guide to Fashion Career Planning STUDIO* available at www.bloomsburyfashioncentral.com. The key elements are:

1. Summary of Chapter 1 text
2. Quiz
3. Informational interview activity

   a. Initial contact letter
   b. Informational interview question form
   c. Informational interview report form
   d. Thank-you letter template

4. Career path links
5. Salary information

VIDEO: Tips for Career Exploration

References

Feitelberg, R. (June 23, 2015). Fordham sets first academic degrees in fashion law. *Women's Wear Daily*, p. 11.

O'Neill, B. (2014). Managing labor market changes: Essential skills for entrepreneurs and intrapreneurs. *Journal of Family and Consumer Sciences, 106*(2), 9–15.

Poloian, L. (2013). *Retailing Principles: A Global Outlook*. 2nd ed. New York: Bloomsbury Publishing, Inc.

Saks Incorporated. (n.d.). Store management. Available online: http://www.saksincorporated.com/careers/storemanagement.html

Shay, M. (June 3, 2015). 3 reasons to put your retail experience on your resume. Available online: https://www.linkedin.com/pulse/three-reasons-put-your-retail-experience-resume-matthew-shay

Strugatz, R. (June 10, 2015). ShopStyle banks on bloggers, relaunches influencer network. *Women's Wear Daily*, p. 10.

US Bureau of Labor Statistics. (2014). Occupational outlook handbook. Available online: http://www.bls.gov/ooh/

US Department of Commerce. (2013). The retail services industry in the United States. Available online: http://selectusa.commerce.gov/industry-snapshots/retail-services-industry-united-states

Wong, E. (March 17, 2011). The highest paying retail sales jobs. *Forbes*. Available online: http://www.forbes.com/sites/elainewong/2011/03/17/the-highest-paying-retail-sales-jobs/

CHAPTER 2

PREPARING TO WORK IN THE FASHION INDUSTRY

You need to be a professional before you actually are a professional.

—ALIZA LICHT (2015)

OBJECTIVES

- To identify the skills and qualities most important to employers when hiring new professionals.
- To evaluate personal strengths with respect to industry expectations and identify opportunities for improvement.
- To recognize appropriate behaviors in professional situations.
- To consider essential professional skills and how they relate to specific professional positions in the retail, apparel merchandising, and design complex.

As discussed in Chapter 1, there are many career opportunities available to those interested in fashion. From design, to product development, to merchandising and retailing, to styling, the opportunities are limitless. Given the many areas available in which to start, and build, a professional career, it may be hard to focus on the specific skills needed for each. The good news is that no matter what area of fashion you are interested in, or what area you pursue, there are some common skills that all employers value. This is true even for employers who are not in the fashion industry. This chapter will examine the skills necessary and provide you with examples of how they specifically fit within the fashion industry.

QUALITIES FOR SUCCESS

Whether you aspire to enter the retail management, sales, apparel merchandising, product design and development, or promotion and marketing area of fashion, certain key professional skills should be developed as you prepare yourself for a successful career. Developing these skills, and being able to recognize them and to market yourself based on your mastery of them, will serve you well as you seek work experience, an internship, or an entry-level position. Regardless of the particular aspect of the fashion business that interests you, there are key personal qualities that are essential.

These qualities are not exclusive to any one career focus and are certainly applicable to fashion professions, whether they be in retailing, product development, design, or merchandising. In fact, whatever career ultimately awaits you, these qualities will contribute to success. Future employers expect you to have these qualities and will scrutinize you during the interview process as they seek to recognize them in you. Furthermore, these capabilities will be observed and evaluated as you make your way in an entry-level position. The successful demonstration of these qualities will be instrumental in your obtaining an entry-level position and in your career advancement. Box 2.1 lists the top ten qualities that employers seek, in order of importance, as published in the *2015 Job Outlook* of the National Association of Colleges and Employers.

Before discussing each of these qualities in depth, there is an important point to keep in mind about success. Being successful does not mean that you will never fail. Most successful leaders can cite numerous failures that have paved their roads to success. H. Lee Scott, president and chief executive officer (CEO) of Walmart Stores, announced at the 2004 National Retail Federation Annual Convention and Expo that "it is more

---

BOX 2.1 Top Ten Attributes Employers Look for on a Résumé

1. Leadership skills (tied with #2)
2. Ability to work in a team structure (tied with #1)
3. Communication skills (written)
4. Problem-solving skills
5. Strong work ethic
6. Analytical/quantitative skills
7. Technical knowledge related to the job
8. Communication skills (verbal)
9. Initiative
10. Computer skills

Source: Reprinted with permission from *2015 Job Outlook*, the National Association of Colleges and Employers, copyright holder. Available: *https://www.naceweb.org/about-us/press/class-2015-skills-qualities-employers-want.aspx*

dangerous not to test than to test and fail." He noted that one can never know what opportunities might be missed when one does not take a risk. Being able to recognize "successful failures" is an important process of growth and development. The experiences that come from failed endeavors, and the ability to learn from one's mistakes, are of tremendous value.

The following section discusses each of the traits important to employers as listed in Box 2.1.

Leadership Skills

Employers not only expect you to be able to follow directions, they expect you to be able to lead others effectively when you give directions. Effective leadership involves taking initiative, providing motivation to complete tasks, accepting responsibility regardless of the outcome, and rewarding members of your team. Many new college graduates fall short in the area of leadership as they are evaluating their skills and producing their résumés. Do not let this happen to you. Take opportunities to be a leader. Become involved in professional, extracurricular, and academic organizations. Do not be content to simply join organizations, because anyone can become a member. Accept the challenge of holding an office, organizing an event, or implementing a new program.

Employers are particularly interested in hearing about leadership skills that you have developed in addition to your academic endeavors. A particularly helpful website for identifying and developing leadership qualities is http://www.nwlink.com/~donclark/index.html. A link to this leadership site is provided on this book's accompanying website (www.bloomsburycentral.com), which also includes a quiz to help you identify your leadership style. As you become an executive, your leadership skills will become as important, if not more so, as your industry/product knowledge. The career of Michelle Crooks-Smith, Senior Manager at Best Buy, profiled in Chapter 9 in Careers Up Close 9.1, illustrates the importance of leadership to success.

An area of leadership that is becoming increasingly important to employers is volunteerism. Make an effort to become involved in your community. Employers want to know what you have done to improve not only your life but also the lives of other people. Most corporations encourage their employees to participate in volunteer activities and will be impressed to know that you have taken the initiative to get involved on your own. There is no better indication of leadership than evidence that you have given of yourself. Volunteering may be just the thing that differentiates you from many other applicants for a position. It says something about your character and work ethic, and indicates an unselfish, team-oriented, outcome-based value system.

There are many books available at bookstores and in libraries that focus on the topic of leadership. Opportunities to learn about leadership and gain experiences in leadership roles are widely available through workshops, college courses, and extracurricular organizations. Take advantage of the resources available to you, and strive to assess your leadership acumen and improve your leadership skills.

Ability to Work in a Team Structure

If you have had any type of work experience, you have probably had to work with a team of people. Or, if you have not had prior work experience, chances are you have been part of a group project in one or more of your college classes. Your ability to demonstrate this trait to employers will be extremely important as you seek an internship and your first professional position. You should demonstrate this ability in your résumé, cover letter, and interviews. Employers will want to know about your group experiences and what you have learned from working with a team. Many employers may ask you to describe a successful team experience you had and what factors contributed to its success. It is also common to be asked in an interview about a team experience that was not positive and what you could have done differently for the group to have been more successful. Regardless of what questions you have to answer about working in a team/group structure, you should be prepared to demonstrate this trait. For example, when working on a group project, what was your personal contribution to the success of the team and your role in demonstrating cooperation and leadership skills?

On a note related to team dynamics, your comfort level in working with people who are different from you should be high. The fashion industry is a global industry. Workplace environments are composed of individuals from diverse cultural backgrounds, representing various nationalities. Furthermore, today's workplace environments recognize and value the infusion of diversity of race, physical ability, and sexual orientation among their employees. Depending on your own background and life experiences, you have a unique perspective on life, interpersonal relationships, and values. Your ability to approach interpersonal relationships with co-workers, clients, and customers in an open-minded fashion that exhibits respect for others and appreciation of diversity will enhance your career progress in this industry. If you have the opportunity to seek international study or travel, interact with diverse populations, and learn about languages and cultures that are not native to you, you should definitely make an effort to do so. Most colleges and universities offer global diversity-focused courses and international markets courses. These academic offerings can expand your knowledge regarding diverse populations.

In a presentation entitled "Leadership in a World of Extremes" at the 2004 National Retail Federation Convention and Expo, Ming Tsai, global vice president of retail for IBM, explained that "diversity runs deeper." He noted that household norms are changing. We no longer expect households to be composed of a mother, father, two children, and a dog. Ethnicity has different meanings today than in the past, and the layers of ethnicity run wider and deeper than ever. Additionally, age is increasingly a diversity factor, with individuals living longer, activities changing throughout active life spans, and market power shifting as baby boomers age and new generations of young people grow up accustomed to affluent lifestyles.

Keep in mind that fashion evolves through a diffusion process. Furthermore, the retailing industry is increasingly global, requiring cross-cultural communication and international trade for optimum productivity and competitive advantage. The greater your knowledge of global issues and your understanding of cultural, racial, physical, and social issues, the better prepared you will be to function successfully in an environment of diverse populations, especially in an industry that thrives on rapid change.

Communication Skills (Writing/Editing Ability)

Your ability to communicate effectively, proficiently, and professionally through written reports will be imperative in any career path you follow. The ability to write well means paying attention to sentence structure, grammar, punctuation, and spelling. Written reports you prepare at work are not only a reflection of you but obviously are representative of the employer. Any report that you prepare—and, for that matter, even the emails you send—should be well written and professional. If you know writing is not one of your strong suits, seek help in college at the student writing lab or from friends who are good writers. Another way to develop your writing skills is by reading, paying particular attention to the manner and style of the writing.

At work, and in school for that matter, you should always read correspondences (e.g., letters and emails) and reports at least twice before sending or submitting them. It is also advisable to use the spell-check feature in the word-processing program—remembering that this feature will only correct misspelled words and not misused words, such as *their* used for *there*. In addition to reading the document and using the spell-check, you may also want to have a co-worker read your documents for typos and grammar errors. Also, as you begin your career search, remember that your résumé and cover letter is the first written document future employers will see, which is why it is so important for those to be perfectly written. This will be discussed more in Chapter 6, which helps you prepare a professional application that includes a cover letter and a résumé.

Problem-Solving and Decision-Making Abilities

Overall, retailers are looking for employees who can make good decisions and solve problems. Whether the quality is expressed as analytical ability, effective teamwork, or innovative and creative thinking, the bottom line is that a successful employee must be able to solve problems. In the fashion industry, problems occur every day, and each day's problems are different, requiring unique and creative solutions. Problems range from dealing with difficult customers, to determining how to increase sales, to dealing with a shipment that has been damaged in transit. What do you do when you cannot deliver goods to your customers, or for reasons beyond your control you cannot follow through on an agreement with a client? You must consider alternatives, make a decision, and follow through to solve a problem. Effective problem solving develops through experience, teamwork, good listening skills, and knowledge-based competencies. It is important to think reflectively, recognize long-term implications, and communicate ideas when solving problems.

Problems present themselves on a regular basis to professionals in all aspects of the fashion industry. Decision making and problem solving both involve creating alternative solutions that meet the needs of your customers or clients, ideally resulting in repeat business.

Strong Work Ethic

The topic of ethics is so important to the process of professional development that we have devoted an entire chapter of this book to it (see Chapter 9). Employers want to employ people who have a strong work ethic, who hold values that match those of the company, who will be honest in their dealings both inside the company and with external constituents, and who uphold principles of fairness and trust.

Analytical Skills

Analytical skills, which typically relate to your adeptness at manipulating numbers and using formulas, are an important component of your problem-solving ability. All professionals in retail-related fields need to understand how to calculate the bottom line—that is, profit. Buyers in particular must be skilled at manipulating numbers in order to determine stock levels, reorders, markup on merchandise, and so on. Designers and product developers must determine product and materials costs, as well as understand measurements for the products. The technical design field requires careful precision when entering and interpreting computer-generated data. Merchandisers will need to calculate sales per square foot, selling cost percent, and sales increases and decreases from year to year. Managers are responsible for interpreting sales figures for their associates and departments, as well as working with planned sales in their areas.

Although mathematical acumen and an ability with numbers generally come to mind when analytical skills are mentioned, this concept actually involves much more. For example, managers and sales associates also need to be able to use analytical skills to assess store environments, interpret consumer behaviors, and evaluate promotional strategies. Knowledge of computer applications, such as Microsoft Excel® that involve creating and using spreadsheets, will enhance your personal marketability. The better you are at math, logical thinking, and data analysis, the more effective you are likely to be as a retailer, merchandiser, or product designer.

Technical Knowledge

In the fashion industry, technical knowledge can also refer to product knowledge. Any salesperson will tell you that the most important component of their job, except for the relationships they build with their clients, is their understanding of the product they are selling. With clothing, for example, there are numerous factors involved in the product, including fabric type, quality, durability, fit, sizing, styling details, finishes, and color availability—to name a few. If you are a fashion wholesaler, some of the items you will need to know concerning your product are delivery dates to the retailer, country of manufacturer, construction processes, order quantity minimums, and pre-packaging specifications. Designers and product developers need technical information concerning fabric construction (e.g., woven versus knit) and its qualities (e.g., durability, stretch capabilities, colorfastness), seam types (e.g., welt versus flat-felled), stitches (e.g., straight, overlock, zigzag), sizing (e.g., junior versus misses), and fit specifications (e.g., seam lengths, tolerances).

Related to technical and product knowledge is the ability to speak in the industry's lingo. For example, if a wholesale rep tells you as an entry-level buyer, "The terms are 2/10, net 30, which allows most of our retailers to keystone their product," would you know what that means? Activities included in the accompanying *Guide to Fashion Career Planning*

STUDIO (www.bloomsburyfashioncentral.com) help you to identify and define some common terms associated with the fashion industry.

Communication Skills (Verbal)

Every successful executive must be able to communicate effectively. This ability includes informal communication with colleagues, written communication, and presentation skills. A terrific idea may never be realized if you are not able to communicate it effectively to the people who are responsible for implementation. Often, you will be the "front person" for the company—the one who interacts with customers, clients, vendors, or manufacturers. The ability to adapt your communication style to best accommodate a given situation will serve you well. As a student, you will often be required to deliver presentations as components of course projects. Recognize the value of these presentations and embrace the opportunity to practice presentation skills and provide examples to prospective employers to best demonstrate those.

Communicate clearly—and also keep your communication professional at all times. You are a representative of the company that has hired you, and your actions are a reflection of the company. Customers, clients, account holders, and other acquaintances will base their perceptions of your company on your ability to communicate. Co-workers, too, are influenced by your communication skills. While completing her internship at a corporate headquarters of a large national specialty store, one student observed the importance of professional communication within the company. As an intern who had been advised to be professional at all times, this student was surprised at the lack of professional behavior she saw exhibited at a department meeting. She observed people gossiping about co-workers and carrying on conversations while the speaker was talking. The unprofessional environment left the intern with a poor impression of the company. The inability of corporate leaders to communicate and model appropriate professional demeanor was likely to negatively influence the morale of their employees. It certainly reduced the level of respect for the organization held by this particular intern.

Whether you are being interviewed, performing your job with colleagues, or working with company clients, your communication style will be evaluated. Most young professionals observe that communication is one of the top priorities in any business. On an average day, merchandisers are likely to speak to many different people within the business. These people might include sales reps, buyers, sales associates, department managers, and store managers, as well as customers. The professionalism of your communication abilities will affect your growth in a company and is a highly visible, continually scrutinized component of your professional profile.

Initiative

Are you a self-starter? Your ability to initiate activities and bring closure to your tasks is valued by employers. Look for tasks that need to be done and volunteer to do them. Step up when opportunities arise. Many of the jobs you take on will not be glamorous, but the initiative you show by doing what needs to be done will be noticed.

Self-motivation is a qualification particularly necessary for independent fashion sales reps. Because many reps' bosses live in different cities, they cannot possibly check up on their employees' daily activities. Most sales reps do not have a time clock that keeps track of daily work hours. Usually reps travel extensively and set their own schedules. Therefore, a sales rep's success is dependent on his or her personal initiative.

Proficiency with Computer Software Programs

At minimum, all entry-level fashion professionals should be proficient with a word-processing program, presentation software, and a spreadsheet program, and also have a general knowledge of database uses. Product development and design positions will also require the use of CAD programs such as Adobe Illustrator. Having experience using web-design software and being savvy with social media applications will also be a plus.

During college, you should take advantage of every opportunity available to learn computer software programs so that you can demonstrate your knowledge of their application for the industry. For example, spreadsheet programs are most often used in buying to develop merchandise plans and include such calculations as planned markups, markdowns, sell-through projections, and open-to-buy dollars. Database programs can help in organizing customer and client information and can be especially helpful to wholesalers, who may have thousands of clients in any one season. Databases can also be used to organize suppliers of certain materials and items needed for designers, such as fabrics and notions. Computer-aided design (CAD) programs such as Adobe Illustrator allow product developers and designers to easily manipulate ideas electronically, making it a much more efficient way to design clothing than the old-school method of drawing on paper. CAD can also be useful to visual merchandisers developing floor sets for a retail chain such as Target or Kohl's. The profile of Deidre Manna-Bratten in Careers

Up Close 2.1 provides an excellent example of how important computer skills can be when combined with the other professional traits discussed in this chapter.

In order to demonstrate your computer software skills to future employers, all fashion portfolios should have examples of work being done electronically on as many of these programs as possible. For fashion business students, that may mean including a six-month buying plan done on a spreadsheet along with slides from a presentation that was given to explain the plan. Design students might include concepts and prototypes illustrated with one or more of the major computer-aided design programs along with a database printout of sourcing companies. Regardless of the field of interest, all fashion students can demonstrate their knowledge of computer program usage through the presentation of a professional portfolio, which can now most easily be generated electronically (see Chapter 4).

While the previous section examines the ten skills that all employers identified as most important in the NACE 2015 survey, there are other skills particularly important in the fashion industry that also deserve some discussion.

Planning, Prioritizing, and Organizing

Are you able to conceive of an idea, plan for its implementation, and then carry it out? This process of planning and execution will serve you well as you enter the professional arena and are required to identify or troubleshoot problems, generate workable solutions, and ultimately solve existing problems. Recruiters and human resource managers continually link the success (or failure) of employees to organizational skills. The ability to plan what needs to be done, prioritize tasks, and organize that information is essential for successful execution. In the fast moving, ever-changing field of fashion, professionals must develop a "sense of urgency" and organize their daily schedules accordingly. Most successful young professionals cite good organization as a top priority contributing to their effectiveness on the job. Not only must you be able to organize your tasks, you must appropriately prioritize them. A popular interview technique involves an in-basket exercise in which the interviewee is asked to assess the items in the in-basket and prioritize them according to their urgency. Are you confident in your ability to prioritize effectively? If not, begin now to practice this important skill.

If learning to be organized is a challenge for you, there are numerous strategies that you can develop to improve your organization. One effective practice is to carry a small notebook or some type of digital assistant (e.g., your phone or electronic tablet) with you and use it to record important information. Keeping a record of what needs to be done and, when practical, how to do it will provide a point of reference, enabling you to record your progress as well as serving as a reminder that you need to stay on task. Upon completing an internship in the corporate office of a large apparel retailer, one student realized that the notebook she had used throughout her internship had been her most valuable resource every day. She knew that she would have been overwhelmed with all of the details and new information for which she was responsible, and she did not want to overburden her supervisor and co-workers with repetitive questions, so she wrote notes about everything in her notebook. She found this tool to be infinitely valuable in keeping herself organized. She had information—and often answers—right at her fingertips. It also gave her a sense of accomplishment to review all the work she had completed and the skills she had acquired. Additionally, she recognized the benefit of having a detailed log of completed tasks, measureable outcomes, and acquired skills to draw upon when updating her résumé and portfolio.

Using a planner to stay organized is also important in documenting everything from phone calls and shipment dates to important details about clients, team members, and buyers you work with. Because you will be responsible for following through with all of the many decisions you make and directives you receive, it is essential to write information down.

Many of the projects that you complete as a college student will require these abilities. As you complete such projects, document the strategies you have identified that contribute to your ability to prioritize, organize, plan, and execute. These opportunities will serve you well as you seek to relay evidence to prospective employers that you possess such skills.

Obtaining and Processing Information

As a college student, this is a quality and a skill that you probably practice daily. In order to complete assignments for class, you have to know where to obtain the information you need, whether that be in your textbook, class notes, online, at the library, or from another individual. Once you obtain the information required for your assignment, you then process the information and decide how it can be used, or not, to effectively complete your assignment.

Completing tasks at work will be very similar except that you may not already have the ability to easily obtain the information or even know *where* to obtain the information. If you are given such a task by others, make sure you have clarified exactly the type of information that person needs and ask him or her for suggestions if you are unsure of where to start. Clarifying your assignment up front and asking pertinent questions should make your job easier and also help to ensure that you provide the correct information.

If you find yourself in a situation where the person assigning your task has not clarified the type of information you need or where to find it, one of the first things you can do is to ask your co-workers or a supervisor for advice. It is likely that one of them has had a need for similar information, or, if not, they may know someone who has. You can also use the Internet to search for information, but remember to verify that any information you take from an online site is credible and reliable—this is a skill you should learn and practice in college. Other valuable resources for information, depending on what you need, are public and university libraries, which have librarians who specialize in a variety of information databases and written materials.

Once you have obtained the information you need to complete your task, you will need to interpret that information as it relates to your situation. For example, how can the data be used to verify a particular finding, answer a specific question, or project sales based on a particular demographic profile? In other words, given the information you have obtained, how does it apply to the situation at hand and why is it important to your employer?

Consider this specific example. As a designer, you may be asked to gather information on the extracurricular activities of teenage girls in the Midwest whose parents are in a certain income bracket. After collecting the information, you will then propose several designs for the activities you identified, keeping the income information you collected in mind (which will obviously affect the price you can charge for the garments). Would you know where to find this information?

Being able to obtain information and succinctly interpret it, either verbally or in writing, is something every executive is required to do. As an entry-level employee, the more you can do to make your bosses' jobs easier, the more likely it is you will be recognized with your own advancement.

Selling Ability (Influencing Others)

In a fashion career, you may be required to sell a product, sell an idea, or, in the case of an interview, sell yourself. Selling ability and writing ability may be your most important professional skills to master—at least for getting your foot in the door.

Retailing is the level at which products and consumers meet. When retailing is successful, products are sold to consumers. Product designers and merchandisers, as well as retailers, must be able to recognize how to sell their products. Future executives need to be able to sell ideas and influence others. Sales will take place at every corporate level and in every company division in some form. Designers and product developers must sell the production team on their ideas, sales representatives must persistently appeal to buyers as they compete with other labels for store space, buyers must convince managers that merchandise is exciting and salable, visual merchandisers use displays to enhance and encourage sales, and so on.

As a sales rep, the importance of product knowledge is key to effective selling. From the materials in a dress to retail pricing to current special pricing offered by the manufacturer, your credibility as a salesperson—and, ultimately, your success in your career—depends on product knowledge. In addition to product knowledge, you must cultivate personal relationships with each of your clients. People skills are absolutely crucial to effective selling. Most sales reps will tell you that "people buy from people they like," so making an effort to learn about clients and show attention to detail regarding their preferences are key.

A former student who is now a sales rep with a major health food line identifies several key strategies that improve selling skills. First, she practices the ABCs of business—"Always Be Closing!" Closing the sale in outside sales is different from a store close, because the outside sales close takes more initiative on your part. Second, upselling is a great skill to acquire. For example, if a store client currently carries only one or two SKUs (stock-keeping units) from your line, make an effort to get the top-selling items into that store. Third, patience is important in selling. It takes some people a while to warm up to a new salesperson, so do not give up! Finally, always assume the sale; that is, talk to buyers as if they are already going to bring your product into their stores.

Experience in sales is essential to success in any aspect of this business. Future professionals should seek opportunities to develop and refine selling skills. Selling merchandise directly to customers is an excellent way to enhance communication skills and to gain an understanding of retailers, corporate structure, the retail calendar, and other professional positions available within the company.

An abundance of sales opportunities exists. Check the classified advertisements in your local paper, the signs posted in many retail establishments, and the websites of retailers. Many positions are available for part-time employment and for summer and holiday breaks (which are great opportunities for students). Keep in mind that a sales associate's primary role is to offer service to the retailer's customers. Customers will appreciate friendly store employees who can communicate with them by acknowledging their presence in the store, providing accurate and informative information about the products, offering suggestions to the customer, and coordinating merchandise items. Knowledge of this ultimate goal for all products—sales—will enhance your ability to design, produce, promote, and buy.

Assertiveness

Assertiveness is an asset for many positions in the industry. The fast-paced nature of fashion requires that successful professionals speak up and act with confidence. Roles you may hold within the industry may require you to convince others to purchase products or services, or to buy into concepts you have created. You will often have a limited time to make a meaningful or memorable impression. If you don't speak up or state your case with gusto, you may miss the opportunity entirely. For example, if you have developed a new product or a new design for a garment, but you cannot defend your reasoning for doing so, it is likely your design will never make it to production.

In a fashion career, you will represent the company employing you. You must exude confidence in this role. Your body language and verbal behaviors speak volumes about your confidence and assertiveness. Walking and sitting with excellent posture, offering your hand for a handshake when being introduced to people, speaking clearly and in a strong voice when you talk, and simply being willing to speak up when you have an important contribution to make in a meeting or conversation are all indications of assertiveness. You may need to take control of a situation, offer leadership in a crisis, or communicate at a crucial moment. Assertiveness will enable you to be the person who can handle these tasks.

Willingness to Accept Challenges

When the task-at-hand seems impossible to complete, that is the time to decide *you* are just the person to see the project through. Kelly Rademacher Schur, who completed an internship with Victoria's Secret, was advised by her supervisor, "Go in with a positive attitude, be willing to jump into anything, and always give 150 percent." Throughout her internship, Kelly was given opportunities to make decisions that affected 700 stores. She accepted the challenge and emerged from the experience with a high confidence level and a feeling of "I can do this!"

As a new entry-level employee, it can be intimidating to supervise 30 employees, assume responsibility for a multimillion-dollar inventory, or make a trend presentation to the CEO and board of directors. If you establish a track record of accepting challenges—and preparing yourself to reach success—you will be much more comfortable moving into roles of greater responsibility as your career progresses.

Creativity

Design, product development, and merchandising depend on creativity to differentiate one product or store from the next. Creative promotions encourage consumers to take a second look at products and consider purchasing them. Aesthetically pleasing environments enhance the consumer appeal of a store or showroom, brands, and products. Careers in visual display and design require knowledge of design principles and elements and a particularly good understanding of color theory. Individuals who can "see" products or store layouts in new and exciting ways enable their companies to effectively position themselves within a special niche.

Although obvious for visual fields such as merchandising, display, and design, creativity is an important skill for other retailers, too. Merchandising professionals must solve problems creatively in order to keep their customers happy. For example, buyers may not be able to receive orders that they request from vendors, producers may desire an outcome that the stylist cannot build, or customers may not be satisfied with the environment or selection of a given store. As a result, merchandisers must be creative with suggestions for alternative solutions so that the customers, clients, and company being represented all end up satisfied with the business transaction.

Flexibility

A successful professional must learn to always be willing (and ready) to implement Plan B. In other words, "B" flexible. In a fast-paced, ever-changing working environment, the plan that was set to roll last night is often outdated or inappropriate by morning. This is a fact with which we all must live. People with rigid, unyielding plans will end up watching the world pass them by. Fortunately, people who have a knack for adapting to change will thrive in today's business and creative environments.

For example, a former student who became a merchandise analyst for Lord and Taylor recalled a situation when, during her internship in the visual merchandising department of DKNY, a window display was planned in which dry cleaning hangers would be the main props. It was her responsibility to research the availability, cost, and sourcing of the hangers (a perfect example requiring the skills of gathering information and applying it, as discussed previously). After learning that a certain minimum order would need to be placed with the hanger supplier—resulting in significantly more cost than was budgeted for the window—the initial window display was scrapped and an alternate display concept was used. The visual design team must be ready with more than one idea and must be flexible to adapt to changing merchandise, availability of props, and the evolution of themes that will best fit the store's promotional strategy.

Loyalty

Employers desire employees who are trustworthy and loyal. Loyalty involves maintaining confidentiality of records, fairness to clients and constituents, and integrity as you interact with customers and coworkers. A good way to demonstrate loyalty to prospective employers is to choose your words carefully when you speak about former employers. How do you refer to the company or a former supervisor? Do you speak highly of the opportunities that you were offered there or are you negative about the experience? Recruiters are likely to assume that the attitudes you develop toward former coworkers and supervisors will be similar to the attitudes you display toward them.

Another important way to demonstrate the characteristic of loyalty is through the work that is displayed in your portfolio. Be certain that you exhibit only those examples that are approved for wide distribution. Many company documents are considered secure and privileged information. You need to carefully honor the trust that has been extended to you during work experiences.

Loyalty does not necessarily mean that you must make a long-term commitment to work exclusively for a certain company. Loyalty does, however, mean: "Don't burn bridges." Although long-term commitment might be a trait associated with loyalty, you should keep in mind that you can exhibit loyalty even in a short-term professional relationship with a company. You can do this by exercising discretion, being honest about your plans for the future and your goals for the present, and maintaining confidentiality of records whenever appropriate. When you part ways with a company, leave on good terms, issue your resignation with plenty of notice, and behave professionally through your very last day of work. Familiarize yourself with the expectations of your company and find opportunities to demonstrate loyalty.

Negotiation

Negotiation skills are a particularly important type of communication ability that lead to a win-win situation when resolving conflict and making decisions affecting your company. Successful negotiation requires that you know the facts, the position of your company, and the bottom line concerning terms you have the authority to agree to or approve. Win-win negotiating requires that you consider the needs of those with whom you are negotiating; it requires that you compromise occasionally and generate creative solutions often. Good listening skills, creative problem solving, and an ability to anticipate alternate outcomes all contribute to successful negotiation skills.

Generally, the process of buying comes to mind when mentioning negotiation skills. Although buyers and sales representatives need to be particularly skilled at negotiating, other retail-oriented professionals negotiate as well. For example, Emily Ellerbrock Ketch, sales coordinator for Tommy Hilfiger, regularly negotiates space. As a merchandiser, she is responsible for positioning her company's merchandise in the best possible location in each store. She must convince store managers and buyers that her merchandise needs the space she desires, and negotiations must be effective because a cordial relationship between her company and the store is essential.

Physical and Emotional Fitness

Stamina is essential for a successful career in retailing, merchandising, and design! As with most exciting professions, you will periodically work long hours and need to be able to handle a fairly heavy dose of stress. Many people thrive in a physically and emotionally demanding environment. Preparing for a week of work is accurately compared to training for an athletic event—or at least getting fit. Full working days can be tiring, and you may find that the first several weeks of a full-time job or an internship are exhausting. Be prepared for this, and recognize that you may need additional physical "training."

An exciting career can also be emotionally demanding. Your ability to handle stress will directly affect your emotional and physical fitness for any job. The adage, "Don't bring your problems to work," truly applies to careers in fashion. It is important for you to anticipate the stress that is likely to come with a full-time work experience. The change from being a full-time student to a full-time professional employee is significant. You will face more structure throughout your day as well as increased responsibilities, particularly involving supervision of other people. These changes are often accompanied by geographic moves and shifts in your support network. Anticipate these major life changes so you can introduce coping mechanisms that will help you adjust to the career phase of your life.

Willingness to Relocate

Many opportunities for advancement depend on location and ability to relocate. Being willing to live in new geographic areas will open possibilities for your career growth that are not possible if you are geographically limited. Certain locations have an abundance of career opportunities in a variety of retailing and apparel merchandising niches. New York City, Chicago, Los Angeles, Dallas, and Atlanta are cities in which career positions from stylist to buyer to showroom sales abound. Many more opportunities for career growth and variety can be found in a large city than in a small town. Although opportunities exist in the retailing and apparel merchandising industry in virtually every location on the globe, the scope of opportunities changes with respect to the geographic location. Furthermore, the specific company you are working for may limit your geographic choices. Walmart's corporate office is in Bentonville, Arkansas; The Target Corporation is headquartered in Minneapolis, Minnesota; the JCPenney corporate office is in Plano, Texas; and offices of The Limited Brands are in Columbus, Ohio. Specific corporate office positions will require that you live within commuting distance from the office sites.

Ability to Work under Pressure

Retailers and other professionals in fashion often have many important tasks that seem to all need to be completed at once. An ability to develop a sense of urgency means that you can prioritize which tasks must be done right away, which tasks you need to do yourself, and which tasks can be delegated for others to complete—and you can carry those out in a calm and effective manner. Christine Wittenbrink learned the importance of working under pressure while she was an intern at the Fashion Office in AmericasMart, the apparel market in Atlanta, Georgia. Particularly during market weeks, she needed to complete everything that needed to be done in preparation for fashion shows while the environment in which she worked was hectic and people around her were often frantic. Her ability to work under pressure allowed her to take care of the business at hand, complete tasks in a prioritized manner, and present a final product that was an impressive reflection of her professional talents. She notes that one's personality is an important element of how well one can work with short deadlines and overlapping projects. An enthusiastic and outgoing individual with a high energy level is best suited to work in an environment that requires working under pressure. In addition, she emphasizes the importance of being able to exert authority when appropriate, delegate work when necessary, and think on your feet when things get hectic.

The career profiles of Deidre Manna-Bratten and Aaron Sturgill in Careers Up Close 2.1 and 2.2 illustrate the importance of many of the traits just discussed. Their career profiles also include invaluable advice concerning career choices, advancement, and the importance of professionalism.

CAREERS UP CLOSE 2.1
DEIDRE MANNA-BRATTEN
Print Project Manager—Creative Services
Lucky Brand

Deidre Manna-Bratten had her sights on Los Angeles for a career even before she graduated with a major in textiles, apparel, and merchandising and a minor in journalism. While her classmates were busy interviewing for local internships with department and discount stores, Deidre made a road trip to LA over spring break and secured her summer internship at GUESS?, Inc. within their Retail Buying department. By the time she completed her internship with GUESS?, she was convinced her future was on the west coast; after graduation, Deidre packed up her car, drove across the country, and never looked back.

Deidre has since gained extensive experience in showroom sales, which involves managing all aspects of customer relationships, from initial contact to product development to sell-through at retail. Not only are her communication skills essential, but she also draws on analytical and time-management skills to best take care of her many accounts. She has represented and sold several women's clothing companies, including Romeo and Juliet Couture, where her main responsibility was volume sales and off-loading of the line through Loehmanns and Neiman Marcus Last Call. In addition, she managed and curated a licensing venture with the *Gossip Girl* TV show and has also been the in-house marketing person helping to launch two e-commerce websites.

As Deidre's career has advanced, she has become increasingly interested in marketing and has developed extensive experience in both print and web. She has held the position of Associate Marketing Manager for Mattel, Inc. and is currently the Print Project Manager in Creative Services for Lucky Brand in Los Angeles. This position carries numerous important responsibilities—including coordination among cross-functional teams, such as copywriters, graphic designers, and visual designers—concerning marketing strategies and retail and digital alignments of aesthetics and messaging. She works closely with the Art Director on artwork approvals to ensure brand/identity alignment. She also reviews monthly seasonal plans and deliverables with Visual Communications, Merchandising, the Art Director, and the Creative Director. While managing the coordination of all print collateral for Lucky Brand (e.g., headquarters, wholesale, digital-wholesale, retail, and outlets) can be very stressful at times, Deidre embraces the challenge. She especially enjoys being a part of the creative process without being the actual executer/designer. This position also requires her to draw on her analytical skills and consumer-behavior insights to ensure all promotional messaging and aesthetics are aligned for the brand. It is helpful that she is cognizant of design programs and processes when managing designers because she understands what their job entails and has an idea of the time frame they need to execute plans.

In addition to her professional positions, Deidre also recognizes the importance of giving back to her community and has volunteered with the L.A. Downtown Women's Center for over five years. Here she began as an individual volunteer and has since been "promoted" to the role of Kitchen Leader where she leads a variety of professional groups in meal preparation for 120 women about two times per month.

Looking back over her career thus far, Deidre has this advice to offer to new graduates wishing to pursue a career in fashion:

1. Be prepared to start from the bottom and work your way up if you want to go the corporate route.
2. Get an internship that is within a company vs. retail store . . . the textbooks only show you so much!
3. Do not be afraid to ask for guidance from your peers. Most people genuinely want to help and educate if you are sincerely interested.
4. Networking is important within this industry and because it is a really small industry, be nice to everyone!
5. This is a fast-paced industry, so you must be able to roll with the punches, attitudes, and ongoing changes.
6. Don't pursue fashion because you think it's glamorous . . . because it's not!

One of the most important pieces of advice Deidre offers is be willing to learn all avenues of the fashion industry—meaning, if you want to be a buyer but there is a merchandiser position or a sales position open, go for it. Taking various positions will give you a well-rounded understanding of how the business works.

Deidre learned most of the computer programs she uses during college and she has continued to use them in various jobs (e.g., Adobe Photoshop for image manipulation, InDesign for line sheet creations or items that need text, etc.), and she always has been computer savvy and had an interest in technology, which she has found helpful. She has held various positions within the industry, and is very proud of her diverse experience and skill set. She realizes that some people want to start off as an Assistant "something" and work their way up the traditional career ladder. However, she states: "I wanted to know everything and how all the pieces fit together in the bigger picture. I have been able to continue my learning and understanding of the industry as a whole because of the many hats I have worn." For example, understanding the industry calendars allows her to better plan marketing strategies and print collateral in her role as a Project Manager with Lucky Brand.

In the future, Deidre is interested in developing a program to educate future graduates about what the apparel world has to offer. Currently she is in the midst of launching her own Public Relations/Branding & Marketing firm called ETCETERA Los Angeles with a friend who has run a PR showroom for ten years. This consulting business offers business-related insight to designers concerning pricing, line development, retail placement, and marketing. End result? She hopes to work for herself in order to have the flexibility and freedom to nurture a family and to continue with her creative endeavors personally and professionally while serving the Los Angeles community.

CAREERS UP CLOSE 2.2
AARON STURGILL
Assistant Director, Career and Leadership Development Center for Hospitality, Merchandising, Recreation
Ohio University

Transitions and mentoring are key themes in Aaron Sturgill's career. With an undergraduate degree in biology nearly completed, Aaron faced an important life choice: continue on the path toward veterinary medicine or make a big change toward a fashion career. At this crossroads, Aaron recognized his love for fashion and determined that he could enhance his life satisfaction by following his heart. Aaron sought advice from people who could inform him about careers in fashion as well as the academic paths to take him there. His decision to pursue a master's degree in apparel, textiles, and merchandising from Ohio University enabled him to gain an advanced degree (which proved valuable in providing credentials to take on college-level teaching) and learn the content needed for access to career positions in the fashion industry.

As a novice to the fashion industry, Aaron knew that an internship would contribute positively to his professional profile; however, an internship didn't fit into his graduate program. He did, however, draw upon restaurant and customer service work experience to demonstrate applicable skills and knowledge when he began his job search. With limited work experience, Aaron capitalized on his perseverance, his belief in himself, and his quest to gain as much knowledge as possible. Early in his career search, he was rejected for an internship opportunity. He sought, and listened to, feedback and then was able to understand that during the application process, he needed to focus on the position at hand—and emphasize his qualifications for that particular position. In his first interview, he reflects, the goals he stated for himself did not fit well with the position for which he was applying. Looking back, Aaron acknowledges, it is obvious why he wasn't hired.

Undeterred, Aaron re-evaluated his goals, résumé, and interviewing strategies. Ultimately, Aaron was successful in a second bid for a manager-in-training (MIT) program with Kohl's®—and had the enviable need to turn down offers from two other companies. He progressed to assistant manager positions at increasingly larger stores and added college recruiting and new employee mentoring to his repertoire. After several years in retail management, Aaron again faced a fork in the road; he valued his management position and could continue career progress, but he was also ready for a new adventure. Interestingly, the new opportunity to join Ohio University's Career and Leadership Development Center team arose because of the wealth of experiences his earlier career provided.

Aaron's diverse experiences have served him well for his current career coaching work. He has developed important networking skills as a retail manager and recruiter that translate into his responsibilities cultivating corporate partners for the Ohio University Career and Leadership Center. Likewise, his experiences mentoring new employees position him with strong credibility as he coaches prospective employees (students) seeking work experiences, internships, and entry-level positions.

Aaron draws from his own career's twists and turns to mentor students as they identify personal interests, career goals, and job search plans. His advice to those in the job market is that "the job you interview for today is your focus and where you need to be engaged." He urges students to seek feedback and draw upon their courage to take second chances. Living this advice, Aaron continues to find new ways to capitalize upon his knowledge and skills.

SETTING GOALS FOR YOURSELF

Once you have explored work experience opportunities and career options, identified areas of interest to you, and considered your strengths, the practice of setting goals will enable you to maximize your potential. Living without goals is similar to planning a trip without a road map. You are much better able to plan your day-to-day strategy when you have identified where you want to go and how you can go about getting there.

Goal setting often presents itself as an overwhelming task for students, but keep in mind that you don't have to set goals that will last a lifetime; your goals can, and probably will, change. If you have some idea of what interests you, or of what you think you might like to try, investigate that area. Identify what you like to do and what you don't like to do. Consider how you might incorporate activities that are enjoyable into your career plans while simultaneously eliminating those you find unpleasant (but keep in mind that all jobs have some distasteful aspects). Plan a strategy for the present. As your goals change and evolve—which they should— modify your strategy. The important thing is to begin with a plan by setting goals. Your life experiences will shape the path of your goal planning, and you should strive to be open-minded with respect to new, previously unearthed possibilities. Clearly established and well-thought-out strategies, leading to identified goals, will serve as a road map for your successful progress through the career landscape.

Short-Term versus Long-Term Goals

Goal setting should be a continual process. To maintain ongoing progress in personal and professional development, new goals should be identified as other goals are being met. Regardless of the complexity of your goals and the length of time involved in accomplishing them, identifying specific tasks necessary to realize those goals will be helpful in your progress to complete them.

Short-term goals are typically defined as goals that can be realized within one year's time. Some short-term goals, such as completing a term paper, may be accomplished within a matter of weeks. Typical tasks associated with this goal would include conducting research on the topic, developing a thesis for your paper, organizing your thoughts, and producing a series of drafts. Other short-term goals may be more complex, involving a greater number of specific tasks toward their completion. For example, the goal of securing an internship for the summer would likely involve researching a number of opportunities, developing a cover letter and résumé, contacting the representatives of potential internship sites, coordinating interviews, waiting for offers, and selecting from among the options that are ultimately presented. Short-term goals are associated with clear timetables and concrete outcomes. If you complete the tasks necessary to meet your short-term goals, the results (completion of the goals) are predictable.

The outcomes associated with long-term goals tend to be more abstract. Long-term goals may be planned for a period of five to ten years or may be lifetime achievement goals. A long-term goal for today's college student may be to become a buyer or a fashion director. Short-term goals can be set and accomplished in the near future that will position you to make progress toward a long-term goal. For example, academic course choices, summer work experiences, strategic networking opportunities, and information gathering can be strategically directed toward the long-term goal of becoming a fashion director. Many aspects of life are apt to change as the time frame for long-term goals unfolds; technologies, personal interests and responsibilities, knowledge of career requirements, opportunities, and attitudes toward lifetime priorities will all probably change. For these reasons, long-term goals should be continually reassessed. It is reasonable to expect that long-term goals will be revised, refined, and restated numerous times. Short-term goals should be set to coincide with progress toward long-term goals.

Goals can be used as conversation points with prospective employers, academic advisors, and mentors. When you interact with others, share your short-term and long-term goals. Simply having such goals demonstrates your initiative and work ethic. Experienced professionals with whom you interact will likely be able to offer helpful advice regarding ways to achieve your goals—and may even suggest additional goals to include in your list. You will also be positioned to determine whether opportunities that are presented to you will be instrumental in helping you achieve your goals. Without goals, it is impossible to assess a given opportunity's value toward achieving your lifetime ambitions.

Making the Most of the Qualities You Possess

We often are asked by students, "How do I set goals if I don't know what I really want to do?" This is a great question and definitely one with merit. The best place to begin with any type of professional goal-setting is with an assessment of your personal strengths. This will also give you a chance to readily identify the qualities that are most characteristic of you.

There are many ways to assess yours strengths. For example, you can simply sit down and make a list of what you believe your particular strengths are based on your experiences, whether those are work experiences or personal experiences. What have you learned about yourself in school or on the job? What are you "good at"?

A second way to assess your strengths is to ask your friends and family members. Since they know you best, ask them what they believe are two of your best characteristics. When they give you the answer, keep a list of what they tell you and look for commonalities. Also, believe what they tell you. Once you have your list, review it and identify ways in which those characteristics would be important in your career. For example, if you find that others think you are "outgoing," that is certainly a characteristic and quality that a successful salesperson has or has strongly developed, given the nature of their professional responsibilities. Another way to use the list is to compare it to the qualities you would assign yourself. Do they match? The areas that you identified in yourself may be areas for improvement if others did not pick up on those.

One resource we have found to be especially helpful in the assessment of strengths, and which is actually used by many successful companies in developing their teams, is *StrengthsFinder 2.0* (Rath, 2007). *StrengthsFinder 2.0* helps identify your key talents and also presents a plan of action for developing those talents. Rath's (2007) premise is that no amount of training will make you excel at your weaknesses; therefore, one's time is better spent developing the strengths and talents that come naturally. Pursuing a career that allows you to use your innate strengths will also make you happier and more likely to be successful.

Regardless of the method(s) you use for identifying and assessing your strengths, doing so will provide you with a clearer picture of some short-term and long-term goals. Seek opportunities that will enable you to practice the professional characteristics that you have not yet fully developed, ones that are of particular interest to you, and ones that you know are particularly important for your desired career path. Note those qualities that are particularly reflective of you, and begin to establish goals for the future that capitalize on your greatest strengths. The more familiar you are with the personal qualities that you possess, the better able you will be to set goals that are realistic for you and that will yield satisfying outcomes as you pursue them. Because no one can be good at all things, and because you will not enjoy doing the same things that others do, developing the strengths and interests *you* have not only allows you to be *you*, it also provides the best avenue to your success. Remember, too, that it will be important to re-visit your goals and perhaps re-adjust those as opportunities present themselves and as you mature in both your professional and personal lives. Chapter 10 provides additional discussion on this topic.

Personal versus Professional Goals

Typically, college students are facing major transitions in life. It is likely that you are considering both goals that include extracurricular and personal interests and professional goals, which are work and career related. Both are important and should be addressed. Eileen McDargh, author of *Work for a Living and Still Be Free to Live*, notes that "there is as much 'success' in catching a trout, comforting a friend, or kneeling before whatever Higher Power you profess, as there is in making a killing on Wall Street, heading up a corporation, or closing a crucial sale" (1999, p. 112). McDargh advocates exploring those things that make you feel "alive" with the same passion that you explore those things that make you "successful." In fact, it is counterproductive to work toward a successful career at the expense of your personal life. A balance between career and personal activities is usually more fulfilling and less stressful than a career-dominated life plan.

Projects

1. Refer to the accompanying *Guide to Fashion Career Planning STUDIO* available at www.bloomsburyfashioncentral.com for a step-by-step process to analyze your competencies with respect to the qualities for success listed in this chapter. What are your areas of strength? What are your challenges for improvement? How can you capitalize on your strengths? How can you improve your areas of weakness?

2. Set goals (activity and related forms found in *Guide to Fashion Career Planning STUDIO*, available at www.bloomsburyfashioncentral.com):

   a. Begin with a self-assessment, or SWOT analysis. SWOT stands for "strengths, weaknesses, opportunities, threats." You should frequently evaluate your strengths and weaknesses, and also the opportunities that are available to you and the threats that serve as barriers to your progress.

b. Ask your instructor, academic advisor, employer, and peers to review your SWOT and ask for their reactions. Do they agree with your stated assessment? Do they offer different insights or perspectives? Take the opportunity to reflect on the content of the feedback that has been offered to you.

c. Articulate a set of long-term goals. Include a time frame within which you will work to accomplish these goals. Consider which short-term goals will be important for you to achieve as you progress toward these long-term goals.

d. Make a list of short-term goals. Define specific tasks that will enable you to accomplish these short-term goals.

e. As you continue your academic studies and embark on work experiences, document your achievements and make plans for improvement with respect to your strengths, weaknesses, and progress toward goals.

Questions for Discussion

1. Which professional skills do you demonstrate on a regular basis? Explain how you demonstrate these skills.

2. Which of your professional skills have you best developed? How have you developed them? Which skills do you most need to improve? What evidence can you offer that leads you to know that you need improvement? What strategies can you implement to achieve improvement?

3. Identify your ideal work environment. Does this environment have a good fit with any of the career paths described in Chapter 1? What are your top priorities for the environment of your job?

4. As you think ahead toward a work experience, internship, or post-graduation career position, what geographic locations provide the most opportunity for you?

a. Is geographic location a factor in your career success?

b. Are you limited by geographic restraints in reaching your career goals? If so, what plans do you have to confront this limitation?

5. How will you combine your personal and professional goals? Are there any conflicts you can identify between these two areas? If so, what are they and how will you deal with them?

6. How do you see loyalty as a factor in your career plans? How will you demonstrate loyalty yet seek new opportunities for career growth?

7. Can you be too flexible? Explain.

STUDIO Activities

Visit the *Guide to Fashion Career Planning STUDIO* available at www.bloomsburyfashioncentral.com. The key elements of this chapter are:

1. Summary of Chapter 2 text
2. Quiz
3. Personal qualities assessment
4. Goal-setting exercises:
   a. SWOT analysis
   b. Long-term goals
   c. Short-term goals

VIDEO: Dress and Appearance in Today's World

References

Licht, A. (2015). *Leave your mark: Land your dream job. Kill it in your career. Rock social media*. New York: Grand Central Publishing.

McDargh, E. (1999). *Work for a living and still be free to live*. Rev. ed. Wilsonville, OR: BookPartners, Inc.

Rath, T. (2007). *StrengthsFinder 2.0*. New York: Gallup Press.

CHAPTER 3

IDENTIFYING AND BRANDING YOUR PROFESSIONAL PROFILE

It's great to be known for your shoes, better to be known for your sole.

—KENNETH COLE (2003)

OBJECTIVES

- To identify, and develop within yourself, the personal qualities of a professional.
- To establish a plan to promote the professionalism you possess.
- To develop a process for mapping out a professionally relevant personal profile.
- To define the term "personal brand" and to identify ways that your brand can be established.
- To identify ways to promote yourself in the career marketplace with distinctive and memorable strategies.
- To incorporate ongoing communication strategies that convey your brand—and express current and potential contributions to businesses and organizations with which you seek to interact and work.
- To identify assessment strategies for evaluating the fit between your career goals, your personal brand, and your current as well as aspirational places of employment.
- To incorporate a professionally relevant social media presence into your personal brand strategy.

DEVELOPING A PROFESSIONAL PROFILE

Your academic training, your technical skills, and your various life experiences contribute to your strengths, which translate to your professional preparation. As a college student, you are preparing for a fulfilling and satisfying career, full of exciting employment opportunities. As a future professional, you are wise to develop yourself, both personally and professionally, as well as academically. The transition from full-time student to career-track professional is significant and challenging. Preparing to make this transition will position you well to accept the challenges and opportunities that await you.

Professionalism—a word that describes the personal behaviors, standards, knowledge, and presentation of a person who has an identified role within an organization—is usually associated with a career position. In 1967, Helen G. Hurd noted in "Who is A Professional?" that the term *professional* (noun) loses its meaning if applied widely across job categories. Hurd defined professionals as those who not only know the content of their fields, keep current with new developments, and belong to relevant associations, but who are also aware of events—locally, regionally, nationally, and globally—that help them understand the larger contexts of their fields. A professional seeks employment as a career, with expectations of gaining experiences that contribute to advancements and greater responsibilities. Furthermore, professionals expect to (and can) find personal satisfaction throughout their careers. Hurd (1967) offers five elements possessed by real professionals: a) a sense of history, b) an awareness of emerging patterns of relationships (e.g., interdependence and cooperation rather than independence and isolation), c) an understanding of the complexity of the world, d) continual personal growth and development, and e) a willingness to offer assistance to others with respect to their expertise. These elements are relevant today, and their application to fashion professionals are explored in this chapter and throughout this book.

In 2015, a simple Google search reveals over forty million books on the topic of professionalism. Virtually every career track offers a set of standards for practice. Your familiarity with the expectations of fashion professionals will position you to emerge as sought-after in the job search process.

When seeking employment, particularly at the entry level, aspiring professionals should be conscious of how valuable the experiences that they will encounter are. There is no substitute for experience, particularly in an industry as dynamic as the field of fashion. Whether your aspirations are toward design, product development, sales, merchandising, styling, manufacturing, management, or teaching, experience in as many facets of the industry as possible not only will increase your knowledge of the interdependence of the industry, but also will provide the advantage of learning firsthand about career possibilities that you might not otherwise have considered.

Professionals, according to *Webster's Dictionary*, are "engaged in, or worthy of the high standards of a professional." Drawing upon this generic definition, the following section explores several criteria that contribute to professionalism. Box 3.1 highlights key behaviors that exemplify professional actions and attitudes.

Body of Knowledge

The cumulative information and skills that you possess is your "body of knowledge." As a student seeking to educate yourself in a specific discipline, you are refining your body of knowledge—presumably so that you will be an attractive candidate for the job market. Professionals have developed skills and expertise that allow them to show leadership in their

---

BOX 3.1 Key Characteristics of 21st-Century Professionals

1. Always be kind. Some days are stressful; everyone has moments when they aren't at their best. Strive to respond with kindness—it is often returned, frequently appreciated, and always appropriate.

2. Value your colleagues; endeavor to build diverse teams. Time and again it is proven that outcomes and creative solutions are enhanced when diverse perspectives contribute to problem solving. Recognize that all people have valuable contributions. Empower yourself by building teams that reflect the global environment in which we live and work. Seek insight from people who have different backgrounds and experiences from yourself—that way you will expand your understanding of the world.

3. Be a receptacle of knowledge. In addition to the "how to do it" work of your job, be sure to keep up with the news in trade journals such as *Women's Wear Daily* as

well as global events. Consider starting each day with a summary of national and world events (such as theSkimm.com).

4. Be aware of the vision, mission, and code of ethics for your company and your disciplines' professional organization(s)—and ensure that your own codes fit with your company. Know your workplace; be in a position to reflect its culture as you carry out daily activities. Consider the workplace mission as you set goals for yourself.

5. Practice strong communication strategies. Interacting with others is impossible to avoid. An ability to communicate clearly, appropriately, and in a way that reflects your organization's image provides credibility. Communication in a variety of formats and with widely different audiences is expected in professional settings. Effective communication must be practiced on a regular basis.

---

organizations and make their own advancement in the industries where they work. As a future professional, you are acquiring skills and knowledge that contribute to your mastery of the retailing and apparel merchandising disciplines. Knowledge of retailing principles, textiles, manufacturing processes, merchandising mathematics, promotional strategies, and so on prepares you to interact successfully in the merchandising industry. Although basic knowledge of these and related areas positions you to embark on a career in this industry, advanced knowledge that comes with experience will enable you to grow in your career and accept greater responsibilities as time goes on. The knowledge that you gain academically, as evidenced by an earned degree from a college or university, is likely to be viewed by recruiters as an "entry ticket" to your lifelong career.

Value for Lifelong Learning

We live in a dynamic world. When you graduate and embark on a career full-time, the educational process will continue in a new setting. New

6. Be trustworthy, reliable, and accurate. You will gain the respect of your co-workers, your supervisor, and your clients through honest actions. Demonstrating follow-through on your assigned tasks is important and expected—do what you say you will do! Also, check over your work; your work is a reflection of the company that has employed you.

7. Volunteer for new opportunities. We tend to gravitate toward activities that are comfortable and to resist those that are unfamiliar, intimidating, and challenging. Going outside of your comfort zone can be exhilarating. Without taking on new experiences, you cannot grow.

8. Seek constructive criticism. It is much sweeter to hear praises than to receive criticism. Nevertheless, as a professional, an ability to accept feedback that can guide improvement will ultimately empower you to be your best self.

9. Acknowledge the good work of others. Recognition feels good. Additionally, your observation of others' successes often results in more highly motivated and loyal coworkers.

10. Seek opportunities for others. Your ability to help others use their best skills for meaningful contributions to the workplace, community, project team, or social network not only positions others for success, but reflects well upon you as a leader.

11. Be a mentor. True professionals recognize that new-to-career colleagues and acquaintances are not competition; rather, they are the future of our industries and disciplines. We owe it to the future to mentor those who will lead after our "shift" is done. In the words of Mary Church Terrell, *lift as you climb.*

technologies, new management theories, changes in global environments and attitudes, and corporate restructuring all provide new opportunities for learning. As you progress through your career, you should expect to observe the environments around you, learn about new innovations, and grow in your knowledge and leadership abilities. For example, the arrival of the Internet has changed the way we shop—and the way we seek jobs. Changes in international trade policies open new markets for fashion, and therefore new opportunities for career experiences. You should seek opportunities to learn about cutting-edge technologies and be able to adapt to change as it occurs. For example, the development of "fast fashion," which is possible because of new capacities in technology, has changed the way retailers respond to consumer demand. Fashion professionals have also needed to adapt to an ever-increasing pace of fashion product development. Professionals not only anticipate but embrace new opportunities for learning throughout their careers and lives.

Commitment to the Company and the Industry

Loyalty is an important characteristic of a professional. When you make employment decisions, you should be committed to that organization. Although it is expected that you will seek additional employment opportunities in the future, you should exercise discretion regarding the commitment you have to your current employer. In fact, your loyalty to a current employer is likely to be evaluated by future employers as you pursue career advances. Loyalty can be measured in such things as length of time with a company (many people advise at least one year commitment to an entry-level position), willingness to take on extra duties or perform tasks that need to be done, and actions as simple as showing up consistently each day on time. Additionally, the way you convey your attitude toward your employer—verbally and through social media—exhibits your loyalty and professionalism.

Awareness and Execution of Professional Communication

Being a professional includes the ability to interact with and communicate effectively with others. In a professional environment, communication often requires diplomacy and careful choice of format. Wise choices with respect to using email, text messaging, telephone conversations, and face-to-face meetings can greatly enhance your professional image as well as your ability to function as a member of your work team.

While a vast amount of business correspondence takes place through email, some communications require a more personal format (e.g., phone call or in-person meeting) and others can be effective with quicker methods, such as text messaging. Being able to discriminate among communication formats and make appropriate selections will heighten the effectiveness of your message. As a general rule, routine daily communication via email is efficient and carries the advantage of written documentation. There are times, however, when email exchanges become excessive and a telephone call or walk down the hall for a conversation can more quickly and pleasantly complete the work being discussed. Similarly, when email correspondence takes on a sour tone, particularly if one or more parties included in the email are expressing frustration or anger, a verbal conversation is recommended.

Typically in a workplace, emails are preferable to text messaging, but when communication needs to be immediate and when the parties engaged in the communication have an established working relationship, text messaging or instant messaging can be highly effective. When using a messaging format, be sure to assess the relationship that you have with the receiver of your communication. Select abbreviations and emoticons with care, and be alert to automatic corrections that can be embarrassing.

Written communication lacks nuances of tone and body language; therefore, there is a greater tendency for misunderstanding compared to verbal conversations. On the other hand, written communication provides a reference and documentation of instructions, details, and timing that cannot be replicated with the same degree of accuracy in verbal conversations. Although telephone and face-to-face communications are more intimate and more animated than script, keep in mind that age, culture, religion, and gender should be considered as potential differentiating factors regarding interpretations of both spoken and body language.

In contexts as global as the fashion industry, it is important to realize that the diverse perspectives of people with whom you interact can affect the perceptions of your message. People who share a given language differ in their regional accents and the slang terms unique to their geographies and generations, and non-native speakers of the workplace language may struggle with literal interpretations of common (but unconventional) expressions. Wangari Maathai describes in her memoir *Unbowed* (2006) the way language can be misconstrued, especially when non-standard figures of speech are involved. As a young girl at boarding school in Kenya, she and her classmates were required to speak and write exclusively in English. She recalls a classmate who used the literal interpretation of the Kikuyu phrase *no tûrar?a mwaki* ("eating fire") to describe her day's activities in a letter home to her mother. The teachers were appalled by the perceived blasphemous lie the girl reported and punished her by placing charcoal instead of dinner on her meal plate—all because of a misunderstood metaphor that, to native Kikuyu speakers, carried the colloquial meaning of "having great fun."

In addition to careful attention about the words used in your communication, you need to be aware of the people who are included in your communication activities. It is very easy to send emails to large groups of people, for example. Sometimes people who reply add additional recipients to the distribution, and sometime replies drop some parties from subsequent communications. Take care to be aware of the protocol expected in your office place with regard to including and omitting colleagues and clients in group email messages. Be careful when you "reply all." A good rule of thumb is to only put into an email what you would be willing to have printed in a widely distributed news source. If you want to say something that you don't want repeated or known, do not put your message in an email. Similarly, learn how to appropriately use blind courtesy copies (see Box 3.2). When you are the blind recipient, take great care not to reply to the group. This was a painful lesson for Bluefield State College's chairman of the Board of Governors, whose gaffe with a "reply all" insulted a large group of college employees and resulted in his resignation (Thomason, 2015). Typically, you should always visibly copy any people who need to know the contents of your email (e.g., an email to George stating that Janelle will complete a task should be copied to Janelle). Likewise, you should generally copy the person on whose behalf you are sending a communication (e.g., when your boss requests that you send information to his client, copy your boss when you do so).

You are likely to face situations where you want to have documentation (i.e., create a "paper trail") of instructions or agreements that are delivered verbally. Diplomacy in communication is particularly important when the relationship with a colleague or client is sensitive—and when you want to confirm the outcome of a negotiated decision or your responsibilities as a team member. We suggest the following strategy for situations when you want to document a verbal conversation. First, take careful notes (written or mental) of the communication. Translate the details into a summary email that you send in a timely manner to your communication partner, and request confirmation (or clarification) of the information you have sent. This way you have written documentation for reference, but have been able to first discuss and negotiate sensitive information without a clutter of tedious (and possibly emotional) emails. This works well when seeking direction as an intern, when meeting with a professor for clarity on an assignment, and for supervising employees— particularly when counseling them on areas of improvement.

BOX 3.2 Guidelines for Blind Email Copies

1. You may use a blind copy to your manager when (a) he or she has asked to be kept closely in the loop about a situation and (b) having his or name on the CC line might intimidate or undermine the person receiving the email. You may also use this approach if a Human Resources or Personnel representative has asked you to do so.

2. Use a blind copy to your coworkers when you want them to have the details of a communication to a client or customer and when the client or customer might be distracted or confused by their names on the CC line.

3. Avoid using blind copies for any "guilty" communication. A guilty communication is one in which you would feel guilty or embarrassed if the primary recipient of the email were to find out that you had sent it to others. Any time a little voice tells you that you may regret sending blind copies, don't do it!

4. When you need other people to know about a situation, but you know that the primary recipient would be upset about those people receiving a CC or BCC, instead email a *summary* of the information to others. Then if the primary recipient asks, "Did you copy anyone on this message?" you can honestly say no. You can add, "However, I did need to summarize what happened for Ms. X and Mr. Y, so they would be aware of the situation."

5. Never use blind copies to damage another person's reputation.

Source: Lynn Gaetner-Johnston, SYNTAX Training, http://www.businesswritingblog.com
Printed with permission.

Personal Contribution to the Field

Mentoring is a way of giving back—to the profession, the industry, your alma mater, and those who aspire to reach the goals that you have already achieved. You are likely to have many mentors who guide your professional development and, in turn, you should plan to provide mentorship to others when you have reached a certain level of professional status. In fact, as an upper-class student, you may have multiple opportunities to be a mentor to students who are less experienced than you. Professionals look for ways to make positive contributions to their companies, the industry as a whole, and aspiring professionals. This process includes contribution in professional organizations, where conveniently, much networking and mentoring occurs. Organizations such as the National Retail Federation, the Fashion Group, and the American Marketing Association provide venues offering leadership and educational seminars. Individual professionals who take advantage of these industry events are afforded great networking and information-gathering opportunities that benefit themselves as well as the companies they represent. Memberships in professional organizations enable you to develop a set of credentials that allow you to give back to your company and to the profession.

Career Advancement

Ambition is a character trait associated with professionalism. As you negotiate growth strategies for your career, you should keep in mind that complementary values such as loyalty, commitment, lifelong learning, and knowledge are associated with career advancement. Your ability to set goals will enable you to assess the progress of your career growth. Valuing advancement as opposed to settling for the status quo in a career is a positive reflection of one's professional profile. Career advancement can take many forms. Examples of career advancement include expansion of a sales territory, consistently increasing personal sales and your client base, promotion to a new position, and taking on additional supervisory roles. Additionally, career advancement can be achieved by expanding the scope of the professional activities you perform. Aaron Sturgill has expanded his professional activities by taking on college teaching assignments that complement his work as career coach as Assistant Director in Ohio University's Career and Leadership Center. Other ways to advance professionally include accepting leadership roles in professional associations and serving as chairperson or coordinator for corporate fundraising or community events. All of these activities reflect personal improvement, continual progress, and acceptance of new challenges. Careers Up Close 3.1 highlights the way Leah Rogers advanced her career using personal branding strategies.

CAREERS UP CLOSE 3.1
LEAH ROGERS
Director,
Brand and Agency Management
Nationwide

Love for creativity and boundless enthusiasm are two of Leah Rogers' strengths. She has capitalized upon her passion for visual presentation and her awareness of professional protocol throughout a career that has included wardrobe styling, freelance promotional marketing, photography production, creative development, and brand identity leadership. Leah's early experiences in fashion styling honed her ability to combine analytical skills with creative solutions to day-to-day challenges. Leah notes that her knowledge of budgeting and personnel management enables her to oversee business operations while her visionary leadership in high-energy environments engenders the trust of her clients and staff. She has successfully harnessed the characteristics that have positioned her for success as a director of brand and agency management—thus simultaneously communicating her own professional brand while also leading brand identity for her company.

As a director of brand and agency management, Leah collaborates with other members of the corporate senior leadership team to develop strategies that result in clear execution of the company brand. Communications, including advertising and other promotions, client information materials, and community outreach activities, must all be consistent with her company's mission.

She has established a reputation for visionary strategic development, critical decision making, and building high performance teams; furthermore, Leah is aware that each opportunity in her career has resulted from her careful attention to professional performance—and her ability to effectively communicate her capabilities.

Just as a corporate brand supports the reputation of its company, a personal brand presents the professional reputation of the person. Leah recommends that students consider their strengths and interests and harness those criteria as a personal brand is developed. She emphasized the importance of proving in your communication channels that you will provide mutually beneficial contributions to potential employers—evidenced by your being able to articulate what you want to learn as well as what skills and knowledge you are already positioned to offer.

DEVELOPING YOUR PERSONAL BRAND

Your personal brand is unique to you and should provide a foundation for personal networking and marketing as you seek professional opportunities. *Brand*—a word used to describe a particular identifying characteristic, a trade name, or unique kind or variety (e.g., humor, style, professionalism)—is increasingly recognized as a personal, as opposed to a solely corporate, concept.

In 1997, Tom Peters presented the concept of personal branding in his *Fast Company* article, "The Brand Called You." He describes the importance of establishing a personal brand by stating, "It's this simple: You are a brand. You are in charge of your brand. There is no single path to success. And there is no one right way to create the brand called You. Except this: Start today. Or else." In fact, Heather Huhman in a 2015 Glassdoor Blog article included *personal brand and online presence* among the top four items employers seek in applicant résumés. In further support of the value a well-established personal brand has on career opportunities, Dan Schawbel (2009, p. 2) wrote in his book, *Me 2.0*:

Many people may view personal branding as a form of self-promotion and selfishness. In some ways it is, but this doesn't mean it's a bad thing! Developing your brand makes you a more valuable asset, whether to the company you work for, a potential employer, or your own enterprise. Don't forget, it's your future we're talking about. Don't you want to make it a success? Furthermore, by effectively branding yourself, your career success will translate into happiness outside the workplace as well.

For example, MacKenzie King (see Careers Up Close 8.3 in Chapter 8), was able to position herself as an expert in children's clothing behaviors as a result of her honors thesis, "Preschool Boys' and Girls' Clothing Choices: Investigating Their Participation and Influences." She capitalized on this element of her personal brand to land an internship opportunity with 77Kids. Similarly, Alexa Speros (see Careers Up Close 3.2) effectively conveyed her fashion savvy in her career search blog, which communicates her personal brand. Thus, consider your activities, your interests, and your opportunities, and make a strategic plan to promote your professional profile in a memorable, meaningful way. As MacKenzie, Alexa, and Joy Teiken (see Careers Up Close 3.3) have discovered, your personal brand will evolve throughout your career; however, you can manage the way your brand develops.

CAREERS UP CLOSE 3.2
ALEXA SPEROS
Assistant Store Manager
Kohl's Department Store,
Columbus, Ohio

Alexa Speros parlayed years of customer service experience—as a waitress in a family restaurant, health club barista, and sales associate at a clothing store—into a successful internship search. She had learned that she excelled in customer service, so she was confident that an internship with Nordstrom on the sales floor would be a good fit. Fortunately, she offered a highly competitive résumé filled with multiple, related work experiences, and she earned a coveted position as an intern at the east coast Nordstrom flagship store in Tyson's Corner, Virginia.

With a unique and creative promotional strategy, Alexa created a blog that conveys her personal brand, which spring-boarded her toward professional positions that fit her goals. Her blog was, in her words, casual and experimental—a place that presented "pictures and writings about my interest in fashion as a whole, and particularly how I like to take articles of clothing and shoes and jewelry from different price points and create an entire look from head to toe." Alexa used the blog to showcase her talents in studying style looks from *Glamour*, *In Style*, *Vogue*, and *Cosmopolitan* and recreating them at affordable prices. She reflects, "I blogged about how I liked to go shopping at high-end department and specialty stores as well as at mid-level and discount stores, choosing pieces from each place and eventually putting together entire outfits—at a fraction of the cost of what I would see in the pages of the fashion magazines."

The blog itself provided a venue for Alexa to showcase her talents, knowledge, and interests—and also gave her the personal confidence to present herself at job interviews. The preparation of work that Alexa put into her blog provided time to think and reflect upon her professional abilities so that she was well prepared to discuss them in interviews. In fact, during her interview with Nordstrom, she was put into a scenario where she was asked to create outfits for different types of customers, keeping a budget in mind. Obviously, this was an interview task in which Alexa excelled!

During her internship, where she was placed in the boys/infants/toddlers/designer department, she loved the daily interaction with customers and thrived on her ability to meet their needs. Alexa recalls one particular customer, a young mother who was expecting a second child, who came into her department with her son and mother in search of a diaper bag. After offering assistance, which was declined, Alexa left them alone to continue their shopping. Alexa noticed the woman admiring one particular diaper bag—an $800 Burberry item—that had been passed over for

weeks. The customer really seemed to like the bag, but was struggling with the price issue. Alexa knew that was her cue! She proceeded to show this woman and her mom the many features of the diaper bag; most importantly, Alexa pointed out that it didn't resemble an ordinary diaper bag. She highlighted that it was sophisticated in its style and design and could double as a makeup and jewelry bag for travelling when it was no longer needed for the baby. Alexa elaborated on how toiletries and jewelry could fit in the various pockets and slots and how its former life as a diaper bag would be unknown. Alexa also emphasized the quality of the bag, noting that it was so well made that it would last for years to come. The client loved the idea and didn't hesitate any longer, buying a bag that had sat on the shelf for weeks! Alexa recalls, "My heart soared as I knew my manager would be so pleased! Sometimes you have to think out of the box to change the meaning of a particular item; when you take time to understand the customer's needs, you can present the relevant utility of the merchandise!"

The internship was full of hard work, but her activities were exceptional opportunities to learn and grow professionally—and to show her best skills, including customer relations, sales performance analytics, and employee affairs (including scheduling). She was also afforded interactions with vendors, which gave insight into the wholesale aspect of retailing. Alexa's dedication paid off; she quickly emerged as top seller on the floor!

Alexa continues to update her personal blog, and remains dedicated to defining and communicating her personal brand. The image she has created demonstrates a creative, confident, and fashionable professional—and as a bonus for networking and continually seeking career opportunities, presents her current résumé. Her advice about personal branding through blogging is to "choose something you love or have a passion for, and strive to work in that field. It makes a huge difference to engage yourself in something that attracts your creative and passionate side; from there, you will be more accepting to learn the business side!" Alexa's passion for style and presentation—and her ability to apply those in customer service situations—enable her to continually develop an authentic blog that highlights her strengths and personal brand.

Kelly Borth, CEO and chief strategy officer for GREENCREST, presented advice about the strategies of well-branded companies in her 2015 *Smart Business* article. She emphasized the importance of companies being distinctive in their brand identities—and this is true of building a strong personal brand strategy, too. As you seek to define your own brand, consider Borth's advice, which includes being aware (and in front of) the competition, offering an element of surprise, using multiple touch points to deliver your brand experience, having a strong sense of clarity, and evolving with changing times. Joy Teiken's philosophy in developing her brand Joynoelle is highlighted in Careers Up Close 3.3.

CAREERS UP CLOSE 3.3
JOY TEIKEN
Owner, Designer
Joynoelle

Focusing on her love for artistic creation and her love for fashion, Joy Teiken launched Joynoelle in 2000. With Joynoelle, Joy captures a niche in the Minneapolis market offering couture bridal and daily wear fashions produced in her atelier. Joy draws from a love of historic influence and an appreciation for fluid, feminine lines to produce what she refers to as "wearable couture."

"Saying that you want to be a fashion designer is like saying you want to be a rock star," Joy says. "Very few people actually make enough money to support themselves as designers, so I've developed a strategy to generate profits through my bridal designs, and I execute an annual ready-to-wear line to feed my creative passions." Joy notes that she started out as a designer who had a business, but she has developed into a business person who happens to be a designer; in her words, "you have to be able to make money in a business career."

In addition to a sound knowledge of art and skills in fashion design, Joy draws from a wealth of influences and life experiences as she creates modern, yet timeless, couture clothing. Her current role as owner and designer of her own label evolved from experiences that have included international travel and teaching. In fact, teaching others art and fashion design enabled Joy to more fully explore her own interests, talents, and goals. After two years in the Peace Corps, where she taught art to children in Botswana, Africa, and then teaching three-dimensional art at Creative Arts High School in St. Paul, Joy decided to launch her own business and label: Joynoelle. The risk of going into business for herself was a bit daunting to Joy, so it was helpful that she maintained her "day job" as an art teacher—though the dual careers left little time to spare. Within two years, Joy felt that her business was able to support her full time; Joynoelle has been her sole career since 2002. Joy's business endeavors are promoted through her website: http://www.joynoelle .com/, but her reputation for client-centered couture services is the foundation of her business. Joy discloses that ready-to-wear is her true passion, but she recognizes that she would be out of business if she limited her products to RTW. The creativity that she puts into each design in her annual line is an exercise in renewal and rejuvenation for her, but her couture dress business—emphasizing bridal—fuels her company's income.

Joy emphasizes, "I want to be true to my art, but I'm a realist. The goal of my career is to support myself and my family; therefore, I need to be strategic about my priorities and my business activities. For example, when I first started my business, I opened a studio in New York City and traveled there once a month for over a year. I would meet with clients and editors but learned that the day-to-day pace, the expense, and the energy needed to compete in that environment did not fit me. So, I took the New York fashion experience and returned to my Midwestern roots in Minneapolis. Living in Minneapolis allows me to do my work the way I want to." Joy reflects that, through her business, she can embrace the community of Minneapolis, and even give back to local non-profit organizations through proceeds from her annual fashion show. The RTW line enables local fashion design students to fulfill their internship requirements as production assistants—executing product lines, photo shoots, promotional strategies, and the runway show over a six-month period. Mentoring and being part of the Minneapolis community is an important component of Joy's professional portfolio.

Joy's playful, yet classic, designs showcase exquisite workmanship and careful attention to detail. Likewise, Joy prides herself on the level of customer service that she is able to offer her clients. Joy offers a "full bridal experience," meaning that prospective clients first meet with Joy to present their dress needs and share their ideas and expectations about the dress. Joy listens carefully to each client, seeking insight into her personality and even potential limitations (such as a religious venue's sumptuary regulations). Joy is careful to communicate to her clients that all of her designs are original—she may use images for inspiration, but she won't copy another designer's work. Joy says that building the client–designer relationship is a two-way process. Sometimes she even counsels a prospective client that her couture services may not be the best route to securing a dress. Joy explains, "My clients have to trust that they will be pleased with the outcome . . . they must commit to my design before it has been developed and sewn."

Once Joy has an understanding of her client's goals, she begins draping fabrics on the client's body. A "dress up" experience is personalized, with Joy's expertise about colors, shapes, and lines informing her suggestions about what design features will complement the woman's body. The individual couture experience, with the client in front of a mirror, enables the woman herself to see instantly as a design draft emerges. Joy reads the customer reaction, and finally, when there is a dress concept, a series of fittings are arranged. Throughout the fittings, the design often continues to change and evolve. Joy offers the example of a bride who is convinced at the onset that she *must* have a long train, but as the dress emerges, the bride decides the train can be eliminated. This intimate process facilitates a close relationship between Joy and the bride. She forges close friendships, attends weddings, and even receives photos of baby pictures years later. Joy proudly shares that "many women have shared with me that the process of having their dress made was the best part of their wedding planning."

Joy's habit of being present in her studio on a daily basis to work and supervise the atelier operations is similar to an author who has a habit of writing several pages per day to stay involved with the craft. This commitment to designing demonstrates the work ethic that has established Joynoelle as a premier bridal couturier in the Midwest. Similarly, Joy's self-imposed renewal through creative design for a RTW line and show feeds Joy's soul while also supporting her persona as a fashion designer. "I see myself as approachable and 'down to earth'—rather than as a stereotypical wacky designer. I think my clients do too . . . which is important to the way I create a comfortable, trusting environment for women to experience the creation of the most important dress they will ever wear." Joy offers this final bit of advice: "Don't take yourself too seriously. You will have successes, and you will have failures. Especially after the really exciting successes, remember that there will be future challenges—and you need to be ready to face them."

Aliza Licht, the mastermind behind the wildly successful Twitter personality DKNY PR GIRL, offers excellent advice about fashion careers and effective use of social media in her book *Leave Your Mark* (2015). Specifically, she encourages development of personal bios as the first step in establishing your personal brand. Licht (2015, p. 199) advises you to write a bio in third person that includes:

1. Personality/physical attributes
2. Education
3. Career path, including important jobs and titles
4. Hobbies
5. Passions
6. Talents, awards, etc.
7. Marital/family status
8. Affiliations, charity or otherwise

As you refine your bio—which can be used as an elevator speech, as the summary on your Twitter and Facebook profiles, and strategically within your résumés and cover letters—give careful attention to consistency and appropriateness of the information for each intended purpose and audience.

YOUR INTERNET AND SOCIAL MEDIA PRESENCE

Recruiters today expect that their prospective employees have social media accounts. In fact, many employers perform social media or Internet searches as screening tools to determine who should be interviewed. Using social media can enhance your portrayal of the image and characteristics, unique to you, that position you apart from the crowd. Therefore, we encourage professional use of social media, which can and should provide a foundation for personal networking and marketing as you seek professional opportunities.

Social media has the potential to either support your image and brand or negate the positive image you seek to present. According to the 2014 Jobvite Social Recruiting Survey, 93% of recruiters review social profiles of candidates before making hiring decisions. The survey (2014, p. 10) results list the following items recruiters look for in candidates' social networks:

- professional experience
- length of professional tenure
- industry-related posts
- mutual connections
- specific hard skills
- cultural fit
- examples of written or design work

Most often, candidates' online profiles are inconsequential; however, if there is an influence, it is usually negative for the candidates. Specifically, Jobvite (2014) cites use of profanity; spelling and grammar mistakes; and posts regarding sex, illegal drug use, alcohol, and guns as negative influences on final hiring decisions. On a positive note, material about volunteering and making charitable donations carries supportive hiring influence. Be aware and be wise about the way your image is conveyed in all forms of social media.

Be aware of your social presence so that you are in the driver's seat in terms of what surfaces. Pay particular attention to the characteristics that define and promote your personal brand, and endeavor to document these through your online posts. Beth Backes, Director of the Curriculum and Technology Center and Online Learning at Ohio University's Patton College, suggests conducting a self-search using multiple search engines.

The results that you observe are the same that will be viewed by your potential employers. If you are happy with the results, keep up the good work; if you are not satisfied, you have the opportunity to manage your online presence—and you should immediately take action. Additionally, to optimize the promotion of your personal brand, Backes recommends use of multiple social media platforms with unified themes and visual images. A word of caution—ensure that you present accurate and honest information about yourself and your work on social media. That is, be careful not to borrow intellectual property (e.g., logos, catch phrases, fashion designs) to be presented as your own. Be sure to properly cite your sources and resources; exhibit creativity through your unique work and products.

Companies are using social media to promote their products as well as to learn about customers and employees, including recruitment. Corporate presence on social networking sites has increased dramatically in recent years. In 2014, 80 percent of *Fortune* 500 companies were on Facebook, and 83 percent had active Twitter accounts, according to Nora Ganim Barnes and Ava Lescault of the University of Massachusetts Dartmouth (2014). This figure reflects an increase of 10 percent from the prior year. Lesser-known platforms are used as well. Barnes and Lescault (2014) reported that Foursquare's use increased by 42% in 2014, growth in Pinterest was 27%, and the adoption rate of Instagram grew by 12%.

Use these networking opportunities to your advantage, and be aware of the reach that social sites have with respect to merging your private and professional lives. Today, it is essential that you incorporate social media into your personal brand promotional strategies. Furthermore, social media site benefits are reciprocal; who you follow is as important as your brand and who follows you. That is, your deliberate strategy to follow people and companies who support your brand and purpose reflects and further supports your professional image. The 2014 Jobvite survey results show that recruiters review the mutual connections of their prospective employees and use sites to evaluate design work as well as writing skills. With this in mind, be sure to follow as many professionally relevant sites as possible. You will gain valuable information, breaking news, and trending broadcasts while at the same time sending the message of your professional activity. See www.bloomsburyfashioncentral.com for links to relevant fashion sites. Furthermore, be careful to take the time to portray accuracy, strong examples of your work, and good communication abilities in your online and electronic media sites. In the section that follows, some of the most widely used social media platforms are described, with particular attention given to ways that you can effectively use them as tools to build your personal brand in a professionally relevant manner.

Facebook

Facebook is unquestionably the most widely used social media platform in the world. While Facebook was originally launched purely for its social networking function, companies and organizations now use the network for marketing and recruiting. Because many people develop a Facebook presence long before they begin professional work, a good first step in building your brand strategy is to comb through your Facebook page to edit its content, untag inappropriate photos, and generally give yourself a makeover. You may want to consider launching a separate Facebook page that contains only professional posts and links (but do realize that while you can enhance the privacy settings on your personal page, anything that is "out there" can be shared and retrieved).

LinkedIn

Recruiters expect you to have a LinkedIn presence; it is the most widely used professional networking site. There are over 400 million users, worldwide, on the LinkedIn platform (LinkedIn, 2015). Think of your LinkedIn site as a public cover letter. Most career coaches insist that a LinkedIn account is essential for both job seeking and career networking. Companies and recruiters are on LinkedIn, too. In addition to setting up your professional profile, LinkedIn allows you to follow companies who are established on LinkedIn. Be sure to review the presence of companies—in the fashion industry as well as other trending market forces— to gain insight into their culture and performance indicators as well as job opportunities. When you connect with others or when your profile is viewed by others, those people can see your LinkedIn connections— which will likely be used to evaluate your professional abilities, including savvy and professionalism. LinkedIn is well known for its opportunities to endorse people (for countless skills such as leadership, public speaking, retailing, marketing, fashion, etc.), which is typically a reciprocal activity. You should make connections with professors, supervisors, job colleagues, and people with whom you volunteer. Do your part to provide endorsements for others, and request (if they don't do so automatically) that they make endorsements for you. An additional, helpful feature offered by LinkedIn is the recommendation letter. People with whom you are connected can upload recommendation letters onto your profile. While you are focused on building your personal brand, consider the influential and credible people you know who could provide professional recommendations on your LinkedIn profile. Keep in mind that it does take effort for others to do this for you, so provide your résumé, descriptions of your work and activities, and plenty of lead time when requesting this service (and then be sure to send a personal letter of thanks!).

You can also support your job search with LinkedIn tools such as the Alumni Tool. Using this LinkedIn resource, you can search where graduates of your school (or any other school) live and work. You can focus your search to specific careers, majors, locations, and employers as you seek to expand your network.

Twitter

Twitter has become somewhat of an institution of instant news. With Twitter, you are in control of the messages you send—and they must be short (140 characters). The challenge with Twitter is gaining followers, because only people who follow you will receive your tweets. Therefore, as you develop your brand and provide resources (résumé, email, business card) to others, be sure to indicate your Twitter account. Tweets can be "favored" and retweeted, so be sure what you post is information that you want to go public. Beth Backes suggests having separate personal and professional Twitter accounts, particularly if you enjoy using Twitter socially. Even if you do keep your professional account separate, keep in mind that your personal information is easily accessible.

Twitter introduces the phenomenon of the hashtag: the pound sign (#) preceding a word or phrase on a specific topic. When you create a hashtag that others adopt and repeat, a trending effect on Twitter results. Hashtags, however, are complicated, and if used, should be selected with care (see Box 3.3). YouTube, Mashable, and other informational sites provide insight and instructions for using hashtags. We encourage you to carefully investigate this tool and use it wisely in your personal branding campaign.

The nature of Twitter and tweeting introduces complexity for its management—particularly when desiring to create a forum that will gain followers while also heightening the recognition of your personal brand. Savvy management of Twitter accounts can optimize the effect of your brand promotion scheme. Apps such as Tweetdeck and Hootsuite enable you to plan ahead with tweets that will be automatically released at times that are likely to generate substantial views.

Google+

Google+ is a social networking site similar to Facebook, but with features for connecting with others in a variety of ways and for multiple purposes. Essentially, it is a competitor of both Facebook and Twitter. Google+ account holders create Google Profiles and generate Google Buzz. There are Circles, Hangouts, Sparks, and Huddles, which provide platforms for different types

BOX 3.3 Selecting a Hashtag to Promote Your Personal Brand

Hashtags associated with Twitter can be fun, effective ways to support your social media presence. The following tips can help you select a hashtag that reflects your personal brand.

1. Make it exciting. To be memorable, and to encourage interaction, it is important for your hashtag to emote excitement. Hashtags should not repeat your brand name (Twitter username) but should convey your concept. For example, Ben & Jerry's #CaptureEuphoria slogan fits nicely with the feelings associated with eating their ice cream. Similarly, Nike's #MakeItCount and Charmin's #tweetfromtheseat reflect memorable and entertaining brand associations.

2. Be original. Do some research (use Twitter, Instagram, Google+, and Facebook) to ensure that your hashtag isn't already in use. Consider using resources such as Walls.io, where you can create a free trial wall to test your hashtag across ten platforms.

3. Test it before going live. You want your hashtag to be memorable in a positive way. Sometimes well-intentioned hashtags evoke ambiguous and even inappropriate messages. In order to reduce the aftermath of an embarrassing hashtag—such as Susan Boyle's album launch with #Susanalbumparty—carefully read your proposed hashtag and ask for feedback from others.

4. Keep it short. As with all Twitter posts, keep your hashtag short. Fewer than ten characters is optimal, but if you must use more, make sure that your message is easy to remember and does not contain tricky spelling. Using a combination of capital and lowercase letters also helps receivers of your message to understand and repeat it.

5. Develop a strategy for trending. Once you establish a unique and memorable hashtag that positively reflects your personal brand, you will want to incorporate it into your promotional strategy. Include your hashtag on your résumé, business card, and email signature line. Use your hashtag at opportune times when you tweet, and encourage your friends to pick up on your hashtag so that it generates momentum.

6. Evaluate your hashtag and make changes if necessary. Give your hashtag some time to develop, but limit that evaluation time to several months. Consider the feedback and re-tweets that were generated by your hashtag and determine whether it was effective. Ask for feedback from people you trust, and be objective about its positive and negative outcomes. Remember, even highly experienced advertising agencies must re-evaluate and refine their promotional strategies.

of group interactions. You may have used a Google Hangout for group work in an academic setting or for cross-department collaborations in a work site. Like the other social networking platforms, you have the opportunity to personalize your site, and your profile. Therefore, G+ provides an additional potential touch point to promote your personal brand.

Instagram

Photo and video sharing is the key purpose of Instagram. Features such as blogging and linking to other social network sites are also affiliated with Instagram, making it a useful app for reaching wide audiences with the images you share. Similarly, you are able to view countless images posted by others. Therefore, Instagram can be a useful way to enhance your brand through visual images. Blogging that supports the visual story can accompany photo and video posts.

Snapchat

Snapchat is a popular visual communication medium that provides instant images through a text-message type format, but with the unique feature that the image is not saved to the sender's or receiver's device. The Snapchat app must be downloaded to a mobile device, and then images can be shared among members in the network. You can follow companies on Snapchat in addition to sending out your own images to your contacts. Some examples of companies using Snapchat include American Apparel, American Eagle, Journey Shoes, and *Seventeen*.

Pinterest

Another popular visual networking tool is Pinterest. The action associated with Pinterest is "pinning" images on your wall. Pinterest allows its members to identify categories of interest and pin items, creating trend boards and other brand-oriented collections.

YouTube

The popular video posting site YouTube can be an excellent complement to the brand promotion activities in your portfolio. Consider posting fashion shows, examples of informational presentations, and other professional demonstrations that enhance your ability to communicate your skills and knowledge. As you seek to incorporate YouTube into your brand plans, take the time to generate a consistent and appropriate introduction and include slide elements such as background colors, font for written text, voice for verbal content, and music—which is useful in establishing and reinforcing image and mood. You should also be aware that you can control the "follow up video" that rolls in a YouTube feed at the conclusion of the video you promote by using playlists. A playlist provides an automatic next video. While you can't control the last video a viewer might ultimately reach, most viewers will seek to watch the video you promote and turn the screen off shortly after the next one starts.

Your management of the next video after your feature video eliminates the possibility of an inappropriate video popping up after your image and being associated with you.

Foursquare

Foursquare is a mobile app with the purpose of providing local information to its user. The idea is that the app stores information about the user's preferences and experiences, and then provides desirable information about local activities and events relevant for the individual person. Businesses seek to establish presence on Foursquare to market their goods and services. Using Foursquare can expand consumers' knowledge of opportunities in their midst. Entrepreneurs and professional consultants are likely to find advantages to including Foursquare among their personal branding tools.

Blogging

Blogs are essentially self-published written features. With the ease of access that the Internet provides, many people have embraced blogs as quick, helpful information sites. Likewise, people who possess knowledge and want to share information, or who seek interactions with likeminded readers, have launched blogs as a means to communicate. Numerous host sites have availed themselves to bloggers. Aspiring professionals have adopted blog formats to promote themselves, to disseminate ideas, or to investigate issues. Some blogs have become so widely followed that their popularity has spun off into books, television shows, and movies. If you have unique ideas or are seeking a way to communicate your brand image—particularly from a consulting or knowledge-based perspective—blogging is an ideal social media forum.

Tumblr

Tumblr is a mix of Instagram and blogging; it is a microblogging social networking platform owned by Yahoo! There are literally hundreds of millions of blogs hosted on Tumblr. It provides users with the ability to upload multimedia into blog posts. Additionally, Tumblr interfaces with Facebook and Twitter.

QR Codes

QR (Quick Response) codes are the square icons that can be printed on anything: music posters, corporate advertisements, sales receipts, business cards, résumés, and so on. Each unique QR code is easily

FIGURE 3.1
QR Code

generated with a free application accessible via the Internet, such as at www.qrstuff.com, https://www.qr-code-generator.com, and https://scan.me. When you generate a QR code through the web-based tool, you identify an address to associate with the code. You could select your portfolio or blog address, your email address, a YouTube video, or your LinkedIn or Facebook page. You can also direct viewers to Twitter, telephone numbers, pdf documents (such as your résumé), or contact details. The opportunities to link a QR code to important information that you control are seemingly endless. See the QR code in Figure 3.1; with a QR reader (which you can download as an app to a mobile device), this code takes you directly to www.bloomsburyfashioncentral.com, where you can access the *Guide to Fashion Career Planning STUDIO.*

As you identify and portray your personal and professional brand, consider including QR codes on your materials so that you are consistently directing viewers in your network to information about yourself. Similarly, when you network, be sure that you have a QR reader on your mobile device so that you can capture information on handouts, brochures, and business cards in an organized (and safe from loss) way.

Resources for Social Media

Fortunately, there are numerous free and easily accessible resources to assist you in building your professional brand presence using social media. The website www.bloomsburyfashioncentral.com provides links to many useful resources. In particular, we recommend that you consult Lynda.com, which provides tutorials and online videos to learn the skills of social media execution. Lynda.com offers the additional advantage of posting certificates on your LinkedIn site for workshop module completion—a great way to indicate your professional acumen and value for lifelong learning.

Projects

1. Check your social media presence (Google yourself). Can you find yourself? Does the message you find match the professional message you want to convey? Why or why not? If not, outline the steps that you need to take to achieve a better alignment.
2. Review social media—find "best practices," good examples, and poor examples. Identify the specific elements that support your categorization scheme.

BOX 3.4 Getting Started—Your Social Media Brand Campaign

- Start out with five to seven key words that define YOU. These words are your reference for promoting your desired brand. Consistently use these keywords to increase the likelihood of your posts rising to the top in a search and to emphasize your focused image. Select your words carefully; be aware that some words can take viewers to visual images that are not consistent with your intended message.

- Use the same name and photo or image as your profile identifiers. Carefully select a "standard" profile visual that is professional and reflects the brand you have defined. Similarly, determine the appearance of your name and use that consistently throughout your social media sites. Repetitive use of the same identifying name and visual serves two purposes—it will reinforce that the site is "you" (especially if your name is shared by other Internet users) and it will further confirm your brand message.

- Select an "elevator speech bio." As with your visual identifier, use the same biographical description of yourself on each social media platform. This is a way to convey your professional image, reputation, experiences, and skills. When you proceed with interviews, cold calls, or other face-to-face forms of communication, draw from this description to elaborate about yourself. Pull from this bio in your cover letters. This is your opportunity to define your brand—then manage your posts to strategically document your brand image.

- Select hashtags carefully. Avoid ambiguous interpretations when using hashtags. Consider how the news of Prime Minister Margaret Thatcher's death in 2013 was erroneously interpreted as Cher's passing through the wide distribution of #nowthatchersdead. Judicious use of capitalization can clarify hashtag meanings (e.g., #nowThatchersDead).

- Develop mobile-friendly pages for blogs and websites. Search engines increasingly favor websites that display well on mobile devices; therefore, you have two advantages with such compliance. First, mobile-friendly pages are easy for readers to navigate on phones and tablets. Second, your website will gain prioritization by search engines when your keywords are searched.

- Search for yourself regularly. A self-search (simply enter your name into a search engine) allows you to monitor your media image. The outcomes of a self-search inform you about the way your brand is communicated and interpreted—especially by strangers. Be sure to use multiple search engines for maximum insight. Use the results to manage your brand through deliberate and strategic changes in your social media activities.

Source: Beth Backes, Director of the Curriculum and Technology Center and Online Learning in The Gladys W. and David H. Patton College of Education, Ohio University.

Printed with permission.

3. Develop a personal blog; identify the purpose of your blog, and execute a strategy to provide information and gain followers.

4. Create your elevator speech. Refine this elevator speech to include biographical information as well as aspirational career goals. Work to incorporate your elevator speech into multiple channels that promote your personal brand (e.g., résumé, cover letters, Twitter, Facebook, Instagram, Tumblr, etc.)

Questions for Discussion

1. What are the best examples of social media campaigns that you can think of? What makes them great? Are the examples you mention mostly companies or individual people? What are the different elements that distinguish a successful campaign for a company versus a person? What are the similar elements?

2. What are some examples of poor examples of social media campaigns? What made them weak, and what suggestions can you offer to improve them?

3. How do you expect to use social media? Is your plan different from your current use? Explain.

STUDiO Activities

Visit the *Guide to Fashion Career Planning STUDIO* available at www.bloomsburyfashioncentral.com. The key elements are:

1. Summary of Chapter 3 text
2. Quiz
3. Written Communication Exercises
4. Launch your personal-branding social media campaign
5. Recovering from a PR disaster

VIDEO: Elevator Speech

References

Barnes, N. G. & Lescault, A. M. (2014). The 2014 *Fortune* 500 and social media: LinkedIn dominates as use of newer tools explodes. Available online: http://www.umassd.edu/cmr/socialmediaresearch/2014fortune500andsocialmedia/

Borth, K. (2015, June 1). 10 things great, well-branded companies do. *Smart Business.* Available online: http://www.sbnonline.com/article/10-things-great-well-branded-companies-do-consistently/

Cole, K. (2003). *Footnotes: What you stand for is more important than what you stand in.* New York: Simon & Schuster.

Huhman, H. (February 25, 2015). 4 things employers look for in résumés. Glassdoor Blog. Available online: http://www.glassdoor.com/blog/4-employers-resumes/

Hurd, H. G. (1967). Who is a professional? *Journal of Cooperative Extension*, 5(3), 77–84.

Jobvite. (2014). Social recruiting survey. Available online: http://web.jobvite.com/FY15_SEM_2014SocialRecruitingSurvey_LP.html?utm_source=google&utm_medium=cpc&utm_term=%2Bjobvite%20%2Bsocial%20%2Brecruiting%20%2Bsurvey&utm_content=2014socialrecruitingsurvey&utm_campaign=search_jobvitecorporate

Licht, A. (2015). *Leave your mark: Land your dream job. Kill it in your career. Rock social media*. New York: Grand Central Publishing.

LinkedIn. (2015). About us. Available online: https://press.linkedin.com/about-linkedin

Maathai, W. (2006). *Unbowed: A memoir*. New York: Random House, Inc.

Peters, T. (1997, August 31). The brand called you. *Fast Company*. Available online: http://www.fastcompany.com/28905/brand-called-you

Schawbel, D. (2009). *Me 2.0: Build a powerful brand to achieve career success*. New York: Kaplan.

Thomason, A. (May 1, 2015). Errant 'reply all' dooms Bluefield State College's board chairman. *The Chronicle of Higher Education*. Available online: http://chronicle.com/blogs/ticker/errant-reply/98201

CHAPTER 4

DEVELOPING YOUR PROFESSIONAL PORTFOLIO

Use what talents you possess: The woods would be very silent if no birds sang there except those that sang best . . .

—HENRY VAN DYKE

OBJECTIVES

- To identify various types of portfolios used to promote your professional growth and profile.
- To learn how to use portfolios for personal assessment, career search, and professional advancement.
- To participate in the process of self-assessment using a portfolio.
- To develop a professional portfolio suitable for presentation to employers.
- To initiate an ongoing portfolio development process that will enhance your professional career.

THE PROFESSIONAL PORTFOLIO

A portfolio is an organized collection of documents that provides evidence of personal accomplishments. Traditionally, designers and others whose careers require visual examples have compiled portfolios. Today, most professional people recognize the benefits of portfolio use. Both the process of coordinating the elements comprising the portfolio and the presentation of the portfolio (during an interview or employment review) are important contributors to professional growth. Fashion business students can use a portfolio to visually communicate their abilities, which definitely increases students' abilities to sell their talents, beyond simply discussing their work.

Why Create a Portfolio?

As you prepare yourself academically for a career in the fashion industry, you are amassing excellent examples that you can use to document your skills, knowledge, and personal strengths. Creating a portfolio provides you with a systematic mechanism for evaluating your work. You can identify the specific skills for which your work provides documented examples, such as fashion illustration, product and surface pattern design, retail math, trend analysis, and management. Your portfolio can also reflect knowledge that you possess—for instance, with respect to application of color theory, principles and elements of design, historic dress, and global apparel industries. Personal strengths that can be emphasized in your portfolio might include attention to detail, organization, leadership, and perseverance. Your portfolio allows you to assemble and organize a comprehensive presentation of your professional profile. Jeromy Coleman's profile in Careers Up Close 4.1 provides information about the types of work products that can be displayed in portfolios to demonstrate your skills.

CAREERS UP CLOSE 4.1
JEROMY Q. COLEMAN
Photo Stylist
Abercrombie & Fitch®

As an undergraduate student studying fashion, Jeromy Coleman set his sights on a career where he could be creative *and* where he could capitalize on his organization and technical skills. To best prepare himself to meet his goals, he joined student organizations and took leadership positions. For example, he was instrumental in producing the annual Fashion Associates Club's annual Mom's Weekend Fashion Show, securing donations from local businesses and establishing corporate sponsors. His academic activities and fashion courses prepared him for a key internship with professional stylist Lani Steinhouse at Hero Wardrobe in New York City, where Jeromy confirmed that a career as a stylist was his goal.

Gaining insight into the details of a commercial costume shop provided a strong foundation for understanding the work of fashion stylists. Capitalizing upon his knowledge of day-to-day stylist work and the networking contacts during the internship, Jeromy successfully transitioned to an entry-level position as an assistant photo stylist upon graduation. He reflects that classes in Adobe Photoshop, trend forecasting, and retail buying all prepared him for his first job.

His dedication to learning the work, persistence, and ability to watch and learn quickly has supported his ongoing career growth. As we know, the area of fashion is very fickle and a fast market, so staying on your toes is definitely a necessity. Now as a lead photo stylist, Jeromy styles the entire Abercrombie and Fitch® male website and has contributed to email and social media presence for the A&F brand. Jeromy recalls, "When starting as a stylist for Abercrombie and Fitch, I had no formal photography training. It wasn't until I started my job that my bosses were really able to show me what our cameras and Photoshop were actually capable of doing." He shares insight about his work as a stylist by explaining, "You're creating 'behind the scenes' magic. It's that openness of the mind and attention to detail that really has helped me grow as a stylist. With the huge expansion of the e-comm industry, I am able to take my knowledge of Photoshop and my training with DSLRs (digital single-lens reflex) and really grow with the industry."

Jeromy offers advice to aspiring stylists, whether it be flat photography, on figure models, or food presentation: "You must start every day ready for a challenge. Don't be afraid of change or starting something new. Don't be afraid to take risks and to adapt. Remember there is always someone waiting in the wings who is ready to take your place, so always put your best foot forward. We work in an industry of some of the most creative and artistic minds, so don't ever stop pushing your creative limits."

In an interview situation, a prospective employer will want to see evidence of an entry-level applicant's success through internships and other practical experience as well as academic coursework. A well-planned and neatly presented professional portfolio is a useful vehicle for personal promotion. As you continue to gain experiences and develop professionally, updating the portfolio as well as the résumé will be important. The portfolio is, essentially, an expanded résumé that provides the documentation for accomplishments you will list on your résumé and discuss in interviews. You should review your portfolio regularly and use it as you evaluate your progress toward goals, set new goals, and consider upwardly mobile career moves. In addition, your portfolio can be used for periodic employment evaluations as well as during interviews for new positions. The sole person responsible for compiling its documentation is its author—you. You may be the only person who, at a later date, remembers and has evidence of your work. Your portfolio is an ideal way to document your academic and career progress. See Careers Up Close 4.2 to gain insight from Stephanie Clark; use this information to consider how blogging and social media work might be presented in a portfolio.

CAREERS UP CLOSE 4.2
STEPHANIE CLARK
Account Coordinator
Zocalo Group, Chicago, Illinois

Stephanie Clark was well on her way to becoming a successful young professional by the time she began college. She started writing her beauty blog, *In Her Makeup Bag*, to help inspire budget-conscious individuals with an interest in cosmetics; it allowed Stephanie a way to combine her love of makeup and social media during college. As she developed her writing skills, she also increased her blog followers, which eventually led to a larger presence on social media.

Realizing that she wanted to pursue social media as a career path, Stephanie decided early on to build a unified body of work centered on that goal. She approached each class project as an opportunity to add a professional piece to her merchandising portfolio, emphasizing her talents in social media, marketing, and fashion. For example, she developed a business and marketing plan for a proposed line of cosmetics, helped produce a fashion photo shoot for *True Star Magazine*, and even put together a team marketing plan that was presented to the Museum of Contemporary Art in Chicago. These projects not only showcased Stephanie's business and marketing ability, but they also indicated to future employers her ability to work individually, with a partner, and within a larger team.

Stephanie also sought out valuable work experience during college in line with her interests. Following her sophomore year, she worked as a makeup artist/sales associate at a local beauty boutique in Chicago where she learned about small businesses and was able to have a variety of roles within her position. That same summer, she also took on a marketing internship at Mark Shale, a high-end clothing store in downtown Chicago, where she worked for the director of marketing and helped with social media, website development, print photo shoots, and numerous merchandising projects. During her junior and senior years of school, Stephanie worked as an assistant to the senior director of marketing at Columbia College Chicago. Along with teaching her valuable skills in traditional marketing and advertising, it was also an opportunity to gain professional experience in social media: One of her many responsibilities was running the Twitter and Instagram accounts for Columbia's event programs, which was helpful in adding value to her résumé.

Based on her work experiences up until this point, Stephanie decided that pursuing a career in social media would be the smartest choice. During the spring semester of her senior year, she was presented an opportunity to shadow a social media strategist at R/GA—a renowned advertising agency with offices in Chicago. Stephanie quickly realized this could jumpstart her career and inquired about a summer internship, which she eventually interviewed for and secured. The summer following her college graduation, she interned at R/GA with the copywriting and social media teams and learned the inner workings of the fast-paced advertising industry.

Given her academic record and work experience, Stephanie had numerous opportunities and offers following this summer internship; however, she kept her goals in mind and did not accept offers that did not reflect those goals. She searched for jobs through a variety of channels: networking with former coworkers and employers, recruiting agencies (Wunderland Group, Paladin, The LaSalle Group, and Advanced Resources), LinkedIn, as well as other job search websites. After a couple of months of vetting positions within the marketing industry, she stumbled upon a job listing for a community manager internship at Zocalo Group, a mid-sized social media/word-of-mouth marketing agency in downtown Chicago. Although she was seeking a full-time job offer, she interviewed for the internship knowing it was exactly the type of experience she wanted. Around the same time, she also sought out a full-time position with a smaller, more specialized social media agency. Soon she had two offers on the table and had to decide between a full-time, salaried position and a paid internship. Stephanie quickly negotiated with the two companies, weighing the pros and cons and having conversations with both management teams. Luckily, a full-time account coordinator position opened up at Zocalo Group, which confirmed her decision to go there. For Stephanie's job search, it was most important to understand 1) the position she wanted, 2) the type of company she wanted to work for, and 3) that having a little patience can reap big benefits.

Another important professional skill that Stephanie developed during college was that of networking. Through each job, volunteer opportunity, class, and internship, Stephanie built lasting relationships with both professors and her classmates/coworkers. As she did so, she also kept her social media profile professional and continually updated and highlighted her experiences on LinkedIn. By the time she was ready to begin her career, she had many peers, mentors, and bosses she could rely on to provide excellent references and sound career advice. Additionally, Stephanie's ability to juggle all of her obligations successfully while maintaining a 3.9 GPA spoke volumes about her work ethic and time management skills.

At Zocalo Group, Stephanie continues to develop her professional skills and responsibilities. Working at an agency offers new experiences and challenges every day, providing many opportunities for personal and professional growth: the fast-paced, team-oriented environment has taught her essential time management and communication skills, as well as the importance of being a self-starter. To students wishing to work in social media and marketing, she recommends:

- Getting your foot in the door: No matter how much work you put into developing your résumé and portfolio, it doesn't have impact if your email isn't opened. Reach out to friends, coworkers, and past employers to figure out what companies you'd like to work for, then ask about informational interviews or opportunities to shadow or intern.
- Don't discredit job search websites: Networking is important, but it's worthwhile to tap into all available resources when looking for a job. Post your résumé to online resources like Glassdoor.com (where Stephanie found her first job as a posted opening), Indeed, Smart Recruiters, and so on, and don't be afraid to work with recruiting agencies.
- Keep your profiles updated: To stay top-of-mind with past coworkers and employers,

update your LinkedIn and other social media profiles as often as you can—even the smallest changes help for search results. This is especially important for LinkedIn, as your profile jumps to the top of search results every time it's updated.

- On motivation: Don't get too discouraged if the perfect position doesn't appear right away. Stephanie gave herself a window of three months to find a job—even if it didn't end up being exactly what she was looking for—so that she wouldn't lose motivation and fall out of the mindset of working.

- One last thought from Stephanie: "You might surprise yourself and realize the job you set out for wasn't what you actually wanted."

We recommend that students begin to develop a portfolio documenting academic and practical experiences and accomplishments early in the collegiate experience. Portfolios are works in progress. It is important that you allow the portfolio to develop by adding new elements and deleting outdated items as progress is made through college and into a career. Initially, as you begin your portfolio, include as much information as possible; save all projects, papers, exams, and other academic assignments for possible inclusion in a portfolio. As the portfolio develops, it should be streamlined so that it becomes a positive reflection of appropriate elements of your work. From all of the work that you save, you can determine which items to include and which to leave out.

Types of Portfolios

There are three basic types of portfolios: assessment portfolios, interview enhancement (career search) portfolios, and performance review and evaluation (career enhancement) portfolios. Most students will benefit from preparing both assessment and interview enhancement portfolios. Each of these should be used separately, as appropriate. Familiarity with the portfolio development process will enable you to transition your interview enhancement portfolio into a performance review and evaluation portfolio as you embark on your career.

All three types of portfolios may be maintained and presented electronically or in hard-copy form. You may wish to construct both—one portfolio that you can carry with you and use to keep original documents, and another, electronic, version that is available on the Internet. An electronic version (e-portfolio) allows you to simply provide a URL to prospective employers so that they can review your work at their convenience. Many students also like to carry a tablet computer with them to career fairs and interviews because they are easily transported and they make it very easy to access their materials.

Assessment Portfolios

Assessment portfolios are compiled primarily to demonstrate growth and accomplishments over a period of time. Students are increasingly required to compile assessment portfolios in their programs of study so that universities can measure the student learning that is taking place (Paulins, 1998; Paulins & Graham, 1999). You may be required to complete an assessment portfolio as a component of your coursework. This is a useful tool for self-evaluation, as well as a collective tool for program faculty to evaluate the progress of their students. Items compiled in an assessment portfolio should be representative of early and later work so that changes in depth of knowledge, application of information or theory, and experience can be demonstrated.

For example, an effective assessment portfolio may contain versions of résumés from sophomore, junior, and senior years, each of which demonstrate growth of experience and improved résumé-writing skills. Students may wish to include examples of papers that indicate improved writing ability over time. Illustrations of designs from an introductory class contrasted with a senior project provide evidence of mastery of skill.

What is the benefit, for students, of compiling an assessment portfolio? A portfolio can provide you with a look at yourself through a "different" lens, provide you immediate access to examples of your best work, and also provide you an outline of personal accomplishments. Looking through your portfolio can help identify areas you need to improve concerning your self-growth and career development. Knowing which skills are important to professionals in your particular field and assessing how your portfolio does or does not reflect those can be extremely helpful in setting goals, identifying career opportunities, and preparing answers for interview questions.

Although it is true that portfolios used primarily for assessment will not be presented at interviews, you can gain a tremendous amount of insight into your own skills, knowledge, and learning processes through compiling such a portfolio. The concept of reflection, which is a process of taking the time to review, consider, and evaluate experiences, is key to the benefit of assessment portfolios. The process of compiling past and current documents that represent your learning experiences is a valuable tool for self-reflection. Self-reflection is an important exercise prior to presenting yourself in an interview. Interview questions such as "What did you learn in college?" "What are your most valuable personal skills?" and "Why should I hire you?" will be easier to answer after completing an assessment portfolio and reflecting on its content.

Interview Enhancement Portfolios

Traditionally, portfolios have been prepared to enhance an interview presentation during a career search. Designers, models, and professionals in visually oriented career paths have long recognized the advantage of displaying examples of their work. Today virtually all professional people can successfully use a portfolio as an extension of the personal interview. The nature of the fashion profession lends itself particularly well to portfolios because so much of the work professionals do involves visual presentation and creativity. The potential is great for those in the fashion industry to present exciting, interesting, and visually appealing work in a professional portfolio.

If a portfolio has been developed for the purpose of interview enhancement, it must be extremely well organized, of a reasonable size, and presented appropriately in the interview. When presenting yourself through a portfolio, only high-quality and error-free work should be included. Refer to Chapter 3 and seek ways to present, reflect, and enhance your personal brand through your portfolio. You want to be careful not to clutter your "message" with extraneous examples. When your portfolio is placed online, it will have to stand alone without a lot of explanation from you. However, when you meet with an interviewer in person, you should be prepared to offer specific explanations of work in the portfolio and articulately relate the item to skills needed for the position in question.

Students have indicated that having a portfolio helped them be prepared to go through the interview process because the portfolio serves as a starting point for conversations and provides illustrations of their abilities that are applicable to the fashion industry (Adomaitis, 2003). For example, reviewing a particular document in your portfolio with a prospective employer might lead to a conversation about your problem-solving abilities. According to Adomaitis (2003), portfolios should be used to showcase your best work. The portfolio serves as a record of your work and can help you prepare for interviews if you consider the work you've chosen to place in the portfolio with an eye to the skills the position requires.

Stephanie Clark (see Careers Up Close 4.2 in this chapter), a recent fashion business graduate, used a portfolio when she interviewed for internships and permanent positions. One of the key components of her portfolio was sample pages from a semester-long project in her Merchandising class, which required her to design and implement a plan for a product line from concept to consumer. This project also involved planning the marketing campaign and proposing a merchandising assortment for retail. Figure 4.1 provides an example of her work. Providing

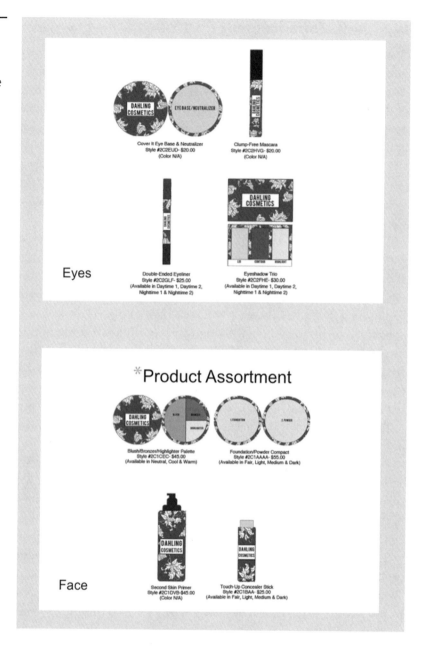

this particular example helped Stephanie demonstrate several professional skills. For example, the packaging design represents her ability to think creatively, illustrate her designs with relevant computer programs, and use effective and appropriate marketing techniques for promoting her cosmetic line. The overall layout and presentation of the pages also represent her ability to effectively and professionally present an idea, which was especially important given Stephanie's interest in marketing and social media.

Performance Review and Evaluation Portfolios

Similar to an interview enhancement portfolio, an updated portfolio can and should be used for periodic evaluations with your supervisor. As you take on new responsibilities and gain new skills and knowledge, you should maintain the process of portfolio development. Your interview enhancement portfolio can transition into a portfolio that can be used to document specific work you have accomplished in your career. When it is time for performance review and evaluation, using a portfolio that served you well when interviewing will again give you an edge in documenting your career performance. It is unlikely that anyone other than you will note each of the specific contributions that you make to the company in your career position. Your ability to organize your accomplishments, illustrate them in your portfolio, and present them to your supervisor will reflect the level of commitment you have to your career growth. Your ability to identify your accomplishments will demonstrate to a prospective supervisor an affinity for self-analysis and improvement.

In fact, your ability to develop portfolios may be tested in a job interview. For example, you might be assigned project-based work in an interview, such as developing a new product design, portraying a proposed fashion line, or leading an advertising campaign. If you have done work like this in courses, you should include them in your portfolio, and be prepared to demonstrate your ability to develop similar projects under pressure.

Organization and Presentation of the Portfolio

Just as a résumé must be customized to fit the career path and specific position for which you are applying, portfolios should be organized to promote the most appropriate items that you wish to exhibit for each situation. Items for the portfolio must be selected with care. Only work that is relevant to the purpose of the portfolio (assessment, career search, or career enhancement) should be presented. Assessment portfolios should include benchmark documents that demonstrate growth and learning. You should include only your best work in a career search portfolio that will accompany you on interviews. When preparing a portfolio for an employment review process, focus on work that you have completed for that company, and contributions that you have made in your career at your current position.

Each item that you include in your portfolio should be positioned in such a way that the reader can easily identify its purpose. Portfolio content will vary depending on the type of position and company that you are targeting. Employers in general want to see evidence of work—both academic coursework and on-site experiences—that fits with their needs and desires for employees.

Generally, items such as examples of trend and concept boards that you have created, reproductions of work you have done that demonstrate your visual display ability, and documents such as spreadsheets that show your analytical ability and knowledge of specific computer programs are appropriate to include and are of interest to recruiters. Documents that highlight your creativity and problem-solving skills will enhance your portfolio. A clear and organized portfolio itself becomes a product that demonstrates many of the skills and professional characteristics that are desirable to recruiters. As you compile and organize your portfolio's contents, consider the whole package that you will be presenting. Brief explanations accompanying your projects and documents will help guide the reader—and will prompt you to offer more detailed explanations in an interview.

Format of the Portfolio

Traditional portfolios, containing hard copies of materials, may contain items of non-uniform size and shape, so they should be created with convenience, organization, and neatness in mind. It is difficult for recruiters and potential supervisors to see the quality of the work in your portfolio if the presentation is sloppy or unprofessional. It is important for a portfolio to have an attractive presentation, with items appearing in an orderly fashion to tell a "story" of your accomplishments, knowledge, and skills. Jane Kenner and Rebecca Greer (1995) offer the following guidelines for preparing a portfolio, which are relevant regardless of the format chosen:

- First, establish the purpose and goals for the portfolio.
- The portfolio should look professional and attractive.
- Portfolio materials should be clearly written in concise language and with an eye-appealing format.
- Materials in the portfolio should be focused on the purpose intended.
- The portfolio should be of a convenient size, large enough to show work but small enough to carry easily if you plan to have a hard copy.
- The portfolio should have consistent page orientation, either vertical or horizontal.

Online and Electronic Portfolios

Today an e-portfolio offers many advantages over the traditional "hard copy" paper portfolios of the past. Table 4.1 summarizes these

TABLE 4.1

ADVANTAGES AND FEATURES OF E- AND DIGITAL PORTFOLIOS

E-portfolio	Hard Copy, Traditional Portfolio
Easily available online with Internet access for editing and viewing	Has to be physically transported to be viewed by others
Easily edited and manipulated for layout	Any editing requires reprinting, which can be time consuming and costly; formatting and actual appearance of pages not always readily visible until printed
"Live" document available for manipulation and collaboration with others	Collaboration with others means physical mark-ups once document is printed and distributed
It is an enduring document (as long as it is updated regularly as software and hardware evolve)	Can deteriorate over time
Provides overview of growth over time concerning skill set and use of technology; may be easier to organize and categorize	Does not readily demonstrate skill set concerning technology use; more cumbersome to organize and categorize to show growth

advantages. In addition to the advantages listed, there are many formats and platforms available to help users more easily design a professional e-portfolio online. Table 4.2 lists some popular platforms and provides a link to each site. Tutorials are available for most of the sites, and if you are naturally intuitive concerning technology, you should find each of the popular platforms easy to use.

In considering the platforms presented in Table 4.2, we particularly like Portfolium because of its ease of use and the continuity it provides students in building a body of work. Exploring this site will allow you to see the many ways in which students and professionals in a variety of fields showcase various projects. For students, Portfolium is a convenient way to keep a record of work, including class projects, volunteer experiences, and professional/work history. Recently we had the opportunity to interview the founder and CEO of Portfolium, Adam Markowitz. His expert advice concerning all matters of electronic portfolios, including excellent examples of portfolios, is presented in Box 4.1.

FOUR PLATFORMS FOR E- AND DIGITAL PORTFOLIOS

1. WordPress. Popular as a blogging site; can also be used successfully for showcasing work. To keep your portfolio from looking like a blog post, see this tutorial, which is especially helpful: http://michaelseery.com/home/wp-content/uploads/2012/01/Wordpress-for-E-Portfolios.pdf

2. Google Docs. Allows you a platform to store word-processed documents, presentations, and spreadsheets. Documents can be brought into e-portfolio and presentation software. An extensive tutorial that is primarily aimed at education applications, but that also provides a good overview, is available here: https://sites.google.com/site/eportfolioapps/overview/levels

3. *Portfolium*. Discussed in the text of this chapter, Portfolium provides a platform to showcase skills and experiences through a visual medium. It allows you to bring the bullet points on your résumé to life and enables you to collaborate with others. As an added bonus, the company has internship and campus founder/representative opportunities available through their website.

4. *Pathbrite*. This platform provides a place for students and professionals to present their body of work or their specific projects (school or business). The website is free to join and has many resources to help with designing a digital portfolio, including a blog with useful information.

Source: Donston-Miller, D. (July 9, 2013). 7 ways to create e-portfolios. *InformationWeekly*. Available online: http://www.informationweek.com/software/7-ways-to-create-e-portfolios/d/d-id/1110673?page_number=1

BOX 4.1 Interview with Adam Markowitz, Founder and CEO of Portfolium

Q: What are the top three skills employers are looking for on young professionals' résumés?

AM: The core of what employers are looking for actually lies beneath any particular list of skills or résumé. Employers are looking for a type of self-driven, self-reliant persona, and there are two primary personas that we've found to make incredible hires: They are what I refer to as "hackers" and "makers."

A hacker can be a graphic artist or designer, a coder, a marketer, an event planner—anyone who can "hack" their way to a solution or end result with great resourcefulness and resolve. A maker is really the same kind of person, but where the hacker's domain is virtual, the maker's domain is physical.

Makers are the people inhabiting fab labs, design studios, hacker-spaces, and 3D printing labs. They create things because they're innovative and passionate. The next generation of great talent is a generation of doers, and they stand out as the most desirable candidates for employers across all industries.

Q: Often students have a hard time taking their experiences and demonstrating those in a portfolio. Could you provide some specific examples of things students can put in their portfolios to illustrate the skills you have just identified (e.g., how would they demonstrate "problem-solving" skills)?

AM: The content within a student's portfolio essentially demonstrates and proves the skills they'd otherwise list on their résumé. The process of creating a portfolio entry allows a student to step back, deconstruct their approach, and walk through the phases of their project or experience from inception to outcome. They can even tag key stakeholders and point to tangible results—something that's more easily accomplished in a digital environment. When a student lists "problem-solving" as a skill on their résumé, they're bound to hear an interviewer ask, "Can you give me an example of when and how you used your problem-solving skills?" Think of a portfolio entry as the visual proof of the well thought-out verbal response to that question. In many cases, the portfolio entry could even speak for itself, which makes e-portfolios an incredibly powerful tool for interview situations.

E-portfolio networks are unique in that a student who is unsure where to begin can easily browse the network to see how others are proving their problem-solving skills (as well as other skills) and whether they've been able to secure an employment opportunity. They can even reach out and connect with these people based on their shared skillsets and experiences. Common portfolio entries showcasing "problem-solving" skills, as well as demonstrating the "maker/hacker" personas, include:

Capstone course projects and creations

Labs/experiments

Writing samples and reports

Hobbies, sports, and extracurricular projects

Research papers, posters

Designs and prototypes

Internship experiences

Students can even import content such as photos, video, documents, presentations, audio, and other mediums to showcase these actual work samples.

Here are some example student portfolios:

https://portfolium.com/howard
Chemical Engineering

https://portfolium.com/dwilli58
Architecture

https://portfolium.com/jvalleci
Structural Engineering

https://portfolium.com/SarahBednar
Computer Engineering

https://portfolium.com/kirk1016
Graphic Design

https://portfolium.com/rohanzrath
Industrial Engineering

continued

BOX 4.1 Interview with Adam Markowitz, Founder and CEO of Portfolium (*continued*)

https://portfolium.com/jnguy186
Art& Design

https://portfolium.com/priyanka
_archimedium
UI/UX Design

https://portfolium.com/LeahArabella
Animation

https://portfolium.com/allysonfaiman
Journalism

https://portfolium.com/thanhvu
Aerospace Engineering

https://portfolium.com/RicardoGuia
Engineering Management

https://portfolium.com/kflanigan
Fashion Design

https://portfolium.com/melissagamboa
Psychology

https://portfolium.com/caitlinmcphers
Marketing

https://portfolium.com/btand001
Hospitality & Tourism

https://portfolium.com/kristakaye
Dance

https://portfolium.com/Johanna
Charpentier
Business & Entrepreneurship

Q: Can you speak to the importance of having a professional electronic portfolio? How important is it to the job search and how much importance do you see employers placing on them in identifying job candidates?

AM: The Millennial generation, also known as "Gen Yers," has been continuously mislabeled by authors, bloggers, and influencers as "entitled" and "narcissistic." In reality, the Millennial generation is filled with hackers, makers, and doers—the most desirable personas for employers and recruiters across every major industry. This is a generation that cares more about the work they will be doing at a company and the impact their work will have on society as a whole than they do about their starting salary.

The doers that make up this generation aren't going to simply wait or look for opportunities to make an impact; they're going to create opportunities of their own. With the world's information at their fingertips and countless opportunities to learn and hone their skills both inside and outside of the classroom, we're going to see one of the most multitalented pool of job candidates ever. These kinds of multifaceted skillsets, coupled with the initiative and work ethic of a promising generation, will not translate well onto a traditional résumé.

Employers are already combing the Internet's competency marketplaces, seeking great new talent. It's of utmost importance for young job seekers and future job seekers to maintain their academic and professional brands online. Résumés aren't disappearing just yet, but the writing is on the wall. All one has to do is imagine what the recruiting and interviewing process looks like ten years from now. Experts agree: An interactive, easy to use, portfolio of work samples and proof of skills will be at the center of this process.

Q: What about a student's GPA and degree?

AM: The lack of transparency about what knowledge, skills, and abilities certain credentials actually represent makes it difficult for employers to trust credentials, transcripts, and résumés to lead them to the skilled workforce they need. The individuals who make things less difficult for employers will find themselves in the lead when it comes to finding great opportunities.

Q: What importance do you see employers placing on e-portfolios?

AM: This is a fantastic topic, because the truth is if you ask an employer if they wish to see e-portfolios from applicants, they'll most likely give you a funny look (unless they're hiring artists and it's a typical component in the application process) and say "no." However, ask that same employer if they'd like to see "relevant work samples" from a candidate or if they'd like to see "proof of a candidate's skills," and nine times out of ten they'll say "absolutely." This is important because although employers might not refer to what they're looking for as "an e-portfolio," an e-portfolio is the ideal medium for delivering to them exactly what they want.

Q: Please provide any other information you think is important for students to know.

AM: If you take a step back and look at college from an input vs. output standpoint, the inputs are quite extensive: years of lecture, assignments, homework, projects, papers, exams (not to mention financial debt), etc. What about the output, though? Hopefully, there's a job, but what else is there? There's a framed degree and a transcript, but I'd argue there's a lot more.

Think about that when you're wondering if you should have a portfolio—or what to put in your portfolio. It's the cumulative output of your years of hard work. Don't sell yourself short—you're more than a résumé. You're more than a GPA, and you're definitely more than just a framed piece of paper on the wall. Now all you have to do is prove it!

Note: Adam Markowitz is the Founder and CEO of Portfolium. Adam founded Portfolium when he had difficulty finding a job after graduating in 2008, at the height of the economic recession. Convinced he was more than just a diploma on the wall, a résumé, a LinkedIn profile, and a GPA, Adam put together a portfolio of his academic work and projects, complete with photos and captions (it took about an hour), brought that into his next interview, and it made all the difference! He says: "I was able to prove my passion and dedication, and the interviewer got to know me on a deeper level. I was working on NASA's Space Shuttle Program a couple of weeks later! See proof in my Portfolium entry."

As you progress in your career, you can continue to build your portfolio online to show your growth to future employees. Other e-portfolio sites will offer similar features, so it is entirely a personal choice concerning which platform you choose. Before you choose, you may want to check with your school to see what platforms they recommend and whether there is a platform that interfaces with the online learning systems used by your professors.

CONTENTS OF THE PORTFOLIO

Once the purpose of the portfolio has been determined (assessment vs. career search vs. career enhancement), and the format has been selected, the contents must be identified. Each person possesses an individual set of goals, personal strengths, knowledge base, skill set, talents, interests, and experiences. Each of these items shapes the portfolio that will be created to exhibit a professional profile. Therefore, there is no set rule to follow that will tell you what, exactly, to include in your portfolio. As a student, you should continually set aside possible additions for your portfolio. If you wait, the task of compiling portfolio documents becomes overwhelming, and it is easy to forget all of the projects that have been completed over time. Furthermore, you should be prepared with an updated portfolio at all times, because you never know when you might need to present your work unexpectedly.

How do you determine what your portfolio should contain? Remember that the portfolio is, in essence, an expanded résumé. You should use the portfolio to:

- Demonstrate examples of your work. This can be done through photographs, letters of thanks or commendation, and examples of course projects and work experiences that emphasize your skills.
- Illustrate growth and development in your professional preparation. As you gain work experiences and refine your career goals, your professional portfolio will evolve. Keep in mind that each person who reviews your portfolio may have a different approach. Some people will want to peruse the visual elements, such as pictures; others will want to read explanations of your work. Your task is to present all of the items that might be desired for review in a manner that allows the reader to easily access the elements that interest him or her.

Ask your professor, peers, and even interviewers for feedback about your portfolio. Strive to improve yourself and your portfolio presentation by considering constructive criticism as you continue to develop your portfolio and seek experiences in the fashion industry.

We recommend that you begin your portfolio with a summary of your strengths and skills, a reflective goal statement, and an updated résumé, and then progress to course projects, evidence of work experience, a statement emphasizing your ethical base, and letters of recommendation.

Summary of Strengths and Skills

After compiling your portfolio elements, you should be able to assess the themes emerging with respect to the strengths and skills you are documenting. A summary that describes these strengths and skills, and that refers to the specific documents that further illustrate them, provides the reader of your portfolio with an introduction and overview to your professional profile. The summary should tie all of the visual elements of the portfolio together, present a theme for your portfolio, and guide the reader to specific items in your portfolio that document your experiences, strengths, and skills.

Even though this is a summary of the work that is included in your portfolio, it should appear near the front, as an introduction to your work. The summary should be written clearly and concisely. Correct grammar and sentence structure are important components of a high-quality summary. The summary should be proofread and free from errors.

Reflective Goal Statement

Prospective employers realize that goal setting is an important step in career growth. Your documented ability to set and articulate goals can enhance your professional profile. Establishing a plan to accomplish your goals will provide direction in your professional development and will inform prospective employers about your plans for the future. Keep the goal statement at a professional level. While we all must also recognize our personal goals, these are not appropriately shared in a professional portfolio.

Through review of your portfolio, employers will have the opportunity to consider whether your goals can be met through the opportunities that they offer, so be certain that your goals are fully developed but do not limit your employment options. On the other hand, clear communication between you and prospective employers will enable you to be fully informed with respect to the degree to which your goals can be met with each employment option.

Updated Résumé

Although your résumé should be presented to prospective employers separately, including a copy in your portfolio is a good idea. In fact, if you use a hard copy portfolio, you may wish to keep extra copies of your résumé in your portfolio so that you can distribute them efficiently.

As you progress toward your educational and professional goals, your résumé will change to reflect updated work experiences and skills. The latest edition of your résumé should be presented in the professional portfolio. Résumé development is thoroughly covered in Chapter 6.

Course Projects

Many of the projects and assignments that you complete in classes offer valuable evidence of your accomplishments and skills. Prospective employers will welcome the opportunity to view your work, and the projects that you include will offer a catalyst for you to discuss yourself in an interview.

For example, you can begin a dialogue about your ability to work with others or as a member of a team by describing a group project that you have included in your portfolio. You could expand on your leadership ability by describing how you took a leadership role in the project. You could talk about your affinity for figures by describing the six-month plan that you have included in your portfolio. This might lead to a discussion about your goal to become a buyer. Check Box 4.1 to get ideas from other professionals' online portfolios about which of your projects you want to include, how your projects can illustrate your specific skills, and an explanation from Adam Markowitz about why it's important to exhibit what you've done.

Evidence of Work Experience

As you gain work experience that will enhance your professional profile, include evidence of such in your portfolio. You may wish to include photographs illustrating visual displays you developed, letters of appreciation from customers or supervisors, and supervisor evaluations (see portfolio links in Box 4.1 for some specific examples of how to cite work experiences.)

One word of caution concerning your portfolio, particularly ones that are accessible online: Be certain to avoid including proprietary information that you may have had access to during an internship or work experience. This might include information about vendors, sales figures, design sketches, or color swatches. Companies typically forbid employees to share these items—sometimes such information may not be removed from the premises—and it would be unethical to include such information in your portfolio. Nevertheless, you can demonstrate your ability to complete appropriate and informative documentation of your on-site career preparation. If you have any doubts about whether to include evidence of your work with an employer, be sure to ask the appropriate company representative before completing (and especially before distributing or publishing) your portfolio.

Statement of Ethical Base

Character education has been a hot topic in higher education for the past decade. It is likely that you have completed courses that focused on ethics or had ethics components. In this age of corporate scandals and questionable practices at the workplace, employers are interested in learning about your ethical perspective. You may choose to write a personal work philosophy, incorporate a statement addressing ethics in your goals, or construct a personal code of ethics. Since many college programs now include ethics courses, you might have an opportunity to include a project from such a class. Regardless of what you choose to include, it is recommended that some form of your work speak to the topic of ethics in your portfolio. Chapter 9 contains guidance on the development of personal codes of ethics and information about considering and presenting your values and ethics.

Letters of Recommendation

Letters of recommendation can offer additional support for you by emphasizing your abilities and expertise. Professors and previous employers may be in a position to write a letter of recommendation on your behalf. Positive letters can point out skills and talents that might not be otherwise evident in your portfolio, such as your tendency to work hard and never be absent. Authors of recommendation letters often speak to the character of their subjects and can offer insight into the attitudes, values, and behaviors that you exhibit. If you plan to post your letters on an electronic portfolio site or any other type of public domain, you may want to ask permission to do so from the people who wrote them.

COPYRIGHTING YOUR PORTFOLIO

Because your work is disseminated worldwide when your portfolio is posted on the Internet, it is worthwhile to give notice regarding the copyright of your work. All original unpublished works of which you are the author are recognized under the authority of copyright (as long as you did not produce the work for hire or as part of your employment). In other words, your original unpublished works are automatically copyrighted, and technically you do not need to indicate the copyright on your work. However, it can be difficult to distinguish what work has been published and what hasn't when work is copied and distributed electronically. Essentially, once you copy and distribute your work you have published it.

It is simple to give notice that your work is copyrighted, and your notice will indicate publicly that your work is owned by you and should not be copied. Therefore, we recommend that you publicly copyright your unpublished portfolio and your electronic and web-based portfolio versions. This can be accomplished by noting on your cover page: "Unpublished work © 2015 Your Name." Notice of copyright should be made on the electronic version of your portfolio, and each page of your web-based portfolio should carry notice of copyright with the date of its creation, also ("© 2015 Your Name").

CONTINUOUS QUALITY IMPROVEMENT OF THE PORTFOLIO

Establish a Schedule for Portfolio Review and Revision

Once you have successfully used your portfolio to secure a job, it is very easy to put your portfolio away and ignore it until you decide to pursue another position, or until another position presents itself. We encourage you not to fall into this habit. As you gain experience and complete significant projects, take the time to update the content of your portfolio to reflect your new skills. One of the advantages to having everything online in an e-portfolio is that it is easily accessible and relatively easy to update. If you take the time to do this, you will be prepared when the next opportunity comes along and will not have to stress out about getting your materials together.

Keeping your portfolio up to date along with your social media profile (e.g., LinkedIn) will give you advantages that you may otherwise miss when it comes to advancing your career. Remember that many employers use social media sites and online portfolio websites such as Portfolium.com to identify qualified candidates for company openings. Even if you have not initiated a job search, you do not want to miss the chance to explore the job market, given the chance.

If you are one to keep a to-do list and a calendar of tasks, we suggest you review your portfolio at least once a month. Ask yourself if you have acquired any new skills over the past month that could be added, or if you have completed significant projects/training that should be included. Try to schedule at least an hour or two each month for updating your online presence, including your portfolio. Depending on how long the updates are taking, you can adjust this time. Do not wait until you *have* to do the update (e.g., a great opportunity comes along!) because you will probably not do your best work, you will forget something, or, quite simply, the task of updating it will become overwhelming and very time consuming—especially if it has been a year or so since you have looked at it.

Seek Feedback on Your Portfolio

As discussed throughout this text, and as mentioned by many of the professionals interviewed for the Careers Up Close profiles, seeking out mentors and asking others for help with your professional development and career growth is highly recommended. As you begin to develop a portfolio, and as you continue its update, seek out others who can give you feedback concerning the content, layout, and presentation. This can be the mentor(s) you are working with, colleagues, and other superiors whose opinions you value. People who make hiring decisions within your company and field are obviously very valuable sources.

Whoever you decide to ask, have them tell you what skills they see demonstrated by your portfolio and adjust your content as applicable. You can also ask them to comment on the layout in general and the ease with which they were able to peruse your pages. While you may think the actual content of your portfolio is what others will view as most important, it is actually more important that others can quickly scan and easily navigate the portfolio and that it portrays professionalism in its layout. Just as we mentioned with your résumé, reviewers of your portfolio will most likely do a quick scan of its contents to determine your qualifications and their interests in pursuing more information.

Projects

1. Review the goals that you identified in Chapter 2. For each goal, identify documents that need to be included in a portfolio to supply evidence that these goals have been achieved.
2. Review the top five professional strengths that you identified previously. How will you document these strengths in your portfolio?
3. What are your strongest areas of knowledge? Strategize how these will be presented in your portfolio.
4. Make a list of items that you should include in an assessment portfolio.
5. Make a list of items that you should include in a professional enhancement portfolio.
6. Begin the project of portfolio development:
   a. Define your purpose.
   b. Select the items that you will include in the portfolio.
   c. Compile the items in your portfolio and organize them appropriately.
   d. Write a summary for the introduction of your portfolio.
7. Analyze the portfolio that you have created. Does it have a professional look? Are the items well organized, clearly labeled, and easy to access? Do all of the items make sense in terms of reflecting your professional profile and helping you meet your goals?
8. Present your portfolio. Whether or not this is an assignment for class, gather an audience (friends, family, even ask your professor)

and make a presentation of your portfolio. This is great preparation for the interview—where you will want to be at ease with incorporating your portfolio examples into your interview conversations and responses.

9. Transform your portfolio into an electronic format using Portfolium.com.

Questions for Discussion

1. Review your assessment portfolio, or the items that you would include in one. What are your strongest areas of growth over time? In what areas can you set goals for improvement? How did you determine these responses?

2. Create a list of criteria that you would expect to see in a professional portfolio. How would you evaluate the quality of those criteria?

3. Review the portfolio that you have created. How did you decide what to leave in and what to remove?

4. Describe in detail the skills, talent, and knowledge that you have represented in your portfolio. Are those items clearly evident to others who review your portfolio? How did you arrive at this conclusion?

5. How do the documents that you have chosen to include in your assessment portfolio differ from those in your professional enhancement portfolio?

6. What changes do you need to make in order to successfully transform your hard-copy portfolio into an electronic format?

STUD!O Activities

Visit the *Guide to Fashion Career Planning STUDIO* available at www.bloomsburyfashioncentral.com. The key elements are:

1. Summary of Chapter 4 text
2. Quiz
3. Portfolio Development/Components
4. Examples of Portfolios
5. Developing Your Portfolio
6. Portfolio Evaluation Rubric

VIDEO: Using Your Portfolio in an Interview

References

Adomaitis, A. D. (2003, November 10). Retail merchandising portfolio: Preparing students for industry. Paper presented at the annual meeting of the International Textiles and Apparel Association, Savannah, GA. In: *Proceedings of the International Textiles and Apparel Association* 2003. Available online: http://www.itaaonline.org

Donston-Miller, D. (July 9, 2013). 7 ways to create e-portfolios. *Information Weekly*. Available online: http://www.informationweek.com/software/7-ways-to-create-e-portfolios/d/d-id/1110673?page_number=1

Kenner, J. O., & Greer, R. (1995, Spring). The portfolio concept: Make it work for you. *The Candle*, 10–11.

Paulins, V. A. (1998). Assessment through portfolios in retail merchandising. *Journal of Family and Consumer Sciences*, 90(4), 82–87.

Paulins, V. A., & Graham, A. (1999, June). An assessment plan for family and consumer sciences programs: Using portfolios. Paper presented at the annual meeting of the American Association of Family and Consumer Sciences, Seattle, WA.

CHAPTER 5

THE JOB SEARCH AND NETWORKING

Open up your eyes and mind to possibilities. Be comfortably uncomfortable and put yourself out there! Shake hands and meet new people. Establish and grow your network.

—MELISSA K. MARTIN, EXECUTIVE DIRECTOR OF PHI UPSILON OMICRON, INC.

OBJECTIVES

- To identify resources available for conducting a successful job search.
- To identify the advantages and disadvantages of each job search resource.
- To identify networking opportunities available for your job search.
- To compile a list of contacts to aid in your job search.
- To conduct and analyze current research on prospective employers.
- To develop guidelines for professional behavior at job fairs.
- To develop a strategy for conducting a job search in a market different from your current one.
- To identify alternative methods for the job search when having difficulty finding a job.
- To formulate a plan for conducting a successful job search in the fashion industry.

IDENTIFYING RESOURCES FOR FINDING A JOB

Two of the most fundamental questions that students have concerning their job search are what to do and where to begin. Consider the job search advice provided in Box 5.1 and then proceed with the chapter, which is designed to help you get started with your search.

BOX 5.1 Job Search Proverbs

- Only you can find your dream job. Don't depend on anyone else to hand it to you on a silver platter.
- Your college owes you nothing other than a great education. Your diploma does not come with a guarantee of a great job. That is something you will have to secure on your own.
- Seek work you love. You will be spending the greater portion of your life working. Make it an enjoyable experience.
- You are infinitely better off making $25,000 and happy than making $50,000 and miserable. No, the extra $25,000 is really not worth the misery. Happiness is priceless.
- Extracurricular activities count. Whether a club or athletics, it shows you are a well-rounded person. And it may be your best opportunity to exhibit leadership skills.
- Experience is experience. You gain new experiences every day. You do not have to be paid for it to be considered valid experience.
- A part-time job during school is a great way to pay the bills and gain some experience. But don't let it take priority over your education or your eventual entry-level job search. Remember what you came for.
- Grades do matter. If you are reading this early, keep your grades high. If late, you will need to provide potential employers with a very good reason if you have not maintained at least a 3.0 ("B" average) or above.
- Keep your ethical standards high and this will soon become one of your most admired qualities, because very few remain honest to such standards. Do not let yours down. Be the exception rather than the rule.
- The truth is still the truth even when everyone else abandons it. Stand for honesty and truth in all you do.
- Don't be afraid to ask questions. Many people may be willing to help, but first you must be willing to ask for their help.
- Develop the necessary computer skills for your field or industry of interest. If you are not sure what they are, check out current job postings.
- Thoroughly research each employer you pursue. It is not enough just to show up for the on-campus interviews and hope for the best.
- The most qualified person does not necessarily get the job. The person with the best job search skills will typically get the job over the most qualified person.
- Job search is a game, complete with a defined set of rules. You need to play by the rules. But to win, you will need to push those rules to the limits.
- Remember that managers hire people who are like them. Do your best to reflect common attributes.
- Always think about meeting the needs of others. This is the only way to meet your own personal needs.
- Nervousness is common and to be expected. It helps you stay on your toes.
- You are unique. There is no one else out there exactly like you. Learn to recognize your unique strengths so that you can communicate them to others.

continued

The job search environment ebbs and flows along with the economy and current market conditions; however, as a college student, you have many resources available to you to enhance the likelihood of receiving multiple offers, even in a lackluster economy. You should take advantage of all of them, so that when you leave campus, your support system will be solidly in place. Recruiters continually evaluate and modify the ways that they reach out to college students—typically in response to the changing technologies and communication methods used by current students. Box 5.2 shows recent trends in recruiter activities, which should serve as a guide as you determine job search resources and strategies. Following is a discussion of some of the more common resources available to college students.

BOX 5.2 Recruiting Methods of Employers

According to the National Association of Colleges and Employers (NACE, 2013, 2014), key changes in company recruiting methods between 2011 and 2015 have been:

- 64.7% are using more social networks.
- 60.9% are using more technology in general.

- 42.4% have initiated a change in their branding.
- 32.1% are attending more career fairs.
- On the other hand, 23.9% are attending fewer career fairs.
- 20.1% are doing less travel.
- Meanwhile, 19.6% are doing more travel.

Sources: National Association of Colleges and Employers. (2013). *Job outlook 2014*. Bethlehem, PA: NACEWeb Publications. Available online: http://www.uab.edu/careerservices/images/NACE_Job_Outlook_2014.pdf; National Association of Colleges and Employers. (2014). *Job outlook 2015*. Bethlehem, PA: NACEWeb Publications. Available online: https://www.umuc.edu/upload/NACE-Job-Outlook-2015.pdf

The Internet and Social Networking Sites

Although not exclusive to college students, the Internet is indisputably the most popular, and easily accessible, resource for a job search. LinkedIn is the number-one social networking site for job seekers. In fact, if you are looking for a position—whether a temporary work experience, an internship, or a permanent job—you should have a presence on LinkedIn. Through LinkedIn, you can connect with companies as well as individual people. Many recruiters are on LinkedIn and use their connections as resources to hire. In additional to networking connections, LinkedIn offers access to blogs and job coaching articles.

Other sites provide a multitude of functions. Jobvite is a website that serves employers; people seeking jobs can register on Jobvite.com and upload résumés. Jobvite conducts market research and publishes information about current markets for a variety of employment fields. Websites such as www.monster.com and www.careerbuilder.com offer multiple job listings in a variety of fields. In addition, most company websites include a section on employment opportunities. Company profiles available online are a good place to begin your research. Refer to the activity at the back of this chapter for guidelines on how to conduct research into a prospective employer. A particularly good site to use in conducting research while completing this activity is www.hoovers.com. Box 5.3 contains a list of websites that promote fashion jobs.

Although the Internet makes it particularly easy to fire off cover letters and résumés via email, you should view the Internet as just one tool in your job search and not as an exclusive means to an end. As is true with any of the previously discussed job-search resources, you will greatly increase your chances of success by using all methods available to you. Most openings posted online will elicit a phenomenal number of responses, so it may be unrealistic to expect that this is how you will find your job. On the other hand, most entry-level positions will require

---

BOX 5.3 Websites for Job Searches

http://www.midwestpersonnelresource.com	http://us.fashionjobs.com/
http://fashionista.com/fashion-careers	https://www.fashion.net/jobs/
http://www.mediabistro.com/	http://www.prcouture.com/
http://www.stylecareers.com/	http://www.fashioncareerexpo.com
http://www.creativejobscentral.com/fashion-jobs	

online submission of résumés and applications, and you will need to use the Internet to research information about the companies where you want to work.

College Leadership and Career Placement Offices

When it comes to a job search, one of the major advantages you have as a college student is the college placement office. Here you will find resources such as books, magazines, company reports, videos, alumnus lists, and a database of prospective employers looking for people in your major. It is likely that this office will also have listings of companies scheduling on-campus interviews for soon-to-be graduates. Generally, career counselors are available who specialize in your specific major and entry-level employment opportunities.

If you have not visited this office on your campus, now is the time to do so. Most campus career centers serve students as early as their first term on campus—and actually encourage students to utilize their resources long before they engage in job searches. In addition to placement assistance, campus centers typically offer resources such as personal skill and interest inventories to help you identify the type of job and career that will fit your interests. Early confirmation of the college major and related job path that will be a good fit for you will enhance your ability to prepare and execute your career strategy. Do not wait until you are in the last semester of your senior year to familiarize yourself with their services.

Employment Fairs

Most college campuses hold career fairs. Common career fair themes include internship fairs, summer employment fairs, or entry-level employment fairs. Regardless of the type of fair, prior to attending it, find out which companies will be there and do your homework. Research each company and prepare a short introduction of yourself, including your name, major, and career interests. Practice your introduction with friends, looking them in the eye, giving them firm handshakes, and handing them copies of your résumé, just as you will the recruiter.

Because a career fair can be somewhat intimidating to first-time attendees, it is never too early to begin attending them. The more fairs you attend, the more comfortable you will be when meeting the recruiters and the more information you will have about different companies and the careers they offer. Also, by speaking with the recruiters each time they come to campus, you will establish a rapport with them, which can give you an advantage over others when you are ready to interview for a position. See Careers Up Close 5.1, in which Beth Bonarrigo shares her career experiences as a campus recruiter.

CAREERS UP CLOSE 5.1
BETH BONARRIGO
Former Senior Campus Recruiter
Target

Upon college graduation, Beth Bonarrigo put her double major—in retail merchandising and business administration—to work as an HR Executive Team Leader at Target. Beth's strong ability to cultivate relationships with people from diverse backgrounds and experiences positions her well for the job responsibilities of a campus recruiter—and enables her to implement Target core values. While an HR Executive Team Leader, Beth was responsible for maintaining an open door culture and executing company retention programs. She had to ensure that all legal standards and company policies were followed as well as make sure that all employees received timely feedback with respect to their work activities. Beth reflects that leading teams of people toward a common mission is challenging and also rewarding. While at Ohio University, Beth gained a lot of real world experience working in group projects, which helped her become a more successful leader at Target. Beth believes the most successful leaders are those who can build trust with others by being accountable, work well with

others regardless of their background, react to change and ambiguity with confidence, and foster a sense of urgency.

To effectively lead and motivate team members, Beth implemented training workshops and also incorporated "learning moments" into the daily routine. For example, when an employee was not modeling the Target Brand she would reflect on their training and use it as a teachable moment for not only the team member but also the leader. Beth's role as a mentor who modeled the Target mission, and her demonstrated success guiding employees through their core functions, placed her as a candidate for promotion to her most recent job as Senior Campus Recruiter. In that capacity, Beth continued to lead teams of people and expanded her network to college career centers and faculty members. Beth represented Target as a career employment option as well as a college partner within academic programs. For example, Beth often facilitated Target Case Studies, which are implemented within retailing, merchandising, and marketing courses—enabling students to gain insight and experience working on real-world challenges as they network with Target executives.

Working from the Columbus, Ohio office, Beth oversaw eight store districts comprised of eighty stores and two distribution centers. She worked in partnership with twenty colleges and universities across Ohio, Kentucky, and Southern Indiana. Within this region, Beth delivered training to store, district, and regional managers to ensure execution of campus recruitment strategies, processes, and programs. In addition, she facilitated the ten-week Target summer internship program for more than sixty potential Executive Team Leader (ETL) candidates each year.

In 2015, Beth is focused on her family and parenting a young daughter. During a life transition time, Beth continues to maintain networking and contacts within the HR field and fashion industry. She anticipates that her strong network, along with her keen skills in cultivating and maintaining connections with people, will enable her to reenter the field at the appropriate time.

Beth advises college students to start their networking strategies early, and to reach out to company recruiters when they visit your campus. Beth shares, "As a recruiter, I believe it is so important to not only research your employers of choice prior to attending a career fair but to also be open to learning about new roles and opportunities by meeting and networking with different people. When I was graduating from Ohio University, I never would have thought I would have ended up working for Target, and it turned out to be a wonderful experience; I was given the opportunity to meet amazing people and do something I was extremely passionate about." Beth's final advice to college students is "make sure you utilize all your resources on campus—from your career services office to professors to recent graduates—not only for networking opportunities but mentorship as well."

In addition to career fairs on campus, you should be alert to fairs held near your college or university that are specifically aimed at fashion merchandising and retailing students. For example, the Fashion Group International (FGI) sponsors career days that provide students with the opportunity to bring their résumés, complete applications, hear speakers, and compete in fashion shows. Needless to say, these days provide excellent networking opportunities for those who attend. Examples of such fairs include the FGI Career Day Chicago and the Dallas Market Career Day, both of which are attended by about a thousand students each year. The National Retail Federation sponsors career fairs for students whose universities hold memberships in the organization. Even if you do not live near a major city, or have affiliation with a college program, you may still be able to attend student events. *Teen Vogue* sponsors an annual Fashion University workshop each spring—available to successful applicants. Ask your professors for more information, or visit the Fashion Group International website at www.fgi.org and the National Retail Federation at www.nrf.com. The fashion trade journal *Women's Wear Daily* sponsors a Fashion Career Expo in New York City (see www.fashioncareerexpo.com). Their website enables you to register and upload your résumé in anticipation of career networking and job search activities with the companies who recruit through their venue.

The activities section at the end of this chapter and the accompanying website (www.bloomsburyfashioncentral.com) provide an in-depth activity to guide you through participating in a career fair. Also check with your college placement office to see if they offer workshops to help prepare students for a career fair. Box 5.4 presents guidelines for preparation, attendance, and follow-up activities associated with career fairs.

BOX 5.4 Career Fair Guide

Prepare for the Career Fair

1. Identify and research employers.

   - Seek information from your college or university so you know which companies will participate in the career fair.
   - Conduct an Internet search to learn about the companies. Also, many companies will provide information to the career office on campus. See whether these are available—especially because these materials are obviously the ones company reps think are most important.
   - Prepare conversation starters and questions for each company with which you plan to connect. (Avoid the dreaded, "So what does your company do?" or "What positions are you looking for?")
   - If companies you are interested in hold "pre job fair" workshops, go!

2. Prepare your résumé.

   - Utilize resources such as workshops and seek feedback about your résumé (see Chapter 6).
   - Keep your résumé general (rather than specific for a certain company or position) because you will be distributing it widely.

   - Carry your résumé in a nice folder or padfolio; this enables you to look professional and keep the materials you pick up organized.

3. Prepare your introduction.

   - Develop a personal presentation that highlights your major, class status, knowledge and interest in the industry and the company at hand, and how your skills would be an asset to it.
   - When doing your research, if you find a company that you are especially interested in, consider sending your résumé or a brief introductory email to the recruiters prior to meeting them in person. This gives you the perfect introduction and makes them more likely to remember you.

4. Dress appropriately.

   - Men should wear suits or sport coats, and an appropriate tie.
   - Women should consider fashionable suits or blazers; pantyhose; closed-toe, low-heeled shoes; and minimal (non-distracting) make-up, jewelry, and perfume.
   - All students should have well-fitting and pressed clothing, polished shoes, groomed hair, and clean hands and nails (you will be shaking hands!).

continued

BOX 5.4 Career Fair Guide (*continued*)

At the Career Fair

1. Be strategic with your time.
   - Plan your day to allow enough time to visit both the key employers that you are targeting and also others who are present. Go as early as possible—sometimes the recruiters are unable to stay the entire time.
   - Stay open-minded—visit and consider companies beyond those that you have identified as most promising.
   - Visit a few "B list" companies first so that you are "warmed up" for your interaction with "first choice" companies.
   - Be patient with employers who are busy.
2. Make a good first impression.
   - Appear professional in all ways.
   - Greet the employer and introduce yourself.
   - Make eye contact.
   - Shake hands and smile.
3. Demonstrate your knowledge of the company.
   - Communicate to the employer that you have done your research by discussing current events and activities relative to the company at hand.
   - Be sure to work into the conversation how you may fit into their organization.
   - Clarify through discussions with the recruiters what opportunities exist for someone with your credentials and interests.
4. Do not be distracted by giveaways. Although the swag is fun, be sure to focus on the purpose of your visit to the career fair. Don't get loaded down with freebies and compromise your professional presentation.
5. Remember names and companies.
   - Be sure to get the recruiters' names and business cards.
   - Take notes about your conversations; making quick notes on the backs of their business cards is a good strategy.
6. When distributing résumés, do not be put off if recruiters do not take résumés; a recent trend is for recruiters to use career fairs for networking only. In this case, consider having a business card that you can offer. Be sure to take their card, and follow up with an email and attached résumé!

Follow Up After the Career Fair

1. Stay organized.
   - Review your notes and reflect upon what you learned about the different organizations.
   - Keep track of business cards; organize them along with your notes.
   - Consider developing a spreadsheet to keep track of the contact and company information that you have collected. Use the spreadsheet to record when you make contact, submit applications, and hear back from companies. (See Chapters 5 and 7 website materials for a spreadsheet at www.bloomsburyfashioncentral.com.)
2. Follow up
   - Send a résumé or other information as soon as possible.
   - Send a thank you note to the recruiters; be sure to mention your discussion

at the career fair, your qualifications, and your interest in the organization.

3. Evaluate your experience and plan for the next step.

- What went well? What could be improved? What preparation was particularly helpful? Did you receive any questions that were difficult to answer? How will you change and improve your next career fair experience? Were you able to explain your career goals? How was your self-presentation received?

- Consider practice interviews at a career center in anticipation for the next step beyond the career fair meet-and-greet.

Professors

Although some students would rather walk over a bed of hot coals than visit a professor's office, your professors should prove to be valuable resources in your job search. In fact, many employers, including alumni, often find new hires through college faculty. Alumni and others in the community regularly call professors for referrals to fill vacancies in their companies. Your professors will be best able to match you with an employer if you have made yourself and your career interests known to them. As a courtesy, you should also provide your professors with a résumé so that they will have ready access to your experiences and your career objectives when employers call. Connecting with your professors, as well as with the alumni who are connected with them, is a good way to enable quick reference of your work experiences, job activities, and campus leadership positions (which should be listed). Many professors are willing to provide endorsements on LinkedIn that can document your academic accomplishments and work ethic. Professors are interested in seeing their students succeed and most are willing to help with a career search.

Professional and Student Associations

Most majors on campus have student associations, clubs, or honor societies serving the interests of their members (e.g., American Marketing Association, Kappa Omicron Nu, Phi Upsilon Omicron). In addition, depending on the locale of the university, there are often professional associations nearby that accept student members (e.g., Fashion Group International, which has chapters in many major cities across the country, and the National Retail Federation student association, which is accessible if your college/university holds membership). Join organizations both on- and off-campus whenever possible because they can provide invaluable experience in building a professional network.

Keeping in mind the truth of the adage, "It's not what you know, but rather whom you know," you should take advantage of every opportunity that membership in such a group offers. Services often include a directory with contact information for each member, seminars, workshops, guest speaker events, and website access. Many times your membership also includes the particular trade publication for that association. Such publications not only contain the latest trends in the industry, but also may include a classified section listing job opportunities—typically available on the Internet. If you are unsure of the groups that are active on your campus, most colleges have a student association office that can provide this information. You could also ask your fellow classmates or your professors for help, or check your college website for a listing. It is quite common that the contacts and friends you make through student organizations while in college will provide job leads for you well into the future.

Your membership in any of these groups, particularly professional organizations, will greatly increase your chances of a successful job search when the time comes. As Brian Krueger, Founder and CEO of CollegeGrad.com and author of *The Networking by Association Technique* (2003) notes, meetings of professional organizations are a networking contact dream. All of the people at the meeting are walking, talking, breathing network contacts, and they are all in your field. Additionally, most of these professionals will feel a certain obligation to help others like you get started. Of course, you will have to do your part by effectively interacting with them, but the more meetings you attend, the more comfortable you will become with talking to others about yourself and your career goals. The more people you can talk to, and get to know, the better your chances will be of landing that perfect job. Remember, too, as emphasized below, that the best time to look for contacts is when you do not *need* to look for contacts. In other words, don't wait until the last term of your senior year to start networking. Three rules of networking are:

1. The best time to look for contacts is when you are not looking for contacts.
2. You never know who you are really talking to.
3. Always ask for names of other contacts.

As you become skilled conversing with others and gathering contacts, make sure that you follow up on each contact given to you by your network associates. When contacting a potential job lead, you should state your name and also give them the name of the person who referred you.

Remember that you are now making a "warm call" rather than a "cold call," which should make you feel more comfortable and also make the person you are calling more receptive. Box 5.5 contains guidance for networking in public venues such as professional conferences.

BOX 5.5 Own the Room at Your Next Networking Event as a Student, Intern, and Recent Graduate
by William Frierson

We live in a busy world, and college students are no exception. Today's young adults have hectic schedules and are oftentimes running between classes, work, extracurricular activities and social time with friends. It may seem tough to fit one more thing into this schedule; however, it is important to make time for networking as well. Networking will help you to gain experience now and will be beneficial in the long run for your career. As a student, intern, or recent graduate, it can be intimidating to stand in a room full of unfamiliar faces that have more professional experience than you do. Here are a few quick tips to help you own the room and stand out like a pro at your next networking event.

Remember to Make Eye Contact:

Looking someone straight in the eye is extremely important for connecting during the networking process. While this may seem intimidating at first, making eye contact is crucial for conveying confidence and appearing friendly. This tip is a must for everyone and should be kept in mind at all times when networking.

Come Prepared:

This tip sounds self-explanatory; however, the more prepared you are, the better you will feel. Spend some time doing research prior to the event to determine the audience that will be attending, and make sure to dress professionally. In addition to this, it is helpful to bring résumés and business cards with you in the event that one of your new contacts asks for more information. Depending on where you are in your professional career, the business card design and information will vary. When crafting your résumé, remember to include the basics, such as contact information, links to your social media and personal website, as well as relevant skills, work experience, achievements and awards, and a summary that includes your career goals.

Have an Introduction:

Chances are, one of the first questions someone will ask is "Tell me about yourself," or "What do you do?" This is the time to give an elevator pitch. Don't make it too lengthy; just be prepared to share a sentence or two regarding your current position and any career goals. When exchanging introductions, make sure to ask the other person what they do as well to engage in a two-way conversation.

Speak Up:

Don't be afraid to talk! Just because you are a student or intern doesn't mean you need to be shy. Speaking up and contributing relevant insight to a conversation demonstrates industry knowledge. As a best practice, stay up to date with news from blogs and online

continued

Internships

The number one place that employers find new hires is through their company internship programs. Therefore, the chance to complete an internship, or co-operative education experience, as they are sometimes called, is arguably one of the most valuable opportunities available to college students in terms of their professional development. In fact, given the competitive nature of today's job market, it is not uncommon for a student to complete more than one of these experiences. You should talk with your academic advisor about such opportunities early in your college career. (Note: Recognizing how important the internship experience is for you as a college student, we have devoted Chapter 8 to a discussion of these experiences; however, they cannot go without a brief discussion here in terms of the job search.)

Most fashion programs offer college credit for completing an internship, or co-op, because they are the best way to gain "real-world" experience while exploring opportunities in a chosen field of interest. An internship may also be your "in" to an entry-level or leadership training program with a company. It is quite common for companies to extend offers for permanent positions to students who successfully complete internships. Many students complete their internships between their junior and senior years of college—imagine the pressure that is eliminated by coming back to school for your senior year with a job offer already in place.

It bears mentioning that while internships are designed to help you identify what you want to do upon graduation, they can sometimes be even more valuable by helping you identify what you do *not* want to do. This is a common occurrence, and it is far better to find out during an internship that a particular position is not for you, than to realize this three months into your first job.

Remember, if you find yourself in an internship that is not interesting or challenging, you should still maintain a positive attitude and strive to do the best job possible. You never know when you may again encounter the people you are working for, or with, during your internship! The fashion field tends to be a "small world," even in big cities. Also, keep yourself open to exploring other opportunities within the company that may interest you. Perhaps you have found during the internship that buying is not a career for you. However, in working with the marketing department, you have discovered that you are quite interested in promotion. In that case, find out who is in charge of the marketing department and let your interests be known to them. Another excellent source for job leads during your internship experience is through the relationships you may build with the vendors and manufacturer reps servicing your internship site. Some of the most successful manufacturer reps were recruited out of a retail or fashion merchandising setting.

If you are doing your internship for college credit, and you find yourself unhappy, you should discuss your discontent with your college internship supervisor. Your supervisor will be able to offer advice and may even be able to speak with the company's internship coordinator to identify other tasks for you. Regardless, keep your positive attitude and remember that the main purposes of the internship are to explore different career opportunities and gain real-world experience.

Newspapers and Trade Publications

Interestingly, newspapers and trade publications are increasingly less popular choices for employers looking for new hires, with the advent of the Internet and social media technologies. However, you should not discount these sources completely when conducting a job search. You should be aware that it is not uncommon for newspaper ads to generate 200 responses per ad. Major newspapers such as the *Chicago Tribune* sometimes receive up to 2,000 responses to a single ad. This means your chances may be one in 2,000 of landing that job. Given these odds, newspapers and trade journals should definitely not be your sole source of job leads. If you do want to use them, remember that most major newspapers now provide both printed classified sections and postings on the paper's website. Usually, the electronic version contains more job postings than the printed version—and they are updated more frequently as well as more readily accessible. With the print versions, there is usually a particular day of the week that focuses on careers, so be sure to get that day's newspaper. These career sections not only offer job postings but also contain valuable articles related to conducting a successful job search. If nothing else, perusal of the classified section will give you a good idea of who is advertising positions and the types of positions within a company. Classified ads in trade journals, such as *Women's Wear Daily* (www.wwd.com), may also help you identify positions that you either may not have considered or did not know existed. If you find something that is new to you, and that sounds interesting, do your research to find out what such a position entails and the qualifications needed.

Other Contacts (Your Personal Network)

As previously discussed, networking is one of the most effective ways to find a job. Morgan Baker wisely advises, "Connections will be your biggest asset, so never burn any bridges." Similarly, Kelly Burt Deasy observes that her career has advanced through recommendations presented by people in her network—from a variety of positions and companies in the industry. She reflects that job opportunities really depend on networking, so "always be aware of the impression that you make on others—you are likely to find the next job by being recommended by someone with whom you have worked." In fact, you are more likely to find a job through someone you know than through any other means discussed in this text. Chiquita Cooper's experiences with networking in her sales rep position are portrayed in Careers Up Close 5.2. (See Chapter 6 for insight into Kelly Burt Deasy's career in Careers Up Close 6.1; see Chapter 8 for more information about Morgan Baker's internships in Careers Up Close 8.2.)

Included in your network should be not only professional contacts but other people, such as friends and their family, people you have worked with, people you meet socially, those serving as your references, neighbors, and even your own family members. When you begin your job search, you should let everyone know about your search and the career goals you have set for yourself. Meet with people and ask for their advice. Also, ask for the names of other people who might be able to assist you. The more people that you have looking out for you, the better. You may be surprised at who will offer that one lead you need. Box 5.6 presents activities designed to help you develop and implement a networking strategy. Because a personal network of contacts is so important, there is an activity included at the end of the chapter and on the STUDIO website (www.bloomsburyfashioncentral.com) to help you generate such a list. Also, refer to Table 5.1, which provides an overview of the types of contacts found in a typical network, and what their role can be with regard to helping you with your job search. A great way to expand and draw upon your network is to conduct informational interviews—these interviews might lead to internships or jobs but, more importantly, they are ways for you to make connections with people who can give you advice and connect you to other people who may be looking to hire someone just like you. See Box 5.7 for Amanda C. Brooks' guidelines on conducting informational interviews.

CAREERS UP CLOSE 5.2
CHIQUITA COOPER
Business Development Manager
Erica Lyons/Crimzon Rose

To best prepare herself for a career in fashion business during her undergraduate studies, Chiquita majored in textiles, apparel, and merchandising, and minored in marketing. As her studies progressed, Chiquita became increasingly interested in Buying as a career, initially as she took her first retail math course, and then moreso when she interned at Burdines as a Department Manager. The internship sealed her interest in working on the merchandising side of the industry rather than in-store management. Approaching graduation, Chiquita pursued an entry-level opportunity with Burdines (now Macy's) Department Store in Florida, where she was accepted into their highly competitive buying program after a series of interviews and her excellent analytical math tests. Because she scored 100% on her math test, she was given the opportunity to explore the Executive Training Program rather than continuing on the Store Management track. Initially, she had been selected to interview with Burdines based on her professional application packet (cover letter, résumé), which also included a high GPA. Her willingness to relocate to Florida from Northern Illinois, where she had to leave family and lifelong friends, was also key.

Chiquita excelled at Burdines in her entry-level buying position and was promoted to an Associate Buyer within two years. In her initial buying position, Chiquita was given sole responsibility for $4.0 million of business, including the development of seasonal sales, merchandising, and marketing plans; she also managed markdowns and turnover while negotiating with vendors to maintain gross margin. As she advanced in her career, her communication skills became increasingly important as she coordinated communications among product development, the corporate office, distribution, and Burdines' store locations to ensure the consistent flow of trend-right products needed to maximize retail sales. During this time, she also gained experience mentoring others and managing business categories, including women's apparel, swimwear, and, as an Associate Buyer, handbags and jewelry.

After five years in buying, Chiquita accepted a vendor position as Regional Sales Director with 1928 Jewelry Company, where she managed several national and regional department store accounts totaling $14.0 million in annual sales. The coordination of her own sales, the sales of her team, training of store merchandisers to ensure proper merchandise execution, and communication with key store management were key to her success. She also monitored industry trends and performed competitive analysis to ensure 1928 Jewelry remained updated and relevant. This position was a home-based position, so there was a huge adjustment learning to work from home. Chiquita found her greatest challenge was learning to shut down the computer at the end of the day and resisting the temptation to continue working through the evening. She also had to adjust to working alone all day when she was used to being in an office environment. She overcame these challenges by setting a daily ending time after touching base with her regional counterparts to stay informed of their business.

Currently, Chiquita is a Business Development Manager with Erica Lyons/Crimzon Rose, where her responsibilities, while similar to those at 1928, also include collaboration with the production team on quality issues, production timelines, sample reviews, and costing forecasts. She also manages excess inventory by partnering with off-price retailers (e.g., TJ Maxx, Ross) to maximize sell-off while minimizing loss.

As you consider Chiquita's career, it is apparent that analytical skills have been extremely important. However, communication skills, including negotiation, selling, and coaching, have been just as important, especially as she has advanced to executive positions. Analysis is her favorite part of managing a retail business. For her, there is a sense of accomplishment in understanding the decisions needed to drive sales and in solving the challenges of addressing unfavorable results.

Reflecting on her career thus far, Chiquita reports the least favorite time in her career was transitioning from retail buying to wholesale manufacturing and making the adjustment to the difference in the approach to the business. For example, retailers partner with vendors for guidance and help in managing their retail business; vendors work for the retailers to help manage the retailer's business and also to grow their own wholesale companies. However, Chiquita recognizes how the Internet and technology have made things easier. Rather than having to spend an entire day printing and faxing orders to vendors, she uses email, Skype, and online meetings to make decision making a timely process; new technologies provide the ability to react faster to business needs.

Chiquita believes one of the main qualities necessary to be successful in the retail and wholesale corporate industry is to be self-driven and disciplined. This quality is important because the primary responsibility is to create a business within a company using industry data. This includes analyzing trends, considering past sales history, gathering customer feedback, and using current business to make decisions and predictions that will align with the company's goals: to increase sales while driving profitability. As an example, Chiquita's first area of responsibility as a wholesaler was in fashion jewelry. Her brand was Charter Club; the customer profile was a 35–60-year-old woman. Because she was only 24, Chiquita had to discipline herself to focus on what her customers' needs would be and remove her own personal taste and opinions from the decision-making process.

Chiquita advises those wanting to work in the industry to learn about the different positions within each side of the business (wholesale and retail). Identify what you enjoy doing and focus on a career opportunity around that. For example, for someone analytical, the field of sales or buying may be the best fit, whereas a more creative and visionary person would probably be best suited to the design or marketing aspect of the industry. She also points out that networking and maintaining relationships are key to having a successful career. Both of her vendor opportunities were due to having established strong business relationships with sales managers. When those same managers had positions available, Chiquita was considered because they knew of her work

ethic, passion, and integrity. Chiquita emphasizes how important it is to always give 100% because you never know where casual or professional encounters can lead you.

There is one last thing Chiquita wants others to know about the industry. While retailing can be a grueling career, with the need to work late hours and travel, there are obviously many people who successfully manage both career and family lives. In Chiquita's case, entering into the vendor/wholesale side allowed her to have a home-based office, which was a great bonus in raising a family. She spent nine years working from home and, while the travel was more than when she worked in a corporate office, the flexibility it gave her was more beneficial to having a healthy work/life balance. After all, she says, "It's just fashion, we're not saving lives . . . just aesthetically enriching them!"

BOX 5.6 Job Search Networking: How to Start Today

What you know will sustain your career, but *who* you know can launch it. Furthermore, in your network, who *they* know counts. Here are some guidelines for expanding and tapping into your network for the purpose of career growth:

- Document who you know. Make a list of the people you know and note their roles in your career search. For example, perhaps the woman who employed you as a babysitter is a buyer; your manicurist may have a brother who is a sales rep; your neighbor may have a cousin who is a stylist.
- Get in the habit of introducing yourself. Develop an "elevator speech." Be sure to be prepared to share your goals and career aspirations. Offer your business

card, and request business cards from people you meet. You literally might meet someone on an elevator—or on an airplane, in line at the post office, while waiting at a restaurant, etc.

- Ask your acquaintances about themselves—and *listen*. Learning about the people in your network will give you the insight to tap into them as resources—plus you will benefit from hearing advice and learning about their career journeys. You may find out that someone you know is familiar with the city where you want to live, or has family members who work in the industry you seek to join.
- Reach out to acquaintances and prospective acquaintances. Use LinkedIn,

continued

BOX 5.6 Job Search Networking: How to Start Today *(continued)*

and include personal messages in your connection request. Make a phone call, or send an email or LinkedIn message, following a script such as this: "My friend, Sylvia Smith, in Los Angeles recommended that I contact you. I am seeking a stylist position and Sylvia suggested that you could offer advice. I'm looking for an internship in New York or another major city. When would be a good time for us to chat?" You should be sure to ask, "Who do you know that I should be talking to?"

- Follow up! Once you have met a new acquaintance, follow up with an email or a hand-written note. Send a message to a new connection on LinkedIn. Mention in your note how you met, and present a request to keep the communication going. For example, "Marcus, we met last week during a flight to Chicago. Thank you for sharing insights about a district manager's job. I am preparing my application for the MIT position in Atlanta. Would you be willing to review my résumé? I've attached it here for your convenience; it is also posted on LinkedIn."

TABLE 5.1

TYPES OF CONTACTS FOUND IN YOUR NETWORK AND WHAT YOU CAN ASK OF THEM

Contact	What they can do	What they cannot do
Friends and family	Give you names	Give leads for every industry
	Comment about your personal characteristics	Serve as professional references
Professional references	Identify leads for you	Give leads for every industry
	Comment about your work ethic and key skills	Increasingly, laws are limiting references as to what information can be legally shared—check with each reference concerning this
People with whom you have worked	Comment about your work ethic and skills	Know a lot about all the companies in which you are interested
	Refer you to others	
People you meet socially	Refer you to others	Comment about your work ethic
	Refer to you as a likeable person	Always do what they say they will do
	Provide on-the-spot informational interviews	

WHAT TO DO IF YOU CAN'T FIND A JOB

Depending on your geographic location, the industry niche you seek, your GPA, and the current economy, the market for college graduates can vary substantially. The good news is that the fashion industry, retailing, and commerce is a solid business with strong prospects for careers. Fashion merchandise, retail consumption, and related marketing activities are not about to cease in our global economy. It is important, however, to keep abreast of the trends that shape how these activities change and evolve—that is where the best opportunities for career growth will emerge. This means that you may have to work hard to find a job and keep your options open. It may also take you somewhat longer to land the job of your dreams than you desire. If you find yourself in this situation, it is extremely important that you remain optimistic and not give up on your efforts. Perseverance truly pays off. Having a strong network of people to offer leads, provide you with feedback, and provide moral support will enhance your job search experience.

Interview As Much As Possible

When asked to give advice to students seeking jobs, the employer members of NACE reported that students were not signing up in great numbers for on-campus interviews. Unfortunately, college students are sometimes perceived as apathetic toward on-campus recruiters. The fact is that there are employers interviewing on campus and students need to take advantage of every opportunity available. As Aaron Sturgill notes in his Careers Up Close 2.2 profile in Chapter 2, simply being at the right place at the right time—by showing up and attending recruiter events—can elevate your position in a job search. Remember that each interview, regardless of the outcome, provides a learning opportunity and will better prepare you for the next interview.

Assess Your Job Search Efforts

If you find yourself becoming discouraged with your job search, now is a great time to assess your search efforts to date. This assessment allows you to ask yourself if you have really done everything you can do to find a job. Take a critical look at what you have done and what you may have missed. (The website for this textbook provides a career search quiz to help with your assessment.) In your assessment, you should ask yourself if you are expecting too much or being too demanding. For example, a student asked us to review her résumé because she was having a hard time getting an interview even though she had a very high grade point average (GPA), great leadership experiences in student associations, and quite a bit of practical experience. One had only to look as far as the second line of her résumé, under her name, where it stated: *Will not consider any positions starting at under $30,000 a year*! Even though this is a reasonable limit, being so bold with the statement is off-putting to recruiters and others who screen résumés. It is important to remain flexible and realistic in your job search. Although prospective employers want to know your goals and objectives, being too demanding, particularly in an uncertain economy, will not be viewed favorably.

You should also make sure that you are presenting yourself in the most professional way possible to each prospective employer, and to all members of your network. Common mistakes that students often make in this area involve unprofessional voice mail messages and email addresses. Check to be sure that you are not projecting the wrong image through these means. Your answering machine message should not include music, slang terms, or anything else that might send the wrong signal to a caller. Messages such as "Yo, leave a message," or "We're not here, call back!" (which are actual messages we have encountered when calling students) are not appropriate. Although they may amuse your friends, they will certainly turn off potential employers. Similarly, voice mail messages you leave for others should be professional. Box 5.8 provides a list of simple hints to follow when using voice mail. Lastly, check your email address to be sure it does not say something about you that would turn off an employer. Again, having received numerous emails from students, we have found this mistake to be quite common. Email addresses such as *partygirl*, *shotqueen*, or *beerdrinking1* are not a good idea. When in doubt, simply use your first initial and last name for your address (e.g., jhillery@xyz.edu).

BOX 5.8 Sending Messages Using Voice Mail, Email, and Web-Based Messaging

During your job search, you will undoubtedly need to leave messages for prospective employers. Whether telephone voice mail, email, or web-based messaging, you must keep in mind the professional nature of your correspondence. Even with a text message, use discretion and seek to portray a professional image.

Your goals for messages, regardless of the media, are the same. You want to be:

- Clear
- Informative
- Efficient
- Professional

Identify yourself. Always state who you are (spell your name if voice message). Providing proper spelling of your name is extremely helpful. Most names aren't easily determined by voice message. This also helps make YOU recognizable and memorable in future interactions.

Briefly describe the purpose for your message. Refer to a web job posting (by date and the publication or website) or mention a mutual acquaintance who suggested you make the contact.

If you are leaving a voice message:

- Speak slowly and clearly. Rushing through a message makes it difficult for the receiver to decipher and write your information. You want to avoid having the recipient re-listen to your message multiple times.
- State the day and time of your call. This is a helpful reference and courteous information to provide.
- Eliminate unnecessary return calls. Leave a message to explain the purpose of your contact. An informative message, such as "I am calling to check the status of my application" or "I will be in town next week and would like to stop in to meet you in person," tells the person exactly what you want. That way, the recipient of your message can respond even if you never make person-to-person contact.

- Leave an email address. Using the tips above, spell your email address and offer that method of reply.
- Be brief. There are likely to be many phone messages and emails for your contact each day. Keep yours brief and include only the necessary details.
- Leave your phone number. Repeat it at the end of your message, slowly, including your area code. This will save time and energy in case your résumé or previous correspondence has been lost or misplaced. You cannot assume that caller ID is activated. Be sure to indicate whether a text message is an option on your phone. Also leave pertinent information such as, "I will be unavailable from 9 to 10 a.m."

If you are sending an email message:

- Follow the guidelines above. It is often a good idea to indicate in your voice message that you will send an email with details.
- Check your spelling and avoid casual jargon and abbreviations. Keep in mind that you are engaging in professional communication. Use complete sentences and avoid "textspeak" (e.g., Pls c my attached resume).
- Blind copy yourself so that you have a quick reference of your communication.

continued

Use a Temporary Employment Agency

If, after a critical assessment of your job search, you feel you have done everything you can to find a job, yet you are still unsuccessful, there are some other options you can consider while continuing your search for that perfect job. In a tough job market, you may want to consider taking a temporary position in your area of interest. A temporary position, much like an internship, allows you to gain valuable experience and may also prove to be an "in" to the company should it need to fill a permanent position. A temporary position is also a great way to add to your network and contacts that can help you find a job. If you are hired as a "temp" for a company, it is perfectly appropriate to let everyone there know about your career goals and objectives. Many of your co-workers probably know others in the industry in which you are interested and may prove to be valuable leads for you at other companies.

Volunteer

Another option to consider is doing volunteer work. Beth Watson, a graduate of the marketing program at Northern Illinois University, discovered first-hand how volunteering within the community can help students land their "dream" position. When the retailer of her choice came to campus to interview students, Beth was disappointed that she did not make the short-list to interview for the company's internship program. However, one month later, while she was volunteering with the Glass Slipper Project in Chicago (a nonprofit organization that distributes gently used prom dresses to underprivileged high school girls), she met and worked with a store manager from the same retailer. Based on this experience, she began an internship with the company and is now an assistant store manager for one of the most successful retailers in the country. Similarly, students who volunteer to assist with fashion shows at AmericasMart in Atlanta are afforded the opportunity to network with staff who hire students for their internship program.

Take a Job in the Service Industry

You may also need to take a job that will simply "pay the bills" while you are conducting your job search. Many college graduates continue to wait tables, bartend, or do various other service jobs until they land that perfect first job. People who have worked as a server or bartender can tell you that these jobs helped them develop valuable skills. Not only do service jobs help perfect customer-service skills, but they also develop teamwork, organizational, and interpersonal communication skills, and many other skills that will be valuable in any field. They also give you the opportunity to network—and, specifically, to tell a lot of people that you are looking for a job. As stated before, you never know with whom you are talking when you work with the public.

Consider Relocating to a Different Area

Because economic conditions, and resulting job opportunities, can differ greatly from one region of the country to another, you may want to consider moving. Although many recent college graduates are somewhat apprehensive about leaving their friends and family behind to take a job in another city or state, others find the opportunity quite rewarding and often comment that the move was the best decision they ever made concerning their professional development. In considering a move, you can start by reading financial reports, trade publications, and out-of-state newspapers (typically available online through your university or local library) to help you identify markets where jobs are more plentiful. The Internet is also a great source for conducting research about other areas. And talk to your network contacts. Many of them probably know someone who is working in another state or city, and they may provide you with a valuable link to the new area you are considering.

To help you get started, the activities section at the end of the chapter contains an exercise to help you research the employment market in another area. If you find yourself somewhat anxious about making such a move, remember that you are not necessarily making a lifetime commitment to stay in the new location. Commonly, once you obtain some experience, you will be more attractive to potential employers in the market you have left, and you can return there if you so desire. Remember, nothing ventured, nothing gained! (See Box 10.4 in Chapter 10, which discusses how to successfully relocate to another area.)

In a tough job market, and even in a good one, it is quite common to become frustrated with a job search. If at a later point you find yourself in this situation, reread this chapter and review Table 5.2, which presents common myths about the job search today. Be sure you are not buying into any of these erroneous statements. Being persistent, optimistic, and flexible will eventually pay off! As your job search continues, one of the most important things you can do is to remain true to yourself and your passions regardless of what field you wish to enter. The majority of the time, after weeks of interviewing, sending out résumés, and networking—just when students and recent college graduates are ready to give up—their hard work comes to fruition. They may even receive multiple job offers in the same week! What a great feeling when the question then becomes, "Which job will I take?" rather than "Will I have a job to take?"

TABLE 5.2

COMMON MYTHS ABOUT THE JOB SEARCH

Myth	Fact
If I am sending out cover letters and résumés, it will result in interviews.	You will need to follow up on every résumé that you send out, requesting an interview and expressing your interest in the position. You must be proactive and persistent, not passive! Opportunities will slip by if you wait for employers to contact you.
There are no positions available at the companies I am interested in because there are none advertised.	Most experts agree that only about 15–25 percent of jobs are advertised in some type of medium. An overwhelming majority of jobs are part of a "hidden" job market and are filled through referrals made through networking. Make every effort to network and find people who work at the companies you would like to work for. They can provide you with the leads you need.
I have no experience specific to my field, so no employers will consider me.	Most employers, particularly when hiring for entry-level positions, will consider your enthusiasm for the position and potential to learn and advance within their organization. Sell yourself using the many transferable skills that all employers are looking for (e.g., leadership, communication skills, time management, organizational skills).

continued

TABLE 5.2

COMMON MYTHS ABOUT THE JOB SEARCH
(CONTINUED)

Myth	Fact
I have no control over the job search—it is the employers who are in control.	You are the one who is in charge of your job search! It is up to you to follow up on leads, make multiple points of contact, prepare for your interviews, and send thank-you letters.
If I go to school, get good grades, and obtain a four-year degree, I will get a good job.	Your degree does not guarantee you, nor does it entitle you to, a well-paying job. It *prepares* you for one. Those who have the best job search and interviewing skills, and who are able to establish a good rapport with the interviewers, will usually get the best jobs.
I do not have definite career plans, so it will be hard for me to get a job.	Developing a career is a lifelong process. It is probable that you will change careers as many as four or five times over the course of your life. While you should always have a set of career goals, it is highly likely that these will change as you learn new skills and identify new areas of interest. Most importantly, show a keen interest in the opportunity for which you presently seek.
Most times people find their jobs through "lucky" breaks.	What often appears as luck is a matter of the person being prepared and working hard to have the chance to secure the job.
A high-paying job will make me happy.	A high-paying job that does not match your goals and interests will only result in job dissatisfaction. Having a job that pays less, but is one that you enjoy, is a far better choice. Remember, too, that you are more likely to succeed at something that you enjoy doing.
Lowering my salary requests, or not negotiating a higher salary, will make me more attractive to an employer.	As long as your demands are comparable with industry standards, you should stick to them. Agreeing to a lower salary will make you look desperate for a job and will most likely cause you to be unhappy in the position because you feel you were cheated out of the salary you deserve.
I should take the first job offer that comes along in case nothing else does.	You should only take the first offer if you are completely satisfied with it. However, there are several factors that you should critically assess before deciding on an offer. Accepting the first offer may be right for you, but you should never do so just because you think nothing else will come along. If finances are a concern, consider taking a temporary job (e.g., waiting tables), until a better offer comes your way.
Others, including my parents and friends, know what's best for me.	You know yourself better than anyone. Although you may want to consider the advice of others, *you* should ultimately make any decision about your career. Follow your instincts—they are usually right!

WHAT IS A PROFESSIONAL NETWORK?

Think of a spider web when you are picturing the ideal professional network. Successful networks draw from social contacts, including family members; academic teachers and peers; work colleagues; acquaintances from volunteering; and fellow members of organizations such as churches, synagogues, and mosques. A professional network, specifically, should be constructed for the purpose of advancing your connections to people who can advocate for you and further connect you to career growth opportunities. Not everyone in your professional network may be positioned to offer you a job, but they might be able to steer you in the direction of a job, introduce you to someone who is hiring, connect you with someone who can provide guidance for entering your chosen career, or give you moral support. A professional network cannot be too big!

Mentors

Mentoring is viewed as a special one-on-one relationship between a senior, experienced professional (the mentor) and a younger or newer-to-career person (the mentee or the protégé). There are several philosophies regarding effective mentoring relationships—some people believe that mentoring only emerges organically, and others argue that mentors can be productive when a formal relationship is established. For example, some organizations actually assign mentors to new employees. Others support formal relationships that emerge when new employees invite senior leaders to serve as their mentors. Still other successful mentoring relationships simply happen naturally and are not formalized in any way.

Regardless of the way in which a relationship might be established with a mentor, you are encouraged to seek at least one—and preferably multiple—mentors throughout your career. Mentoring is such an important topic that we present insights throughout this book—particularly in Chapter 10.

Developmental Networks

When mentoring expands to include multiple people who are positioned to offer insight and advice, the result is a developmental network that serves a novice professional.

Social Contacts

Mentoring and developmental networks are entities that traditionally emerge from professional relationships; however, it is important not to discount the social contacts that provide essential career guidance and support. All of the people you know, and also people *they* know, can comprise your developmental network.

NETWORKING AS A LIFELONG ACTIVITY

You will continue networking and cultivating your professional contacts long after completing collegiate work experiences. While you are in college, be sure to make optimal use of the resources on campus and set the standard for making connections as you meet and work with new people.

As You Approach Graduation

Be sure to draw upon the advice provided in Chapter 3 to build your personal brand. In anticipation of your graduation, use social media, college placement offices, and internship experiences to refine your professional profile. Be sure to attend employment fairs and consult with academic advisors and faculty mentors as you navigate the first steps in your career.

As a New Professional

Many graduates mistakenly assume that they forfeit the university career and leadership resources upon graduation, but, in fact, you should plan to stay connected to these important resources. Additionally, when you have embarked on your first career job, be sure to join professional organizations where you can meet other new career people as well as seasoned professionals who are positioned to serve as mentors and guides. An added benefit of professional organization membership is the access to lifelong learning activities and potential mentors. Professional organizations typically host networking luncheons and happy hour events, sponsor featured speakers, and invite prestigious members of the business and political communities. Women in Business clubs emphasize empowerment of female professionals, Toastmasters provides opportunities to polish public speaking skills, and Rotary International engages its members in global service activities. Professional organizations offer the added benefit of social support to the professional development and networking that are inherent in their memberships.

Projects

1. Researching a prospective employer. One of the most important things you need to do when embarking on a job search is to conduct research into companies that you are considering as prospective employers. Complete the following exercise for each company you are interested in pursuing. Although information is available from a variety of sources, one of the best is www.hoovers.com. Log onto this website and collect the following information related to each retailing or apparel merchandising company for whom you would be interested in working.

a. Current state of the industry and trends for the future
b. Top companies in the industry
c. General overview of the company
d. Major developments, trends, and issues at the company
e. Key executives at the company

Summarize your findings in a 2- to 3-page report, including a discussion about implications for employment with this company. Keep your report for referral when writing a cover letter and interviewing with the firm. Remember, this information can be valuable in formulating questions to ask at an interview.

2. Career fair and internship fair assignment. Choose one of these fairs to attend on your campus, if possible. Before going to the fair, look over a list of the companies that will be there, review the positions they are offering (if available), and do your research. Your campus placement office should have many resources to help you with this process. You can also conduct research using the Internet at the company sites and at sites such as www.hoovers.com, as you did for Project 1, above. At the fair, you should talk to at least three employers. Get a business card from each, and type up a brief synopsis of your conversations. The synopsis should include a summary of the conversation, a brief description of the available position, why (or why not) you would be interested in the internship, and a brief reaction to the encounter. Also note any follow-up that was agreed upon. The website accompanying this text, www.bloomsburyfashioncentral.com, provides a template for this report.

3. Visit with a professor. Make an appointment with a professor who teaches in your major to discuss career opportunities in your field. Before your visit, prepare a list of questions. Ask about typical positions secured by graduating seniors, employers who commonly interview on campus and the types of positions they offer, the skills employers are especially interested in, and positions held by the program's alumni. You may also want to let the professor know about your career interests and ask for the names of any contacts he or she may have. Prepare a brief report to summarize the findings from your meeting.

4. Job and internship search in a different market. Identify a job market that interests you that is in a different location from where you currently live. Prepare a brief report, including the following:

a. Name and description of the city or area

b. Explanation of why you are interested in this city or area

c. Comparison of the cost-of-living in this city or area versus your current location

d. Major companies located in this city or area

e. Examples of specific job opportunities you have found using the Internet, newspapers, or other sources

f. A specific plan for conducting a job search in this city or area

g. Advantages and disadvantages of relocating to this city or area

5. Networking Activity. Often, people looking for a job make the mistake of being too conservative when identifying a network for assistance. Do not limit yourselves only to professional contacts. Everyone you know should be considered a source of job leads. Generate your own personal contact list. People to include in your network:

- Past employers. List all the people you have previously worked for and with, even if it was in jobs that you feel are not directly related to your current job search. Don't forget to include people for whom you may have done odd jobs, such as lawn mowing, babysitting, or errands.

- Your professional references. List all those who will be serving as personal references for you (see Chapter 6 for further discussion of personal references).

- Internship supervisors and co-workers. List all of your supervisors, people you met, and people you worked with at your internship. If applicable, you should also include the people you know in the human resources department.

- People you know from school. List friends, professors, coaches, counselors, fellow students in your major, alumni, fellow members of your sorority or fraternity, and members of your professional and student organizations.

- People who you know from volunteer activities. List all people you have met while doing volunteer work.

- Friends from home and their families. List all of your friends from home and their parents and other adult family members. Also include your neighbors and their family members.

- Current employer and co-workers. List all the people from your current job that you consider co-workers, and your supervisors. Also include others with whom you may not work directly but whom you know from this job.

- Customers and clients. If you have worked in a service position, your customers and clients may be of some assistance to you in your job search. List all customers and clients whom you know from past and previous jobs.

- Your family. List family members, including your parents, adult siblings, aunts, uncles, cousins, and grandparents. Although they cannot serve as professional references for you, they can be a great help when it comes to job leads.
- People whom you have met socially. List all the people to whom you have been introduced at social functions. Include those you may have conversed with on the train, while standing in line at the movies, or while shopping.

Questions for Discussion

1. What types of services are available at your college or university placement/career services office to assist in your job search?
2. What are some questions you could ask recruiters at a job fair? What are some questions they might ask you?
3. List three organizations on your campus that you would be interested in joining. What are the requirements for membership? What are some of the activities they sponsor?
4. What are some ways that membership in student and professional organizations could help you personally (e.g., what are some skills you need to develop)?
5. List three companies that offer internships that interest you. How can you find out more about these internships?
6. What are some of the advantages to using the Internet as a job search resource? Can you think of any disadvantages?
7. What are the three job search sites on the Internet that you think are most helpful? What are the strengths of these sites over others you have visited?
8. What is the major newspaper in your area that could be useful in your job search? Under what category or categories in the classified section would you find jobs that interest you?
9. Why do you think networking is an important part of the job search? What do you think are the major advantages to networking over other job search strategies?
10. What are some of the major groups or organizations in your area that would offer you the best networking opportunities?
11. Besides those discussed in this book, can you think of other strategies for finding a job or an internship? How have your friends or classmates found jobs and internships?
12. What are some jobs you could do while searching for an entry-level career position? What transferable skills would these jobs offer you? How might one of these jobs help you find your first professional career position?

13. In reviewing the job search proverbs presented in this chapter, identify and discuss (a) the five that you most agree with and (b) the five you least agree with.

STUDiO Activities

Visit the *Guide to Fashion Career Planning STUDIO* available at www.bloomsburyfashioncentral.com. The key elements are:

1. Summary of Chapter 5 text

2. Quiz

3. Career-fair attire assessment

  a. Career-fair attire critique form

4. Career-fair contact information log

5. Company contact information and career-fair report form

6. Finding a Mentor

VIDEO: Your Handshake

References

Brooks, A. (2015). *Always pack a party dress and other lessons learned from a (half) life in fashion*. New York: Blue Rider Press.

Krueger, B. (2015) *Job search proverbs*. Available online: www.collegegrad.com

Krueger, B. (2003, January 13) *The networking by association technique: Job search tip of the week*. Available online: www.collegegrad.com

National Association of Colleges and Employers. (2013). *Job outlook 2014*. Bethlehem, PA: NACEWeb Publications. Available online: http://www.uab.edu/careerservices/images/NACE_Job_Outlook_2014.pdf

National Association of Colleges and Employers. (2014). *Job outlook 2015*. Bethlehem, PA: NACEWeb Publications. Available online: https://www.umuc.edu/upload/NACE-Job-Outlook-2015.pdf

CHAPTER 6
RÉSUMÉS AND COVER LETTERS

If you haven't had a few dents in your résumé, you haven't tried.

—ANDREW "TWIGGY" FORREST

OBJECTIVES

- To identify pertinent information for preparing professional résumés and cover letters.
- To identify the appropriate format for professional résumés and cover letters.
- To construct a professional résumé, reference page, and accompanying cover letter.

Cover letters and résumés create the first impression you will make on prospective employers. Therefore, their appearance and accuracy are extremely important. You will find that the extra effort involved in presenting neat, attractive, well-formatted, and high-quality documents (e.g., laser-printed hard copies) will pay off. Be sure to purchase light-colored or white premium paper appropriate for representing your professional profile. Above all, any written correspondence—and, in particular, the cover letter and résumé—should be completely error free.

Although they are submitted together, both the letter and the résumé should be able to stand alone. Each should contain relevant information for employers enabling them to know something about you and how to contact you. This chapter provides detailed information that will help you construct professional, personalized résumés and cover letters.

RÉSUMÉS

Résumé writing has long been considered an arduous task. Because summarizing education, work experiences, activities, and references all at one time is overwhelming, résumés are better developed over time. A comprehensive, well-refined résumé is certainly preferable to one that has been quickly compiled. You will find it helpful in the long run to begin your résumé as your collegiate and work experience career begins, and to update and adjust it as new opportunities are encountered and leadership skills are enhanced. The advantages of developing a résumé early in your academic career include:

- Increased accuracy in reporting dates, job duties, and specific leadership experiences (rather than writing from memory).
- The convenience of having a "work in progress" (rather than starting from scratch at the last minute).
- Time to experiment with various formats.
- An opportunity to formulate and organize your goals as well as identify personal areas for improvement through revision.

Formats of Résumés

The résumé is your calling card, and should be tailored to each type of position you are seeking (e.g., management trainee, internship). You should think of your résumé as a one-page advertisement of you.

A résumé should focus on educational preparation, previous work experience, leadership activities, and references. Although résumé formats are not as strictly prescribed as letter formats, generally there have been two types of résumés: the chronological format and the functional format. Today, more creative formats are also being accepted, which we will also discuss.

Functional Format

The functional format provides the opportunity to list education and work experience entries in order of importance, with the most significant, not the most recent, listed first. It generally deemphasizes places of employment and concentrates on specific skills, qualifications, and accomplishments. On a functional résumé, you might find categories such as *Managerial Skills*, *Technical Skills*, and *Accomplishments*. A functional résumé is best suited to people with a variety of specialized skills or many different and short-lived positions. It is not recommended for college students and recent graduates.

Chronological Format

The chronological format is the most common and also the most desirable type of résumé for college students and recent graduates. Beginning with your most recent experience, it lists your education, followed by your employers, job titles, dates, and responsibilities. Figure 6.1 provides an example of the chronological format.

FIGURE 6.1
Chronological
Résumé

Maria Vasquez
Mvasquez1@hotmail.com

Present Address	Permanent Address
321 River Street	22154 Valley View Lane
Athens, OH 45701	New Concord, OH 43721
(740) 555-5505	(740) 555-5555

EDUCATION
Ohio University, Athens, Ohio
Candidate for **Bachelor of Science in Human and Consumer Sciences**
Major: Fashion Retail Merchandising —Minor: Marketing
Major GPA: 3.97   Overall GPA: 3.6   Dean's List
Degree Expected: June 2015   Financing 40% of education

HONORS
Mary P. Cosbey Award, 2014
—Awarded to Consumer Science Major most likely to make
outstanding contribution to profession
Phi Kappa Phi Academic Honor Society, 2014
Mortar Board National Honor Society, 2014
Golden Key Honorary Society, 2013
Kappa Omicron Nu Honorary Society, 2013

PROFESSIONAL EXPERIENCE

June 2004–Aug. 2004   **Internship**
MARSHALL FIELD'S, Chicago, IL
• Gained valuable insight into the overall operations of a large retail
department store
• Monitored daily departmental sales and goals
• Assistant to the Department Manager for entire departmental
operations
• Assisted Manager with the hiring, training, and scheduling of sales
associates
• Performed operational duties including interstore transfers,
Returns-to-vendors, and seasonal markdowns
• Assisted visual merchandising team with creative merchandise
displays
• Communicated weekly with buyers and vendors

Academic Breaks   **Sales Associate**
2011–2015   THE LIMITED, Sunset Mall, Zanesville, OH
• Consistently met or exceeded daily sales goals while providing
exceptional customer service
• Increased sales through the use of creative and unique
merchandising displays

OTHER EXPERIENCE

Academic Years   **Server**
2013–2015   CRAIG'S FINE DINING, Athens, OH
• Demanding clientele in a fast-paced environment provided
opportunity to enhance interpersonal communication skills

LEADERSHIP ACTIVITIES

2014–2015   Phi Kappa Phi Academic Honor Society
• Vice President
2011–present   Fashion Associates Student Organization
• Secretary 2014–2015

Creative Format

It is increasingly prevalent for those in artistic fields such as graphic
design and fashion to present their résumés in more expressive formats.
If done correctly, the creative format will combine the two previously
discussed formats. The resulting résumé will often resemble an info-
graphic, which is a kind of diagram used to present statistics and figures
on a given topic. Although the creative format will look different, it is
still important to follow the basic guidelines presented in this chapter
in both the type of information you provide (e.g., your skills and work

experience) and the way in which you present it (e.g., action words, professional lingo). Figure 6.2 presents an example of this format that is also available in the accompanying *Guide to Fashion Careers STUDIO* (www.bloomsburyfashioncentral.com).

FIGURE 6.2
Creative Résumé

LAUREN
DODD SMITH

myemail@provider.com   212-555-1212   **Lauren Dodd Smith**   linkedin.com/me/laurendoddsmith

- EXPERIENCE -

01. **Sears Holdings Management Corporation**
Hoffman Estates, Illinois, 2011-14

SOCIAL MEDIA AND DIGITAL DESIGN STRATEGY MANAGER

2014

- Promoted to position to create and oversee social media campaigns and calendar cadence.

CREATIVE MANAGER, STORE ENVIRONMENT DESIGN

2011-14

- Spearheaded the design of shop concepts, fixtures and displays including the high-profile Kardashian Kollection
- Designed and developed Aesthetic Standards, In-aisle Presentation Standards, and Fixture Roll-out Books for Sears and Kmart.
- Provided creative direction to construction, business units, and all levels of leadership to ensure successful implementation and adherence to corporate design standards.
- Directed shop renderings for new fixture and shop designs, and reviewed store construction plans to improve merchandise marketing and overall store layout.

02. **Driving Fore Profit**
FOUNDER/STORE ENVIRONMENT DESIGN CREATIVE DIRECTOR

Fort Myers, Florida, and Chicago, Illinois, 2004-11

- Recruited and consulted small and large retail stores and chains in visual merchandising, displays, interior design, and logo design.
- Ensured creative displays and products supported client business needs and goals.
- Presented visual design seminars at The PGA Show and Methodist University.

PROFILE

Creative brand leader whose retail visual marketing expertise drives sales and optimizes inventory. Leader with proven success shepherding projects from concept creation to successful in-store installation. Experience across retail business leads to visual design strategies that integrate successfully with overall company initiatives and financial goals.

SKILLS

Brand Management; Store Design; Visual Merchandising; Inventory Optimization; Staff Development & Training; Public Speaking; Fixture Development; Forecasting & Market Analysis; Plan-o-Grams; Strategic Planning; Budgeting & Financials; Vendor Interaction; Change Management; Loss Control / Shrinkage; Logo Design

COMPUTER SKILLS
Adobe Creative Suite (Photoshop, Illustrator, InDesign, Acrobat Pro); Microsoft Office Suite (Excel, PowerPoint, Word, Publisher); Retail Software Systems (JDA)

EDUCATION, TRAINING AND CERTIFICATION

DIRECT MARKETING ASSOCIATION CERTIFIED MARKETING PROFESSIONAL, 2012

BACHELOR OF SCIENCE: TEXTILES, APPAREL & MERCHANDISING, NORTHERN ILLINOIS UNIVERSITY
DEKALB, ILLINOIS, 2010

ASSOCIATE OF ARTS IN DESIGN, EDISON COLLEGE
FORT MYERS, FLORIDA, 2006

continued

LAUREN
Lauren Dodd Smith
DODD SMITH

- EXPERIENCE -

03. Target Stores

EXECUTIVE INTERN

2008

- Optimized inventory by correcting end-cap merchandising and creating and implementing forms to track placement and sales

04. Chico's FAS Inc.

VISUAL MANAGER FLAGSHIP STORE, CORPORATE VISUAL DESIGN TEAM

Fort Myers, Florida, 2003-04

- Developed and designed window displays for flagship store, monthly window update, and plan-o-gram update including visuals for all 465 stores in the chain.

- Trained store leadership on the visual standards required to deliver execution and drive consistency across the chain, and trained new store leaders in visual merchandising before grand openings.

05. Stein Mart

REGIONAL VISUAL MERCHANDISE MANAGER

Southwest Florida, 2001-03

- Creative lead for visual merchandising standards in three top-grossing Southwest Florida retail stores, including training department leaders in visual standards and guidelines.

- As part of new store opening team, led start-to-finish prop creation and helped to set up stores.

06. Additional Department Store Visual Merchandising Experience

1999-2002

Jo-Ann Fabric and Craft Stores, Burdines Department Stores, Robb & Stucky Interiors

- Created store layouts, stack-outs and window displays, and oversaw graphics, artwork and other visual elements.

- More details available upon request

FIGURE 6.2
Creative Résumé (continued)

Components of the Chronological Résumé

Because the chronological format has traditionally been preferred for college students and recent graduates, we will focus on it for our discussion. However, as mentioned, other methods of formatting résumés may be perfectly acceptable, especially as you progress in your career. If you have questions about the preferred format for your résumé, check with the career resources office at your university.

Name and Contact Information

Your name should be the first item listed on your résumé under a top margin of at least three-quarters of an inch. Next, include both your current and permanent addresses and a phone number. When relevant, include the precise date that you will be leaving your temporary or school address. Often employers will try to reach you after you have moved, and you do not want to miss an opportunity because the employer cannot find you. On a related note, if you place a copy of your résumé on file with your career planning office, remember to update your contact information periodically.

Directly under your name, along with your address and phone number, you should include your email address. This address should be an account that you routinely check, and the email name should be professional. The best approach is to use your first initial followed by your last name (e.g., *jsmith@yahoo.com*). Recruiters will notice unprofessional email names (e.g., *partygirl*, *@cuteone*) and many use those to screen out what may have otherwise been qualified candidates.

Objective

Traditionally, résumés often began with the heading *Career Objective*, or something to that effect. Although this segment may give some direction to an employer about your goals and desired position, more often the objective becomes extra baggage on the résumé—or worse, too restrictive, blocking consideration of the job seeker for other opportunities that may be available within the hiring organization. A poorly written objective may also work against you by turning off an employer before he or she reaches the sections of the résumé that list your credentials. Recruiters, too, have indicated that an all-encompassing objective doesn't narrow the desired career path or position adequately, and a very focused objective may eliminate you from consideration of another position. Furthermore, an objective often will not provide any information about you that the employer doesn't already know. For example, consider the following objective: *Seeking a challenging position with a profitable company with opportunities for advancement.* Who *doesn't* want this type of position, especially if you consider the alternative: an unchallenging position with an unprofitable company with no opportunities for advancement! It is better to tailor your cover letter to express your desired position within the given company and list your background facts in the résumé.

One exception to this advice is when you visit a career fair. You will not be able to write a letter to each employer, and you may want to distribute a large number of résumés. In such a situation, employers will want to know whether you are seeking an internship, an entry-level job, or summer break employment. This information should be listed in the objective section of your résumé and needs to be direct. For example, a good objective would be: *Seeking an internship in retail merchandising.* You may wish to further specify: *in summer 2020.*

Personal Mission Statement

Rather than include an objective on your résumé, we posit that a personal mission statement is much better use of résumé space and something that could set you apart from others. We stress to all students the importance of forming such a statement to drive your career decisions—and life decisions, for that matter. Because we have devoted an entire section in Chapter 9 to this subject, we encourage you to review that information and complete the assignments provided, so that your own personal mission statement can be included on your résumé. Figure 6.3 provides an example of a résumé that includes a personal mission statement.

Education

The educational institutions that you have attended should be listed in order with most recent first. Generally you would include only those institutions where you received, or will receive, a degree. Likely, your university experience will be listed as current, and you should focus on your major, any minors, and the degree that you expect to earn. A notation indicating the expected date of your graduation (e.g., *Expected Graduation: June 2017*) is preferable to postdating your résumé (e.g., *BS Retail Management: June 2017*). This style points out to the employer that you are currently a student seeking a work experience, an internship, or a full-time position in a future context rather than disguising the fact that your graduation has not yet occurred. Remember, plans are made, but until an event actually happens, one should not report it as fact.

Whether to list high school information is another area of confusion for many students. If you are enrolled in a university, it is implied that you have earned a high school diploma or its equivalency, so unless the high school has some particular merit toward your career preparation (such as a vocational focus or other specialized course of study, military academy, or such), listing the high school is unnecessary. Applicants who have not engaged in education beyond the secondary level should list the high school graduation date or the date the general education development (GED) degree was received to demonstrate that level of education.

FIGURE 6.3
Résumé with Mission
Statement

Andrea Westcott   resume
awestcott1@gmail.com

321 River Street
Oklahoma City, OK 55996
(899) 555-5505

Decision maker with vision for building strong relationships among work teams including outside
partners to achieve maximum results. Intuitive ability for uncovering opportunities.

SKILLS PROFILE
- Strong analytical skills to aide in the accuracy of decisions
- Experience with leadership in working with teams and groups
- Impeccable work ethic and personal initiative with a powerful drive for success
- Extremely flexible with scheduling and easily adapts to changes in work environment
- Robust understanding of Fashion Forecasting and identifying market trends

WORK EXPERIENCE

Category Management/Merchandising Assistant Buyer home accessories
Hobby Lobby Oklahoma City, OK June 2014– present
- Implemented 75 test items for store with average 82% sell-through to date
- Manage assortment plans and Excel files for merchandise allocation nationwide
- Collaborate with marketing department planning promotions and advertisements

Wholesale Intern
Miss Missy Sportswear, Chicago IL Feb. 2014- May 2014
- Maintained calendar of appointments for over 600 accounts
- Coordinated presentation of merchandise during market week
- Managed and fulfilled orders for retailer customers
- Merchandised market-week booth and assisted with sales to retail buyers

EDUCATION
Ohio University, Athens, OH
Bachelor of Science in Human and Consumer Sciences, June 2014
Major: Retail Merchandising
Minor: Business Administration
Study Abroad: Paris and London Spring 2013

LEADERSHIP ACTIVITIES AND AWARDS
- Performance Award, 2015
- Volunteer, New Beginnings Animal Shelter – January 2015 - Present
- Intern of the year award, June 2014
- Ann Paulins Merchandising Student Award, June 2014

SYSTEM KNOWLEDGE
- Microsoft Office: Outlook, Word, Excel, PowerPoint
- Allocation Systems: JDA, EFAS, DCM, Retek, E3

Space permitting, you may also include coursework that supports your
career objective in this section. Additionally, if you have paid for all or a percentage of your education, you should include a line stating this. This percentage should include any part of your education that you have personally
financed (through your cash and student loans) and any grants and schol-
arships you have received. If you have paid for a large percentage of your
education, employers will definitely ask you about this and will most likely
be impressed because of it. (And yes, those student loans you have taken
out do count in the portion of school you have financed!) In addition to the
nuts and bolts of academic credentials, Kelly Burt Deasy's profile in Careers
Up Close 6.1 provides insight into the types of educational experiences that
you should consider highlighting in your cover letter and résumé.

CAREERS UP CLOSE 6.1
KELLY BURT DEASY
Director of Trend and Design
Cost Plus World Market

Global exposure and awareness are a key trend among today's college students—and fuel their potential for personal growth and opportunities in fashion-forward careers such as in trend and design, says Kelly Burt Deasy. She observes that the world around us is full of information that can both spark innovation in product design and also inform designers and product developers about future direction. She urges students who are considering careers in trend to keep eyes and ears open at all times, noting that not everyone looks, dresses, talks, acts, and thinks like you do. Understanding diverse perspectives is essential to diminishing ethnocentrism. In her work as director of trend and design, Kelly travels extensively and searches for inspiration from many sources. Then, she is responsible for translating and presenting her observations of global trends into forecasts that buyers and senior merchants incorporate into their seasonal product lines. She draws upon her education in fashion merchandising and her years of experience

In her senior-level position leading trend, Kelly works closely with buyers who take her samples, images, patterns, colors, and ideas to their factories where product prototypes are developed. The buyers continue to work with Kelly to evaluate prototypes that are tweaked, refined, and eventually launched through retail venues. Kelly reflects that interns and new employees can use their observational skills to position themselves for career growth. She emphasizes the importance of understanding that influential coworkers and supervisors watch for professional behaviors, including being present and engaged, dressing and speaking appropriately, and interacting with others positively.

In her role directing trend, Kelly's knowledge of the job responsibilities of others within the company is crucial; she urges new employees to be sure to learn what the buyer does, how finance interfaces with the fashion operation, strategies implemented by the promotional division, and human resources procedures. Your interest in the "big picture" of your work environment will be noticed—and will inform you in ways that will enhance your ability to perform your job. Kelly's job is to communicate and convince buyers and company leaders (who invest the financial resources) about the *next big thing*. She must earn the trust of her colleagues through professional and accurate work.

Kelly advises, "don't take your experiences—even everyday activities—for granted. Be curious and excited about your world; get to know the people who work alongside you, especially to learn about their different experiences, codes of ethics, life expectations, values, and ideas." She also urges aspiring fashion professionals to be keenly aware of the effects that the world around you (local and global) has on fashion.

Grade Point Average

One of the most common questions related to educational information on a résumé is whether to list one's grade point average (GPA). Some employers rely on GPAs to screen potential employees, while others focus more directly on work experiences, special skills, or the interview to narrow job applicants. A good rule of thumb is that a GPA that meets or exceeds a Dean's List designation is a positive reflection of one's academic preparation and should be listed. If your overall GPA is average, or not a source of pride to you, it may be better left off the résumé. Consider, however, including your *major* GPA if it is considerably better than your *overall* GPA. This is often the case and occurs for a number of reasons. For example, if a student has changed majors, he or she may begin receiving higher grades in the new major because the subject matter comes more easily or is more interesting to the student. If you have done well in your required major courses, you can designate this on your résumé as your *major* GPA. If you do not list a GPA, employers who wish to know this will ask, but you should not eliminate yourself from a pool of applicants by listing on your résumé a weakness rather than a strength. You may want to seek information regarding the expectations of the company to which you are applying before making a final determination about this item.

Work Experience

The fact that you have engaged in previous work experience sends the message to the employer that you have successfully held a job and are likely to be familiar with work environments. Be sure to list, as comprehensively as practical, the employment that you have experienced. Often entry-level applicants attempt to shorten their résumés by deleting what they consider to be nonrelated work experiences. A summer lifeguarding job or a waitstaff position during the school year are representative of your work ethic, your ability to manage your time, and your willingness to accept responsibility. These seasonal and part-time jobs, while likely different in task from the job you will be seeking upon graduation, have enabled you to develop professional skills upon which you can now rely. Include as much information as space allows, and remember that if you have a good deal of "odd job" experience, on which you do not have room to expand, you can simply list the job titles and dates of employment.

Although it is somewhat of a departure from the traditional chronological format, it is perfectly acceptable to separate your work experience into two sections: one titled *Relevant/Professional Experience* and the other titled *Other/Work Experience* (see Figure 6.1 for an example). Under the *Relevant/Professional Experience* section, list all employment, including internships, that are related to fashion, retailing, apparel merchandising, and product design. The *Other/Work Experience* section would include positions such as a lifeguard, waitstaff, or camp counselor. For each job, and particularly for those more directly related to the position you are seeking, include bullet statements indicating the specific achievements and responsibilities included in your duties, with the most important and relevant listed first. Use action verbs, such as *organized, maintained, developed*, and *directed*. (See Box 6.1 for a list of action words.) Choose words that tell the employer what you achieved (*managed and coordinated the scheduling of 25 sales personnel*) rather than what your tasks and responsibilities were supposed to be (*responsible for scheduling*). Use quantitative, results-oriented information as much as possible. Careers Up Close 6.2, highlighting Molly Doyle and Katie Cawley, contains examples of work experience tasks that can be included in cover letters and résumés.

CAREERS UP CLOSE 6.2
MOLLY DOYLE AND KATIE CAWLEY

MOLLY DOYLE
Regional Sales Manager, Cejon-Steve Madden-Betsey Johnson-Big Buddha Accessories

When Molly Doyle was an assistant buyer trainee with Shillito Rikes, she was determined to make her mark by demonstrating her retail merchandising skills and her work ethic. In particular, she recalls her first week on the job when the defective and return-to-vendor room needed to be organized. No assistant had been in the area for some time and there were hundreds of pairs of shoes to be organized, returned to vendors, and some marked out of stock. There were mismatched shoes, many worn and returned shoes, and defectives. Obviously, this was not a desirable job; however, someone needed to do it. Molly recognized this as an opportunity to step forward and demonstrate that she was not afraid of a little hard work and, furthermore, that she could approach this task with creativity and good humor. The organization and cleaning of the shoe department took the better part of four working days. The work wasn't difficult, but it was messy, dusty, and tedious. It definitely was not part of the training program she was expecting. When her work was completed, the shoe debit room was in sparkling shape. Molly was recognized for the rest of her trainee experience as the "girl who actually got the shoe stockroom straightened out." The buyer she was assigned to looked to that accomplishment as a reference for moving forward in the program.

Molly has used this example repeatedly in her professional life as a great reason to volunteer and execute the jobs no one wants to do. Over the years, Molly has mentored new career professionals with an enduring message: "Demonstrate your tenacity by volunteering for every job and performing it with exceptional professionalism and competency." As regional sales manager for Cejon-Steve Madden-Betsey Johnson-Big Buddha Accessories, she had the unique opportunity to mentor countless interns in both the New York and Cincinnati offices, including her own daughter, Katie Cawley, who now holds the position of Sales Manager at Steve Madden, Cincinnati.

KATIE CAWLEY
Sales Manager at Steve Madden

A career in fashion appealed to Katie Cawley from an early age as she watched Molly balance career and family—and navigate successfully through a lucrative and productive career path in sales. Katie noted that a fashion sales career is a lot of hard work, but also exciting, ever changing, and often fun. Katie developed a strong worth ethic as a part-time employee assisting her mother Molly during high school and college. Key things Katie learned from Molly are:

- Trust your gut instinct. Retail is a fast-paced industry and trusting your gut can help you react quickly.
- Speak your mind—chances are, if you are thinking it, so is someone else.
- Don't be afraid to negotiate with employers for benefits (pay increase, more vacation, etc.). Your employers are buying moments of your life, so make the job worth it.
- Pick up the phone. For those growing up in the tech world, email is second nature—it's fast and easy—but so much more can be learned from a phone call.

Now an intern supervisor herself, Katie reflects that attention to details and willingness to do what it takes to execute the work of the company are important qualities that interns need to demonstrate. Internships and early career work experiences provide chances for inexperienced but ambitious future fashion professionals to build work skills that translate well on résumés and provide much-needed experiences, positioning students for early career success. In fact, interns have the opportunity to become integral members of their sales team, developing relationships with clients and engaging in customer service activities that keep the business strong.

For example, a few past interns in the New York office enthusiastically engaged with buyers during market and showroom appointments. They were forthright in introducing themselves, asking buyers questions and clarifying any points a buyer made during the meetings. Many were responsible for picture, note, and pricing follow-up after appointments. They would send info via email and this would allow them to establish contact and the beginnings of a relationship with buyers in key accounts. On more than one occasion, these interactions led to references and future employment.

Both Molly and Katie emphasize that when interns are available to help with seemingly mundane tasks, they have more time to focus on the business activities requiring their attention, and the interns are able to observe the showroom atmosphere and the buying procedures taking place. They agree on the following advice offered to the many students they mentor each year: "Be willing to work hard and do what it takes to get the job done."

BOX 6.1 Action Words for Résumés

accelerated	consulted	expedited	organized	scheduled
accomplished	contributed	experienced	originated	secured
achieved	controlled	explored	participated	selected
administered	coordinated	facilitated	persuaded	served
advised	created	forecasted	planned	simplified
analyzed	critiqued	formulated	presented	solved
applied	decreased	generated	prioritized	stimulated
approved	defined	guided	projection	streamlined
assembled	delegated	identified	produced	structured
assessed	delivered	implemented	promoted	summarized
assigned	demonstrated	improved	proved	supervised
assisted	designed	increased	provided	supported
attained	developed	influenced	recommended	synthesized
balanced	devised	initiated	reconciled	trained
briefed	directed	interacted	recorded	translated
built	earned	interpreted	recruited	transported
calculated	edited	introduced	redesigned	tutored
clarified	encouraged	launched	reduced	updated
coached	enforced	led	referred	upgraded
collaborated	enhanced	maintained	refined	utilized
collected	ensured	managed	reinforced	validated
compiled	established	marketed	represented	verified
completed	evaluated	monitored	researched	volunteered
conceived	examined	motivated	resolved	wrote
conducted	exceeded	negotiated	responsible	
consolidated	executed	obtained	restored	
constructed	expanded	operated	revamped	

When describing your responsibilities, consider also that it is increasingly common practice for employers to electronically scan résumés that they receive; your résumé may be submitted electronically in the first place. Therefore, the action words that you include on your résumé should be ones that are key to the field in which you are applying and to the job description given by the company. Doing so shows a potential employer that you have experience with the skills they require, you have customized your résumé to their position, and you are knowledgeable in the field's lingo. Additionally, your résumé will surface when employers use keyword searches to match applicants with their needs.

Activities

Employers, invariably, are seeking students who have unique and outstanding professional qualities. These qualities include, but are not limited to, a willingness to accept responsibilities, an ability to prioritize, an ability to motivate others, a sense of appropriateness, mature judgment, and time and conflict management. Often the area that separates the exceptional applicant from all of the good ones is activities.

A positive trend in this section is to include such activities under the heading of *Leadership Activities*. Of course, the heading must be tailored to your individual strengths and may be entitled *Activities/Honors*, instead, as applicable. (Note that in Figure 6.1, a separate *Honors* section has been placed directly after *Education*). If your goal is to obtain an exceptional internship or a first-rate entry-level position, it is imperative that you develop leadership skills. It is not enough to join clubs and other organizations. Rather, you must be willing to accept leadership responsibilities and take up the challenge of organizing and motivating members. Such activities not only will provide material for discussion at interviews and in cover letters, but they also will enable the development of important skills such as time management, conflict resolution, creative organization, and public speaking.

If you have not yet identified activities that fit this category, begin now to develop yourself professionally as a leader. In addition to professional associations and extracurricular activities, volunteerism is a terrific way to gain leadership experience. Not only does volunteerism indicate that you are able to budget your time and organize activities, it also demonstrates that you are willing to give back to your community and provide a necessary service to others. Increasingly, employers are interested in your history of community service and, in fact, many employers have indicated that they look for these types of activities on a résumé before looking for anything else. By all means, the activities section should emphasize quality over quantity!

References

A practice has emerged in which prospective employees construct a résumé and insert the final line, *References available upon request*. This is often done to keep the length of the résumé at one page; however, it is advised that this statement be omitted. Although there is no consensus about the practice of including references with an initial contact, if you wish to do so, simply include a reference list as a second page accompanying the résumé. This is a simple convenience on your part, and eliminates the need for employers to contact you subsequently to obtain a list of references. Virtually all employers check references, and their possession of a list of your references may accelerate your employment procedure. Because the references will need to be continued on a second page and are considered a separate item from the résumé, you may prefer to state *References Attached* at the bottom of the résumé.

When listing references, be sure to identify the title and job position of each person you have selected to represent you. This is particularly important when listing gender-neutral names, as phone calls or letters from the employer will likely result in asking for Ms., Mr., or Dr. Additionally, the reference person's professional position may give an indication of the relationship between you and that person. It is also helpful to include a brief statement along with the person's contact information that delineates his or her relationship to you. If one of your references has changed jobs since working with you, you should indicate this by stating *formerly with XYZ company*. This will allow the reader of your résumé to more easily identify that person's relationship to you.

In selecting references, avoid family members and purely personal references, particularly if you have work experience. It is essential to ask people whom you plan to list as references if you may use their names. Your reference people will also appreciate receiving a copy of your résumé for their files. Obviously, you should seek those whom you believe will offer a favorable reference for you, and you should plan to perform to a standard that is worthy of high recommendation. Your reference list should parallel the experiences that you have listed on your résumé. Intuitive employers will question the absence of supervisors representing major work experiences on your résumé. Be prepared to explain the absence of a recent supervisor, should you decide to omit such a person. Furthermore, current and recent students should include an academic reference, as this is your most recent and concentrated experience. The importance of identifying professors, mentors, current and former managers, and others with whom you work and interact on a regular basis for the purpose of providing references cannot be overemphasized. If you presently are not aware of such a person, begin now to make yourself known to your professors, seek mentors who can guide your professional development and provide testament to your character, and establish positive working relationships with your supervisors.

FIGURE 6.4

Reference Page

REFERENCES

Maria Vasquez
Mvasquez1@hotmail.com

Present Address	**Permanent Address**
321 River Street	22154 Valley View Lane
Athens, OH 45701	New Concord, OH 43721
(740) 55-5505	(740) 555-5555

Ms. Ellen Sampson
Department Manager, Internship Supervisor
Marshall Field's
111 North State Street
Chicago, Illinois 60602
(312) 555-5555
esampson@marshallfields.com

Dr. Ann Paulins, Associate Professor
Director, School of Human and Consumer Sciences
Ohio University
Tupper Hall
Athens, Ohio 45701
(740) 555-5655
annpaulins@ohiou.edu

Craig Schultz, Owner
Craig's Fine Dining
444 University Avenue
Athens, Ohio 45702
(740) 505-5555
craig@eatingwell.com

Dr. Martin Panzer, Professor
Phi Kappa Phi Advisor
Department of Marketing
Barsema Hall
Athens, Ohio 45701
(740)555-5656
Mpanzer@ohiou.edu

One final comment on the reference page—be sure that the complete and matching heading from your résumé appears at the top of the reference page. Without this identifying information, it could be disastrous for the references to be separated from your résumé. Additionally, the reference sheet is likely to be removed from the résumé for the purpose of checking references, and it is best that you provide the necessary identification on the page. A sample reference page is provided in Figure 6.4.

Other Items to Consider

Avoid personal information when constructing a résumé, such as age, gender, race, marital status, family members, height, weight, and physical challenges. Also, do not put a picture on your résumé. In the age of LinkedIn and other social media, pictures and images are readily available should employers want to see those. Mention of these criteria may eliminate you from the candidate pool or unnecessarily call attention to irrelevant information. These personal characteristics are not related to your preparation for the job, professional experiences and skills, or ability to perform the tasks necessary for the prospective position and therefore do not enhance your professional profile. Additionally, some companies will automatically toss your résumé if it includes a picture because the law does not allow them to discriminate based on race, gender, age, or appearance. Even the chance of an impropriety is not a chance most employers are willing to take, and pictures make that more likely.

Most entry-level résumés are approximately one page long. It is easier for potential employers to scan résumés that are concise and clearly presented than those that are lengthy. However, do not leave off key information that may contribute to your landing a job. You will also notice that some of the examples we are providing are longer than one page, which is typical as you move forward with your career.

When condensing descriptive information on your résumé, remember that you may benefit by moving some items to your letter and expanding on certain experiences in that format. Recruiters generally emphasize a one-page limit, particularly for entry-level jobs that have numerous applicants. Remember, most recruiters will spend only ten seconds scanning a résumé before making a decision about the candidate. Make your résumé as easy to scan as possible.

Some students will have difficulty fitting their experiences and activities on one page, but others may find that they are having a hard time filling up the page. If this is the case, consider adding additional headings to the résumé. For example, the résumé might include the heading *Specialized Skills*, under which could be listed knowledge of particular computer programs, such as Excel or PowerPoint, or a second language that you speak, (e.g., *fluent in Spanish*). A heading with *Related Coursework* is another option and would include any courses taken that are directly related to the position sought. Don't assume that employers know that a fashion/retailing/apparel merchandising major or a design major requires the completion of numerous business or marketing courses. This is not the case, and you may be selling yourself short by not communicating this information. This is especially true for designers. If you have taken business courses, or any type of consumer behavior classes, this may be a huge advantage for you.

As professional experiences increase through internships or specialized opportunities, you may begin to eliminate some of the more distant unrelated experiences that had previously occupied space. Another section that may often be condensed is *Activities*. List only those items that you can relate to specific skills that will enhance your ability to perform the position you are seeking. Many students include a good deal of "fluff" in this section that is easily spotted by employers.

Project 1 at the end of this chapter is designed to get you started on constructing your résumé. A number of activities related to résumés are also included on the accompanying *Guide to Fashion Career Planning STUDIO* website (www.bloomsburyfashioncentral.com), including a résumé checklist. After completing your résumé, evaluate your document with the checklist as well as with the information in Box 6.2, which outlines "pet peeves" found on résumés.

COVER LETTERS

A cover letter should always accompany a résumé. The letter is your opportunity to personalize and sell yourself to an employer. Its contents are subjective, whereas the items listed on the résumé are objective. Your letter provides a prospective employer with the opportunity to analyze you before meeting you in person because it can illustrate your written communication skills, organization skills, attention to detail, career philosophy, and focus, as well as your technical knowledge and management style.

The letter serves as an introduction for the writer. It should provide a reason for the employer to more closely examine your résumé. The letter is likely to enhance your résumé, but it has the potential to detract from it. The letter can be quite revealing—or misleading—if it is not carefully constructed. Used effectively, a letter personalizes the application and allows you to point out your unique and special qualities. It, like the résumé, is an important screening device, so be sure that yours represents you well.

A well-written letter is direct, providing the purpose for your correspondence early on. The tone should be confident, with specific examples offered to substantiate claims that you make about yourself. Good writing will help your letter stand out above the crowd and allow the employer to focus on the content rather than be distracted by poor sentence structure or grammar and spelling mistakes. Avoid being too wordy, but do not fill the letter with overly simple sentences. In constructing your letter, evaluate it for organization, flow of ideas, and accuracy. Above all, honesty is essential. Too many prospective employees are tempted to embellish their experiences and skills, which ultimately leads to embarrassment following reference checks or during an interview.

General Format

Proper letter-writing format should be used for all professional correspondence. The use of correct structure demonstrates an attention to detail and a willingness on your part to make the effort to present yourself professionally. Résumés are formatted to best suit the situation at hand, and it is best to seek opinions of respected professionals in your field for feedback regarding résumé styles. Typos, poor sentence structure, misspelled words, and grammatical errors are unacceptable in letters and résumés and will most certainly eliminate you from consideration. Both letters and résumés should be presented in a single-spaced format when submitted as hard copies. Professional letters should be written in either full block, block, or modified block format. In this text, we chose to present full block format. The advantage of full block format is that it is simpler to format in a word processing system because there are no indents.

Regardless of the specific format selected, necessary elements in a professional letter include the heading, inside address, salutation, body, close, and signature block. Special notations may be used when you provide an attachment or enclosure (such as your résumé), when you send a copy of the letter to a third party, or when you have used a typist. Figure 6.6 provides an example of a cover letter written in block format that you can refer to when reading through the following sections explaining each component of the cover letter. The letter in Figure 6.5 addresses the applicant's credentials in light of the specific requirements in a job advertisement, whereas the letter in Figure 6.6 takes a more general approach. In addition, the *STUDIO* website accompanying this book provides examples of cover letters.

Contents and Components

Heading

The heading provides your address, your phone number (optional), and the date. You should not include your name in the heading unless you are using personalized stationery that displays your name, which we recommend. If you are writing professional correspondence on behalf of a business, the heading is generally preprinted or preformatted on a template, and you simply supply the date for each letter. However, *never* use company stationery for the purpose of writing a cover letter. This is in poor taste and is probably contrary to company policy.

899 Acoma Ave.
Columbus, OH 43210

Ms. Martha Johnson, CEO
Miss Martha Ltd.
1440 Atlanta Apparel Mart
Atlanta, GA 70607

May 13, 2015

Dear Ms. Johnson:

I am writing this letter in response to your advertisement for a Showroom Assistant in the May 12 issue of the *Atlanta Journal*. As you will note from the attached resume, I will graduate with a Bachelor of Science in Textiles and Clothing from The Ohio State University in June 2015.

My credentials match with those you have listed in your advertisement as I am outlining below:

Strong problem-solving and organizational skills: As president of my sorority, I am constantly required to resolve difficult interpersonal and procedural problems. I also plan, schedule, and moderate weekly meetings with other sorority executive board members, and distribute and enforce sorority rules and regulations in a "firm but fair" manner.

Strong customer orientation and attention to detail: For the past 18 months, I have worked in Target's Customer Service Department. In that capacity, I respond in a calm and professional manner to the complaints of dissatisfied (and often irate) customers. I also answer the telephone, issue refunds, place Internet orders, and respond to questions from vendors and warehouse personnel. In 17 months I have never received a customer complaint and have maintained a 100% accurate cash drawer.

Self-motivated, assertive person with a positive attitude: I have maintained an above-average grade point average while attending school full-time, working an average of 25 hours per week, and participating in a number of professional and community service activities. I am equally adept at assuming leadership roles, operating in a cooperative team environment, and working independently.

You can be assured that I will apply the same level of enthusiasm to my position as a Showroom Assistant at Miss Martha Ltd. I appreciate your attention to my application and look forward to speaking with you about this exciting opportunity.

Sincerely,

Janice Albertson

Janice Albertson

FIGURE 6.5
Cover Letter
Matched to Job
Announcement

Inside Address

The inside address is that of the receiver of the letter and is the same as the address on the mailing envelope. The inside address should contain the name, title, and position of the person whom you expect to read the letter. If you do not know the name of the appropriate individual to receive the letter, you should find out. It takes little effort to make a telephone call or consult a resource such as the career services office, the Internet, or company literature. A personalized address and salutation will demonstrate that you have made an effort to determine who will

44-A Lincoln Highway
DeKalb, IL 60115

Ms. Kim Rankin, College Recruiter
Neiman Marcus
1 LBJ Highway
Dallas, Texas 78092

July 17, 2014

Dear Ms Rankin:

Because of my strong interest in a management career with an upscale fashion retailer, I was immediately drawn to your recent advertisement for a department manager. A background in retail management, a proven record of achieving results, and my level of enthusiasm make me a qualified candidate to join the Neiman Marcus team.

My interest in retailing started in DECA in high school and developed further through a variety of retail and merchandising positions while I was pursuing my Textiles, Apparel, and Merchandising degree at Northern Illinois University. In researching the tip retailers in the country, Neiman Marcus emerged as having an excellent training program, a reputation for exemplary customer service, and a sound market position. This is exactly the type of retailing environment I seek.

The enclosed resume highlights my qualifications, which match those you seek in a department manager. You will also note that I was recognized as the top salesperson in my store in 2014 and was instrumental in writing the new-employee handbook. Based on customer and supervisor feedback, I am confident that I have the skills needed to succeed in the retail management. Additionally, I have a true interest in working for Neiman Marcus.

Would you please consider my request for an interview so that we may discuss my qualifications further? I will call you next week to see if a meeting can be arranged. Should you need to reach me prior to that, please feel free to contact me at (815) 565-5656, or kallen@niuniv.edu.

Thank you very much for considering my application. I look forward to talking with you.

Sincerely,

Karen C. Allen

Karen C. Allen

Encolsure

read your letter. You should include a title, such as Mr., Ms., Mrs., or Dr., in front of the name of the receiver on the inside address. Make the effort to identify the correct title, and use that in the salutation as well. The professional position of the receiver should be identified on the second line of the heading. Do your homework to ensure that the position you list is correct. Above all, take extra care to be certain that the name of your addressee is correctly spelled. In some situations, particularly with very large companies, the application process for internships or entry-level positions requires a more anonymous submission. If the contact person is not identifiable, address the letter as the advertisement for the position directs (e.g., "Attention Human Resources"). Similarly, if you are not able to determine the appropriate title of the receiver, use Mr. or Ms. if the gender is obvious. If in doubt, use only the name of the receiver.

Salutation

The salutation begins with *Dear* and includes the title of the reader and his or her last name. The first name of the reader is not included in the salutation except in the case where an appropriate title (Mr. or Ms.) cannot be determined. In this case, use the full name (e.g., "Dear Lee Jones"). Occasionally, situations arise for which a name is not available. For instance, you may find a lead via a newspaper advertisement that lists an address but no name. If you find yourself in a situation in which you cannot identify a name, use a salutation such as *Attention Human Resources Manager* or *To whom it may concern* as a last resort.

The salutation ends with a colon (:) rather than a comma. On more familiar correspondence, such as professional letters you write to colleagues or clients with whom you are acquainted, it is permissible to address the salutation using the first name and a comma. When applying for a position, however, it is always best to use a more formal approach.

Body

The opening paragraph of your letter should begin with an introductory statement describing the position that you are seeking. It is best to state the purpose for your correspondence right away. It is frustrating for the reader to have to guess the purpose of the letter or to be unclear about the position being sought. It is helpful to include referral information, particularly if someone suggested that you contact the receiver of the letter or if you are responding to an advertisement. Briefly include background information about yourself that correlates to your compatibility with such a position.

Use the next paragraph or two to describe your specific interests and qualifications as they relate to the position announcement. This is the section of the letter in which you should highlight your achievements and elaborate on opportunities you have had that make you stand above the crowd. Employers, as they seek to fill positions, are looking for individuals who have something to offer them that no one else has. Be sure to explain what makes you different from (and better than) all of the other job applicants. Although you may be tempted to expound your virtues, remember that the reader has only a finite amount of time. Limit the content of your letter to key items that you can relate to the necessary qualifications for the job desired.

In the closing paragraph of your letter, you will want to reiterate your excitement for and interest in the position for which you are applying, and offer information to the employer regarding your availability for an interview. Be sure that your telephone number, email address, and any other relevant contact information is included in the letter as well as on your résumé, and offer any necessary information that may be of use to the employer when contacting you.

If you know you will be out of town during a certain week or in the geographic area in which the company is located, let them know. Do not be too restrictive as to the time of day during which you may be reached. If you will not be available until late in the afternoon, rather than suggesting that the employer wait until then to call you, use voice-mail and indicate in the letter that you would appreciate a message to which you will promptly respond. If you go this route, be sure to check your messages throughout each day. If you do not hear from the prospective employer within a week to ten days from the time you expect your letter to have arrived, it is wise for you to contact the employer. If you desire, you may indicate in your closing paragraph that you will call; however, do not be too specific about the day or time in which you plan to make the call. You will be setting yourself up for failure should an event occur that precludes you from following through on this promise.

With the increasing use of electronic communication today, it is appropriate to suggest that an employer may most efficiently use email to contact you. Again, be certain to check your messages daily and, as mentioned previously, make sure your email address is a professional one.

Close

The close, sometimes referred to as the "complimentary close," should be appropriate for the letter. *Sincerely*, *Sincerely yours*, and *Respectfully yours* are three common and suitable closes. If you use a close longer than one word, capitalize only the first word.

Signature Block

Your signature is the final personal touch of the letter, and your name appears in this section only. Your name should appear twice, once type-written and once as a signature. Leave four single-spaced lines between the close and your typewritten name to sign the letter. Be sure that you sign the letter in blue or black ink, as this is one additional example of your attention to detail. Some people suggest that it is best to sign in blue ink; otherwise your cover letter may look like a copy, and not an original cover letter. However, the choice of ink color may strictly be a matter of your preference. Sometimes cover letters are sent via email, and in that case you will not actually sign your letter. You should have a signature block just as in a hard copy or PDF attachment; however, you do not need to present your name in typeface twice.

General Letter-Writing Tips

Like most things in life, the adage "practice makes perfect" applies to letter writing, too. As you write your cover letter, and as you review and edit it, consider the tone being presented. The letter should be upbeat, enthusiastic, and positive. You, as the writer, should come across as confident, reliable, and capable. As you construct sentences, vary your writing style to avoid beginning sentences with and overusing the word "I." Even though, obviously, the letter focuses on you, vary the presentation of your accomplishments to make the letter interesting. Avoid wishy-washy statements such as "I feel . . ." and "I think . . ." These statements do not exude confidence the way a definitive statement does. ("I believe that my qualifications are acceptable for the demands of this job" versus "My qualifications are perfectly matched to the demands of the job.")

Be careful, also, to avoid slang use of English in your written communication. Common errors include statements such as "I would like to get with you in an interview . . ." and "since I live in Chicago . . ." and so on. Better approaches include: "I would like to arrange an interview . . ." and "because I live in Chicago . . ." It is not enough to communicate your message effectively; you must impress the reader with your professional style and attention to detail. Table 6.1 provides a list of word choices for cover letter writing.

Good writing style depends on variety as much as syntax, so it is helpful to refer to resources that offer ideas for words, phraseology, and structure. Seek words that imply your aptitude for management and responsibility. Label your accomplishments with words such as "challenge" and "opportunity," and reflect upon previous employment or academic

---

TABLE 6.1

BETTER WORD CHOICES FOR COVER LETTER WRITING

Instead of	Use	Instead of	Use
Anxious	Looking forward to	Had to	Had the opportunity to
Since	Because	Do	Complete
Set up	Arrange	Get back to you	Promptly return
Starting	Beginning	Hope to	Plan to or Expect to
Come in	Schedule	Can	May or Shall
Have	Possess	Would like	Expect
Had	Completed	Feel	Believe

opportunities as positive experiences. Use appropriately descriptive action verbs (see Figure 6.4) representing the level of responsibility that you have undertaken. You will find projects at the end of the chapter and on the accompanying website (www.bloomsburycentral.com) to help you compose an effective cover letter. After completing your cover letter, you will find a checklist in the *Guide to Fashion Career Planning STUDIO* (www.bloomsburyfashioncentral.com) to evaluate your document.

Sending Your Letter

If you are using "snail mail" to send your cover letter and résumé, the size and type of envelope you select for mailing is one additional detail worth considering. Cover letters and résumés should be sent in an envelope no smaller than a standard business envelope (9 by 4 inches). Most stationery available for letters and résumés will include matching business-size envelopes. The cover letter and résumé should be folded together, cover letter on top, with two folds. There are two acceptable methods to follow when folding the documents. The most common is the inside-fold method: Looking down on the letter, fold from the bottom up approximately one third of the way up the page, then fold the top down over the first fold so that the documents fit into a business envelope. The top fold should be placed so that the top edge of the paper is not flush with the first fold but rather is inset about half an inch from the folded edge. The outside-fold method produces an accordion fold. The advantage of the outside-fold is that the letter heading is immediately visible when the envelope is opened. The first fold is made identical to the first fold of the inside-fold method, but the documents are folded *back* rather than forward in the second fold. Regardless of the type of fold made, the documents should be placed in the envelope so that the letter will be face up and right side up when it is opened.

You may wish to make the extra effort to send your cover letter and résumé in a large envelope. This strategy provides the advantage of delivering an unfolded cover letter and résumé. In addition to the more pristine appearance of your documents, the receiver may be more apt to open a large envelope first.

Employers increasingly accept, and often require, electronically submitted résumés and cover letters. In fact, many employers will now ask that your application materials be submitted by that method. If you find yourself in that situation, it is essential that the guidelines presented by the potential employer be followed precisely. Consider the following statement from Roland Hearns, vice president of recruitment and placement for Saks Incorporated, in a public presentation: "I was once receiving 500 résumés per week in response to an MBA Internship advertised on our website. Retailing students, even at the MBA level, are facing new and increasing levels of competition in today's career marketplace." Generally, employers will ask that you submit your résumé electronically. Some employers will ask that you email your résumé and cover letter as an attached document, which is easily done through any email program. Before sending your résumé, you should save it in a pdf format, which assures the formatting will remain intact during the transmission, and also makes it less likely that others can edit what you are sending. Regardless of how you send your résumé, you should always include a cover letter, even if that means providing it as an email message. If you send an email, see Box 7.1 in Chapter 7, which discusses professionalism in email. We recommend that you compose a brief professional email message and attach your formal cover letter, along with your résumé.

As mentioned at the beginning of this chapter, preparing a résumé and cover letter can be quite a demanding task. However, by starting early, reading through the chapter guidelines, working through the projects we have provided, and looking at the many examples you can find both here and online, you should have both a winning résumé and a cover letter that will be sure to set you apart from other candidates! Review the information in Box 6.3 for a summary of the activities related to résumé and cover letter writing that you should revisit regularly. Remember, once you have created a basic, strong résumé and cover letter, you can easily update these documents as you expand your experiences and leadership skills throughout your career.

BOX 6.3 Landing Your Perfect Job

- Review your goals concerning a career. Now is the time to be specific in thinking about what it is you want to do. While flexibility is important in many regards, your goals should be specific and outline what you want. Setting goals prior to your job search helps you focus and will help ensure a successful outcome.
- Revisit your online presence. Almost all employers will expect you to have an online presence and will at the least check your LinkedIn profile. Google your name to make sure nothing un-

expected comes up that could hurt your reputation and clean up anything you find that does not reflect "Brand You." Also make it a habit to post items on your LinkedIn page, Twitter account, and other social media that promote your brand.

- Revamp your résumé. Review the chapter on résumé writing and customize your résumé to match each position for which you apply. Update any skills and experiences using key words that match those found in the job announcement.

continued

BOX 6.3 Landing Your Perfect Job *(continued)*

- Leverage your experiences (even the bad ones). Everyone has had a job that they are not particularly proud of or one that was not what they expected. Perhaps you had a bad experience with an internship that didn't exactly deliver as promised and you ended up making coffee and answering the phone more than anything else. Use such experiences to reflect on what you learned and demonstrate your growth. The transferable skills you can demonstrate in such experiences will speak well for you; when you accentuate the positive, it tells an employer you are a step closer to knowing exactly what it is you want to do in a career. Thus, you can be more productive in a position with them.

- Put yourself out there. Networking is one of the most important things you can do to advance yourself and your career (see Chapter 5). People are generally open to helping others with their career exploration and especially like to share their experiences—*if* you ask. College alumni groups and LinkedIn are great places to start. Social media makes this much easier today; however, there is still no better way to connect with someone than face time. Find groups online or in person that fit your interests and dive in!

Source: http://www.businessnewsdaily.com

Printed with permission.

Projects

1. Résumé development. Prepare a résumé worksheet by completing the following entries and questions. After completing the worksheet, construct a professional résumé and reference page. Be sure to refer back to the Résumé Checklist online in the *Guide to Fashion Career Planning STUDIO* and the list of "Pet Peeves" in Box 6.2. For your convenience, the accompanying *STUDIO* website also provides examples, résumé templates, and exercises to help you practice writing an effective résumé.

    a. Current address, telephone, and email address

    b. Permanent address

    c. Education

- Institution
- Name of major
- Name of degree
- Year of graduation
- Grade point average (if desirable)
- Percentage of education you paid for (if applicable)

d. Work experience (for each previous job)

- Job title
- Duties
- Duration (time frame) of experience
- Major learning opportunities
- Activities or leadership experiences: For each of the items listed in this section, write a statement indicating how the item relates to the job opportunity you are seeking.
- References: Who can serve as references for you? Why would each person be a good reference?

2. Cover letter development. Locate a job or internship announcement matching your interests and qualifications. Based on the announcement, complete the following worksheet (an example is given to show you how to start). Once you have completed the worksheet, construct a professional cover letter based on your outline. Be sure to refer back to Table 6.1 ("Better Word Choices for Cover Letter Writing"), and the Cover Letter Checklist found on the *STUDIO* website. Also note that the website (www.bloomsburycentral.com) contains examples, templates for your cover letter, and drafts to help you practice writing an effective cover letter.

Job or Internship Requirements	*Your Qualifications*
1. Two years' retail experience	1. Worked as a sales associate at The Limited; two years at the Gap® as Assistant Manager
2.	2.
3.	3.

3. Combining résumé, reference page, and cover letter. Locate a job or internship announcement matching your interests and qualifications. Based on the announcement, construct a résumé, reference page, and cover letter specific to the position. You may wish to use the formats provided on the website (www.bloomsburycentral .com).

4. Checking résumé, cover letter, and reference page. Using the checklists provided, check at least two of your classmates' résumés, cover letters, and reference pages. Provide them with positive, as well as constructive, feedback. After your classmates have checked your materials, make the changes you believe are necessary and then take the résumé and cover letter to your campus career planning office to obtain additional feedback.

5. Construct an "aspirational résumé." Refer to your goals. Construct an "aspirational résumé"—that is, a résumé that is a reflection of where you want to be five years in the future. What steps will you need to take to achieve this aspiration?

Questions for Discussion

1. What are some advantages of a functional format résumé? Of a chronological format? Of the creative format?
2. Do you agree or disagree with the idea that generally an objective is not necessary on a résumé?
3. What can an employer learn about you from reading your mission statement?
4. Do you think employers should consider your GPA when reviewing your résumé? Why or why not?
5. What are some transferable skills you might gain from the following positions that would be important for a job in retailing, merchandising, or design?
   a. Babysitter
   b. Lawn care person
   c. Lifeguard
   d. Restaurant server
   e. Fast-food counter help
   f. Bartender
   g. Pet- or house-sitter
   h. Receptionist
   i. Caddy
   j. Office- or house-cleaner
6. Why do you think employers are interested in activities or volunteerism when reviewing your résumé?
7. Do you think employers should have the freedom to call any employer you have listed on your résumé for a reference? Why or why not?
8. If your résumé does a great job of presenting your credentials and qualifications, why do you think it is necessary to include a cover letter with it?
9. Can you think of some strategies to enable your résumé to stand out from those of other applicants?

STUDIO Activities

Visit the *Guide to Fashion Career Planning STUDIO* available at www
.bloomsburyfashioncentral.com. The key elements are:

1. Summary of Chapter 6 text
2. Quiz
3. Résumé development
   a. Résumé Examples
   b. Résumé Editing
   c. Résumé worksheet
   d. Résumé checklist
4. Cover letter development
   a. Cover letter Editing
   b. Cover letter editing activity
   c. Cover letter worksheet
   d. Cover letter template
   e. Cover letter checklist

VIDEO: Résumé Critique

CHAPTER 7
INTERVIEWING

My interviewing style and my approach to things is that, yes, it's okay to be sincere; it's okay to be yourself; it's okay to be real.

—EDDIE TRUNK

OBJECTIVES

- To recognize the importance of projecting a professional image when interviewing.
- To develop confidence with respect to a variety of interviewing situations and common interviewing questions.
- To identify and implement personal strategies leading to success in interviews.
- To apply telephone etiquette and email etiquette appropriate to requesting, scheduling, and participating in an interview.
- To identify common types of interview settings, including online video-enhanced interviews.
- To employ appropriate wardrobe and appearance practices for an interview.
- To enhance oral communication skills appropriate for a professional setting.
- To effectively evaluate an interview.
- To construct a professional thank-you letter for follow-up after an interview.

The direct result of a successfully written cover letter and résumé—and the next step in your search for employment or an internship—is an interview. The interview is your opportunity to showcase your personal style and your oral communication skills. Although you have likely made a first impression with your résumé and cover letter, the first few minutes of an interview will create a lasting impression of your professional profile. Your professional "package" will be evaluated—your manners, appearance and hygiene, linguistic skills, ability to analyze situations and think on your feet, and expressed knowledge of and interest in the company.

One of the most common errors of prospective employees is too little preparation for the interview. Employers expect interviewees to have a genuine interest in their companies. This interest should extend to a knowledge of the organization's history, structure, geographic territory, subsidiaries or divisions, and information available on a recent annual report. Many employers furnish company literature to career service offices, and the Internet makes it very easy to find more information. Students and recent graduates should seek this information! Additionally, employers who visit university campuses may offer company presentations prior to interviewing opportunities. It is essential that you attend such presentations both to obtain information and to inquire informally about the nature of the company.

Keep in mind that interviewing, like anything else in life, improves with practice. Although interviewees often feel inhibited and lack confidence in early interviews, the experience gained from assessing experiences will serve as preparation to improve in the future. A recent retail merchandising student recalled that her early interviews were not positive experiences. Upon reflection, she acknowledged that she had, indeed, not prepared herself as she should have, resulting in lackluster interest by employers. As she continued to interview, however, she noticed an improved confidence in herself along with an ability to anticipate questions and better articulate responses. Following several disappointing interviews, she hit her stride and eventually landed a prestigious internship with Saks Fifth Avenue, where she is currently successfully working her way up the merchandising career ladder. The moral of the story: Keep at it, keep practicing; interviewing becomes easier.

ESTABLISHING VERBAL CONTACT

Although much business correspondence today is done through email, and sometimes even text messages, if you have not previously spoken to the person with whom you will be interviewing, you may need to make an initial verbal contact to arrange the interview. This initial contact establishes an impression in the same manner as letters, résumés, and interviews. A verbal impression is typically stronger and longer lasting than the impression that accompanies a written item. Therefore, it is important to exhibit confidence and self-assurance when you speak with a potential employer.

Telephone Calls to Make Initial Contact

When making your initial contact by telephone, rehearse what you will say. One advantage of a telephone call compared to a face-to-face encounter is that you can use notes. Decide what you want to say and how you will say it, and write it down if you believe it will help you. Your professionalism over the telephone *will* be evaluated.

If you have not yet determined the appropriate person to receive your letter and résumé, your first telephone contact will be to establish the recipient of correspondence. Identify yourself, and then state that you are interested in contacting the person who is responsible for receiving résumés and interviewing potential hires. Be sure to request the spelling of that person's name and his/her exact job title. Use this information in your cover letter and for future telephone correspondence. As you place this initial call, be prepared to speak to this person; he or she may be the one who answers the phone, or the office assistant may offer to direct your call. Take advantage of any opportunity you may have to make a positive impression, to initiate a contact, and to establish an interview opportunity.

A typical phone conversation might begin, "Hello, my name is Ann Paulins. I am interested in contacting the manager of human resources. May I have this person's name?" After receiving the name and double-checking the precise spelling, be sure to obtain the correct job position title. Also identify the appropriate personal title (Ms., Mrs., Mr., Dr.), particularly if you have been given a gender-neutral name. We also suggest double-checking the personal title, as names commonly don't identify gender or the person may go by another title such as Doctor. The conversation should continue, "Thank you. Is that Ms. Jones?" Then, "What is Ms. Jones' job title?"

Another alternative is to ask whether the information you are seeking is available online through the company website. For example, "Does the company website list Ms. Jones' email address? If so, I am happy to look that up myself." Make sure that you have researched and obtained as much information as you can from the Internet and are only calling to get the remaining difficult-to-obtain details. The people you speak with will appreciate your willingness to save them time, and it also demonstrates your ability to problem-solve.

Telephone Call to Request an Interview

A week or so after you have sent a letter, you should follow up with a telephone call. The purpose of this call is to reinforce contact with the employer and to request an interview. You should ask for the person who has been identified as the recipient of your letter. When you place your call, one of two scenarios will most likely occur. You will either be connected to that person, or you will be asked to leave a message because the person is unable to take your call. If you can leave a message with a person, ask if there is a better time for you to call again. When leaving a message, restate your name and spell it, provide your telephone number and the time frame in which you will be able to receive a call, and a brief message such as "I am calling with regard to the status of my application for an internship." If you have been told a good time to call back, note that time and *do* call again. This will indicate a strong commitment on your part to establish contact with the potential employer.

The preferable result, of course, is to connect with the intended recipient of your call. If this is achieved, do not expect that he or she will automatically remember your letter or your résumé. Approach the conversation in a manner that will allow the employer to identify your application materials and converse with you without having to "be in the dark" about who you are and what you want. Such a conversation could begin, "Hello, I am Ann Paulins. I sent a letter and résumé to you last week indicating my interest in your designers' assistant position. Have you had an opportunity to review it?" The conversation from this point on is an important initial contact for you, and you will be able to demonstrate your ability to carry on a conversation and think on your feet. Be prepared for either event: that the person has read and is familiar with your résumé or that your résumé has not made it across the desk yet. As the conversation warrants, reiterate your interest in the company and your desire to visit with the employer in person. The employer may take control of the conversation, or he/she may expect you to do most of the talking. Anticipate various telephone scenarios, and even practice your responses with friends. This is another area in which practice leads to improvement—and ultimately, leads to confidence, a genuine interest in connecting, and an ability to think on the go that is evident over the phone.

If you are unable to talk with the desired person or if you are denied an interview, do not give up. If you are truly interested in employment opportunities with the company, you should continue to correspond professionally with the appropriate representatives of the company. Listen to the reason(s) they offer about why you have not achieved your goals with the company. Are there currently no openings, are your qualifications inadequate, is their division being downsized, or is the personnel manager currently preoccupied with other business? Respond accordingly to the given reason. Set a plan for yourself to remedy any personal inadequacies (such as finishing your degree, completing a merchandising math course, or obtaining more in-store merchandising experience) and reposition your application to demonstrate an interest and ability in fulfilling their needs.

In the event that you are unable to contact the person or if your telephone messages go unreturned—do not give up! Perseverance really does pay off. Be persistent and polite as you go after the job of your dreams. Keep calling. Several former students have marveled in the fact that they were persistent enough to finally be invited to participate in an interview, and when the interview occurred, the employers commented that their persistence was impressive (and the employers knew who the resilient students were!). Do not place telephone calls to the point of being a nuisance, but do exhibit enough perseverance to demonstrate that you are genuinely interested in the company and are committed to waiting until there is an opening or an opportunity to interview for a position. It may be helpful to remember H. Jackson Brown Jr.'s (author of *The Complete Life's Little Instruction Book*) "Two Rules of Perseverance":

Rule # 1. Take one more step.

Rule # 2. When you don't think you can take one more step, refer to Rule #1.

Receiving a Telephone Call

The ideal situation following distribution of your résumé, whether it be via email or telephone, is receiving a call from the prospective employer. Be prepared to receive a professional business telephone call after you have sent out your very first résumé. Begin answering your telephone professionally *every time*, and encourage anyone else who may be answering your phone (e.g., roommates or friends) to do the same. For example, answer your phone saying, "Hello, this is _____ (state your name)." You are most likely to receive a business call between the hours of 8 a.m. and 5 p.m., but these hours are certainly not limited, particularly given the popularity today of business cell phones. On a cell phone, you often have the advantage of caller identification, so it is likely you will know when the company is calling you back. However, this may not always be the case, so you should always assume that any unknown number coming into your phone may be a potential career opportunity.

In the case that you receive a call at a time that is not convenient, let the call go to your voice mail. Also, if you are in a place where your cell signal is weak, if it is noisy, or if you are driving, you should also let the call go to voice mail. One recruiter tells a rather humorous story of calling a student in the evening; when the call was answered, it was apparent the student was at a bar and intoxicated. Needless to say, this made professional communication with the student impossible, and the student was not offered an interview.

Because some of your calls will inevitably end up going to voice mail, make sure that your outgoing message is brief and professional. This message should identify the telephone number to the caller and request a message be left. Including your name in the message is also an option. An example of a generic, but professional, telephone message would be, "You have reached 000-111-2222. I am not available to take your call, so please leave a brief message along with your name and telephone number so that I may return your call promptly." When recording your greeting, speak slowly and clearly. After recording your message, call your own phone and listen to the message to ensure it recorded well and is easily understood.

When conducting a job search, it is especially important to check your phone messages often and return calls right away. Once prospective employers decide to contact you, you cannot afford to miss an opportunity because of a breakdown in communication.

In the case that you are receiving phone calls on a landline phone that is shared by others, you should be accessible when the phone call arrives, if at all possible, and able to pick up the phone quickly. Do not fall into the habit of keeping callers waiting on the line. As professors, we often return telephone calls during the hours of 9 a.m. and noon. As you might expect, many of the recipients of our return calls are students. While the vast majority of people with whom we speak are courteous and willing to take messages when necessary, a variety of unprofessional responses have been encountered. One common response to a request to speak with someone when calling a residence is "He's/she's asleep." While honest, this blunt response does not contribute positively to one's professional profile. Other calls result in being placed on "hold" seemingly long enough to do short errands before picking up the line. Further frustration for the caller occurs upon requesting that a message be taken. Apparently many households no longer make a practice of locating a pen and pencil near the telephone. Remember, these are return phone calls, meaning the recipients of these calls have initiated contact and have requested that someone call them back! These offenses are forgivable in most contexts, but within your job search, they may be lethal.

If you do have a shared number, such as a landline phone, inform your roommates or family members that you are expecting potential employers to be calling you, and instruct them in the telephone etiquette to which you expect they will adhere. Begin today to practice telephone etiquette yourself, and you will easily become accustomed to speaking professionally on the phone. A simple phrase such as "Susan is unavailable right now. May I take a message?" is a catch-all for any situation which prevents the intended recipient of a call to come to the telephone, and it is much more professional than "Susan is in the shower; can she call you back?"

Establishing Contact Via Email

Email is the go-to form of communication in the business world, accounting for 929 million mailbox accounts in 2013; by the end of 2017, that number is expected to reach over 1.1 billion (Radicati, 2013). Perhaps the biggest advantage email offers for job seekers is the ability to perfect what is said in an initial contact before making that contact. It also allows the potential interviewer the ability to receive information at their convenience versus taking a phone call when they may be distracted with other tasks. However, despite the many advantages of email, it can also kill a job search quickly if it is not used properly.

All email communication should be written in the same professional manner that you would write a business letter, such as your cover letter. However, there are some specific considerations with email correspondence. Following the guidelines as outlined in Box 7.1 will increase the chances that your email will be noticed and that you will get a positive response. Remember that *every* form of communication you have with a potential interviewer is being examined for professionalism. All communication provides a preview to the employer as to how well you will represent their company once you ace your interview and are hired.

PREPARING FOR THE INTERVIEW

In preparation for an interview, you must familiarize yourself with the company. For retail companies and apparel (and other product) manufacturers, there is no substitute for first-person interaction with the store or the product. Visit as many Kmart® stores as possible if you are going to interview with Kmart®. Examine Liz Claiborne products if you are going to interview with Liz Claiborne.

After a recent interview with a recruiter for a large retailing chain, a student commented that she felt confident in replying in the affirmative when asked had she ever shopped in the store. She had been stumped, however, when asked what one change she would make, given the opportunity. An interview question such as this requires great familiarity with the company and the store, as well as critical thinking ability. When gathering information about a company, go beyond the written history and the informative brochures to delve into the heart of the business—the store or the product—and research the company yourself from the perspective of a consumer. Shop in the store or for the products yourself, talk to people who are frequent customers, and research the company creatively as you prepare for an interview. This firsthand knowledge of

BOX 7.1 Guide to Writing Professional Email

1. Subject line. Include a subject that gives the recipient an idea of what the email message concerns, that will entice the reader to open the message, and that will also make it easy to find in the inbox later. Depending on the circumstances, this could contain your name, your school, or the name of the person who has introduced you. Regardless of the subject you use, remember to keep it short—five to seven words is a good guideline. Examples:

   - Prada Internship Applicant Julie Hillery
   - Ohio State Fellow Alumnus applicant Julie Hillery
   - Julie Hillery—we met through Ann Paulins

2. Salutation. If you do not know the person, the safest salutation is "Dear Mr. Johnson." You can also use "Hello Mr. Johnson" or "Good morning/afternoon Mr. Johnson." If you know the person well, it may be acceptable to use "Hi," but remember this is a professional correspondence and thus all components of the email should appear as such.

3. Message body. The first or second line of your email should get directly to the point of why you are writing, which should be preceded only by a brief greeting. A few examples include:

   - "I hope this finds you well and that you are enjoying your day. I am writing to inquire about an internship with your company. Would you possibly have five minutes to connect with me on the phone so that I may learn more about that opportunity and tell you why I am so interested in the position?"
   - "It was great to meet you last night at the networking event. I would love the opportunity to talk with you more about the openings available because my three years of retail merchandising experience make me a perfect match for those."

   Obviously there are many possible opening lines, depending on your specific circumstances. Regardless, always get to the point and keep your email short. Because everyone is extremely busy, with full inboxes that they likely check on the small screens of their phones, your brevity will be much appreciated.

4. Use bullet points, numbers, and spacing wisely. In addition to keeping your email brief, use formatting to make the message easy to read. If you have two or three main points to make, use bullet points or numbering to list those. For ease of reading, be sure to include blank lines between the salutation, each paragraph, and the closing. In addition, use a font size that is no less than 11 point.

5. Closing. As with the salutation, the closing should also be traditional. Close the email with "Sincerely," "Respectfully," "Thank you," or something similar. Leave two blank lines before your name and include your electronic signature.

6. Signature. All email programs make it easy to compose an electronic signature. Yours should include your full name and contact information. You may also include a title, such as appears in the example below. If you have a Twitter account or a website, that can also be included.

   Julie Johnson, Intern Candidate
   The Ohio State University
   C: 000-111-2222
   Email: jjjohnson@myemail.com

BOX 7.2 Researching a Prospective Employer

These are the things you should know about a company *before* your interview:

- Location of the company's home office
- Size of the company, including number of employees, subsidiaries, and divisions
- How long in business
- Major competition
- Reputation of the company
- Whether privately or publicly owned
- Technology systems in place
- Geographic locations

- Potential or recent growth
- Current events in the news
- Annual stock growth during the past five years
- Current stock price
- Target customers
- Price points of products
- Products and services offered
- Current employees that you know
- Formal versus on-the-job training
- Typical career path at the company

the company will impress the interviewer and will demonstrate more than a superficial awareness of current market performance and industry trends. In talking with many college recruiters over the years, we have repeatedly heard them mention that the biggest mistake students make in interviews is having little or no knowledge about the company. Box 7.2 provides the guidelines for researching a company with which you have an interview.

As you are preparing for the interview, identify a focus in your self-presentation. If you are interviewing for an internship or an entry-level job, define your own objectives for the experience. Employers want to know what you expect to learn, what you can contribute to the company, where your interests lie, and the goals you have set for yourself. Being able to confidently answer these questions will demonstrate a level of personal preparation that is in keeping with corporate expectations. Focus not only on your strengths and areas of expertise but also on the areas within the company that interest you and in which you hope to work and learn. Recruiters will have difficulty identifying a place for you if you have not defined your goals and objectives and if you are simply "willing to do anything." Even though you should be open-minded enough to pitch in and do what needs to be done on the job, in an interview you will serve yourself better when you focus on a particular job or department and are able to articulate your particular professional goals. As you plan your future and prepare for interview questions, set realistic goals for yourself. Being unrealistic, overblown, or overly general in the accomplishments you expect for yourself may indicate to the employer that you lack knowledge of the company hierarchy and aren't a team player.

Most importantly, in preparation for your interview, know what you have to offer the company. You are, after all, selling yourself. In a recent study, Dr. Phil Gardner, Director of Research for the Collegiate Employment Research Institute at Michigan State University, surveyed 815 employers inquiring about the professional skills of liberal arts college students. On a positive note, employers reported that the students were equipped with needed workplace competencies, yet they were not able to clearly articulate and demonstrate their abilities in order to perform well in the job search and interview process (Chan & Derry, 2013). Remember, your interview is literally a sales job for your complete "package," and you will be evaluated accordingly. No detail is too small as you plan your appearance, your responses, your questions, and your nonverbal cues, including posture, gait, eye contact, and handshake.

Interview Tests

It is common, particularly for entry-level interviews, to be required to participate in a series of tests. Tests range from mandatory drug tests required of all employees to pen-and-pencil or computer-based tests that are reminiscent of academic exams. Chiquita Cooper, who is profiled in Chapter 5, recalls that she was given an opportunity to pursue a merchandising/buying career path with Burdines (now Macy's) because she scored 100% on the retail math test given as part of her interview process. Although some recruiters will say that there is no way to prepare for such a test, you can review information from your retail math courses before taking analytical tests. Students should be familiar with sales reports that include this year's (TY) and last year's (LY) sales, stock-to-sales ratios, and inventory figures. In addition, knowledge of different zones—hot, warm, and cold—within the United States is important for merchandising positions.

Additionally, it is likely that you will be subjected to a leadership/skills inventory test that might include problem solving, preferences, and abilities. Your familiarity with your strengths and weaknesses should enable you to better identify your own preferences. Personal analysis of your skills and abilities may prove valuable as you navigate the questions on the interview tests. As discussed in Chapter 2, one tool we recommend for doing this accompanies the book *StrengthsFinder* by Tom Rath. Regardless of the amount of preparation that you can undertake, your awareness of the likelihood of being subjected to a test should reduce your anxiety level during your interview.

Your Interview Wardrobe

Appearance is important. When you visit the company, observe the appropriate attire and tailor your wardrobe to fit the company culture.

Remember that an interview is a professional occasion; when in doubt, lean toward conservative attire over casual. Several years ago, an Ohio University student landed an internship with a visual merchandising department—a competitive position for which there were multiple applicants. She confided that during her interview she became quite uncomfortable when she realized that the employer and members of the visual merchandising team were all dressed in jeans and tennis shoes. Having been duly instructed as to proper interview attire, this student appeared in a conservative suit, dressed for a "corporate interview." Although this extreme difference in dress resulted in her feeling ill prepared, she later learned that her appearance had influenced the decision to offer her the internship. The director of visual merchandising later commented to her that he was extremely impressed by her professionalism and the care that she had taken to prepare herself for the interview. Even though she ended up wearing jeans and tennis shoes every day of her internship, this student discovered that she had landed the job because of her professional appearance and preparation for the interview.

When interviewing with companies that are fashion focused, it is perfectly appropriate to display a fashionable appearance. This can be accomplished, however, without compromising good taste and professional behavior. We recall a student who attended a retail career fair at Purdue University. She wore a tailored suit in a shade of green that made her stand out in a sea of navy and black suits. Recruiters at the conference even commented to her that they appreciated her fashion sense and willingness to break out of the "corporate" appearance mold. This dress style worked—as she was remembered for exhibiting a relatively daring fashion sense while at the same time her appearance (in terms of the style of the suit, grooming, and choice of accessories) was professional and appropriate.

It is a good idea to avoid clothes and accessories that will draw emphasis away from what you are saying. Be cautious of flashy clothes, dangling earrings, hair in your face, shoes you can't walk in, and other distracting items. At a panel discussion during a recent Purdue University Retail Management Career, recruiters offered this valuable advice: "If you question what you're wearing, don't wear it." Be sure to consider the appearance of your hands, nails, teeth, and hair, in addition to your wardrobe. When your appearance or attire is noticed and recalled by the interviewer as a point of interest, it is not likely a good thing. It is more likely that a midriff-baring shirt, a low-cut blouse, or five-inch heels will be remembered because of their inappropriate presence during an interview than that a conservative interview suit will be recalled. It is better to have your interview associated with your positive characteristics and your fit with the company than with an embarrassing visual faux pas. The

STUDIO website (www.bloomsburycentral.com) provides an activity to help you discern appropriate and inappropriate interview outfits.

A last word of caution concerning your appearance for the interview. There has been an increasing trend for young adults to have multiple tattoos or piercings. A recent study (Blanton, 2014) found nearly half of women under age 35 have gotten ink, which is almost double their male counterparts (47 percent vs. 25 percent); more liberals (26 percent) have tattoos compared to conservatives (18 percent); and 73 percent of registered voters reported they would hire someone who had a visible tattoo. However, although tattoos and other body modifications are becoming more socially acceptable, you should still avoid revealing them in an interview or in a corporate setting. Choose an interview outfit that covers tattoos, and consider removing jewelry in nontraditional piercings (e.g., nose, tongue; earrings for men).

Behavior in the Interview

Many nonverbal messages are communicated during face-to-face and virtual interviews. Be aware that these facial and bodily gestures convey a lot of information to the interviewer. When you sit up straight and lean slightly forward, you indicate that you are an active and interested participant in the interview. Slouching back in a chair sends the opposite message. Extending your hand and offering a firm handshake exudes confidence and professionalism. Waiting to take a seat until invited to do so shows courtesy and respect. Eye contact throughout the interview demonstrates your interest in the topic and your attention to the interviewer.

In addition to the nonverbal messages that you send, your behaviors should be planned with a professional demeanor in mind. Never chew gum during an interview, even on the phone. This behavior is completely unprofessional and considered offensive to many people. Gum or any type of distraction (such as clicking a ballpoint pen or tapping your feet) will detract from the focus of the interview—you and your qualifications—and will shift the focus to your deficiencies. We do not advise smoking or drinking alcoholic beverages during interviews, even if you are offered and your interviewer chooses to imbibe.

Responding to Interview Questions

It is often said that the best interviews are essentially conversations rather than question-and-answer sessions. This is true, and your ability to communicate in a conversational manner will contribute to the effectiveness of the interview. Be aware that the level of development of your social skills will be clearly evident in an interview. Many of the questions employers ask will direct you to offer examples of experiences you have had in which you had to solve problems, take responsibility for your actions, and evaluate your strategies. If you are able to relate such experiences to situations that will be an asset to the company, you are on the right track.

As you prepare yourself for the interview, anticipate questions that may be asked and prepare logical, insightful answers. All employers, regardless of the field, are looking for employees who know how to solve problems. You are likely to be asked questions that require you to analyze situations, plan actions, and generate results. "Behavioral interviews" or "targeted selection questions," as they are often called by recruiters, require you to draw from your personal and professional experience, your ethics, your creativity, your analytical ability, and your communication skills to respond effectively. When asked a question such as, "Give me an example of a situation in which you made a decision that you had to stand by, even though that might have been difficult," the interviewer is looking for an insightful response demonstrating that responsibility has been taken and that you have accepted ownership for your decision. You should be prepared to draw from your experiences and relate your responses to specific tasks that you might be expected to perform on the job. Important qualities that you should strive to demonstrate via your response include leadership, the ability to motivate people, responsibility, an appreciation of conflicting opinions, an ability to resolve conflict, an ability to prioritize, and potential for personal growth. Responses to questions such as this must be well thought out and genuine. Do not feel that you must offer examples that always have "happy endings." Prospective employers will be more receptive to answers demonstrating an ability to learn from your mistakes than to responses that are simple, flip, or superficial. An interview allows you (forces you, really) to recall experiences and evaluate your actions to demonstrate how you will be effective at making decisions for the company. Your experiences may not be direct results of retailing, design, or merchandising experiences, but you should provide enough insight to explain how your experience does relate.

A student recently recounted an interview question asking her to describe an experience that she had come to regret. This difficult question was most likely posed to give an opportunity for the student to provide insight into her character, values, and ability to learn from her mistakes and to analyze situations. Not surprisingly, she was unsure of the motive behind the question, and she was not certain how to answer. The student later realized that she had interpreted the question in a literal sense, and considered the term "regret" to mean "dwelling on a mistake that cannot be changed." The student responded in the interview that she did not make it a practice to harbor regrets, but rather to accept situations that were in the past and consequently unchangeable. Upon further analysis of the interview, the student concluded that the interview had not ended well, and likely the reason was this misinterpretation of the "regret" question. The question sought a response that showed her ability to own, reflect upon, and learn from her mistakes, but her response had indicated a lack of ownership for her actions and an unwillingness to learn from her mistakes. On the other hand, another student had responded to the same question that as a lifeguard manager the previous summer she had implemented a "no holidays off" policy to address the problem of having too few employees on the busiest days of the summer. She was obligated, she explained, to stand by this policy but realized as the summer wore on that a better approach could be implemented in the future. The next summer, she modified the policy so that days off had to be approved by a certain date with the understanding that lifeguards were responsible for finding their own substitutes. Although she regretted the policy decision she had implemented the first year, she learned from the experience, was willing to take ownership of a decision even though it turned out not to be optimal, and did not compromise her credibility the first year on the job by changing the policy midseason. The next year, she reported, her new policy improved morale among the employees and also helped solve the problem of sufficient staffing. Experiences such as lifeguarding, while not a part of the retail or apparel industry, have direct application to skills necessary for success in retail management and virtually all other job positions.

One of the mistakes many students make is to think they will not be considered for a job simply because they have no direct experience in retailing. Although it is most desirable to have some retail experience when applying for an entry-level merchandising position, if you do not have direct experience, you should at least be able to identify skills you have developed in your prior jobs that are directly related to those needed to be successful in retailing. (See Discussion Question 5 in Chapter 6, which provides the opportunity to identify transferable skills from jobs typically held by college students that are not fashion related.)

Appropriate Interview Questions

As you prepare for interviews, it is important that you be aware that there are legal limitations regarding what an interviewer may ask of you. Interview conversations should remain on a professional level at all times, and you should be alert to questions that are legal but that lead to responses that reveal more information than an interviewer is legally able to ask. Personal questions, such as your age, marital status, and parenting obligations are not permissible by law. In other words, an interviewer may not ask you if you are married. An interviewer can, however, ask you, "Where do you see yourself in five years?"

In anticipation of interview questions and conversations, familiarize yourself with appropriate and inappropriate topics as defined by law. Furthermore, develop strategies for responses to typical interview questions that do not reveal personal information that it is not necessary for interviewers to know. Responding to illegal questions is certainly awkward, but the informed and prepared interviewee will have an advantage over one who is naïve. Sometimes interviewers ask unlawful questions because they are unaware of proper hiring procedures. Often inexperienced interviewees offer responses to legitimate questions that are more detailed than necessary. The common interview question, "Where do you see yourself in three to five years?" is innocent and legal enough, but the response may yield more information than one need offer in an interview. For example, if you reply that you hope to be settled down with a family in addition to stating your career aspirations, your interviewer may (perhaps mistakenly) interpret that your priorities are not focused on career growth with that company. When responding to questions of this nature, it is best to stick to professional topics, such as anticipated position in the company, level of responsibility related to the position, and specific accomplishments that may be achieved on the job. Avoid personal information, such as anticipated change in marital status or parental responsibilities, as these are not relevant to your ability to perform in the workplace. Comments made by interviewees about personal issues may be considered along with other applicant criteria. Experienced and productive interviewers are trained to wield as much information as possible from their interview encounters. The savvy applicant will recognize topics to elaborate and emphasize and those to avoid.

When you are asked questions that are not legal or appropriate, you should respond at your discretion. You may reply, "That is an inappropriate question that I prefer not to answer," or you may answer the question. Obviously, your experience in the interview situation will inform your impression of the company and should contribute to your decision about whether to continue to pursue employment there.

Honesty in the Interview

Ethical behavior, as discussed in Chapter 9, includes a commitment to honesty. It is necessary to be completely honest when formulating responses to anticipated questions. Do not fabricate information during an interview, particularly regarding employment history. The interviewer relies on information gathered during the interview to make placement decisions and, in some cases, to abide by company policies. Making false statements during an interview is sufficient grounds for termination, a situation that in the long run will be more detrimental to you than the advantage of making a false statement in the first place. If you anticipate some "sticky situations" that you will be expected to explain, prepare responses thoughtfully and with your, and the company's, best interest at heart. If you describe yourself as an outgoing leader who is willing to take on responsibility, what will you say when the interviewer asks what you have done to demonstrate the traits you possess?

Although you must be honest, you should present yourself and your experiences in a positive manner at all times. You should take time to evaluate your work opportunities and to identify positive aspects of bad experiences. It is much better to make lemonade than be stuck with sour lemons! We advocate a "no excuses" philosophy for assessing one's experiences. That is, do not make excuses for the mistakes, unfortunate circumstances, and problems that you have encountered. There is nothing worse in an interview than presenting an "It's not my fault" attitude. Rather, you should take ownership of the situation and demonstrate the maturity to realize and accept the benefits along with the consequences of any experience.

One important part of an interview is to speak well of previous employers. If you cannot honestly do this, then phrase any references to former employers in a careful manner. You will give a better impression of yourself if you comment that you "had a valuable learning opportunity as an employee of Doomsday Discounters" rather than elaborating that the manager was crazy, the employees were given no direction, and the pay was lousy. A student encountered this dilemma when interviewing for an internship position. She had had previous experience with a large, well-respected specialty retailer and was asked, "Why did you leave that job?" Wanting to be completely honest, the student replied that she did not get along well with the manager, and she felt that she could not work with this particular manager anymore. Furthermore, the student continued to discuss some of the specific circumstances surrounding the manager's performance. The interviewer, the student reported, did not seem interested in pursuing the interview any further, and the company did not offer her an internship. Providing complete, revealing information elaborating on perceptions and judgments of people extraneous to the interview is inappropriate. You must be careful about what you say and how you say it, as interpretation is the name of the game for interviewers. The student would not have compromised her honesty had she responded that the specialty-retailing job was beneficial for her, but that she hopes to expand her retail opportunities and learn about other facets of the industry. If asked specifically about management styles or previous supervisors, the student could reply that she has had opportunities to observe various management techniques, and has a good understanding of the importance of clear communication and the important role personality plays in effective management. Prospective employers expect that you will be as insightful—or disrespectful—about the opportunities they have to offer as you have been about your previous opportunities. Furthermore, as an employee of their company, you will be serving as an ambassador for them. They expect that you will handle delicate situations that may occur in your prospective job with the same courtesy and tact you exhibit in the interview. What you say and *how* you say it makes all the difference!

As you are responding to questions in an interview, you may feel as though you should have a quick answer for every question. Because interviews tend to be situations that make people nervous, you may tend to speak quickly as well. Do not be concerned if you need to take a few moments to collect your thoughts and develop an articulate answer. After all, you can prepare for the interview very well, but you may not be able to anticipate every single question. You will present yourself better if you concentrate on speaking clearly and reflecting on your answer momentarily before you speak than if you jump in and begin speaking before you have thought the idea through. Remember, too, that it is perfectly appropriate to ask interviewers to repeat questions or to elaborate on them if you do not fully understand what they are asking. It is better to be clear about a question than to try to guess at what they are asking and wind up giving an inappropriate response. For the most part, interviewers will welcome your asking for clarification because they obviously want information from you concerning a specific topic. You will also demonstrate the ability to ask questions before trying to muddle through something you do not understand. This trait is one that is highly desirable of most employees.

Take the initiative to analyze yourself by preparing responses to typical interview questions. This exercise will prevent you from fumbling over wording and ideas in the actual interview and will require that you assess your work, volunteer, club, and other leadership opportunities to identify both their intrinsic and extrinsic benefits. Once you have thought out responses to typical questions, seek an opportunity to practice an interview that is recorded. This exercise is probably the most intimidating project that our students undertake in their career search strategies courses; however, once it is completed, the pain is quickly forgotten and the value of the exercise is easily realized. You will have no opportunity in a "real" interview to review your verbal interaction, nonverbal behavior, and appearance as you may in a recorded practice interview. Students have observed nervous habits and other personal quirks that they would not have detected without the opportunity of viewing a video. Videos also reveal the positive aspects of your interview techniques, and they may serve to boost your confidence.

You will find a list of common interview questions in Box 7.3 and on the accompanying website. Common topics that provide the basis for many of the questions asked of recent graduates are listed below.

- Summer employment
- Jobs you liked the least
- Future plans
- Why you picked the college you attended
- How you paid for college
- How you are different from others in your major
- What you have learned in school that you can use in your job
- Your willingness to perform routine tasks
- The type of position in which you are interested
- Why you think you will like the work
- What you know about the company
- Your grades and whether they should be considered
- Whether you have ever had problems getting along with others

BOX 7.3 Common Interview Questions

- Are you willing to relocate?
- Describe yourself.
- Describe your ideal job.
- Describe the ideal employee–supervisor relationship.
- Describe a situation in which you learned from a mistake.
- Did you like your former place of employment?
- How have your activities contributed to your ability to do this job?
- Why did you leave your last place of employment?
- Tell me about your previous managers.
- What are your career goals?
- What are your strengths?
- What is your greatest weakness?
- What are your weaknesses?
- What do you know about this company?
- What would you change in our stores?
- What, as a customer, have you observed that is good about our merchandise?
- What have you observed that you would change about our merchandise?
- What do you expect to do in this job?
- What makes you different from the other applicants for this job?
- What is your most prized possession?
- What is your proudest achievement?
- What rewards do you expect to earn in this job?
- Where do you expect to be in 10 (or 5 or 20) years?
- When can you begin work with our company?
- Why did you select your major?
- What were your favorite courses?
- What courses did you not enjoy? Why?
- Why should I hire you?
- Do you have any questions?

Although we are not providing suggested responses for each question, the primary question that our students want to know how to answer is the "money" question: the question about how much money you expect to be paid. Because it is extremely likely that you will have to answer this question or have some discussion about it, the *STUDIO* website accompanying this book provides you with the necessary guidelines and an activity for successfully responding to this question.

Asking Questions of the Interviewer

Near the conclusion of the interview, you will undoubtedly be asked whether you have any questions. You should identify and ask questions, as this will indicate an interest in the company, and you may be able to demonstrate that you have researched the company by asking appropriate questions. Even if you are not asked to present questions, you may certainly take your turn in the interview and seek responses from the interviewer. You will need to think on your feet (so pay attention) and be sure not to ask a question that has already been answered. This is where your notes and attentiveness can be especially useful.

Typical questions that are useful for prospective employees to ask pertain to daily routine, training, compensation, evaluation, career paths, and work environment. You might ask about the typical daily routine for an intern or entry-level position, and particularly whether certain activities, such as visiting the distribution center or accompanying your supervisor to a trade show, might be part of the program. Questions about the structure of the training program for entry-level employees and the evaluation process for new hires should also be of interest to you if these were not already explained. Avoid questions that would be obvious to anyone who had properly researched the company. Do not ask questions about the hierarchy of the corporate ladder, as these are likely published in the company literature, but you may be interested in learning about the typical career path of current employees. Helpful information may be gained by inquiring whether employees tend to work their way up in the company or whether they tend to be hired from the outside. Similarly, you may wish to learn the average length of time a typical employee works for the company and the company's policies regarding continuing education and professional development. You may find it helpful to ask what qualities the interviewer believes are important for the job you hope to obtain. A most important question if you are interviewing for an entry-level position, as opposed to an internship, should concern the reason for the vacancy. Pay attention to the response you receive, as it may give you insight into what you can expect if you take the position. Of course, the most desirable response from the prospective employer is that the position is available due to a promotion. If you find that the vacancy is due to a termination, your next question should be concerned with what you can do, when hired, to avoid the same fate! Box 7.4 provides you with some typical questions you could ask of your interviewer.

It is perfectly appropriate to ask when you might expect to hear from the employer regarding a decision to hire you. This shows that you are interested in following through with the interview process, and the response gives you valuable information. Some recruiters may plan to make hiring decisions in as little as a week, while others may not expect to complete their round of interviews for several months.

When to Bring Up Salary

As a general rule, you should refrain from asking about salary in the first interview. Recruiters know that a well-prepared interviewee will have researched the salary ranges of his or her potential employers, and the first interview is better used to establish a relationship between the company and prospective employee regarding a potential future relationship. If you feel you must inquire about salary, ask about the "range" typically offered at the entry level. The first interview is not a time to negotiate specifics. It is inappropriate to bring up questions about vacation time, holiday policies, and personal days, particularly in a first interview for an entry-level job. Bringing a focus such as this into your interview will indicate to the employer that your priorities are misguided. Although the compensation and benefits package is an important feature in your final consideration of entry-level jobs, you will be better served by keeping the focus of any interview on the mutual benefits of employment based on learning opportunities and professional skills.

INTERVIEW SETTINGS
The Traditional Interview: Face-to-Face

Historically, these have been the most popular types of interviews, and they involve meeting with your interviewer in person. Generally, they will be held on campus, at a store or corporate office, or sometimes in a hotel lobby or coffee shop if the interviewer is from out of town. Regardless of the location, the preceding section has thoroughly discussed both preparation and professional expectations for these traditional types of interviews. However, one word of caution not previously mentioned: If you do meet your interviewer in a setting such as a hotel lobby or coffee shop, do not be distracted by the activity around you. Keep your focus on the interviewer, making eye contact while speaking directly to him or her.

Telephone Interviews

With time and expense for travel a major obstacle in scheduling interviews, telephone interviews are increasingly used, especially for first interviews. Telephone interviews should be prepared for in the same manner as a face-to-face interview, with the exception that you do not need to plan a strategic wardrobe. Do be certain, however, that during a telephone interview you have absolute quiet in your background environment and that there will be no interruptions from your end of the telephone line. Do not respond to call waiting during a telephone interview.

If you receive an interview call unexpectedly, you should NEVER ask the caller if they can call back. If you are caught off guard, ask the caller if they mind holding while you shut the door or change phones to a quieter location. However, do NOT leave the caller on hold for more than 30 seconds! Even if you do not need to change phones or locations, use the time to take a deep breath (get a grip!) and to find the notes you should have readily available. When returning to the phone, thank the caller for holding and then proceed with the interview.

While telephone interviews do not give you the advantage of making a great "appearance" by utilizing positive and professional non-verbal behaviors, you do have the advantage of using notes. Be sure to write down all the items you wish to share with the interviewer. It is a good idea to have a copy of your résumé in front of you and a list of questions you wish to ask. Even though you have crib notes, you will still need to prepare thoroughly and just as well as you would for a face-to-face interview.

During a telephone interview, take special care to speak clearly. Many students have also told us that in preparing to receive a scheduled phone interview, they dressed professionally, just as they would for a face-to-face interview, simply because it put them in the right frame of mind—meaning that dressing like a professional made them feel like a professional, which in turn helped them communicate professionally.

Virtual Interviews

Interviews done virtually via video applications such as Skype are also becoming increasingly common, especially for first interviews. While the preparation is the same as for the telephone interview, and all other interviews for that matter, there are special considerations you should make to present yourself in the most professional way possible. Because the interviewers will be able to see you and your surroundings, you will need to pay special attention to your visual presentation. This requires additional preparation and practice, which Box 7.5 outlines.

BOX 7.5 Nailing the Virtual Interview

1. Use of technology. Make sure your technology works to avoid any embarrassment. Obvious as it sounds, know everything you can about operating the technology before the interview. For example, make sure your camera will turn on as soon as you answer the call and also locate the volume button so that you can adjust it seamlessly as necessary. Additionally, your microphone and webcam should be high quality, assuring a clear picture and voice.

2. Pay attention to the lighting and your background. When selecting a location for your call, make sure the background does not contain anything that will be distracting to the interviewer or portray you in a negative way. It is probably best to sit with your back against a blank wall, if possible, or in an office setting where there are bookshelves or file cabinets behind you. The lighting should also be bright enough to project a good screen image.

3. Avoid distractions. When considering your background, you should also choose a spot that has minimal distractions and potential interruptions. Put pets outside or in an area where they will not be heard; turn off all phones, TVs, and music; and shut your windows to avoid sirens or other noises from the outside. You should also consider putting a "do not disturb" sign on the doors to your room and the outside door. If by chance something does happen (e.g., someone unexpectedly stops by or a child in the house starts crying), apologize to the interviewer and deal with the distraction as quickly and easily as possible. Remain calm and show your ability to handle unexpected matters professionally.

4. Make eye contact. Just as with the in-person interview, you need to look the interviewer in the eye. This is accomplished by looking at the camera and not at the screen of the computer. Many people do

---

continued

BOX 7.5 Nailing the Virtual Interview (continued)

not realize this and you can often set your-self apart by looking into the camera.

5. Convey your enthusiasm for the job. It is more difficult to convey your enthusiasm for the job in a virtual interview. However, you can do this through facial expressions (smile!) and also by telling the interviewer you are excited about the opportunities for specific reasons—those you have found while researching the company.

6. Watch your body language. As is true with all interviews, your body language is important. Very soon after you answer the call, you should acknowledge your inter-viewer with a "virtual handshake." This is a small nod during introductions to acknowl-edge each other. During the interview, do not swivel around in a chair. In fact, con-sider sitting in a straight chair if you know you have a tendency to swivel and fidget. Third, be careful of leaning into the camera too much as it will distort your image and send an unprofessional message. Lastly, sit up straight and avoid too many hand ges-tures, which can also be distracting.

7. Do several dry runs. Practice with your friends and family and have them be hon-est with you on suggestions for improve-ment. They should evaluate your personal appearance, the background, sound, and your speech. Also have them pay special attention to your making eye contact with them. When practicing, have them ask you several interview questions to evaluate your answers, especially concerning the use of "um," "ah," and other space-fillers that are unnecessary. They may not know as much as you about the quality of your answer's content, but they can certainly evaluate your speaking.

8. Dress for success. Your dress for a virtual interview should be professional and no different than your dress for an in-person interview. While the interviewer may only see the upper third of your body, it is important that you are wearing the entire professional outfit. Consider how it will look if you have to get up for some rea-son during the interview or if the camera catches the bottom part of you showing shorts and flip-flops. And, honestly, dress-ing in the complete outfit will make you feel more professional and prepared for your interview.

9. Relax and be yourself. If you have done your research on the company, practiced using your technology, and are dressed professionally, you are ready! Smile, be yourself, and nail the interview so that your next step will be an in-person meeting, resulting in a job or internship offer.

Group Interviews

Group interviews are not commonly conducted as an initial interview; you are more likely to encounter these as part of a second or third interview. As the name suggests, group interviews are primarily used to observe how potential candidates interact with others. Generally the interviewer will give a group of candidates some sort of case study or problem to solve and then make observations of the group dynamics as they work toward a decision. The candidates who emerge as leaders within the group, those who contribute positively to the decisions, and those who offer interesting and insightful alternatives in line with the company's structure will be the ones who will most impress the interviewer. If you find yourself in a group interview, even if you tend to be shy and introverted, you must speak up and contribute to the discussion. If you have done your homework on the company, this is the perfect opportunity to make realistic and logical contributions to the group, justifying those by citing specific information you gathered in your research. If you tend to be an extrovert and a person who likes to take charge, this is the type of interview where you can shine. However, you must also guard against dominating the conversation and being too assertive because while you want to be viewed as a leader, it is also very important that the interviewer sees you as a team player.

Dinner Interviews

Many students view dinner interviews as the most nerve-wracking of all. Understandably so, given all of the elements that you will now have to manage while at the same time appearing professional, carrying on a meaningful conversation, and minding your manners!

The first thing that you need to remember about a dinner interview is that you are not there to eat. As contradictory as this may sound, the purpose of the dinner interview is to observe your behavior in this setting and gauge the type of representative you would be for the company should you be hired and be required to have dinner with clients in the future.

Because it is not in the scope of this book to thoroughly explain dinner etiquette, manners, proper use of silverware, and all of the other nuances involved with having dinner, we encourage you to seek out an etiquette dinner workshop on your campus so you will be best prepared. Repeatedly, over the years, our students who have attended these workshops report them to be one of the more informative experiences they have in preparing for the job search. Many students find that they had no idea how little they knew about "having dinner."

The most common question we get about dinner interviews is whether it is okay to drink alcohol if it is offered and everyone else at the table is doing so. Our stance, for the most part, would be to decline participation. You want to be on the top of your game, and drinking can sometimes impede your ability to be so. However, if your host insists, and you are comfortable having alcohol, allow at most a small glass of wine—*only* if you are of legal age. This will be enough to "fit in" with the group while still allowing you to interview well.

Entertainment Activities as Interviews

You may experience interviews—particularly second interviews—that last the duration of one or two days. These interviews are typically jam-packed with activities and are likely to be exhausting. You should prepare both mentally and physically for marathon interviews. Make sure that you are in good physical shape and have the stamina to remain energetic throughout the entire interview.

Interviews that last throughout the day generally include meals and might even include an entertainment event, such as attending a ball game or an "after hours" get-together. Keep in mind that regardless of the activity, the interview is still going on. Your actions during events away from the corporate environment are as insightful to interviewers as your responses to their formal questions at the office. Your manners, level of professionalism, self-control, and common sense will all be evaluated. Remember, you are interviewing for a position where you may entertain clients and represent the company in a variety of contexts. Your ability to adapt to a variety of situations is being observed. Obviously, your behavior at a ball game as part of your interview, or with a client, will not be the same as your behavior when attending a ball game with your buddies. Never let your guard down; remain professional from the time you make the initial contact with the employer until you have a signed agreement.

To illustrate how important it is to remember that your interview starts during the first contact, consider this story told to a group of students by a corporate recruiter, "Ted." When Ted was looking for his first summer job, he went to a local ice cream parlor to apply for a position he saw advertised. Upon arriving, Ted parked in the back of the parking lot and proceeded into the store to apply. After filling out an application and answering just a few questions, he was surprised to get a job offer on the spot. The reason for such a quick decision? The owner had noticed that Ted chose to park in the back of the lot even though there were spots much closer to the front door. The owner indicated that when she saw Ted leave those spots for customers, she immediately knew he understood who and what was most important to a retailer! Moral of the story: Your interview can start even *before* you make contact.

EVALUATING THE INTERVIEW

A job search, and particularly an interview, is all about fit. The reason many people are unhappy in their careers or lose their jobs is not because of their inability to do the job, but rather because they are not a good fit with the company, its culture, and its employees. Fit is so important that some recruiters have told us that they can tell within five minutes into the interview if a candidate will fit into their workplace culture. When you interview, you have an opportunity to familiarize yourself with the company culture in the same manner that the company learns about you. Remember, not every job is right for every person. Do not be discouraged if an occasional interview does not "click." Keep in mind, also, that the interviewing process is comprehensive, and you can learn from your previous experiences.

You should evaluate the interview from your perspective just as the interviewer undoubtedly will from his or hers. Take notes either during the interview or immediately after so that you can keep track of any information you wish to remember. After several interviews, the information begins to run together, so you are wise to make your notes immediately following the interview, particularly if you are participating in a job fair or some other interview-intense opportunity.

Make a list of positive and negative aspects of the company information you learned and note the way the information was presented in the interview. Reflect on your responses to the questions that were asked, and develop or refine responses to questions that you felt were difficult to answer. As you begin to make your selection regarding an employer of choice, weigh the information gathered through the interview in a manner that is consistent with your goals, values, and personal fit in that company. For your convenience, and to help you with your interview evaluations, the STUDIO website (www.bloomsburycentral.com) provides an interview evaluation form. Download this form and keep it somewhere readily accessible for notes after every interview. This will help you make notes on each company in a uniform manner, making sure you are evaluating the companies on the same factors. Add any items to the form that are not already included that are of special importance to you.

FOLLOWING UP
AFTER THE INTERVIEW

After any type of interview, you should make a point of sending a thank-you letter to the interviewer. Although some employers indicate that this is a gesture that is usually not expected, other employers consider a thank-you letter to be the final component of the interview. A prompt, well-phrased thank-you letter may make the difference between a job offer and unemployment when competition is tight. That is because your thank-you letter is the last influence you can have on the interviewer's impression of you and his or her ultimate decision. In the letter, you should thank the employer for the opportunity of speaking with him or her and also refer back to the interview, reiterating why you are the perfect candidate for the position. You should also address anything that you think may have been perceived as a weakness or potential objections you picked up on during your interview. Remember that the thank-you letter gives you one last chance to sell yourself, so you must tell the interviewer one more time what you can do for the company.

A separate thank-you letter should be sent to every person you met or who participated in your interview. If you participated in a panel interview, then everyone on the panel should receive a letter. The thank-you letter should be laser printed following proper letter format or neatly handwritten. Attention to detail is just as important in the thank-you letter as it has been throughout your job search. Be sure to spell everyone's name correctly and include his or her proper title. It is more important that you send it than how it is formatted, but, as the final impression you will make on the company before any hiring decisions, it should be neatly presented and free of errors.

It has also become increasingly acceptable to send the letter via electronic mail, especially if that is the form of communication you have been using with that particular employer. Email definitely has the advantage of being the most expedient method of delivery. However, you should also send a hard copy of the letter. To be completely effective, the thank-you letter should be sent on the same day or the day after the interview and should be kept to one page ("The Perfect Thank-You Note," 2003). Figure 7.1 provides a sample thank-you letter to use following an initial campus interview, and Figure 7.2 provides one that can be used after a second.

After sending your thank-you letter(s), if you do not hear back from the employer in the time frame provided to you, you can take the initiative to follow up by phone. Before doing so, however, you may want to review the guidelines presented earlier in this chapter for making telephone contacts.

As mentioned and discussed previously, interviewing is usually the area of the career search in which students experience the most anxiety. After each interview, be sure to critically evaluate the experience. In doing so, you may want to use the information in Box 7.6, which provides some general guidelines for successful interviewing. With time and practice, you will soon see each interview as a learning experience, and you may even find that you enjoy interviewing. After all, remember—each interview is *your* opportunity to find out more about prospective employers and what they have to offer *you*!

123 Oak Street
Geneva, IL 60134
jjjames@gmail.com

Ms. Rebecca Wright
College Relations Coordinator
Fashion Department Store
404 Michigan Avenue
Chicago, IL 60603

October 22, 2016

Dear Ms. Wright:

I enjoyed interviewing with you during your recruiting visit to Northern Illinois University today. The management training program you outlined sounds both challenging and rewarding and I look forward to your decision concerning an on-site visit.

As I mentioned during the interview, I will be graduating in December with a Bachelor's degree in Fashion Merchandising. Through my education and experience I have gained many skills, as well as an understanding of retailing concepts and dealing with the general public. I have worked seven years in the retail industry in various positions from Sales Clerk to Assistant Department Manager. My education and work experience would complement the Fashion Department Store's management trainee program.

Thank you again for the opportunity to interview with Fashion Department Store. The interview served to reinforce my strong interest in becoming a part of your management team. I can be reached at (630) 555-5555 or by e-mail at jjjames@gmail.com should you need additional information.

Sincerely,
Jennifer J. James

FIGURE 7.1

Sample Thank-You Letter: Initial Campus Interview

Source: Thank-you letter prepared in part by Northern Illinois University Career Services, DeKalb, IL. This, and other effective letters, are available at www.niu.edu/careerservices. Reprinted with permission.

123 Oak Street
Geneva, IL 60134
jjjames@gmail.com

Ms. Rebecca Wright
College Relations Coordinator
Fashion Department Store
404 Michigan Avenue
Chicago, IL 60603

November 1, 2016

Dear Ms. Wright:

Thank you again for the opportunity to interview for the management training program at Fashion Department Store. I appreciated your hospitality and enjoyed meeting the members of your staff.

The on-site visit and interview convinced me of how compatible my background, interests, and skills are with the goals of Fashion Department Store. As I mentioned during our conversation, my experience as an Assistant Department Manager and as a Retail Sales Associate have prepared me well for entering your management training program. I am confident that my work for you will result in increased profits in the Junior's department within six months of my employment.

Again, thank you for your time and consideration. I look forward to hearing from you concerning your decision.

Cordially,
Jennifer J. James

FIGURE 7.2

Sample Thank-You Letter: On-Site Visit and Second Interview

Source: Thank-you letter prepared in part by Northern Illinois University Career Services, DeKalb, IL. This, and other effective letters, are available at www.niu.edu/careerservices. Reprinted with permission.

BOX 7.6 Tips for Successful Interviewing

- Be prompt. Arrive early and make sure *you* are the one who needs to wait.
- Do not sit until a seat is offered. Waiting to sit until the interviewer asks you to is a sign of respect.
- Dress appropriately. Check out the company's dress code; be conservative rather than too flashy.
- Speak up. Speak clearly and demonstrate your communication strengths.
- Show interest. Speak as though you would like to have the job. Make reference to the research you have done and the personal experiences that you have had with the company.
- Never speak negatively about your last job or previous employer. This will be a poor reflection on you in an interview.
- Be honest. References will most likely be checked. Remember that it is a relatively small industry.
- Be enthusiastic and sincere. Many recruiters look for enthusiasm for the position above anything else.

- Take a résumé with you. You may need to distribute updated résumés or replace one that you have sent previously.
- Bring a portfolio. Make reference to your portfolio during the interview. Use it as a tool to demonstrate your abilities and strengths.
- Smile. Be friendly, but don't joke or laugh too much.
- Execute good eye contact. Maintain eye contact without overemphasizing or staring.
- Thank the interviewer. At the conclusion of the interview, be certain to express appreciation for the time that has been spent with you. Thank the person for meals or other amenities as well.
- Offer to shake hands. Be the one to offer a handshake and close the interview in a positive, professional manner.

Projects

1. Participate in a recorded practice interview. After the interview, view the video to evaluate your eye contact, nonverbal behavior, and appearance, as well as the delivery and quality of your responses. Discuss your observed strengths and weaknesses with others who view the video. Identify areas for improvement and areas that you should strive to showcase in an actual interview.

2. Visit a store location of a company for which you are interested in working. Use this opportunity to observe employees, customers, floor layout, traffic flow, and merchandise assortments. Formulate ten questions that you can ask a recruiter for that company based

on your observations. Make a list of five recommendations that you could make to the recruiter if you were asked. Based on your experience, make a list of reasons that you wish to work for that company. Be prepared to share these reasons in your interview. The same can be done for a product line.

3. Identify a company for which you are interested in working. Follow the guidelines set forth in Box 7.2 to research the company. You may also include any other items you find interesting. Complete a brief report on your findings.

Questions for Discussion

1. Familiarize yourself with the common interview questions listed in Box 7.3. Can you readily and coherently respond to each question? Are you able to substantiate each response? What do you consider to be appropriate and inappropriate responses to each question?

2. Consider the opportunities you are seeking in an upcoming work experience or entry-level position. What are they? What questions can you ask in an interview that will yield information you can use to determine whether the position you are seeking will provide the opportunities you want?

3. Review Box 7.2, which presents an overview of researching a prospective employer. What other things would you like to know about the company?

4. Pick five items from the list in Box 7.2 and explain why you think it is important to know the information in terms of interviewing.

5. Talk to two friends or acquaintances who have recently gone through job interviews. Ask them about their experiences and what advice they would give you based on how their interviews went.

6. Why do you think most people do not send a thank-you letter as a follow-up to an interview?

7. Review the list of common interview topics presented in the chapter. Provide an explanation as to what you think employers would have to gain by your talking about these subjects. For example, why would they want to know how you chose the college that you attend?

8. What are some of the most important things that you would like an employer to ask you about in an interview? What are some strategies for conveying the information in case the employer does not ask you to address these specifically?

STUDIO Activities

Visit the *Guide to Fashion Career Planning STUDIO* available at www
.bloomsburyfashioncentral.com. The key elements are:

1. Summary of Chapter 7 text
2. Quiz
3. Typical interview questions worksheet
4. Interviewing outfits (examples and critique)
5. Interview schedule and follow-up log
6. Interview evaluation form
7. Thank you letter template
8. Professional dress websites
9. Interview assessment form

VIDEO: Interviewing

References

Chan, A. & Derry, T. Eds. (2013). A roadmap for transforming the college-to-career experience: Rethinking success. Available online: http://rethinkingsuccess.wfu .edu/files/2013/05/A-Roadmap-for-Transforming-The-College-to-Career -Experience.pdf

Blanton, D. (March 14, 2014). Fox News poll: Tattoos aren't just for rebels anymore. Available online: FoxNews.com

The perfect thank-you note. (2003, May 25). *Chicago Tribune* (Section 6, Career Builder), p. 1.

Radicati, S. Ed. (2013). Email statistics report 2013–2017. Available online: http:// www.radicati.com/wp/wp-content/uploads/2013/04/Email-Statistics-Report -2013-2017-Executive-Summary.pdf

CHAPTER 8
WORK EXPERIENCES AND INTERNSHIPS

The retail industry is competitive; a great internship can be the thing that sets you apart from the pack.

—AARON STURGILL, ASSISTANT DIRECTOR FOR HOSPITALITY, MERCHANDISING, AND RECREATION IN THE OHIO UNIVERSITY CAREER AND LEADERSHIP DEVELOPMENT CENTER

OBJECTIVES

- To learn about the dynamic fashion industry through hands-on experience and training.
- To develop a systematic career search strategy that results in work experience and internship opportunities that begin prior to or during college and continue after graduation.
- To understand the relationship between academic preparation and work experiences in the fashion industry.
- To apply career search strategies to real-life situations, resulting in industry placement.
- To learn how to interact in a professional manner within company structures.
- To enhance your professional profile, and your résumé, by participating in quality work experiences.
- To better identify your own professional strengths and weaknesses as applied to career preparation.
- To implement strategies that put your strengths and best skills to work for you.
- To develop a set of ambitious, yet realistic, professional goals regarding career planning based on work experiences that inform you.

Internships, co-operative education (co-ops), and work experiences have become commonplace for fashion students. In fact, according to the National Association of Colleges and Employers (NACE, 2015), 95% of employers consider the candidate's work experience when making hiring decisions. Katharine Hansen of Quintessential Careers states in her blog (www.quintcareers.com) that college students "simply must do an internship" (see Box 8.1). Furthermore, college and career center professionals report that students with internships hold strong competitive advantages in their job searches compared to students without internships ("Internship experience," 2010). Internships provide students with experiences related to their academic programs that help them "hit the ground running" when they begin their post-graduation jobs (Ashman, 2013).

Ideally, you will have hands-on work involvement—or even shadowing and observing opportunities—early in (or before) your college experience. The more and varied activities that you pursue as you are preparing yourself academically, the better equipped you will be when it is time to seek a post-graduation career position. The advantages of industry immersion extend from general knowledge of career possibilities to understanding of specific skills and expertise needed for certain jobs. In addition to career insights, people who engage in industry

---

BOX 8.1 Quintessential Careers: College Students: You Simply Must Do an Internship (Better Yet: Multiple Internships)!
by Katharine Hansen

1. Employers increasingly want to see experience in the new college grads they hire.
2. Employers increasingly see their internship programs as the best path for hiring entry-level candidates.
3. You may get paid more when you graduate if you've done one or more internships.
4. You could earn college credit toward your degree.
5. Internships enable you take your career plan for a test drive.
6. You'll gain valuable understanding of your major field and be better able to grasp how your coursework is preparing you to enter your chosen career.
7. You'll develop skills galore.
8. You'll gain confidence.
9. You'll build motivation and work habits.
10. You'll build your network.
11. You will build your résumé.
12. Growing numbers of colleges require internships.
13. You might make money.

Copyright by Quintessential Careers. The original article can be found at: http://www.quintcareers.com/internship_importance.html. Reprinted with permission.

experiences build their résumés, expand their networks of professional contacts, and enhance professional interaction abilities that improve interviewing talents.

Typically, *internships* are culminating work experiences that occur after a significant amount of coursework has been completed toward a major. Internships are generally "full-time" employment situations that last the duration of an academic term. Some colleges and universities make arrangements with companies for students to work in conjunction with their courses. These experiences are often called *co-ops*. Internships and co-ops are, in fact, work experiences. They are formal arrangements that recognize the educational component of experience in the industry. *Work experiences*, sometimes referred to as *field experiences*, are usually shorter in duration than an internship. Work experiences, as opposed to internships, might be weekends only, one week in duration, or project based. A work experience might be a temporary job undertaken during breaks from school. Despite the ways these terms can vary, in this chapter, the terms *internship*, *co-op*, and *work experience* are used interchangeably.

Box 8.2 contains some useful pointers regarding internships and how they add value to your professional profile. Table 8.1 presents a timeline with specific activities and related advice for the purpose of planning appropriate and sequential work experiences throughout your college career. Be sure to refer to the *Guide to Fashion Career Planning STUDIO* website (www.bloomsburyfashioncentral.com), which provides a list of websites that are good sources of leads for internship and work experience programs.

BOX 8.2 Internship 101: Tips and Techniques

The Value of Internships

- Employers sometimes value on-the-job experience more than your major or GPA (Fischer, 2013).
- You will be more competitive in the job market—more than 62 percent of college graduates in 2013 completed at least one internship or co-op (NACE, 2013). Additionally, 96 percent of the survey respondents agree/strongly agree that "students who graduate [from college] without an internship experience are at a competitive disadvantage in the current labor market" (Internships.com, 2010, p. 1).
- Many interns are hired into entry-level positions with the company. According to Internships.com (2010), in 2012, full-time jobs were offered to interns at 69% of companies with 100 or more employees. According to

continued

BOX 8.2 Internship 101: Tips and Techniques (continued)

Internships.com's Spring 2010 Survey of Career Center Professionals, 98 percent of respondents agreed that "employers favor students who have had an internship experience" over their peers who have not had an internship while in college.

Internship Search Tips

- Refer to your career goals when seeking internships.
- Seek information from fellow students who have completed internships.
- Keep your résumé updated as you gain experiences, including courses and new skills.
- Start planning your internship early. Plan more than one internship. Consider how each experience will contribute to your career goals and be prepared to explain that.
- Be open-minded—take a risk on a new place or job category.
- Contact prospective employers to let them know of your interest and to inquire about opportunities.
- Prepare for your interviews by practicing.
- Attend career fairs—even before you are ready to actually apply for internships.
- After interviews, follow up with employers, including sending thank-you notes.
- Assess which opportunities are best for you.
- Ensure that you have as much information as possible (and that it is accurate) about what the internships entail as you consider offers.
- Be prepared to negotiate start and end dates that fit your school calendar.
- Look at your internship(s) as a long interview!

Resources for Internships

- Career and leadership centers on your college campus
- Company websites
- Internship-focused websites
- Web search—enter "fashion internships"
- Publications such as company newsletters, sorority and fraternity magazines, trade journals, and student organization newsletters
- Alumni organizations
- Friends and acquaintances
- Classmates
- LinkedIn discussion groups

TABLE 8.1

TIMELINE FOR EXECUTING
AN INTERNSHIP SEARCH STRATEGY

Time frame	Activity	Tips for implementation

One year in advance of your planned internship	Create a database of prospective internship sites	• Use the Internet to explore many options and opportunities
		
		• Copy and paste websites into your database for quick future reference
		
		• Set up a spreadsheet that includes information such as:
		
		  • is a formal internship offered
		  • compensation for interns (or employees)
		  • whether there are future entry-level positions available for interns
		  • whether (and at what cost) housing is provided
		  • deadline for applications (and seasons in which internship is offered—e.g., summer only; summer & fall, etc.)
		
		• Compare your goals with the experiences offered by each internship site

6 to 8 months in advance of planned internship	Refine your résumé and cover letter; seek advice and feedback from people you trust about your application materials	
6 months in advance of internship	Send application materials to prospective companies	• Most applications will be electronic, so create a folder in your email to save all correspondence (BCC yourself or move items from your SEND folder) • Develop an internship search calendar—note the dates that you submit applications and add notes that prompt you to follow up to check the status of your application

continued

TABLE 8.1

TIMELINE FOR EXECUTING
AN INTERNSHIP SEARCH STRATEGY *(CONTINUED)*

Ideally 3–5 months prior to your internship	Set up interviews	There is a high likelihood that your diligent effort to submit internship applications will result in requests for interviews. Be prepared to participate in telephone interviews. • Prior to the interviews, be sure that you have carefully reviewed the specific company's website • Prepare a list of relevant questions (for which the answers are not readily available on the Internet) • Follow up each interview with a thank-you note (generally email is fine)
Ideally 3–5 months prior to your internship	Consider your offers	Create a spreadsheet that lists comparative information about your offers, including: your fit with the company culture (review your code of ethics and the company's mission, vision, values, and ethics statements); compensation (including potentially housing and food); costs of housing, food, and living; opportunities for advancement beyond the internship; geographic location; whether this is a new learning opportunity or a more familiar experience (and your value of that); diversity of the workplace; workplace climate
Approximately 1–3 months before the internship start date	Make a decision	
Between the time you accept the internship and your start date	Be sure to stay in touch with the company	• Request the offer in writing • Be sure to accept in writing (and save responses/confirmations) • Submit updates—make inquiries about your living arrangements • Engage in conversations with your direct supervisor about your goals; request feedback and ideas for revision and addition • Several weeks in advance, be sure to contact the company and confirm your start date (and time)

UNDERSTANDING THE VALUE
OF WORK EXPERIENCES

Work experience, whether it is a structured internship, temporary employment over school breaks, or a part-time job in addition to your coursework, enables you to learn and practice professional behaviors, gain insight into the fashion industry's myriad career opportunities, develop leadership and time management skills, identify your focused career interests, and apply knowledge that you have gained in your courses. Susan Strickler (2001) surveyed retail students who had graduated from South Dakota State University during a 30-year timespan to determine the value of work experiences toward their career positions. She found that three skills learned during the work experience—stress tolerance, leadership, and organization—were related to their current positions. In 2010, Jessica Hurst and Linda Good reviewed scholarly literature about internships during a 20-year period. They observed five themes (2010, p. 176) regarding internships that are important to consider:

- Internships are a recruiting tool.
- Internships are increasingly endorsed by retailers and educators.
- Internships are sometimes unpaid; the legality of hiring non-paid interns can be an issue for companies.
- Internship programs have been restructured.
- Internships create social structures for the student interns.

These themes resonate with observations and advice about internships offered by students, recent graduates, established career professionals, and industry recruiters.

Today, all students should take advantage of the benefits of temporary employment, such as internships or summer break jobs, especially so that career options—ranging among design, product development, store management, merchandising and buying, brand representation and sales, and visual merchandising—can be experienced firsthand. In addition to providing you with a supplemental income, work experiences allow students to explore various facets of the industry, get a foot in the door with companies where future employment is desirable, and learn firsthand some practical elements of professional development. Work experiences have the potential to introduce diverse experiences that will enhance your résumé and strengthen your professional profile. Your initiative to take on a variety of work experiences demonstrates your desire to learn and grow in a professional direction. See Careers Up Close 8.1, which highlights the way Melissa Martin parlayed an internship into an exciting career in product development.

CAREERS UP CLOSE 8.1
MELISSA MARTIN
Executive Director
Phi Upsilon Omicron, Inc.

A career in product development transitioned to Melissa Martin's current role as Executive Director for the national honor society Phi Upsilon Omicron. This exciting career path began with a prestigious internship with the Textile/Clothing Technology Corporation [TC]² (see www.tc2 .com/). Melissa reflects that the comprehensive nature of her design, merchandising, and textiles program at Western Kentucky University provided the breadth of knowledge she needed in her career, though she personally was more interested in technical design, pattern development, and textile science. She notes that her minor in consumer and family sciences and her leadership in the national honor society Phi Upsilon Omicron (Phi U) further enhanced her résumé. Her Phi U professional service project advisor and mentor encouraged her to apply for a [TC]² internship—an opportunity Melissa would not have pursued without the guidance and suggestion by a former faculty member.

The [TC]² internship program brought ten apparel/textile students from across the US to Cary, NC, for the summer. Melissa recalls being nervous and outside of her comfort zone, but nevertheless, she pushed her fears aside, hopped in the car, and embarked on an amazing educational adventure! This internship program focused on product development technologies, industry supply chain

management, and business planning concepts. [TC]² developed the first 3D Body Scanner utilizing white light technology. There are numerous notable companies who are members of [TC]², including Jockey, Target, Cotton Incorporated, L Brands, and Brooks Brothers. The final project of Melissa's internship was to work in groups to make a Business Plan Proposal to real-world professionals and representatives from member companies. It wasn't your average "class" project—it was an exceptional experience. Going into her internship, Melissa had no idea how much she would get out of it. She reports that, "The icing on the cake was the opportunity to network with top business professionals in the industry. I was able to obtain business cards and could now list actual people on my cover letter and résumé. I applied for jobs everywhere and was happy to name drop if it meant I could at least get called for an interview."

Melissa's career path includes substantial product development work, which she had the skills and network to secure largely because of her internship. Her entry into a post-graduation career and her route to her current leadership position as Executive Director of Phi Upsilon Omicron have taken some twists and turns. Melissa describes her journey:

"After completing my internship, I discovered what most college graduates encounter: I was expected to have 'experience' to get the job . . . but I needed someone to hire me to get more experience. You can graduate Summa Cum Laude and be ready to take on the world, but unfortunately, that doesn't mean you will land your dream job right out of the gate. For those that do—kudos! You are one of the few. For the rest of us, it's about work ethic, paying your dues, putting in the time, and gaining the respect of peers and management alike. Networking and 'who you know' will certainly help land you the interview. However, 'what you know,' your personality style, and interviewing skills will be what get you the job.

"If I'm being honest, one of the best things to happen to me was rejection. Humility can teach you a lot. Through my contacts, I was called for a job in Bayonne, New Jersey, to interview for Maidenform. I was elated! It was my first 'career' interview. They paid for my plane ticket, sent a fancy car to pick me up, and catered in lunch—the works! But I wasn't ready for a position of that caliber, and they could quickly tell, I'm sure. Although I didn't get that job, I still learned a lesson. From there I spent a couple of months applying feverishly for jobs and decided to reach out to my former collegiate and Phi U advisor. She had great working connections with Fruit of the Loom, Inc., a local company to my area. She encouraged me to apply for an entry-level position and was gracious to give me a positive referral. I admittedly had no idea of the scope and reach of this company that was 'in my backyard.' I was interviewed by eleven people over the course of a day, but this time I was prepared! I ditched the cookie-cutter answers, decided to approach the interview as a real and capable future asset, and was later hired as the Assistant Product Manager for Intimate Apparel. Now, I didn't start at the pay level I had always dreamed of and most of my early days were spent measuring underwear—but it gave me a foot in the door and a chance to prove myself. After one year, I was promoted to Associate Product Manager for

Intimate Apparel. It was an exciting time for Fruit of the Loom as Vanity Fair Intimates and Russell Athletic Brands were acquired. As the transition of these brands took place, I saw an opportunity to once again test the limits of my comfort zone. I applied (and this time had experience) and was hired to be the Product Manager for Russell Athletic Team Sports. I quickly went from developing ladies' underwear to collegiate football uniforms. It was an uncertain career move, but proved to be one of my favorite jobs. There was so much to learn, and I enjoyed the challenge and new opportunities. I worked with a great team. So, when I was approached by the company I had interned with about applying for a position—I was humbled and honored, but respectfully declined. I was settled and happy!

"As time went on, I decided that it was time for me to open up to the possibility of my next career move. As luck would have it, I was approached by a former Fruit of the Loom co-worker—and once fellow student—about a job opening with another local company. It was a licensing and branding company, Lifeguard Press, Inc. They had recently signed a contract with designer brand Kate Spade New York and were looking for someone to help with product development and in the support role to the Senior Brand Manager. This position would get me closer to a designer brand than I had ever been but would also take me out of the textiles industry. However, I decided to go for it and was hired as the Product Development Manager. I enjoyed working in such a creative environment and traveling to KSNY offices for presentations. I learned many new things in the area of gifts, stationery, melamine, acrylics, etc., but I still longed for a challenge."

Life often comes full circle. In 2014, Melissa was approached by her Phi U mentors about an interesting career move—to her current position as Executive Director. Melissa notes that her fashion industry career provided the foundation for her to play a role in helping collegiate members realize their potential by serving and supporting the honor society. Melissa's most recent career move provides more flexibility with her young and growing family while keeping each day new and challenging.

Many companies offer internship placements within their organizational structures. It is an advantage for both you and your employer to enter into a work experience arrangement that has a definite starting and ending point—risk is reduced for the employer, who now has a "trial period" to evaluate an employee, and risk is reduced for you, in case you wish to change work environments in a relatively short period of time. While many employment opportunities give preference to a full-time, permanent employee, most employers recognize the value of providing an environment in which a future professional can learn.

An internship should be viewed as a long interview. Think about the parallels—the company has a long (typically 10 to 15 weeks) time to observe and evaluate your work habits and skills, while you also have that period of time to determine whether the particular company or position is right for you. Savvy employers use internships as screening tools that can lead to entry-level positions for top performers. No brief interview can compare to the in-depth observations an employer can make of an intern. Real knowledge of an employee's work habits, attitude, and interpersonal skills is extremely valuable, considering that employers will make a significant financial investment in the people whom they hire.

As a student who seeks a career in a competitive industry, your ability to build your résumé through participation in a variety of hands-on work experiences will reflect well on your future career prospects. A temporary work experience will enable you to take risks that you might not take with a permanent commitment. For example, many merchandising students seek internships in New York City. The location at the heart of the industry and the pace of the city make an experience there desirable. New York City, however, is a big change of culture for many students, who might be unsure of a permanent (or at least long-term) move there. With an internship, you can forge ahead with a temporary experience that exposes you to new environments and excellent learning opportunities without the risk of being stuck in a job or a city that is not a good fit.

It is not wise to commit to a permanent employment position that you are uncertain about. In the long run, it can be detrimental to your career to job hop too much. An internship provides a win-win situation in which you can embark on a temporary "test run"—in a certain segment of the industry, in a new city, or with an unfamiliar employer. Likewise, the employing company does not need to make a permanent or long-term commitment to you. A recent student landed offers for the top two internship sites on his list. He was torn between the two—each offered compensation, good benefits, and new learning experiences that were different from one another and located at opposite sides of the United States. Both opportunities would provide new geographic experiences as well. He re-evaluated the internships' availabilities and realized that one was offered in both summer and fall. In the end, he successfully negotiated postponing one internship until fall, and he embarked on the summer-only internship as originally planned. He learned, upon inquiry, that his résumé and interview had successfully positioned him to negotiate, and the company offering multiple internship schedules was delighted to accommodate his request. Two internships later, he has the benefit of twice the networking, experience, and insight from which to make his first longer-term, entry-level career decision.

An internship is a great way for you to get your foot in the door, particularly in a competitive job market. An intern who proves that he or she is a valuable asset to the company is often first in line when a permanent position becomes available. Experience in a working relationship between the intern and the company considerably lowers the risk of an offer to both parties. The company knows whom it is hiring, in terms of performance expectations and abilities, and you know what the environment is like and whether you have found a good fit for your career aspirations. Morgan Baker (see Careers Up Close 8.2) knew that internships could provide the networking and insight that she needed to plan her post-graduation career. Through her internships, she was able to clarify the work environment that felt best for her, and she had the network and experience to be a successful candidate for her position with the J. C. Penney Company as an Assistant Buyer Trainee. Jeromy Coleman used an internship opportunity to explore New York City, and then he parlayed that experience into a full-time position in Columbus, Ohio—a city he decided was a better fit for him as a permanent home. (See Jeromy's profile in Careers Up Close 4.1 in Chapter 4.) On the other hand, Hannah Klein used an internship in New York as a test to confirm that she wanted to move there permanently upon graduation.

CAREERS UP CLOSE 8.2
MORGAN BAKER
Assistant Buyer Trainee
JCPenney

Morgan Baker always knew she had a knack for fashion, but early on she wasn't sure what she wanted to do for a career. When thinking about selecting a college major, Morgan's search to discover her true passion led to a breakthrough realization—she loved shopping. She recognized the pleasure that shopping experiences hold for her—quality time with her mom, problem-solving that happens during customer service interactions, and even elements of applied mathematics. When Morgan enrolled in the fashion merchandising program at Texas State (where she also earned a minor in business administration), she delighted in her first textiles course and was confident that she would gain the knowledge and experiences she needed to reach her goal of being a buyer. In addition to the classes, Morgan was determined to expand her profile by participating in multiple work experiences.

During her sophomore year, Morgan worked as a Merchandise Team Associate at Saks Off Fifth at the Outlets in San Marcos. There, she learned the back of the house functions within a store. Morgan reports, "I quickly began working on the sets and displays in the store front. I was able to hone in on how merchandise visual representation can impact sales, by putting looks together on mannequins as well as strategically filling the sales floor."

Morgan applied to and was accepted for the JCPenney® Emerging Leader Program, which she completed during the summer prior to junior year. This ten-week Leader-In-Training Program prepares students for the roles and responsibilities of a leader on the store management team. Morgan shares an impressive range of experiences gained from this program: "I performed on and off the floor in managerial positions, worked as a member of HR, created sets, interacted with customers, and led a sales team. I was able to conduct interviews to find new talented associates for the store. Interns work closely with the Merchandise Execution Leader to create visuals, understand brand strategies, and learn product knowledge and specifications to help target current and potential customers. As my big project, I spearheaded the new Joe Fresh Kid's brand rollout in the store, where I was in charge of everything from setting the newly remodeled empty sales floor to organizing employee shifts to complete the rollout. I also helped lead a philanthropy event for the entire district to benefit the North Texas Food Bank."

Morgan realized that an in-store internship provided a strong foundation for her professional profile; she "wanted to know the ins and outs of everything so I could fully understand how my decisions as a buyer would trickle down into a store. JCPenney was an ideal candidate because they were going through many changes when I interned for them and I was able to see how a big box retailer department store reacts to the changing demand of the retail environment."

Morgan notes that her academic preparation, particularly a Buying Principles class, helped her understand the business side of the store. She reflects that pulling reports and seeing the numbers come to life in a real setting put the pieces together of how success works in the retail world. Additionally, the internship included leadership experience. Morgan reports, "I was given the responsibility of leading a team that was 100+ people, an opportunity that I probably could not have been given anywhere else. It was humbling to see all the work and time the employees put into making the store run, and it helped me appreciate what they do."

The summer after Morgan's junior year, she embarked on a second internship at Michaels Support Center (Corporate Office). As a Merchandising Intern, she completed a ten-week structured program that prepares participants for entry-level positions in the buying office as a Category Administrative Associate. Morgan aided all departments in the Framing Division, which includes Table Top Frames, Wall Frames, Wall Decor, and Regional Merchandise. Her responsibilities included setting up SKU information for new products in the system, collaborating with marketing/advertising teams on the production of ads, updating forecasting sheets and assortment plans, and assisting with the setup of new planograms at the Model Store. Her biggest project was to lead the development and execution of a Speed to Market program, using two themes and sixty-four total test stores. Morgan drew from all of her prior experiences as she worked through the product cycle all the way from development to placing the products in stores for customers.

Morgan was able to compare and contrast the two work environments and discovered that the fundamentals learned in stores really helped her succeed in a buying role. "I was able to understand the numbers and statistics we used in making decisions because I used them in evaluating sales reports in stores. The leadership roles I played really developed my confidence so that I was able to take on these huge projects at Michaels comfortably. While the experiences were both in different settings, team work was still a huge common theme." Her multiple experiences helped solidify her goal to become a buyer. Morgan has begun the Assistant Buyer Trainee program where, upon completion, she will be placed in a department as an Assistant Buyer. Morgan approaches her career opportunities with enthusiasm, with aspirations to continue down the buying path and ultimately reach higher leadership positions in the industry.

You have an opportunity to apply concepts that you have learned in your academic program to real-life situations on the job. Jodie Tuchman, who completed an internship with Neiman Marcus in Troy, Michigan, commented that as a result of the job responsibilities associated with her internship, she was better at solving problems. Jodie explained that in her sales position, she was responsible for customer satisfaction when assigned to the selling floor. On one occasion, Jodie had a mother-of-the-bride client who had been expecting an altered dress. The mother-of-the-bride's dress, unfortunately, was not ready when promised, and Jodie had to deal with the situation. She knew that it was her responsibility to provide a satisfactory shopping experience to the customer, so she was required to think on her feet and implement a workable solution to the dilemma at hand. The sales experience that empowered her to solve problems served as a strong foundation for a lucrative career with H. Stern. Similarly, Leah Rogers recalls learning practical skills in college classes that she parlayed into problem-solving skills as a styling intern in Los Angeles. She reflects that early on, learning that "no" is never the answer was an important and pivotal point that has provided a strong foundation for a successful career managing brand identity (see Leah's profile in Careers Up Close 3.1 in Chapter 3). In her leadership roles and interpersonal relationships, Leah knows that it is not an option tell her clients that something cannot be done; rather, she offers multiple suggestions of alternative possibilities—creating positive and opportunity-driven workplace solutions.

HOW TO IDENTIFY APPROPRIATE INTERNSHIPS AND WORK EXPERIENCES

You will have many decisions to make regarding career preparation in the dynamic fashion industry. As we have mentioned in previous chapters, the career niches available for employment are virtually endless. You may be curious about the work environment of a corporate office, you may be well served to expand your experience at the store level, you may want the opportunity to experience a showroom atmosphere or work for a well-known design house, or you might find success as a stylist. It is important for you to refer to your short-term goals, review your résumé, and identify areas of strength and weakness as you strategize your work experience and internship plans. You should consider the types of tasks in your workplace environment as well as the people—and be sure to look for experiences where you can network and find mentors. See Careers Up Close 8.3, where MacKenzie King shares the ways her academic experiences played into her internship placement.

It is becoming commonplace for design, retail, and fashion merchandising students to engage in multiple internships, largely because of the great diversity of job opportunities and the interrelationships common among various jobs. The dynamic nature of the fashion industry makes it a challenge for students to obtain in-depth and well-rounded practical experiences. Thus, the greater the variety and quantity of work experiences and internships that students secure, the more competitive they will be in their career searches. As you prepare to make applications for work experiences, refer to the guidelines presented in Box 8.3, which are particularly relevant when visiting stores. Box 8.4 contains insight into best practices and expectation for merchandising internships compiled by Linda Good, Professor of Retailing at Michigan State University.

CAREERS UP CLOSE 8.3
MACKENZIE KING
Assistant Manager of Business Strategies
American Eagle Outfitters

MacKenzie King realized that she had experience and skills that set her apart from other students—and she was able to successfully promote these unique attributes in ways that opened doors to career opportunities. As she sought an internship, the accomplishment of completing an honors thesis was relevant and impressive. MacKenzie reflects that her honors thesis, "Preschool Boys' and Girls' Clothing Choices: Investigating Their Participation and Influences," was a key reason she secured a prestigious merchandising internship at American Eagle Outfitters. She notes that companies do not just look at majors and GPA; they are looking for something that sets you apart from the rest of the applicants. In fact, her research emphasis on children's clothing strongly supported her internship placement with the (experimental at the time) American Eagle children's brand, 77Kids.

Following her internship, MacKenzie joined American Eagle Outfitters as an assistant buyer for Aerie in the bra department, where she worked for the next two years.

This solid entry-level buying experience positioned MacKenzie for her next and current opportunity as assistant manager of business strategies at American Eagle's outlet division. In this role, she has a more global view of the business. Rather than focusing on a single product, MacKenzie is responsible for analyzing the total store performance; she compiles financials to inform decisions about the most productive placement of products floorsets and maps floorsets to optimize both aesthetics and sales, selects products for promotional photo shoots, and develops store training materials.

MacKenzie thrives on the opportunity to make decisions on behalf of her company. She has transitioned into a role of supervisor and mentor, noting that interns must exhibit hard work, determination, and organization. Buying and merchandising require a great deal of analysis—and tedious re-analysis—that informs daily decisions. In her words, "Having a voice and an educated opinion about the product is what sets you apart from other interns. Financials are typically easy to teach and learn, but you often cannot teach someone to be outspoken and to have a voice. Merchants need to be able to present and defend their business plans to executives."

Caron Stover completed an internship in the Fashion Office at AmericasMart in Atlanta 2002 and has continued a career there; she now holds the title of Vice President–Apparel Tradeshows. Caron notes that there are many opportunities to gain experience in the field, and she suggests that students look for opportunities everywhere—go to stores or malls and ask to help with fashion shows, inquire at stores about the possibility of working there or helping with special projects that might be underway, especially seasonally. Once you have secured a work experience, Caron urges students to make their opportunities worthwhile. She suggests, "Put effort into it and apply it to your future!" Caron advises students to be strategic with the experiences that are secured by giving back to the company what they gave you in an opportunity; then you can move on to other companies and new experiences. She also encourages students to document what they do during a work experience. She suggests that measurable outcomes, such as increased sales volume, press reports, and letters of commendation can be presented in a portfolio and as points of interest in an interview.

The most basic of all experiences necessary for success in the fashion, retailing, merchandising, and design industry are in-store. Morgan

---

BOX 8.3 Job Search and Application Guidelines

When Asking for an Application . . .

1. Dress nicely. Even if employees wear jeans, *you* should dress more professionally.
2. Don't chew gum!
3. Bring your own pen if you plan to fill out the application there.
4. Don't call. Come in person to request an application.
5. Come to get the application yourself. Don't send your parents or a friend.
6. Come in alone. Don't bring friends, children, a boyfriend, or anyone else.
7. Speak as if you would like to have the job.
8. Never speak negatively about your last job.
9. Bring a notebook, PDA, or tablet. Write down information such as when to come back, who to talk to, and (hopefully) the date and time of an interview.
10. Bring a résumé.
11. Be enthusiastic and sincere.
12. If there is a line at the desk, don't get in line; instead, wait until there is no line. If there is never no line, you have come at a bad time, but . . . they are likely to need your help!
13. If you don't qualify for the position, thank the manager anyway and inquire about future opportunities.

On the Application . . .

1. Always fill in something for academic and professional activities and honors if you can. If you have none, work on developing some *now!*
2. For hobbies and activities, put something constructive—*not* "watching TV," "going out," "having fun," etc. (No kidding—these items have appeared on applications!)
3. Be honest about previous experience. References *will* be checked.
4. Print *neatly.*
5. Avoid crumpling or staining the form before you return it.

Baker offers valuable insight, observing, "If someone is going into merchandising and desires to be in a corporate office, whether it's buying, planning or allocating, I would suggest working in a store. To make the best business decisions, you have to understand how your actions will affect the store, which is the face of the company for customers. You are given great responsibilities, learn how to work with and direct a team, and help drive sales for the success of the company. Also, you may find this is where your passion lies and therefore it can benefit you in a great way! Overall, in-store experience really lays the ground work for success in becoming a buyer."

We agree with Morgan's advice and encourage all aspiring fashion professionals to seek significant in-store experiences. These will provide a foundation for growth and knowledge about the customer, about how a workplace functions, and insight into all other facets of the industry. The customer service, personal selling interactions, and hands-on experience with merchandise in the customer transaction phase of retailing are essential. Many corporate office positions—in buying, product development and design, merchandising, and promotions—expect, and often require, prior store experiences. In fact, some internships and entry-level corporate positions build in-store experiences into their training programs.

The type of internship environment is an important consideration that may affect your satisfaction with the experience, but don't be too limited in the options you consider. Morgan Baker emphasizes, "Everyone has a dream job, a company they want to work for, a place they want to be. If you want to get there, you have to work hard for it. You have to take jobs you may not want to because *everyone starts at the bottom*. If you don't keep yourself open to all opportunities, you may end up empty handed. Don't discount the importance of a job or internship based on the company, because it may shoot you into a direction of something better." Paulins (2008) conducted a study among 242 merchandising students who completed internships at stores, corporate settings, and other types of places, such as in showrooms, with stylists, or in PR divisions. In this study, there were significant differences for interns' satisfaction among the types of sites. Specifically, the variety of activities, ability to achieve closure with tasks, autonomy, networking opportunities, and feedback received from supervisors were criteria that contributed to satisfying internships. In this study, corporate offices most consistently offered internships that provided activities resulting in student satisfaction; however, all environments have the potential to do so. In fact, all three internship placement categories were associated with relatively high levels of student satisfaction. Therefore, you should ask about the types of activities and tasks provided and expected in your potential internships.

Seek to obtain internships in environments where you are most likely to receive the opportunities noted here.

Furthermore, as Melissa Martin observes, most employers want to teach you "their" way of doing things before you are positioned to propose new solutions and make decisions. She encourages interns to "share your skill set, but also share how willing and eager you are to learn." Whether in a store, corporate office, or other setting, be sure to be attentive to learning the culture of the place where you are.

There is simply no replacement for the first-hand knowledge and experience of contributing to effectively displaying and selling merchandise in stores. In-store work experiences provide insight into customer needs and demands, effective merchandising techniques and store layouts, and consumer product preferences. In addition, the knowledge developed in the management aspect of a store environment directly transfers to any environmental situation. Keep in mind that without the final point at which merchandise trades hands between the retailer and the consumer (traditionally in a store), all of the other aspects of merchandising would be moot. Even in this age in which more and more merchandise is sold in non-store formats, such as via television, the Internet, telephone, and direct in-home sales, the experience of interacting with many customers in a store environment is irreplaceable and should be valued as a career-enhancing opportunity.

If you have little or no in-store experience, seek a work experience in a store early in your academic career. There is simply no substitute for the hands-on knowledge that can be gained about the retail industry, about fashion products, and about your personal interests and skills. Many times students are surprised by the value that is immediately apparent in a store work experience or internship. There is a tendency for students to associate in-store work with low-level tasks; however, store leadership programs truly provide interns and managers with strategic problem-solving responsibilities. Additionally, Aaron Sturgill reflects that in the retail store environment, there are constant problems to solve—and you never know what problem will emerge on a given day. He notes that there is fun and satisfaction in the process of organizing chaos and solving problems within the constraints of company policy. (See Aaron's Careers Up Close 2.2 profile in Chapter 2.)

Beyond an in-store work experience, the variety and scope of other retail and apparel merchandising internships available are extensive! Virtually all of the career avenues mentioned in Chapter 1 lend themselves to work experience and internship opportunities. Your own interests and initiative set the limits for your experiences as opportunities abound.

COMPENSATION FOR WORK EXPERIENCES AND INTERNSHIPS

One of the most perplexing questions with respect to internship and work experience decisions have to do with compensation. According to Hal Ashman (2013) and a NACE report (2013), students with paid internships report engaging in more professionally relevant workplace activities than students in non-paid internships. For interns in the fashion industry, images from *The Devil Wears Prada* fuel the reputation of mundane and clerical tasks associated with entry-level work. Interestingly, though, in Paulins' (2008) study, while store-based internships were associated with greater levels of satisfaction with pay, compensation itself did not affect the level of satisfaction students had with their internships overall. It is important to carefully analyze your own goals and expectations of an internship site—and be selective as well as realistic. You want to go into an internship with accurate expectations of what you will do and what you will learn. Some non-paid experiences are worth the investment in learning, access to future opportunities, and networking. Other experiences may not be a good fit for your needs.

In 2010, the US Department of Labor updated the Fair Labor Standards Act (originally established in 1938) to include internship programs. Their "Fact Sheet #71: Internship Programs Under the Fair Labor Standards Act" presents six criteria, all of which must be met, to ensure that unpaid interns are not, in fact, simply unpaid employees (which is illegal). These criteria are:

1. The internship, even though it includes actual operation of the facilities of the employer, is similar to training that would be given in an educational environment.
2. The internship experience is for the benefit of the intern.
3. The intern does not displace regular employees, but works under close supervision of existing staff.
4. The employer that provides the training derives no immediate advantage from the activities of the intern, and on occasion its operations may actually be impeded.
5. The intern is not necessarily entitled to a job at the conclusion of the internship.
6. The employer and the intern understand that the intern is not entitled to wages for the time spent in the internship.

Will the experience generate an income for you? This is often a highly personal issue—and a variety of factors play into the necessities of compensation. Negotiation of the terms of your internship, including compensation, takes thought and preparation on your part. The following are some points to consider when making a decision to embark on experiences without compensation.

Value of the Experience

Just as you are making an investment in yourself by earning an academic degree, you are afforded the opportunity to invest in yourself and your future career through completing a work experience. You should consider the value of the experience as you consider the need for compensation. Consider the return on your investment of time when you determine the level of compensation that you need to receive.

Type and Duration of Experience

By definition, a work experience is likely to be more project-based and limited than a full-fledged internship. There are many possibilities for a short-term work experience that may not be worth the investment of a company to compensate you. On the other hand, an internship that involves significant preparation on your part, training and education by the company, and a relatively long-term commitment is more likely to be compensated. Both internships and work experiences can be found for varying lengths of time. In fact, you may embark upon a work experience that is a regular part-time (or even full-time) job. Experiences such as these should certainly be compensated. On the other hand, you may seek a short-term experience that complements a course you are taking (or is a requirement for a course), enhances an area of knowledge that you wish to improve, or provides a unique opportunity that will set you apart from other career candidates. In such cases, you may be willing to forgo compensation.

Internships in segments of the industry such as design houses and public relations firms are almost never paid, while in-store internships are almost always compensated. Furthermore, a short-term, temporary work experience—such as a practicum experience with a total of 40 hours—is much less likely to be compensated than a ten-week, 40-hour-per-week internship.

Your Expenses

The cost of living is a reality of life—and venturing to a new city can be expensive. If you are relocating, you will likely have housing, transportation, and food expenses to cover. You will need to consider whether you can afford the financial investment of these items without compensation from the internship.

Your Contribution to the Company

Consider what your contribution to the day-to-day operations of the company will be. Would the company need to pay someone else to do the job tasks you are doing if you weren't there? If you are assuming an integral role for the company, it is more appropriate to be compensated than if you are an "extra" who is provided an opportunity to primarily observe and learn. Interns who are directly involved in sales generate direct revenue for their companies and are much more likely to receive compensation than interns who fill more peripheral roles.

Competition Level

What is the level of competition for entry-level positions in the particular segment of the industry you are targeting? When entry-level positions are scarce and the field is highly competitive, the investment in work experience without compensation is a better risk than for an industry segment where career positions are plentiful.

Your Goals

How much do you want to engage in the work or internship experience being considered? The fit between what the work opportunity offers and your own career goals is important. The bottom line in decision making should revolve around what you want to do—if you have career aspirations that require this type of experience, you should be more willing to embark on the experience and forgo compensation. If you are offered an internship that is not of particular interest to you and you won't be compensated, you may prefer to keep looking for an alternative opportunity.

BOX 8.4 Best Practices and Expectations for Merchandising Internships

Companies' Expectations of Interns

- Before starting the internship, learn as much about the company as possible by doing extensive company research.
- Do more than you are required to do. Be productive and stay busy. Demonstrate initiative.

- Observe everything. Watch how the "seasoned" employees operate. Analyze why some individuals are more effective and efficient than others.
- Some of the work you do will be routine, but important. Do the routine things as willingly and professionally as

continued

you do the more complex, challenging, and interesting work.

- Read and follow the company rules and policies. They are usually posted; if not, ask.
- Work with your supervisor to find out what your work includes and what your responsibilities are. Ask questions.
- Listen carefully and take notes when you are given verbal instructions. This eliminates the need to ask again at a later date and ensures accuracy during completion of assignments.
- When you are ready for more challenging work, approach your supervisor with some suggestions for potential new responsibilities rather than waiting for the supervisor to suggest new ones.
- Set high standards for yourself. Work as accurately, safely, and quickly as you can.
- Learn from your mistakes; do not try to cover up.
- Have confidence in your ideas. Present them at appropriate times.
- Be tactful; do not offend others. Be friendly, show respect, be honest, and be polite.
- Learn to accept constructive criticism and implement strategies to improve performance.
- At the end of the internship, develop a draft of your updated résumé listing the internship and discuss it with your supervisor.

Expectations of Companies Providing Internships

- Conduct an official introduction of the intern to the management team, identifying the intern's role, position, and responsibilities so other employees are aware of and understand the role of the intern.
- Meet with the intern weekly to discuss training progress and concerns, project status, and developmental opportunities. Provide the intern with specific examples of his or her strengths and weaknesses. Ask the intern for feedback on the internship experience.
- Train the intern with company systems (computer, receiving, etc.).
- Provide the intern with opportunities for the analysis and understanding of company or departmental records.
- When possible, prepare the intern to communicate with vendors, buyers, and purchasing agents.
- Include the intern in company management and district or regional management meetings (or both).
- Include the intern in the processes of management and scheduling of sales associates.
- Expose the intern to advertising, promotion, and public relations activities.
- Assign the intern responsibility for specific projects or departments. Example: Track sales for a department for a period of time (e.g., ten weeks), make inventory suggestions, sales technique suggestions, display suggestions, and other appropriate actions.
- Provide the intern with exposure and experience in all functional areas of the company.
- Involve the intern in pricing and markdown procedures (retail interns).

- Involve the intern in merchandising and display (retail interns).
- Involve the intern in the hiring and selection process.
- Provide the intern with training in sales techniques (or other appropriate functions) and the opportunity to eventually help in the training of new hires.
- At the end of the internship, assist the intern in developing a list of appropriate responsibilities to use when updating the résumé with the internship experience.

Source: Linda K. Good, Professor of Retailing, Michigan State University. Reprinted with permission.

Ultimately, the decision about whether to be compensated for a particular work experience or internship is yours to make. You will need to be strategic with your decision and calculate the opportunity costs of the investment of your time. It is a calculated risk on your part when you embark on an unpaid experience, but the advantage of getting your foot in the door may be well worth the forgone compensation. Keep in mind that any experience you undertake is an investment in your future career.

GATHERING INFORMATION

Resources abound for internship opportunities—and the fields of fashion design, retailing, and apparel merchandising are particularly ripe with a variety of work experience possibilities. The sooner that you begin learning about internship and work experience opportunities that are available, the better equipped you will be to position yourself as a top candidate to secure the positions you desire. For short-term work experiences, a search time frame of a year in advance to immediately preceding your experience may be appropriate. Internship searches should generally be initiated one year in advance of, and no less than six months prior to, your planned experience.

A few key resources are a necessity for you to use in order to arrive at a comprehensive choice of internships and work experiences.

- Teachers and professors
- Career Services office
- Career fairs
- Internet
- Publications
- Previous students/students who are more senior than you
- Previous employers
- Friends and family members
- First-hand inquiry

While we believe strongly that what you know is very important and will propel you forward in your chosen career, it is true that the people whom you know are valuable resources—right at your fingertips. Take advantage of the contacts that can be made through personal networking. Often these are the people who know you best, and who have a good knowledge of your skills and abilities. Kelly Burt Deasy (see Careers Up Close 6.1 in Chapter 6) observes that in her career, from the internship on, the people with whom she has worked—and therefore networked— have been her most significant connections to new career opportunities. Because of workplace interactions, these contact people know firsthand her work ethic, strengths, and experiences. The people who can speak well for you and recommend you in a complimentary way are the best kind of references!

Firsthand inquiry works particularly well for in-store experiences because access is so simple. Dress professionally, carry a portfolio with extra copies of your résumé, be prepared to articulate what your goals are and what type of work experience you are seeking, and visit store locations to speak with managers and gather information. Business cards that direct prospective employers to your online portfolio and website can support your professional presentation. You have an opportunity to make a great first impression through your professional appearance and behaviors. Be sure to observe the workplace atmosphere—if it is a busy time, return when the manager can give attention to you. (See Box 8.3.)

Your preliminary research will yield information regarding whether or not companies that are of interest to you offer formal internship experiences. If a company doesn't offer an internship, don't pass them by. You may be able to be instrumental in starting a program or at least gain experience in a "non-structured" internship.

Keep in mind that the search process, including information gathering and interviewing, is a two-way street. You are searching for an opportunity that fits well into your areas of interest, your career goals, and your personal needs, just as the prospective companies are evaluating the fit you make in fulfilling their needs. The better you have identified what specifically you are looking for in a work experience—what your goals are, where you want to live, what type of company culture you feel comfortable in, and whether you seek compensation for your experience—the better equipped you are to make an informed and rational choice about your future.

Making the Most of Your Contacts

There are potentially valuable contacts all around you. Your ability to identify relationships between the people you meet and your career goals is likely to improve with experience. As we suggested in Chapter 5, take every opportunity to meet people, learn what they do, and share your goals with them. Conversations often lead to discoveries of "I know someone who could help you" or "I know someone who you should call about a job." Several years ago, a student who was in the midst of an internship search was stuck on a plane that was delayed considerably. Usually a plane delay is a frustrating and inconvenient experience, but this student made the most of a potentially bad experience. While sitting on the tarmac for two hours, the student struck up a conversation with her seat neighbor. It was during this conversation that the fellow traveler revealed she was a buyer for a major retail company. The student shared with the buyer her goals to enter the fashion industry and her search for an internship. As a result, the student gained valuable advice from someone who was successful in the industry and came away with her business card and a number of contacts to use toward her internship search. This particular buyer did not have an internship to offer, but she shared information with the student that eventually led to a positive internship experience. Always be prepared to meet new people, share information about yourself that will enable new contacts to understand your goals and needs, and be sure to follow up on information you receive.

Keeping in Touch with Your Contacts

If you have established a work experience several weeks or more in advance of your initial work date, it is important that you maintain contact with your future supervisor. Using LinkedIn is a current and productive way to ensure up-to-date networks—and to expand your network through mutual connections. Because turnover and change are constants in retailing and apparel merchandising, you want to become a familiar person to all of the players at your future work experience site. It is not uncommon for a supervisor who has made arrangements for your work experience to be promoted to a new position across the country—or worse, fired! We have worked with students who have faced just such situations—finding internships in September that will start in June, only to discover in June that the manager is no longer working for the company and no one there knows anything about a student work experience.

Prior to the start date of your work experience, you should maintain regular contact with the supervisor. You can establish this contact by formally acknowledging the experience and your understanding of what it will entail. This can be accomplished through a letter or email. Be certain to state when you will be beginning the experience, what your goals are with respect to the learning outcomes you anticipate accomplishing, and your appreciation for the opportunity to embark on the experience with the company and the supervisor. Finally, seek to become connected through LinkedIn or other professional networking sites so that you can stay in touch and remain current when career changes occur. If your prospective employer is on Twitter, follow him or her—just be sure that your Twitter feed maintains a strictly professional presentation because you might be reciprocally followed.

It can be somewhat awkward to make a telephone call or send an email with no particular content other than "I'm just checking to make sure I still have an internship with you this summer," so we recommend that you build a strategy that will provide context for your contact with the site. Though it sounds trite, if you can be "in the neighborhood," it is a good idea to stop in to say hello and meet the employees who are currently working at your prospective site. The more people who are familiar with you and who know about the plan for your future experience, the less likely you will fall between the cracks if changes in the management structure occur. When you make a telephone call or send an email, establish a reason for the contact. See Box 8.5 for some suggested agenda items that you may wish to use when maintaining contacts with future work experience sites. Keep in mind that you should also stay in contact with a company where you have accepted a position—especially when you have landed the job well before the actual start date.

BOX 8.5 Reasons to Contact Future Work Experience Sites

- Send a copy of your goals to your supervisor.
- Request that your supervisor review your goals and offer you feedback with respect to the probability that you will be able to achieve your goals during the work experience.
- Over time, if you identify new goals, you can contact your supervisor to share the updated information.
- Send an updated résumé for the company files.
- Call to arrange a meeting with your supervisor to discuss your work experience or internship responsibilities.

- Interview your prospective supervisor for a class project.
- Forward information about your internship requirements so that your supervisor can familiarize himself or herself with them.
- Make an appointment to stop in and share your portfolio with your supervisor. Ask your supervisor if there are particular elements in your portfolio that should be enhanced prior to your work experience.
- Discuss with your supervisor the specific projects that you will be able to undertake during your internship.

As you maintain contact with the particular company representative who is the key to your work experience, do not neglect opportunities to establish additional contacts for your network. If an opportunity for work experience does fall through, be prepared to pursue new avenues using the network of contacts that you are building. Remember, the more people who you know, and who know you, the better your chances of being able to select ideal work experience opportunities from a range of possibilities. Furthermore, you probably want to identify multiple work experiences to complete while you are a student, so keep yourself active with a network of contacts.

ENGAGING A CAREER COACH/MENTOR

The people with whom you work are as important to your learning and growth as the positions and work experiences you hold. As we mentioned in Chapter 5, mentors are among the most valuable resources for young professionals. While you are in the workplace, be sure to identify key people (such as managers or senior executives) who can expand your mentoring opportunities by offering you guidance, providing insight, and expanding your network of contacts.

Mentors are valuable in their ability to be confidential guides. They can often offer insight based on their experiences and knowledge of company and industry culture. Seek mentors whose professional behaviors and career accomplishments you admire. Be cognizant that a mentor is positioned to offer you constructive feedback, and you should seek such input to develop a personal continuous quality improvement strategy. It is actually a great benefit—and somewhat rare—to have a caring and trustworthy person give formative direction early in your career. Additionally, your willingness and receptivity to constructive feedback—particularly when you use that feedback to implement improvements in your professional demeanor and skill set—is an admirable quality that can be noted when employers confer with your reference people.

The difference between mentors and career contacts lies in the level of the relationship you establish. A mentor must be someone you can trust and who takes a genuine interest in your career growth. A mentor may or may not work directly with you. Your mentors may be former or current supervisors, professors, or contacts with whom you have maintained close ties. Often a mentoring relationship develops between a senior-level professional with extensive experience and a new, entry-level employee. A supervisory relationship is not necessary, and sometimes the mentoring relationship is strengthened when there is not a supervisory component. Regardless of the specific roles that the mentor and his or her protégé assume, the relationship that they share must be one of mutual respect and trust. Potentially, your mentors will be active resources for you throughout your career.

You should actively seek mentors. While some terrific professional contacts seem to simply happen along, you should strive to contact and cultivate potential mentors. A good place to start is with the supervisor of your work experience or a current professor. Professionals will be able to mentor you only if they believe that you are committed to your career growth, and if their areas of expertise match the goals that you have set for yourself. Your ability to communicate to potential mentors regarding your career aspirations, personal goals, and work ethic will enable prospective mentors to recognize their potential contribution toward your professional development. Be certain to let prospective mentors know who you are!

Be open-minded regarding who might serve as a mentor to you. You may not hit it off well with a supervisor, but that doesn't mean that a valuable mentor is not available in your work environment. Make a point to meet people in all divisions of the companies where you work. The ability of your mentor to offer objective feedback is important. Identifying a mentor who does not work directly with you often enables more candid and objective feedback and advice than would be the case from a mentor who works with you on a day-to-day basis. Ask successful and senior employees about their careers and for advice in yours. Follow up on all opportunities that are presented to you to learn from other professionals. Keep in touch with people so that you will be someone they remember— and perform well so that you are someone whom they think of fondly. Even contacts you make while interviewing can turn into valuable mentors. Follow up on every interview and each introduction to a person in the industry; these interactions will lead to mentoring relationships with some of the contacts that you make.

COORDINATING YOUR GOALS WITH THE JOB REQUIREMENTS

To make the most of a work experience, you must set goals for yourself. Construct a goals plan prior to actually beginning your work experience—you will be too busy actually working once the experience begins to write your goals then. In addition, it is important that you communicate your goals for the work experience to your on-site supervisor. He or she should be able to offer feedback on your goals, let you know if there are any goals that are unrealistic for the experience, or alert you to goal opportunities about which you were unaware. Establishing a plan for your goals before your work experience begins allows you to optimize progress toward them during the time you are working.

Your satisfaction with your internship will depend in part in your ability to set and communicate appropriate and realistic goals during the interview. If you have not yet identified your areas of interest, you need to determine why that is, and eventually you will need to establish a direction (at least for the present) in which you wish to focus. When you are interviewing for work experience opportunities, be certain to ask questions that specifically relate to your goals so that you understand what the company has to offer and so that you can evaluate the fit between the company and your goals. In addition to your personal career and work experience goals, you need to make sure that the work experiences you seek meet academic requirements if they apply. Does your academic program require a certain number of hours to be worked, activities to be performed, etc.? You need to be aware of any work experience requirements and communicate them to prospective companies where you might work. You and the company will be better satisfied at the conclusion of the internship when clear goals have been established and worked toward during the duration of the experience.

MAKING THE MOST OF AN INTERNSHIP OR WORK EXPERIENCE

Begin your internship or work experience with a positive attitude. Remember, you will likely be learning as much or more than you will be contributing to the company's bottom line. Be open-minded and willing to do what needs to be done. In fact, a prevailing theme in most internship programs is the expectation that the intern will work hard—and must be willing to do so. This is your opportunity to demonstrate that you can and are willing to go the extra mile to enhance your professional profile and the position of the company. Internship and work experience positions often are not particularly glamorous, and almost certainly will involve completion of mundane tasks—even running errands and making coffee! Do not let the need for routine task performance deter you from making the most of your experience. In fact, you are challenged to observe the most seasoned, successful professionals in your professional environment. There are few jobs that respected professionals won't participate in themselves—and keep in mind that your job is to make things easier for them. By virtue of your junior position, you are the person

BOX 8.6 Internship Tip: Carry a Notebook, PDA, or Tablet

In a presentation to a class of aspiring interns, one former student noted that the most valuable resource she used throughout the duration of her internship was a small spiral notebook. She carried the notebook with her every place she went, and kept comprehensive notes about what tasks she was assigned, how she was instructed to go about them, and when she completed her work. She referred to the information in that notebook constantly, and it served as a source of security for her because she felt confident that she knew what she needed to do and how to do it, without having to check with her supervisor in a burdensome way. In fact, she mentioned that the process of keeping a notebook kept her organized, and the practice of keeping the notebook offered the added advantage of making a positive impression on her supervisor and the colleagues with whom she worked. She ended up making a great impression—demonstrating her self-sufficiency, organization, innovation, and commitment to learning—by creating a tool that enhanced her internship performance.

Whether your prefer the low-tech pencil and paper approach, or use a personal digital assistant (PDA), tablet, or your smart phone, be sure to write names (with proper spelling), instructions, and other details to which you can refer. The task list apps on electronic devices, the ability to save your own audio messages, and automatic transcription features make note taking—and information access—a simple and therefore indispensible activity.

doing the most learning and observing. Box 8.6 presents advice about taking notes as you are assigned and complete tasks. You will gain the respect and trust of your supervisor and senior colleagues by stepping forward with a positive attitude to complete any and all tasks that need to be done.

In addition to the goals that you will be working to achieve throughout your internship, consider the professional behaviors and practices that you will embody. Your attitude and behaviors will be major components of the evaluations and assessments that your supervisor will make of your performance. A few tips for success at an internship include:

- Seek projects; don't sit around waiting to be told what to do. Students who let supervisors know that they have completed tasks and are ready for another assignment will exhibit a strong work ethic and earn the respect and appreciation of their supervisors. It is likely that your supervisor won't know how long you need to complete projects, and it will be up to you to speak up when you have. There may be times when you have more projects underway than you have time for, too. If this happens, communicate with your supervisor and make sure that he or she knows the progress that you are making on each assignment.

- When in doubt, ask. It is expected that an intern who is learning will have many questions. It is far better to ask questions and confirm the nature of tasks that you are expected to complete than to make costly mistakes. Good judgment is important in this respect, however, because there is a fine line between asking timely and important questions and appearing insecure and pesky. Be aware of the corporate climate, and listen carefully when given instructions. If fact, keep a notepad with you at all times and write information down! That way, you can refer to your own notes rather than ask the same question repeatedly.
- Continue to network throughout your internship. The interviewing, career search, and networking skills that you have developed throughout the process of securing an internship should be continued once you have secured a site for your internship.
- Make the internship your top priority. You need to give 100% to the work experience at hand—particularly when it is a full-time internship. When your attention is divided among other obligations—whether they are personal or scholastic—your performance at the internship, your ability to learn, and your evaluation will likely suffer.
- Avoid using electronic distractions: personal phone conversations, texting, Facebook, and even LinkedIn surfing are inappropriate in a workplace. Your professionalism and commitment to the work environment will be supported through your focus on job-related tasks.

EVALUATING YOUR WORK EXPERIENCES

Throughout your tenure at a work experience site, you should look for specific learning opportunities and evaluate the quality of your experience as well as your own performance. There are a number of methods that you might be required to use to accomplish your evaluation. In addition, you may wish to employ one or more of the suggestions next in preparation for your career development and future interviews.

Keep a Journal

It is a good idea to keep a journal that you can review. By reviewing the progress that you make throughout your experience, comprehensive assessment is possible. You will be amazed at the growth and maturity you can observe in yourself. Excerpts from your journal might be used in your portfolio to document your work experiences and the knowledge you have gained. Reflecting on your journal entries should help you identify your strengths, the aspects of the industry that you have particularly enjoyed, your learning throughout the experience, and a direction for your future that will optimize these.

A word of caution—be certain to keep your journal private. If you use electronic means to record your journal, be sure that it is password protected. If you write by hand in a traditional journal, be sure to keep it at home and write in it there. Never bring a journal to the workplace where it might become lost or, perhaps worse, found by others. It is too likely that you will record one or more entries that are not flattering to the company, your supervisor, or your coworkers. A journal that is left in a break room or an accessible digital journal is very tempting for others to explore. Your discretion is important, and we recommend keeping the journal away from the workplace.

Ask Your Supervisor for Feedback

Few people will be as well equipped as your supervisor to offer you honest and constructive feedback regarding your on-site work performance. In fact, you will be shortchanging yourself if you do not ask your internship/work experience supervisor for an evaluation of your performance. Positive comments will reinforce your areas of strength, and a letter or copy of an evaluation instrument that is positive will be a good addition to your portfolio. There is great value in constructive criticism as well. Advice from an on-site supervisor with respect to areas that you still need to develop or the fit of your personality and interests and this specific work experience is valuable as you plan for your future.

Do not avoid the opportunity to be evaluated by an expert in the field. Although aspects of evaluation are tedious at best, and painful at worst, the long-term benefits of gaining feedback about your professionalism and the success with which you implement knowledge and skills in the workplace are worth the risk. Often the anxiety that precedes an evaluation meeting is worse than the outcome of the meeting itself. Many times, supervisors see more strengths in students' performance than the students expect. Regardless, an objective and informed observation of your work quality (such as can be offered by a supervisor) is invaluable toward your professional development and future goal setting.

Identify the Strengths and Weaknesses of Your Work Experience Site

The process of reviewing the environment in which you completed a work experience will not only enhance your self-assessment process, it will also be helpful to your professors and to students who may wish to pursue internships or work experiences there in the future. Professors are typically very interested in understanding which companies offer outstanding experiences to students, and which companies do relatively little toward student career development. Some companies are better than others with respect to organizing learning opportunities, following through with promises of experiences in various facets of the company operations, and access to upper-level professionals who can offer career guidance and insight into company operations. The information that you provide your professors and peers will help future students seek and accept experiences of the highest quality. In addition, you may help realize improvements for future students if deficiencies that you observe and report are remedied as a result of intervention by professors.

You will probably be asked in an interview to discuss what you liked or disliked about your internship experience. Your forethought on this matter will prepare you to produce thoughtful and articulate responses. You may find that your internship site is interested in seeking feedback about its program. Your ability to construct a detailed list, with examples of your observations of strengths and weaknesses of the site, has the potential to impress the company with your observational skills. Of course, you must practice tact and diplomacy when delivering constructive criticism. Keep in mind that it is a good reflection of the company to seek information and means of improvement. This is, in fact, the type of company many individuals wish to work for, as taking the initiative for long-term improvement is certainly a quality that leads to long-term success.

If your internship or work experience site is not interested in your feedback, do not take that personally. Simply keep the information you have compiled to yourself and use your knowledge of the company priorities as you seek future employment experiences.

Projects

1. Set goals for your work experience. Refer to Chapter 2; determine your strengths and your areas of interest. Prepare goals specific for an internship. Be prepared to share these goals with prospective internships sites. Seek feedback from prospective and secured internship placements. Modify your goals accordingly. (Then be sure to reflect upon your goals after your internship!)

2. Keep a journal. Reflect on a) what you learn, b) what you apply, c) what questions you have, and d) how to seek answers to those questions.

3. Observe and reflect on the ethical environment of your work experience site.

4. Match the skills/tasks that you do as a part of your internship to the academic preparation/courses you have completed. Note the similarities/differences in your applications and expectations.

5. Case Study: Have you encountered any problems/challenges that require you to make important decisions? Describe the problem and present the process of decision making that you embarked upon. Include a list of the advantages and disadvantages of various alternatives you considered.

Questions for Discussion

1. It goes with the territory in fashion and retailing that you will spend some portion of your work experience time as a sales associate. Although this position does not particularly excite a significant number of retailing and apparel merchandising or design students, it is an important learning opportunity. What could you bring to the position of sales associate to enhance your enthusiasm for the job? What could you bring to the position to enhance your professionalism as a representative of your company? How could you enhance the total shopping experience for your customers?

2. Consider the work situations in which you have already participated. If you were in a management capacity, how could you improve employee morale in those situations? How could you improve sales or production capacity in those situations?

3. After embarking on a work experience, what personal and professional strengths can you build upon?

4. Have you identified any areas in the business in which you are more interested now than before your work experience? What about areas of the business in which you are less interested? Why?

5. What criteria have contributed to a successful (and an unsuccessful) work experience for you?

6. What criteria have contributed to a successful (and an unsuccessful) professional mentor for you?

7. What are some specific professional skills you have developed as a result of your work experience?

8. How can you effectively present the work experience that you have completed in a professional portfolio?

STUDiO Activities

Visit the *Guide to Fashion Career Planning STUDIO* available at www.bloomsburyfashioncentral.com. The key elements are:

1. Summary of Chapter 8 text
2. Quiz
3. Work Experience/Internship Planning sheet
4. Internship search in different market

VIDEO: Reflecting on Two Internships

References

Ashman, H. (August 6, 2013). Internships: Why students need them to compete in today's job market. Available online: http://www.woofound.com/blog/posts/internships-why-students-need-them-to-compete-in-today-s-job-market

Hansen, K. (n.d.). College students: You simply must do an internship (better yet: multiple internships)! *Quintessential Careers*. Available online: http://www.quintcareers.com/internship_importance.html

Fischer (March 4, 2013). A college degree sorts job applicants, but employers wish it meant more. *The Chronicle of Higher Education*. Available online: http://chronicle.com/article/The-Employment-Mismatch/137625/#id=overview.

Hurst, J. L., & Good, L. K. (2010). The international review of retail, distribution and consumer research: A 20-year evolution of internships: implications for retail interns, employers and educators. *The International Review of Retail, Distribution and Consumer Research, 20*(1), 175–186.

Internships.com. (June 2010). Internship experience is essential and internship opportunities are improving: New federal guidelines governing unpaid internships are unrealistic [Press Release]. Available online: http://www.internships.com/about/news/internship-experience-is-essential-and-internship-opportunities-are-improving-according-to-internships-com-spring-2010-survey-of-career-center-professionals

National Association of Colleges and Employers (NACE). (2013). Internship and Co-op Survey. Available online: https://www.naceweb.org/uploadedFiles/Content/static-assets/downloads/executive-summary/2013-internship-co-op-survey-executive-summary.pdf

National Association of Colleges and Employers (NACE). (2015). Annual Survey. Available online: https://www.naceweb.org/uploadedFiles/Content/static-assets /downloads/executive-summary/2015-internship-co-op-survey-executive -summary.pdf

Paulins, V. A. (2008) Characteristics of retailing internships contributing to students' reported satisfaction with career development, *Journal of Fashion Marketing and Management, 12*(1), 105–118.

Strickler, S. (2001). What influence does a practicum experience have on a students' future? Poster presented at the International Textiles and Apparel Association, Kansas City, MO.

US Department of Labor. (April 2010). Fact Sheet #71: Internship programs under the Fair Labor Standards Act. Available online: http://www.dol.gov/whd/regs /compliance/whdfs71.htm

CHAPTER 9
PROFESSIONAL ETHICS

Your job will test your ethics—and therefore teach *you ethics—every day.*

—MARIA SHRIVER (2000)

OBJECTIVES

- To understand the concept of ethics and its application in both personal and professional activities.
- To identify and explore the relationship between professionalism and ethics.
- To establish awareness that benefits and consequences accompany actions.
- To develop accountability by encouraging acceptance of responsibility for actions.
- To establish awareness of the relationship, and likely conflict, between profit and ethical behavior.
- To establish awareness of the role that power plays in ethical dilemmas.
- To consider personal mission and vision statements—and their relationships to personal and professional ethics.
- To develop and document personal mission statements and codes of ethics.

THE IMPORTANCE OF ETHICS IN BUSINESS

An important component of professional development, ethics, should be considered by students preparing for careers in any area—and the fashion industry is no exception. Ethics is the practice of what is "right." Most people believe they know the difference between what is right and what is wrong. During the process of social development, children learn to abide by a series of rules that govern their behavior. Well-adjusted adults continue to respond and react to the standards dictated by the society in which they live. But questions of ethics and morality make people think, and often there are no singular, easy answers when ethical conflicts arise. When one clear choice over another is not evident, ethical dilemmas arise. In the professional arena, discussions of ethics—and how to resolve ethical dilemmas—have become frequent. Employee conduct is carefully and increasingly scrutinized today.

The concept of ethics is often associated with feelings, religion, and the law. These associations, though, are potentially erroneous. When led only by feelings, people are as likely to make unethical choices that "feel good" as they are to choose the course that is "right." Although religions support ethical conduct in their members, ethics are not exclusive to religious people. In addition, perspectives of moral "rightness" vary considerably from one religion to another. Cultural perspectives and religious beliefs can present conflicts with respect to ethics among and between people from different backgrounds. Laws, although they present behavior standards, do not always present standards that are ethical. Consider the case of pre–Civil War slavery laws, which allowed and enabled the unethical behaviors and structures of slavery. More recently, the 2015 decision by the Supreme Court of the United States to recognize same-sex marriage as a constitutional right in all of the fifty states reflects an evolution of civil rights and law that was slower to occur than many people's understanding of what was ethically right.

What, then, does it mean to be ethical? An ethical individual is one who avoids behaviors that are morally wrong. Cheating, stealing, lying, and murder are universally considered to be wrong. On the other hand, ethical individuals strive to behave in a manner that endorses virtues, including honesty and respect for others. Virtuous behaviors are those considered to be right. Some values are not universally adopted, but are nevertheless important in today's social and work environments. Consider the values of diversity and human rights: The zeitgeist (spirit of the times), the cultural values, and companies' values inform the way ethics are applied in decision making involving these issues.

An awareness of the role of ethics in a business environment is crucial as you prepare for and enter a career. Ethics are not an issue unless something is at stake; ambiguity occurs when differing perspectives are held about how to resolve conflicts or make decisions. One constant of life is ambiguity, and successful individuals must learn to live with the uncertainty of events that will affect them. We can, however, prepare ourselves to be better able to cope with conflict and uncertainty

BOX 9.1 Ethical Dilemmas

Over 1,150 professionals who were members of The National Council on Family Relations and the American Home Economics Association (now the American Association of Family and Consumer Sciences) responded to a survey asking, "As a professional, have you ever faced a serious ethical dilemma relative to your role?" Seventy percent replied that they had.

The following types of ethical dilemmas were identified by survey respondents:

- Confidentiality
- Lack of professionalism in colleagues
- Sexual misconduct
- Job-related issues
- Research issues
- Academic issues
- Social issues

Source: Knaub, P. K., Weber, M. J., & Russ, R. R. (1994). Ethical dilemmas encountered in Human Environmental Sciences: Implications for ethics education. *Journal of Family and Consumer Sciences, 86*(3), 23–30. Copyright © *Journal of Family and Consumer Sciences*, 1994.

by exploring our own values and determining the comfort levels we associate with certain actions. When faced with ethical dilemmas, or "situations which cause internal conflict in considering what is the 'right' thing to do" (Lee, Weber, & Knaub, 1994, p. 24) it is helpful to be prepared with your response strategy. Knaub, Weber, and Russ (1994) surveyed professionals and found that their own past experiences, personal codes of ethics, emotional biases, the social context, their religious backgrounds, colleagues, parental influence, the literature, workshops, college, professors, and the media all served to influence their actions. Therefore, knowing your own personal values and your emotional biases and drawing from your experiences and influences can prepare you to address and resolve ethical dilemmas within any specific situation. Box 9.1 presents the most frequently identified types of ethical dilemmas faced in the workplace.

Just as ignorance is no excuse for the law, individuals are expected to perform up to the standards established by employers. Most companies provide a written set of guidelines to their employees, containing operating procedures, including those for events such as emergencies and loss prevention, guidelines for dress and appearance, and standards for conduct. Individual employees are responsible for familiarizing themselves with the company's rules and are held accountable to follow them. Ethical behavior requires that an employee live up to the standards set by an employer. Box 9.2 provides a listing of typical company guidelines.

BOX 9.2 Typical Company Guidelines for Dress, Appearance, and Conduct

Dress and Appearance

- Do not wear political or controversial buttons, insignias, or apparel.
- Wear a name badge at all times.
- Tattoos and piercings:
    - Some companies require no visible tattoos.
    - Some companies require no facial piercing.
    - The content of the tattoo, placement of piercing, or amount of either may be restricted.
- For women:
    - Avoid ornate and extreme styles, plunging necklines, halters, short-shorts, and extreme miniskirts.
    - Closed-toe shoes are often required. If open-toe shoes are allowed, a professional pedicure may be required.
    - Capri pants are sometimes prohibited.
    - You may be required to wear hosiery.
- For men:
    - Business-like suits and a jacket at all times may be required.
    - Ties may be required.
- Dress shoes with appropriate hosiery are often required.
- Facial hair is sometimes restricted.

Prohibited Activities (May Be Grounds for Immediate Dismissal)

- Any act of dishonesty or theft
- Falsification of records and documents
- Competing in business with the company
- Divulging trade secrets or proprietary information
- Engaging in conduct that may adversely affect the company or its reputation
- Carrying a weapon on company premises
- Disobeying the company's rules on smoking and/or abuse of controlled substances
- Use of alcohol or controlled substances during working hours
- Insubordination
- Tardiness or absenteeism
- Harassment of employees, colleagues, or clients
- Violation of antitrust
- Violation of employee discount policies
- Noncompliance with store security policies
- Wearing non-purchased merchandise

DEFINING THE BOUNDARIES OF ETHICAL DILEMMAS

Many rules, or company standards, are objective. In other words, behaviors that follow and break the rules are easily defined and observed. It is the responsibility of employees to be familiar with the expectations of their employers to avoid conflict when making decisions regarding behaviors. For example, it is wrong to steal from the company, it is wrong to falsify documents, and it is wrong to dress contrary to the established dress code.

Unfortunately, there are many subjective situations in which rules or standards must be interpreted and personal opinion will vary with respect to the degree of "rightness" or "wrongness" associated with a given action. Is it wrong to take home pens or pencils from work? Is it wrong to "fudge" your timesheet when you are late—even if you stay later to make up the work? Is it wrong to make a "fashion statement" even though your appearance violates company dress policy? Is it wrong to violate company policy if you are satisfying a customer or client? Is it wrong to put your own money in the store cash register at the end of the day so that the till is balanced? Is it wrong to use your employee discount to buy gifts for your friends and family? Do you have a responsibility to speak up when you observe unethical behavior—even if you won't be rewarded for doing so? As individuals, people respond differently to any given stimulus, and this contributes to unique opinions, actions, and often conflict. Experience, culture, religion, family relationships, generational roles, education, influences of mentors, and individual value systems all contribute to one's ethical base. Thus, judgments about what constitutes ethical behavior differ. Most of us, however, will at one time in our working lives be faced with an ethical dilemma—a situation in which the best course of action is not obvious.

In the fashion industry, there are a variety of globally recognized areas where ethics come into play. These range from global issues of human rights for factory workers, emissions and wastes produced in textiles plants, treatment of animals for cosmetics testing as well as use of fur and animal products in fashion, to counterfeit merchandise production, advertising practices, economic issues such as fair trade, and general workplace interpersonal relationship matters. See Box 9.3 for some examples of ethical topics in the fashion industry.

BOX 9.3 Ethical Topics in Fashion

Ethics in the fashion industry include many topics—from workplace honesty and collegiality to issues of fashion product development practices. Advertising campaigns, fair labor standards, and import regulations are often cited in current news as examples where ethical dilemmas arise. Intellectual property of designers, with charges of counterfeiting and illegal appropriation of copyrighted work, present a myriad of ethical challenges in the fashion industry. Opportunities for profit support unethical behavior that occurs in production, manufacturing, transportation, retailing, and promotions. Some of the most widely

continued

BOX 9.3 Ethical Topics in Fashion (*continued*)

recognized ethical dilemmas in the fashion industry include:

Body Image

One of the most visible elements of fashion are the bodies that wear apparel. Dove's beauty campaign celebrating real women is a good example of a positive way to counteract the potentially detrimental effects of an industry where rail-thin models and most advertising campaigns not only celebrate, but even air-brush to unachievable levels of perfection, an ideal yet unrealistic body form.

Advertising

As mentioned above, fashion advertisements often depict images that are not real. Additionally, fashion advertisements can be provocative, and for some viewers, distasteful or obscene. Kenneth Cole's advertising strategies have historically pushed the envelope to generate conversations and thought about controversial issues. Calvin Klein's edgy ad contents have extended from Brooke Shields saying, "Nothing comes between me and my Calvins," in the 1980s to the 2015 campaign that features sexting.

Fur and Animal Products

Animal rights supporters have established widely held expectations that beauty product researchers not harm animals during testing and development. Some consumers make choices not to purchase or wear animal products (e.g., leathers and furs) in keeping with their ethical conscience. Ethical controversies sometimes arise when activists—such as People for Ethical Treatment of Animals (PETA) members—protest use of furs and leathers in fashion lines. A good example is Jane Birkin's request to Hermes to remove her name from the namesake Birkin Bag made from crocodiles.

Branding

Macy's found themselves in the midst of an ethical controversy in 2015 when Republican Candidate Donald Trump's comments about Hispanic immigrants presented a conflict with their support of his namesake clothing brand. As a result of the ethical dilemma, Macy's dropped the Donald Trump brand—but not without receiving first a petition from consumers to drop the label and then a lawsuit from Trump because of the dismissal.

Environmentalism

Today's production and manufacturing companies are increasingly pressured to practice sustainability and responsible stewardship of our world's resources. Processes from textile production to apparel manufacturing, to transportation of finished product, to the "greenness" of the retail store itself are all issues of interest to global consumers. Companies such as Patagonia build their reputations on their sound environmental practices.

Fair Trade

The people who grow textile products, farm or trap fur products, and sew apparel garments are historically marginalized in the global economy. Fair trade is a social movement that supports producers—particularly those in developing countries—to receive their fair share of revenue from the products that they produce. There are increasing numbers of retailers who promote and distribute fair trade items, including fashions, and a growing number of consumers who seek to invest in these often higher-priced products to be satisfied that their ethical consumption supports the producers.

THE ROLE OF PERSONAL VALUES IN ETHICAL JUDGMENTS

Individual judgments with respect to ethical behavior are directly related to individual value systems. You must be familiar with your own personal values in order to make clear and rational judgments regarding ethics. Values are learned. Children adopt values that have been taught, consciously or not, by family members and others in their near environments. Value systems are shaped as individuals develop their personalities, and are nurtured and reinforced by the responses one receives in response to actions. Actions such as cheating and lying may be rewarded with success, power, and other positive reinforcements or may be negatively reinforced via punishment, failure, and exclusion. Personal experiences in conjunction with responses to behaviors result in decidedly varied value systems. Although there is much debate over the appropriateness of teaching values, it is clear that, without a strong value system, sound, well-informed, and courageous decisions in the face of ethical dilemmas cannot be made.

Michael Bugeja introduced the concept of moral absolutes in his book *Living Ethics* (1996). He presented the ideas of Christina Hoff Sommers (1993), who noted that there are some truths that are not personal judgments, but rather truths accepted by all people as clearly right or clearly wrong. These clear standards are considered to be moral absolutes. Included in her list of moral absolutes are truths such as, "it is wrong to mistreat a child," "it is wrong to humiliate someone," "it is wrong to torment an animal," "it is wrong to think only of yourself," "it is wrong to steal, to lie, to break promises," "it is right to be considerate and respectful of others," and "it is right to be charitable and generous." Bugeja added to Sommers' moral absolutes, "it is wrong to prejudge others based on physical or racial features," and "it is wrong to treat human beings like objects or property."

In order to make decisions rooted in ethics, personal values must be developed that are acceptable to those in one's immediate environment. The environment could be a family, social group, or place of employment. The organizational culture—a set of values, traditions, and customs that defines and directs employee behavior—should be explored by potential employees to clarify workplace expectations. In a professional setting, your own values must be adequately defined so that ethical decisions can be made with confidence. When decisions are made about employment options, it is helpful to keep in mind that the interview process is a two-way street. You should strive to find a workplace that has an organizational culture that dovetails well with your own ethical base. In order to do that, you must take the time to explore and confirm that ethical base. See the Careers Up Close 9.1 profile, featuring Michelle Crooks-Smith's description of the way her personal ethics have shaped her career decisions.

CAREERS UP CLOSE 9.1
MICHELLE CROOKS-SMITH
Senior Manager, Merchandising Operations
Best Buy

Leadership always came naturally to Michelle Crooks-Smith; in college she was a member of the Black Student Caucus and the Fashion Industries' Organization. During her career at Target, she took on a leadership role as the Co-Chair of the African American Business Council and Board Member in the community.

Michelle knew she was hooked on the retail industry from her very first internship position as a Sales Associate with Von Maur Department Stores. However, as much as she loved the experience, the ability to touch and feel products, and customer interaction at the store level, she wanted to focus on the many dimensions of the industry behind the scenes. Turning down the highly selective Manager-in-Training program at Marshall Field's, she started her career at Hartmarx in downtown Chicago for a lower-paying position as a Manufacturing Specifications Coordinator. There she learned the dynamics of a corporate environment as well as how to tailor her experiences and relationships into stepping stones for the next opportunity.

Over the years, Michelle developed a vast amount of experience that provided insights into many aspects of retailing. As a Retail

Marketing Associate for Haggar® Clothing Company, Michelle interfaced with employers such as JCPenney®, Kohl's®, and Lord & Taylor in the Chicagoland region to oversee in-store merchandise presentations and educate store employees about the brand. As an Account Coordinator for Readerlink, she further honed her skills in client relationship management and developed a passion for providing a merchandising assortment that was key to customer needs—both her retail customers and the retailers' customers.

In 2006, Michelle joined Target as Senior Merchandise Presentation Expert and was promoted four years later to Manager for Merchandise Presentation. In both of these positions, she led cross-functional teams to achieve optimal visual presentation of the Perishables and Entertainment divisions, then later the Mom & Baby departments, in over 1700 stores. Motivating team members, who brought valuable insights and perspectives from finance, aesthetics, inventory and product allocation, and consumer behavior, required diplomacy and strong communication skills. Developing strong collaboration and a passion for driving results were keys to her success. Michelle encouraged her team to know the business, understanding the same numbers as their merchant (retail-store) partners did, as her team worked together to develop solutions for the most effective store merchandise presentations.

Michelle's strong ability for leading people to reach Target's goals and her individual attention to the growth and development of new employees resulted in several prestigious awards, including an award for mentoring interns and Target's Corporate Values Award, given for fostering an inclusive culture. Michelle shares this about mentoring: "People always sought me out as mentor because they knew I was going to 'keep it real,' meaning the mentee could be comfortable with me knowing I would tell them what they needed to hear, sometimes with corporate jargon or simply tough love. I love identifying gaps in communication or execution so that I can then provide the tools needed for people to be successful. I do research to find common opportunities, prioritize those, and then look for ways to simplify and streamline processes. My mantra is to *work smarter, not harder.*"

After seven years leading merchandise presentation at Target, Michelle was promoted to Manager, Store Operations where she led a team of seven people to develop strategic communications to Target stores nationwide. She developed partnerships among merchandising, supply chains, technology services, digital, business intelligence, facilities and store operations teams at Target headquarters so that coordinated, clear, and actionable information could be distributed to over 1800 stores. In this role, Michelle regularly drew upon her comprehensive knowledge of retail operations, her expertise in relationship building, and her enthusiasm for placing employees in areas that fit their interests and skills.

Some accomplishments of which Michelle is especially proud is rallying for, and achieving, a part-time job share program for working mothers, holding offsite team meetings to strengthen the team bond, and implementing world class support to counterparts in India as well as the stores across the United States.

Michelle joined Best Buy® as Senior Manager, Merchandising Operations in 2014. In this position, she is challenged daily to lead a team of project managers responsible for the execution of every major transition and transformation in 1100 domestic stores, offering customers the latest technology in a fast-paced retail and corporate environment. She takes a lot of skills acquired over almost eight years at Target and applies them in her current role to establish strong cross-functional partnerships with the Visual Merchandising, Space, Fixture Procurement, Labor Management, Merchant and Merchant Operations teams to continuously meet deadlines while ensuring work is completed efficiently at the corporate and store levels.

Michelle advises aspiring retail executives to "go with your gut" and don't doubt the choices you make in your career. Each challenge, high or low moment, mistake, and lesson is an experience to build on. Even if you feel something is not fulfilling your passion, position yourself to gain experiences that will allow you to have a story to tell so that you can move on to the next adventure. Never be afraid to use your knowledge and talent to influence. Always speak up and ask questions; have a voice in the room. If you are not a merchant (e.g., in-store personnel), you may feel like you cannot make decisions for them, but you can influence them by using data, coming up with solutions, and presenting your thoughts. Michelle gives this as an example: "I presented the idea of not moving fixtures around for each apparel transition because it caused additional workload for my team and the stores, and made it hard to shop for the basics. Finally, the idea stuck and was executed because my team leveraged our partners and their resources, presented the facts, set up a test, and got the approval to have a fixed floor pad due to positive results."

Examples of Responsibilities:

TARGET

- Update single store adjacencies via CAD software 1–2 times per year for transitions.
- Ensure the right planograms are tied to each store; factoring planogram footage, product, segmentation needs.

- Build good planograms in pro/space software; apply merchandising best practices that cater to the Target Guest.
- Create visual adjacencies for soft goods, incorporating shopper insights, trends, and presentation ideas gathered while comp shopping.
- Help develop new department prototypes that catered to the modern shopper.
- Write communication to allow stores to understand direction and be able to execute.

BEST BUY

- Maintain positive vendor relationships and communicate needs to ensure flawless and timely execution of key store projects.

Advice from Michelle:

- Find a mentor who complements your style but is the opposite. I find that a mentor who is strong in skills in which I am not offers the most benefit. It is always good to find a "ventor" who you can candidly speak to, but who will still offer support and guidance as you navigate situations.
- If you work the corporate retail route, take advantage of any and all opportunities to work in the store environment if they are offered. Knowledge of how things work in the stores is invaluable when executing your role in the corporate offices.
- Retail is fast paced and ever changing. You need to have patience when things do not go according to plan and you have to start over. Each of those experiences will help develop critical thinking skills for future projects.
- Understand what drives your team members; a one-size-fits-all approach doesn't work. You will find as a leader that you need to cater to individual styles in order to get the best out of team members.
- Challenge the status quo.

In environments where people interact together, unique problems that do not adhere perfectly to the "rules and regulations" are bound to occur. It is within these circumstances that you must rely on your previously developed ethical base to arrive at acceptable and appropriate decisions. Lee, Weber, and Knaub (1994) have identified eight categories of ethical dilemmas commonly experienced by human science professionals. In order of frequency, these are lack of professionalism in colleagues, social issues, job-related issues, confidentiality, academic issues, lack of professionalism in students, research issues, and sexual misconduct. Although categorized as ethical dilemmas encountered specifically by human science professionals, these situations are typical of a diverse selection of professional environments.

APPROACHES TO ETHICS

Ethics are approached in a variety of ways, depending on the circumstances surrounding a given situation. The moral absolutes mentioned earlier are examples of the *virtue approach* to ethics. Using this approach, ethical behavior is equated with virtuous behavior. As ethics are applied to larger groups of people, particularly when ethics are tied to policy making, the *utility approach* (also called *utilitarianism*) is often applied. This approach requires a comparison of benefits to harms, with the ethical choice being the one that provides the greatest benefit with the least amount of harm. In the utilitarian approach, the ends justify the means. The *common good approach* seeks to identify as ethical the choice that advances the common good. Additional approaches to ethics include the *fairness approach* and the *rights approach*. The fairness approach focuses on the need to treat members of a group fairly unless there is a moral reason for disparity. The rights approach relates to fundamental human rights (which may differ among cultures) and seeks to identify the choice that respects individuals and their rights to be respected and treated fairly and equally.

When faced with an ethical dilemma, one should take time to evaluate the situation, consider all sides of the given issue, and refer to appropriate ethical codes when available. Application of a specific approach to ethics may help to focus on an appropriate decision. Although there are generally no "right" or "wrong" responses to ethical dilemmas, some solutions have more (or less) merit than others. To further complicate the ethics issue, one must be prepared to realize that rewards for ethical behavior are often not immediate. In fact, when unethical behavior is prevalent, ethical behavior may be associated with negative short-term feedback. Because attitudes related to ethics are rooted in value systems, the only reward for ethical behavior may be the personal satisfaction associated with doing the right thing.

Using Case Studies to Resolve Ethical Dilemmas

A case study approach is an effective way to go about resolving an ethical dilemma. The case study method of problem solving works well in situations in which more than one possible solution exists, and there is not necessarily a "right" versus a "wrong" solution (Granger, 1996; Rabolt & Miller, 1997, 2008; Silverman, Welty, & Lyons, 1992). The case study approach provides a system for organizing information about a problem and presenting alternative solutions to the problem that can be compared. A case study problem-solving approach requires that first the main issue, or conflict, be identified. Second, the circumstances contributing to the dilemma should be identified. Third, several alternative solutions should be developed, with advantages and disadvantages of each alternative being considered. Finally, in light of all considerations and with respect of the "rules," the solution should be reached. A considerable investment of time, for both research of the situation and thoughtful contemplation, should be devoted to successfully resolve ethical issues.

As you work through ethical dilemma cases, you should first identify whether ethical dilemmas actually exist. To be appropriately prepared to make this determination, you should be familiar with policies of your work environment, should consider what course of action is fair to all parties, and should explore your "gut reaction" to the situation. There may be specific guidelines stipulating appropriate actions and behavior of personnel. It is wise to refer to these guidelines when considering alternative decisions. Furthermore, if one employee ends up with an unfair advantage over other employees—in terms of preferential treatment by management, opportunities for career advancement, or ability to be productive while selling—overall productivity in the work environment is compromised. First reactions to situations often provide a base for further exploration, although they should not be the only consideration given to potential dilemmas. Gut reactions should be given merit; if a situation seems wrong, it probably is. Although no new employee wants to bring every decision before a mentor or manager, such people are excellent resources when particularly difficult situations present themselves. Often, it is helpful to think through a problem and seek advice from a respected person in authority before any action is taken. The JCPenney Business Ethics Policy offers excellent advice: "When in doubt, ask." Box 9.4 provides some news articles that reveal actual ethical dilemmas faced by the fashion industry. Additionally, the *Guide to Fashion Career Planning STUDIO*, available on www.bloomsburyfashioncentral.com, that accompanies this book provides opportunities for you to work through case studies pertaining to ethical dilemmas. Knowledge of current ethical dilemmas, as well as trending news in general, is helpful for the fashion professional. Whether you draw from the cases during interview conversations or use the insight as preparation for your own business decisions, you are encouraged to keep up to date with current industry activities—particularly as they relate to ethics.

BOX 9.4 Cases in Fashion Ethics

Advertising

Edelson, S. (July 2, 2015). Wal-Mart's made in the USA program draws scrutiny. *Women's Wear Daily*, p. 2.

Branding

Rappeport, A. (July 1, 2015). Macy's drops Donald Trump's fashion line over immigrant remarks. *The New York Times*. Available online: http://www.nytimes.com/politics/first-draft/2015/07/01/macys-drops-donald-trumps-fashion-line-over-immigrant-remarks/?_r=0

Counterfeits and Intellectual Property

Ellis, K. (June 24, 2015). US, China boosting efforts in fight against counterfeits. *Women's Wear Daily*, p. 2.

Lieber, C. (December 1, 2014). Why the $600 billion counterfeit industry is still horrible for fashion. *Racked*. Available online: http://www.racked.com/2014/12/1/7566859/counterfeit-fashion-goods-products-museum-exhibit

CSR (Corporate Social Responsibility)

Ellis, K. (June 10, 2015). Fashion industry advising on US responsible sourcing plan. *Women's Wear Daily*, p. 3.

Saini, M. (June 23, 2015). Bangladesh minister's comments spark backlash from brands. *Women's Wear Daily*, p. 8.

Employee Benefits / Employee Issues

Ellis, K. (with contributions by L. Lockwood & S. Edelson). (June 26, 2015). Supreme court upholds Obama Health Care Act. *Women's Wear Daily*, p. 1, 11.

Feitelberg, R. (June 16, 2015). Elie Tahari denies harassment claims. *Women's Wear Daily*, p. 11.

Fur

Williams, A. (July 3, 2015). Fur is back in fashion and debate. *The New York Times*. Available online: http://www.nytimes.com/2015/07/05/fashion/fur-is-back-in-fashion-and-debate.html

Gender and Identity

Zimmerman, E. (June 19, 2015). Benoît Monin: How men react when their masculinity is questioned. Stanford Graduate School of Business. Available online: https://www.gsb.stanford.edu/insights/benoit-monin-how-men-react-when-their-masculinity-questioned

Immigration

Moin, D. (July 2, 2015). Who dumped whom? Lundgren vs. Trump. *Women's Wear Daily*, pp. 1, 3.

Models and Body Image

Friedman, V. (April 6, 2015). Do women take body image cues from models? *The New York Times*, Available online: http://runway.blogs.nytimes.com/2015/04/06/do-women-take-body-image-cues-from-models/?_r=0

Product Recalls

Young, V. M. (June 26, 2015). Lululemon recalls 318K women's tops. *Women's Wear Daily*, p. 3.

Sweatshops / Worker Safety

Kaplan, M. (July 2, 2015). Mass fainting at Cambodia factories brings country's textile industry under scrutiny. *International Business Times*. Available online: http://www.ibtimes.com/mass-fainting-cambodia-factories-brings-countrys-textile-industry-under-scrutiny-1994128

The Decision-Making Process

Once it has been determined that some choice needs to be made, a set of alternative choices should be identified. As these choices are identified, their merits and consequences should be considered. Some questions that should be considered as the process of decision making progresses are:

- What are the positive and negative benefits and consequences that are likely to be associated with the course of action being considered?
- Do any selected courses of action violate company policy?
- Do any selected courses of action violate your own ethical standards?
- Do you personally feel comfortable with the course of action being considered?
- Does the outcome associated with the course of action result in an inappropriate advantage or disadvantage for you or any of the parties involved?
- Would you publicly stand by this course of action?

For more information about the process of ethical decision making, you may wish to review the Markkula Center for Applied Ethics at Santa Clara University website at http://www.scu.edu/ethics.

FACTORS THAT CONTRIBUTE TO ETHICAL DILEMMAS

The ability to seek information when faced with an ethical dilemma is invaluable. You can save yourself a considerable amount of stressful contemplation if you seek information and ask relevant questions. What are the circumstances surrounding the situation at hand? How will morale of company employees be affected by the actions that are taken? These and other questions will lead you to a better understanding of the situations you will face. Sufficient information is necessary to develop creative solutions to dilemmas. Considering the facts of the situation, you will be better prepared to present compromises that create outcomes that are fair to all employees and in the best interest of your company. Whenever possible, consult with trusted colleagues and mentors; they can provide feedback and act as sounding boards as you consider your actions and decisions.

The Profit–Ethics Dilemma

In a business environment, the temptation to violate ethical rules is often strong because of the relationship between unfair play and profit. Profit itself is not unethical, but behaviors exhibited by individuals seeking to achieve profit may be. Companies that condone employees who capitalize on an unfair advantage, such as stockbrokers who maneuver trades based on inside information or designers who unscrupulously secure information about a competitor's upcoming line, may reap short-term profits. These profits, however, arrive at the expense of violating ethical standards, potentially damaging the firm's reputation, and, in some cases, incurring legal retribution.

Employees must be aware of the expectations of their employers. Employers expect their employees to live up to the expectations set forth. Situational dilemmas that arise with profit as a leading motivator for action should be carefully considered. Although companies expect employees to make decisions resulting in the highest possible profit margins, individual employees must remember that they alone are responsible for and must answer to decisions that they have made. Companies further expect that their "good names" will be preserved by all employees. Dr. Laura Schlessinger, a licensed marriage and family counselor, internationally syndicated radio host, and author, encourages her audience to consider, as if viewed retrospectively, the choices they will wish they would have made. Her approach encourages consideration of a perspective that does not necessarily provide immediate gratification, but allows one to determine the extent to which a decision involves one's character and conscience. In her book *How Could You Do That?!: The Abdication of Character, Courage, and Conscience* (1996), Dr. Schlessinger describes the situation of a woman who was distressed at witnessing racial discrimination among her co-workers at a department store. The woman's ethical dilemma—the decision about whether to speak up and voice her disapproval—was further complicated by her knowledge that doing so would likely jeopardize her career with the company. Dr. Schlessinger (1996) relates the situation to the concept of "selling out," sharing the situation of one of her radio callers who made a personal ethical decision. The caller did not "sell out" and betray her ethical stand; but rather than being rewarded for it, she received a reprimand from her workplace manager.

Your comfort level with the ethical environment supported by your employer is an important measure to consider. Success and happiness can be found in very different ways, and personal values are directly related to the feelings of contentment an individual finds in any given situation. Young professionals should be aware that company environments and collective views regarding ethics differ, just as individual value systems and personal ethical codes differ. These conflicts, and the workplace drama that accompanies them, are often referred to as "office politics." Box 9.5 presents advice for navigating office politics.

BOX 9.5 How to Deal with Office Politics

by Jeff Ousborne

Aristotle wrote that "man is by nature a political animal." For evidence, look no further than the workplace. Glad-handing. Gossip. Competing interests. Yet few people proudly self-identify as an office politician, especially at the entry level. "Young people are often idealistic and see politics as pathological," says Richard Shell, professor of legal studies, business ethics, and management at the Wharton School of Business. "They want to be conscientious objectors to office politics, but doing so will limit their effectiveness and leave them marginalized."

Neutrality is not an option: Ignore office politics, and you put your career in peril. Here is what the experts have to say about unleashing your inner political animal.

1. Politics? What Politics?

"Young workers think, 'I'll keep my head down, my nose to the grindstone, and be impervious to everything around me,'" says Wayne Hochwarter, professor of management at Florida State University and expert on organizational behavior. "But your actual job function in the office is only one component of work. You need to be aware of an entire social environment, or you'll end up cut off from reality." Develop your peripheral vision and accept that politics is neither good nor bad. No organization has infinite resources, so inevitably people must jockey for time, money, power, promotions, and recognition. In a word: politics.

2. Press the Flesh

Think you're going to thrive by hunkering down in your cube with your headphones on? Think again. Presidential hopefuls practice real politics—informal campaigning spent shaking hands, chatting at diners, and making personal connections—and so should you. "Nudge yourself to get out, socialize, and network," says Rick Brandon, coauthor of *Survival of the Savvy: High-Integrity Political Tactics for Career and Company Success.* "Build your visibility."

Whether it's a cocktail party or a beer-pong tournament, go. If there's a group of colleagues traveling to hear a speaker across town, join them. Get other people invested in your career—both inside and outside your office. "Think of your contacts and political alliances as a bank account," says Marilyn Puder-York, author of *The Office Survival Guide.* "Make contributions to it regularly."

3. Beware of Cling-Ons

Remember the first day at your new school? Remember that kid who seemed a little too needy, the kid who wanted to be best friends by recess? Well, that kid grew up and works at the company that just hired you. So be friendly, but cautious. "When you join a new organization, hold back a little," says Don Asher, author of *Who Gets Promoted, Who Doesn't, and Why: 10 Things You'd Better Do If You Want to Get Ahead.* "Often, the first thing that happens is that the person with no friends and no power will seek you out, looking for an ally." The takeaway: Take a breath and get a sense of who's who before you commit to a BFF.

4. Cultivate Key Relationships

You know your boss and your immediate colleagues. But how well do you know your boss's assistant? The IT guy? People in finance? The HR department? "Look beyond titles," says

Marie McIntyre, author of *Secrets to Winning at Office Politics*. "For example, many mistakenly assume that people in HR have no power. Well, you'd be surprised at how many problems they solve, how many decisions they influence—even on the level of promotions and layoffs."

Bonus: people in departments such as HR and IT sit on a lot of insider knowledge. When an HR person says, "Don't tell anyone, but . . ." listen up. Get to know people in finance: They manage long-term budgets and know where the company is headed.

Developing relationships outside your division will help you avoid potential conflicts on projects too. "If you know people on the manufacturing end, in marketing, in sales, you'll be able to anticipate their points of view, their needs, and their agendas," says McIntyre. If you understand these competing interests, you'll be able to navigate the wider political landscape. Just be careful not to confuse work friends for real friends.

5. Good Office Gossip

Sure, office gossip has a negative connotation. But it's not always a bad thing. "Gossip is information," says Asher. "If a colleague you trust warns you before a business trip, 'Hey, that guy always hits on women when he travels,' that might be necessary information for you." Just consider the source. Likewise, you can use gossip for good: If a superior compliments one of your colleagues, tell the colleague. She'll remember your kindness. Gossip can be a valuable currency—especially if you have a reputation for being perceptive, trustworthy, and discreet.

When you come across a nugget of information that's genuinely useful to a political ally—a colleague, a networking contact, even a superior—use it to build your alliance: "Normally, I don't share this kind of stuff, but I thought it might help you." That said, keep a couple of rules in mind. First, don't initiate negative gossip or pass it along. Second, be wary of relationships built on too much gossip. "Remember," says Puder-York. "That person who's gossiping with you will probably gossip about you too."

6. Rise Above Conflict

When disagreements arise, try to identify the work-related issue at the source of conflict. If you can't find one, let it go. Head games? Needling? Disengage. "I had a younger client who was working with an older colleague who didn't have a college degree," says McIntyre. "The older guy was always Googling obscure information and quizzing the younger guy, trying to trap him. The younger guy was going to go to his boss about this." Bad idea: Generally, do not use your boss as a playground referee to mediate disputes. An exception: If you know someone is going to trash you to your boss, get to your boss first.

The trick is to not return the trash talk, says Brandon. Instead, be the strategic-thinking grown-up, and you can make your nemesis look like an ass. Go to your supervisor and say: "You might be hearing from Tom. We had a disagreement and neither of us was at our best. But if we need to sit down and talk about this, I'm happy to do so."

7. Guard Against Idea Theft

Yes, colleagues may steal your work—and the credit—so get things time-stamped. That means taking your ideas in their available form and running them by your boss or another person with power before they're due, before the big meeting, before anyone has an

continued

BOX 9.5 How to Deal with Office Politics *(continued)*

opportunity to pull a heist. Just be careful: It might just be the custom and culture in your company for the head of a team or supervisor to take all the credit for group accomplishments. Try to sidestep the chain of command and you could burn a few bridges.

8. Influence, Not Power

Power comes from control over resources, hiring, and firing. Early in your career, you may not have much power. But you can build influence by being knowledgeable, competent, trustworthy, and dependable. That sounds obvious, but you need to think about these qualities strategically: not just as virtues in themselves, but as tools to career advancement.

Your short-term goal is to make yourself someone whose opinion is valuable. Your long-term goal is to become indispensable. "That means anticipating and knowing what your superiors and colleagues need," says Shell. "It might be your special technical knowledge. It might be your willingness to work on weekends. It might be project-specific. But you'll know when people say, 'We can't start the meeting until Jones gets here.' You want to be Jones."

9. Phrases that Pay

When you receive criticism, you can gently push back by asking specific questions. If you're told you need to be more of a team player or do a better job on your weekly reports, be diplomatic: "Thanks for telling me what I need to work on. Can you be specific about how I can improve?" When you need to give criticism, do it in a tactful way that's unlikely to trigger personal conflict. Phrases that pay: "I'd be doing you a real disservice if I didn't bring this up." "I am concerned about _____ and let me tell you why." "I understand what you are saying and how you see the issue. Let me give you my thoughts."

10. If You're a Pawn, Be a Smart One

Backing the wrong candidate—a person, a proposal, a new software platform—can have major consequences. You can often demonstrate your judgment by withholding your opinion, according to Asher. So, two candidates are up for a leadership position, and someone asks you which one you prefer. The correct answer: "I'd be happy to work under both of these people." Honesty is fine—to a point. Executives and managers may say they want truth-telling or "healthy conflict," but in reality, this is politically risky territory for younger employees. So be strategic with your honesty, especially in meetings. "Don't always put your heart and mind on the table," says Asher.

11. Please the People Who Matter Most

It's not enough to get good results: You need to satisfy the people who matter. That may require hard choices, but you have to make them. "When there's a conflict between the two, choose pleasing your boss over pleasing your colleagues and subordinates, or you will never advance," says Asher.

Two prime directives: First, never go over your boss's head without explicit permission. Second, never start a war with your boss. You will lose. Still, keep your first loyalty in the back of your mind: It's not to your boss, your colleagues, or your company. "Your first loyalty has to be to yourself—your brand, your long-term job continuance," says Hochwarter, of Florida State. "That includes your profile outside the company where you work in case you need to move on."

12. Don't Complain

You may be low on the political power chain, but you don't have to be a doormat. The key is to turn complaints into questions. For example, if people are offloading their work onto you, find the substantive business issue in your complaint, then frame it as a request to get the backup you need.

"Prioritizing your work is different from complaining about being overworked," says McIntyre. Don't whine. That's a sure way to enrage your boss. Do go to her and say, "I can help them handle this other work, but could we sit down and I could show you a list of tasks and we could prioritize them?" When others approach you with extra work, say, "I'm glad to help—let me check with my supervisor about that."

13. Toot Your Horn

People need to know what you're doing. "I always hear this complaint: 'People just don't know my contributions,'" says McIntyre. "I always ask, 'Why don't they?'" Here's the point: You cannot rely on your accomplishments to speak for themselves. It's up to you to show people your contributions. But when it comes to self-promotion, think storytelling, not advertisement.

"Weave your accomplishments into brief narratives that communicate passion, energy, and delight," says Peggy Klaus, the author of *Brag!: The Art of Tooting Your Horn Without Blowing It.* If your boss's boss asks how things are going, don't just chirp, "Fine." Use the opportunity to mark a specific triumph: "I've been trying to get this difficult customer on the phone for the last two days and I finally did it. He's really on board with us now and I'm thrilled."

Source: Ousborne, J. (n.d.) How to deal with office politics. *WetFeet.* Available online: http://schools.wetfeet .com/advice-tools/on-the-job/how-to-deal-with-office-politics Reprinted with permission.

Ethics and the Role of Power

> The highest proof of virtue is to possess boundless power without abusing it.
>
> **—LORD THOMAS BABINGTON MACAULAY (1843)**

Power is a phenomenon that affects the environment in which decisions are made. In a business environment, the relative power one possesses is typically related to one's role as a supervisor or subordinate. Obviously, supervisors possess power over subordinate employees. Thus, one may likely believe his or her professional position and potential for growth to be at stake when actions and decisions do not reflect those of the supervisor. Herein lies the relationship between power and ethics.

Supervisors, managers, and leaders in professional situations possess power over the employees who depend on them for evaluations, promotions, wage increases, and recommendations. Along with this power, such professionals must accept the responsibility not to abuse the power associated with their positions. In fact, the roles and responsibilities associated with both supervisors and subordinates should be carefully considered. Up-and-coming executives can practice good leadership ethics through responsible decision making. People in positions of power should be aware of the importance of setting a good example; theirs will be the standard to which subordinates compare their own actions.

Although employees have the responsibility to perform according to established standards within the company and to follow the direction given by the supervisor, subordinates should make certain that any conflicts between these two directives are recognized and resolved. Virtually all companies have specific policies regulating the relationships of supervisors and subordinates. Specifically, companies address issues such as discrimination, sexual harassment, and consensual relationships. Some companies prohibit two members of an immediate family from working together. Most companies discourage romantic relationships between employees, particularly among supervisors and subordinates.

Harassment of fellow employees, most often instigated by a supervisor or employee with greater power in the business organization than the victim, is particularly nonproductive in the work environment. Harassment may take the form of unwanted physical, verbal, visual, or sexual behavior directed against another because of his or her gender, race, age, religion, or disability. Most instances of harassment are illegal as well as unethical, but because of its intimidating and potentially embarrassing nature, victims often suffer through the abuse rather than report it and seek reprieve. Employees, especially executives, have the responsibility to prevent workplace harassment by setting good examples and refusing to tolerate unethical behavior. Individuals who hold positions of power over others must be aware that when workplace ethics become problematic, the supervisor is inevitably in the role of the person who "should have known better."

ETHICS FOR INTERVIEWS

Communication between the parties in employment interviews is important, because each question and every response must be carefully considered. Often, implied meanings of questions and answers are conjectured, and perhaps misinterpreted. Those people responsible for the selection of employees are morally obligated to be familiar with the limits related to legal questions and assumptions that may be made. For example, interviewers should not assume that marital or parental status of individuals will affect their abilities to successfully perform their jobs. Gender, age, sexual orientation, and race discrimination, along with assumptions related to these factors, are widely recognized areas in which the issue of ethics is of concern.

THE RELATIONSHIP BETWEEN ETHICS AND ETIQUETTE

Ethics and etiquette, while undeniably different entities, are related in both business and personal settings. Concepts such as fair treatment of and respect for others, honesty, and the value of charity and generosity are often recognized as moral absolutes (Bugeja, 1996), rules that apply to everyone. The idea of a moral rule is rooted in the theory of ethics, but it is obvious that the concepts of fair treatment, respect, honesty, and generosity are also inherent components of etiquette. Most often, when you carry out an action that is "right" (ethical), it is also the action that is most considerate of other people involved and affected (etiquette). Etiquette, though, goes beyond ethics to establish an environment that encourages interactions and feelings of being at ease in a given situation. According to Emily Post (1984, p. xiii), the purpose of etiquette "is to make the world a pleasanter place to live in, and you a more pleasant person to live with." This is a noble goal to strive toward and, indeed, is the "right thing to do" in both personal and professional environments.

The basic, and most familiar, rules of etiquette prevail in today's business world. It is appreciated when "please," "thank you," and "you're welcome" are used appropriately in conversation. It is good manners, and likely to result in a positive impression, to send thank-you letters and to be punctual with respect to correspondence and requests. A firm handshake is an appropriate action that demonstrates respect for an acquaintance. A smile or simply a nod or other gesture of acknowledgment is a polite way to recognize the presence or recognition of another. Respect for others and an appreciation for alternate points of view are hallmarks of both ethical behavior and good etiquette. When in the company of interviewers, colleagues, supervisors, or subordinates, your attention to good manners will be noticed and is likely to contribute to others' perceptions of your professional profile.

EXPLORING YOUR ETHICAL CONSTRUCT

Have you ever considered your own ethical base? When faced with a situation in which an ethical dilemma might arise, are you prepared to "do the right thing?" Michael Bugeja (1996) encourages students to keep track of their behaviors by recording white lies and other nontruths. This exercise, he says, provides an opportunity for students to consider the potential consequences of their actions, and to quantify the number of times they compromise an ethical ideal. Your own history of behavior is important. Employment applications frequently include questions such as, "Have you ever been convicted of a felony?" If you have a record of shoplifting, you are not likely to be employed by a retailer. To "do the right thing," we must apply ethical principles in all aspects of our daily lives. Refer to Box 9.6, which explores seven myths about ethical principles.

BOX 9.6 Seven Myths about Ethics
by J. Edward Ketz

To be ethical, one must build good habits by applying ethical principles every day, including telling the truth, not stealing, and treating others as you would want them to treat you. Start by learning the seven fundamental myths about ethics.

Myth No. 1: Business ethics. Many people talk about business ethics without realizing that there is no such thing as "business ethics." Ethical principles exist for all walks of life, and these principles do not change as one traverses different venues. Applications might differ, but the principles themselves do not.

Myth No. 2: Professional ethics can be separated from personal ethics. A variation of the first myth is that we can live however we wish in our personal lives as long as we act ethically on the job. Aristotle discards such a juvenile idea when he proclaims that my character is the sum of all my habits. If I lie habitually in my personal life, then I am not building the strength or the character to stand true at the other times.

Myth No. 3: Some things are ethical, some are not. The gist of this myth is that some issues or topics are devoid of ethical content,

but this assertion can be true only if human interaction is absent. Consider the classic make-or-buy analysis taught in management accounting. At first blush, it may appear that this decision analysis is purely technical and devoid of ethical content. But ethics pervades this technical grid in several ways.

The analyst who is working for the firm is receiving compensation to perform a good investigation; doing anything less is stealing from the employer. The investigation and the recommendations presuppose reliable data and disclosure of all important assumptions; anything less is lying. The decision process itself assumes maximization of shareholder profit, constrained by various stakeholder concerns.

Myth No. 4: Ethics is a matter of education alone. To act in an ethical way, a person must understand his or her duties and obligations. Obviously, education has a role to play in instructing folks about their ethical responsibilities. I have learned, however, that education alone does not produce ethical people, for some very highly educated people act thoughtlessly, selfishly, and unethically.

Myth No. 5: Responsibility for ethical education rests with colleges and universities. The calls for more ethics training at colleges and universities make me laugh. I wonder where were the parents, the churches, the K–12 teachers, the Little League coaches, and the Girl Scout leaders?

Myth No. 6: Ethical dilemmas are episodic. This myth takes the tack that ethical problems arise only occasionally during one's life; accordingly, individuals need education about these professional quandaries; armed with the appropriate facts, one becomes capable of solving such predicaments as they occur. Missing the ethical content of daily human interaction increases the chances of not recognizing major ethical episodes when they materialize.

Myth No. 7: You either are an ethical person or you are not. This myth has several problems. The first mistake is that this assertion presumes that education, enforcement, and habit building have no role to play. Clearly, they do. The second problem with this thought is that it assumes perfection, but all people have ethical lapses. (I silently chuckle whenever people inform me that they never lie, because they just did.) What differentiates the two groups is that an ethical person will admit the error, try to make amends, and learn from the transgression. Unethical people cover up the blunder, do not care about the consequences of their sin, and learn nothing from the experience.

J. Edward Ketz, associate professor of accounting at Pennsylvania State University, is author of *Hidden Financial Risk*, a book on accounting scandals and misdeeds.

Source: Reprinted with permission of J. Edward Ketz. ©2003 SmartPros Ltd. All Rights Reserved. Available online: http://accounting.smartpros.com/x38366.xml

Applicants for employment with retailers or in merchandising positions are often asked to complete a psychological or "attitude" questionnaire. Results of such questionnaires contribute to hiring decisions. Responses to these questionnaires offer employers information related to one's value system, beliefs, and behaviors. Although there are no right or wrong responses to the questions posed, one's ethical construct contributes to the pattern of responses. An attitude questionnaire might ask such questions as, "Do you think that it is wrong for an employee to take home a pen from work?" "If someone has stolen money before, can he/she be trusted to handle money in the future?" and "Do you think it is okay to cheat on your income taxes?" Attitude questionnaires frequently ask questions pertaining to use of alcohol, tobacco, and other substances, along with pointed questions regarding one's history of convictions.

Developing a Code of Ethics

A code of ethics is a set of rules guiding the behavior of an individual or a group of people. Codes of ethics may be constructed to address philosophical issues, codes of conduct, or policies. Codes may be categorized as aspirational, educational, or regulatory. The nature of the code, whether it is a corporate code or a personal code, and the culture of the people or individuals for whom the code is constructed, dictates its purpose. Philosophical codes of ethics can also be referred to as aspirational. An aspirational code of ethics presents an individual's or group's values and ideals. The principles to which the person or group aspires are the focus of this type of code. A code of conduct could be considered an educational code of ethics. This type of code would be presented to help its readers make appropriate decisions for the organization or individual the code represents. A policy-related code of ethics is considered regulatory. Such a code of ethics contains detailed rules that govern the conduct of its author or members of the group it represents.

Codes of ethics typically develop from and reflect the values of company vision and mission statements. Vision statements, which present "what the company aspires to be," and mission statements, which articulate "what the company does," are excellent reference points for the development of ethics codes. In essence, the code of ethics provides action and decision making guidelines for the many choices that arise as a company (or you, as an individual) face during day-to-day operations and on the path to the envisioned future. Paulins, Hillery, and Sturgill (2015) developed a process for using personal mission statements and codes of ethics as career search tools. The *Guide to Fashion Career Planning STUDIO*, found at www.bloomsburyfashioncentral.com, contains an exercise for you to identify your core values, transform those values into a personal mission statement, and then develop a code of ethics to guide your decision-making processes. Figures 9.1, 9.2, and 9.3 illustrate the outcomes of these activities.

Many corporations have adopted ethical codes by which they operate and expect their employees to abide. An ethical code is a compilation of statements or rules, or both, that offer guidance and direction to the organization that has generated the code. Members of organizations represented by codes of ethics are compelled to act professionally and within the standards of the codes. Employees often possess certain knowledge and expertise in their professions that might result in a position of disadvantage among the public should standards of ethics not be maintained. Codes of ethics therefore serve as regulatory tools for organizations, and benchmarks by which needs for disciplinary actions may be weighed.

When a member of an organization faces an ethical dilemma, the code of ethics, by providing written guidelines, can be used to help that member decide the best course of action. A code of ethics' effectiveness is constrained by the circumstances under which it is administered. An effective code of ethics must be reflective of the company or organizational culture and must be enforced (Hira, 1996). The concept of creating a code of ethics has been embraced by many businesses and professional organizations. Numerous Internet sources are dedicated to presenting information about organizations' codes of ethics and the process of creating and using codes of ethics. The Markkula Center for Applied Ethics of Santa Clara University has a particularly good website that provides a plethora of information on the topics of ethics, ethical decision making, and ethical codes (http://www.scu.edu/ethics). Markkula's website presents ethics from business, campus, Internet, character, government, and bioethics perspectives. There is even a free app, available for download, to assist with making ethical decisions.

A code of ethics usually begins with a general statement concerning the nature of the organization and the purpose of providing the code of ethics. This introduction is followed by specific belief statements directed toward the expectations of members represented in the organization or business. Codes of ethics may be either brief and general or lengthy and considerably detailed. One of the most comprehensive codes is that of the American Marketing Association (AMA, n.d.). The AMA Ethics Statement addresses responsibilities of marketers with respect to honesty and fairness, rights and duties of parties in the marketing exchange process, and organizational relationships. Their key statements include a) do no harm, b) foster trust in the marketing system, and c) embrace ethical values. Furthermore, the ethical values noted in the AMA code include honesty, responsibility, fairness, respect, transparency, and citizenship. The National Automobile Dealers Association (NADA) has adopted a code of ethics that addresses expectations of professional performance of its members (Box 9.7).

To be optimally effective, it is essential that all members of an organization (or employees of a company) be familiar with its code of ethics. The code should be easily accessible to all employees and should be shared with clients and other constituents of the organization. This reinforces the importance of accountability. The basis for discussion and awareness of ethics, and the reason for constructing a code, is that each person is responsible for his or her own actions. Individuals are expected to follow the rules of conduct set by law, company policy, and common professional courtesy. Individuals will be held accountable for decisions that they make and actions that they take in professional positions.

It is all too easy—and unfortunately fairly common—for employees to lose sight of ethical, or moral, considerations for the advancement of themselves, their division, or their company. Accountability is a reality. A helpful ethical benchmark is present by Kenneth Blanchard and Norman Vincent Peale in their book *The Power of Ethical Management* (1988): Ask yourself, "Is it legal?" "Is it fair?" and "How will it make me feel about myself?" A negative response to any of these questions should

BOX 9.7 National Automobile Dealers Association Code of Ethics

NADA's Code of Ethics is designed to reinforce dealers' personal commitment to quality service and high ethical standards.

As a member of NADA, member dealers subscribe to the following principles and standards. Implicit in this Code is the requirement that NADA members comply fully with all federal, state, and local laws governing their businesses.

We pledge to:

- Operate this business in accord with the highest standards of ethical conduct.
- Treat each customer in a fair, open, and honest manner, and fully comply with all laws that prohibit discrimination.
- Meet the transportation needs of our customers in a knowledgeable and professional manner.
- Represent our products clearly and factually, standing fully behind our warranties, direct and implied, and in all other ways justifying the customer's respect and confidence.
- Advertise our products in a positive, factual, and informative manner.
- Detail charges to assist our customers in understanding repair work and provide written estimates of any service work to be performed, upon request, or as required by law.
- Resolve customer concerns promptly and courteously.
- Put our promises in writing and stand behind them.

Ethics Guide

In addition, NADA has published an Ethics Guide that focuses on four key areas of dealership operations: sales, service, financial services and advertising.

Source: NADA. (n.d.). Code of ethics. Available online: https://www.nada.org/codeofethics/ Reprinted with permission.

lead you to seriously reconsider that particular action. Consider also the ramifications of having your actions publicized for scrutiny by others. Remember, you will be held accountable for your behavior.

When faced with a simple dilemma, people undoubtedly are able to identify the difference between right and wrong. It is when the gray areas present themselves, however, that judgment can be difficult. Codes of ethics, core values, and mission statements exist for these situations. Because of the individual nature of so many decisions that are made on behalf of organizations, the identification of core values, development of a mission statement, and creation of a personal code of ethics can be an excellent beginning to exploring your ethical construct and your value system. These tools can be used as guides for decision making— both at work and in your personal life. By identifying your core values, you can clarify the priorities you hold. Only you can determine *the most*

FIGURE 9.1
Word Diagram
Displaying
Collaboratively
Generated Class
Core Values

Honors Class Mission Statement

We are a community of loyal friends who are committed to education, knowledge, honesty, family, and happiness. Our relationships with one another provide opportunities for us to work with humor in our educational endeavors.

FIGURE 9.2
Mission Statement
Generated
Collaboratively from
Shared Core Values

important things in your life. The words that identify your core values should be predominant in your personal mission statement. The development of a personal code of ethics should be reflective of your mission statement. Through development of these items, you will have an opportunity to identify, prioritize, and operationalize your values.

As you embark on a professional career, you can refer to your own mission statement and code of ethics, along with appropriate organizational codes of ethics, to help guide your career choices and professional decisions. In fact, you may decide to include your mission and ethics statements in your résumé, on your blog, as the document to which a QR code refers, and/or in your portfolio. An example of a class-generated mission statement, drawn from collectively identified core values, is presented in the word diagram in Figure 9.1 and as a mission statement in Figure 9.2. One student's personal code of ethics, which reflects this mission statement, is presented in Figure 9.3.

I will approach my education with integrity; I will be honest in my work and in my relationships.

I value the love of family; I will seek to bring happiness to my family and friends.

I will endeavor to find humor in all situations.

My success is important, but it cannot come at the price of my happiness, or the happiness of my family. I will not jeopardize my personal relationships in the pursuit of personal success.

All people deserve respect; I will strive to enrich my community through valuing, including, and respecting all people.

FIGURE 9.3
Sample Personal
Code of Ethics

Projects

1. Identify a list of moral absolutes. Compare your list with those of your classmates. Do they include additional moral absolutes beyond those you originally identified? Are any moral absolutes listed that you or other classmates do not agree are moral absolutes? Discuss in class.
2. Develop a personal code of ethics. First identify your core values. From those core values, write a one- to two-sentence mission statement. Then, construct your code of ethics to reflect your values and mission statement. Evaluate the elements that you have included in your code and compare your code with those of your classmates. Are there any elements that you included and others did not, or vice versa? Why have you chosen to include or omit the elements that you did?
3. Complete a case study analysis that presents alternative responses to ethical dilemmas presented in the *Guide to Fashion Career Planning STUDIO* (www.bloomsburyfashioncentral.com).

Questions for Discussion

1. Respond to and rank the following situations identifying the level of ethical acceptance you associate with each action: "5" = very unethical, "4" = unethical, "3" = neutral or not sure, "2" = fairly ethical, and "1" = extremely ethical. Discuss whether the situation has ever been relevant for you, the circumstances associated with the situation that might affect your reaction to the degree of the potential ethical dilemma, and consequences resulting from participation in the situation.

    a. Taking credit for participation in a group project in which you did no work
    b. Using a false excuse for missing a mandatory class
    c. Cheating on an exam
    d. Turning in a paper from a "study file" as your own
    e. Turning in the same term paper for two different courses in which you are enrolled
    f. Copying your roommate's class notes without his or her permission
    g. Giving your teacher a gift
    h. Omitting a bibliographic citation in a paper
    i. Inaccurately embellishing your résumé
    j. As a corporate buyer, accepting a personal gift from an apparel representative
    k. Calling in sick to take a day off

l. Returning merchandise to a store that you have already worn

m. Using high-pressure sales to sell merchandise to a customer who you know cannot afford it

n. Scheduling more hours to employees you are friendly with and consequently cutting back hours of other employees

o. Ringing up a sale as if you were the seller when merchandise has been purchased from the "hold" rack

p. Misrepresenting the quality of the merchandise you are selling

2. How, as a manager or supervisor, would you deal with ethical dilemmas among subordinates? How might you respond to unethical behavior of a supervisor?

3. How, in an interview situation, might you deal with unethical questions? Would the existence of unethical questions in an interview affect your interest in the position? What additional factors might play into your decision?

4. Do you expect your professional behavior to be any different as a result of identifying a personal code of ethics? Why or why not?

STUDIO Activities

Visit the *Guide to Fashion Career Planning STUDIO* available at www.bloomsburyfashioncentral.com. The key elements are:

1. Summary of Chapter 9 text
2. Quiz
3. Writing a personal ethics statement
4. Ethics case study activities

   a. Case study form

5. Links to business ethics websites

VIDEO: Handling an Illegal Interview Question

References

American Marketing Association (AMA). (n.d.) Code of Ethics. Available online: http://www.amagvsu.com/statement-of-ethics.html

Blanchard, K., & Peale, N. V. (1988). *The power of ethical management.* New York: Fawcett Crest.

Bugeja, M. J. (1996). *Living ethics: Developing values in mass communication.* Boston: Allyn and Bacon.

Granger, M. M. (1996). *Case studies in merchandising apparel and soft goods.* New York: Fairchild.

Hira, T. K. (1996). Ethics: Personal and professional implications. *Journal of Family and Consumer Sciences, 88*(1), 6–9.

Knaub, P. K., Weber, M. J., & Russ, R. R. (1994). Ethical dilemmas encountered in Human Environmental Sciences: Implications for ethics education. *Journal of Family and Consumer Sciences, 86*(3), 23–30.

Lee, C. L., Weber, M. J., & Knaub, P. K. (1994). Ethical dilemmas of Human Science professionals: Developing case studies for ethics education. *Journal of Family and Consumer Sciences, 86*(4), 23–29.

NADA. (n.d.). Code of ethics. Available online: https://www.nada.org/codeofethics/

Paulins, V. A., Hillery, J. L., & Sturgill, A. (2015). Using personal mission statements and codes of ethics as career search tools. Presented at the International Textiles and Apparel Association Annual Meeting, November 7–11, Santa Fe, NM. Available online: www. itaaonline.org

Post, E. L. (1984). *Emily Post's etiquette: A guide to modern manners* (14th ed.). New York: Harper & Row.

Rabolt, N. J., & Miller, J. K. (1997). *Concepts and cases in retail and merchandise management.* New York: Fairchild.

Rabolt, N. J., & Miller, J. K. (2008). *Concepts and cases in retail and merchandise management* (2nd ed.). New York: Fairchild.

Schlessinger, L. (1996). *How could you do that?!: The abdication of character, courage, and conscience.* New York: HarperCollins.

Shriver, M. (2000). *Ten things I wish I'd known—before I went out into the real world.* New York: Warner Books.

Silverman, R., Welty, W., & Lyon, S. (1992). *Case studies for teacher problem solving* (Instructor's manual). New York: McGraw-Hill.

Sommers, C. H. (September 12, 1993). Teaching the virtues. *Chicago Tribune Magazine* reprint, p. 16.

CHAPTER 10
TRANSITIONING FROM COLLEGE TO CAREER

Your real education begins now.

—UNKNOWN

OBJECTIVES

- To identify and consider key components for personally evaluating a job offer, including all obligations surrounding work–life balance.
- To identify areas and explore tactics for the negotiation of job offers.
- To develop strategies for comparing multiple job offers.
- To identify professional methods for accepting or rejecting a job.
- To recognize the importance of professional behavior during the first year at a new job.
- To realize and recognize the importance of having a mentor and becoming a mentor as your career progresses.
- To consider problem-solving strategies when you find yourself in a job you do not like.
- To explore strategies for career search while working full-time in an entry-level position.
- To identify professional considerations and practices in resigning from your job.
- To identify and realize the value of lifelong learning opportunities.
- To develop strategies for ongoing career evaluation and for making career changes when appropriate.

By the time you reach this chapter, you may have already completed an internship and as a result of that internship, or as a result of your job search, have your first job offer. This chapter explores some of the key considerations as you embark on your career. This is a very exciting time as your hard work and academic achievements are starting to pay off in the form of your first job offers. When searching for your first job experience, review some of the strategies for landing the "perfect" one in Chapter 6, Box 6.3.

Before discussing the specifics surrounding a job offer, such as the responsibilities of the position, starting salary, and benefits, there are some general considerations about your career that are just as important. As you transition from a student to a full-time professional, it may help to ease any anxieties by identifying some of the adjustments you will experience. This is also a good time to understand how your career plans fit with your personal life and your values.

MAKING THE TRANSITION TO FULL-TIME WORK

Perhaps one of the biggest adjustments for recent college graduates is switching roles between being a college student and becoming a full-time professional. Identifying what you value the most in your life and evaluating how your career of choice fits with those values is probably one of the most important considerations to make as you embark on your career. Unfortunately, this step can be overlooked in the excitement of having a job offer and entering the workplace. Before accepting any job offer, you should definitely evaluate, or re-evaluate, your priorities in life. In fact, as you progress through your career, and your life, we encourage you to make this a part of your transitions. Knowing what is most important to you will help guide you to the right decision concerning the job offers you receive and the career moves you make.

As you move through life and your career, you will find that your priorities will change, depending on experiences and personal circumstances. Some of what you value when you are in your twenties will probably not have the same importance to you when you reach mid-life, so re-evaluating your priorities at different stages in your career will be necessary. This does not mean you can always predict what your values will be in the future. It also does not mean that you should be worried about making mistakes with your decisions; things are bound to change anyway. Rather, you should make decisions based on present circumstances and know that you can make adjustments as necessary to best serve the person you will become. If you have been reading the Careers Up Close profiles throughout this book, you may have noticed that many of the professionals' career paths took some unexpected turns, requiring them to make adjustments and take advantage of opportunities that were never anticipated when planning their career right out of college.

Anticipating Daily Routines and Obligations

One thing that can be anticipated, and something that is usually the first major change recent college graduates notice as they enter the workplace, is the difference in their daily routines and schedules. College is typically a time during which students have selected schedules that allow them to work, socialize, study, and attend classes at times best suited to them. For example, if you are a "morning" person, you can plan a schedule that allows you to get the majority of your classes and assignments done by early afternoon. However, once you graduate and begin your career, your schedule will probably be less flexible. Depending on the career you choose, you may have little say in the specific days and hours you work. This will be especially true as you are beginning your career. Your willingness to work nights, weekends, and even overnights (particularly in retailing) will demonstrate your commitment to the company and your desire to advance. Many instances will arise when you will be expected to work extra hours in order to meet deadlines or to solve problems. Adjusting to a 40+ hours workweek that is set by others can be difficult for many entry-level professionals.

As you have worked your way through this book, you have no doubt noticed how many times we mention the importance of researching and gathering as much information as possible about the companies and the careers you are considering. If you have done your homework in this regard, and asked the right questions in your interviews, you should have a good sense of the responsibilities and obligations you will be taking on as a new employee in a particular position at a particular company. This is extremely important in order to weigh your options when considering how the career fits with your life. Specifically, how will this career fit with the other things you value? For example, if having every Sunday available to spend with family or friends is important, you probably do not want to pursue a career in retail management. However, if you would value a weekday off, allowing you to spend some time alone or to avoid crowded stores and traffic, then retailing may be perfect for you! Many people in retailing careers cherish their days off during the week when they can take care of personal obligations and errands without the rush created by everyone else doing the same thing on the weekends.

The Work–Family Balancing Act

Another main career consideration that does not always affect entry-level decisions but nonetheless may become extremely important moving forward is the ability to balance work and family. Many young professionals do not consider this until they marry and want to start a family, at which time they may find it almost impossible to keep up with their career, family, and other obligations. At best, having a successful career along with raising a family and having some type of personal life is extremely hard. Although more employers are providing services to their employees (e.g., onsite child care) to help relieve some of those burdens, it can still be overwhelming at times. As you evaluate career opportunities, this should definitely be something to keep in mind—and even ask about prior to accepting an offer, if this is a concern.

The ability to balance work and family continues to be a major issue among all working parents—even wealthy celebrities such as Victoria Beckham. In an interview published by *Women's Wear Daily*, she addresses this topic, saying, "Sometimes I just want to scream, because I'm not sure how you are meant to do it all. I'm sure there are a lot of working mums out there. It's tough when you're trying to juggle." She admits, "With all the parents meetings and soccer matches, there are a lot of people who help me make all of this possible. I'm not doing any of this on my own" (Feitelberg, 2015).

Collin Wood Perdew, who is profiled in Careers Up Close 10.1, offers this advice concerning work–life balance:

> It can be very challenging, depending on the company culture and your individual team. In the end, you are accountable for your own career success and happiness. It is up to you to find a work–life balance and, if you are not happy, to go elsewhere. I am not saying that you can't have it all, but you definitely have to make choices—i.e., if your goal is to have three children by 30 and to be a stay-at-home mom, it is highly doubtful you will also be a company VP by then. It's all about choices and what is important to you. I have found that every new challenge has made me more informed of what my goals are and what I truly want in life.

You may also recall that Chiquita Cooper, profiled in Chapter 5, also addressed how switching roles between corporate retail and wholesale made it easier to balance work and family.

To further illustrate the complexities of balancing work and family, consider Box 10.1, which presents Dr. Laura McAndrews' research.

BOX 10.1 Work–Life Balance Research

Dr. Laura McAndrews studies the way fashion industry professionals balance career and personal life. She asserts that, in our careers, we don't "climb the *ladder*" but rather we climb the *lattice*. In other words, rather than seeking just one focused career goal, we should take into account various twists and turns that will occur over time. In reality, our lives and career paths offer multiple directions and a myriad of opportunities—being prepared to embrace opportunities and remain flexible when confronted with change enhances the likelihood of satisfaction and happiness in both personal and professional life aspects.

Dr. McAndrews conducted research investigating the internal struggles of five female apparel professionals living in New York City and Philadelphia in 2012. The results, presented in her University of Missouri master's thesis, "Between the Devil and the Deep Blue Sea(m): A Case Study Exploring the Borders between Work and Life Domains Described by Women in the U.S. Apparel Industry," document a tendency for women to deny needing a personal life during career-focused life stages, and subsequently to feel a loss of control and dissatisfaction when confronted with the absence of a fulfilling personal life.

Although struggle may occur with women in other industries, Dr. McAndrews' study focused on women working in the US apparel industry. That is because the uniqueness of the US apparel industry makes it difficult for female professionals to balance career with a personal life. Values and activities women partake in their work domain can be in contrast to values and activities in their life domain. This is different from other female-dominated industries, such as teaching or nursing, where

similar values and activities exist in both the work domain and life domain, such as helping others (McAndrews & Ha-Brookshire, 2013). The activities and values in the work domains found in the apparel industry may be considered more closely related to male-dominated work domains. Thus, women in the apparel industry may face different challenges when managing and crossing their work–life domains than women in other female-dominated industries do. Yet, we know little about how women in the US apparel industry deal with work–life borders.

Consequently, the study was designed to help gain a deep understanding of border-crossing and how this affects work–life balance among women in the apparel industry through the theoretical frameworks of Clark's (2015) work–family border theory. More specifically, this study had two key research questions: (a) to identify the events or situations triggering the participants to cross into their work and life domains; and (b) to understand the nature of the border between work and life domains that influences when, where, and the period of time the border-crossing occurs.

In understanding the border-crossing phenomena of triggering events and effects experienced by women working in the US apparel industry, the results of the study's data analysis revealed *grand view* border-crossing events. The *grand view* border-crossing events were milestones in the women's lives that affected their life situations—for example, having a baby, getting married, or being laid off at their job. These triggering events caused the women to border-cross between their work and life domains.

continued

BOX 10.1 Work–Life Balance Research (continued)

In the grand view of border-crossing events and effects, three themes emerged: (a) chaotic stage, described as a "very consuming" work domain, and "what is my life?" domain, (b) fight stage, described as keeping work and life separate, but "not too separate," and (c) calm stage, described as work and life blending together so that "there is not a clean line."

All the women in the study, at some point of their career and life, described how "work is 90% of my life and it should only be 50%," suggesting a chaotic stage of their lives. Their duties and responsibilities in their work domain seemed to be overwhelming and they would, for instance, "try to let it [work] go but [they] would dream about it." Their work domain consumed what little life domain they tried to have. They described not "know[ing] why [they] felt [they] don't need it [a personal life]." As a result of this consuming work domain and a very small life domain, the women seemed to feel their work domain dictated their life domain.

Because of life triggering events, some women find themselves moving out of the chaotic stage into the fight stage. One woman in the study had recently gotten married and was pregnant with her first child. In this stage, she seemed to fight to balance her work and life domain by creating a rigid border between her domains. To help fight against her work domain interfering with her life domain, she made it difficult for herself to check emails at home. She did not let her work emails come to her personal phone. There was a conscious struggle to keep her work and life domains separate and equal.

Other women may find themselves moving into the calm stage, where there is not such a rigid border between work and life domains and instead the two domains blend together. One woman in the study described how she "didn't want that" life anymore, alluding to not wanting the chaotic stage. In that chaotic stage, she thought about how "it had always been work [that] consumed me" and she was "tired of that lifestyle." The women that were in the calm stage made intentional choices to find a work situation where they had more control. In the study, one woman owned her own clothing boutique and another worked as a consultant in the apparel industry. Both women had previously worked for major US retail brands in product development, production, and sourcing. However, leaving their previous jobs and working for themselves gave them the control and flexibility they needed to also enjoy their life domain.

Though Dr. McAndrews' study identified three stages of women in the apparel industry balancing their work and life, there may be other stages as well. This study suggests three stages (chaotic, fight, and calm) to consider that may help women (and men, for that matter) who wish to enter the apparel industry manage their work and life. The border between work and life needs to be identified and managed by the individual based on his or her life and career goals. Ideally, apparel organizations will understand and support employees' ever-changing strategies for balancing domains.

The outcomes of Dr. McAndrews' research help working women realize that they are not alone in their struggles with work–life balance and also inform all working professionals about ways to negotiate a successful balance. Some suggestions for approaching a healthy

THE JOB OFFER

Once you have considered the previously discussed general career factors, you next need to identify specific items for review before accepting a job offer. It is understandable that after months of preparation and searching for a post-graduation entry-level position, the tendency for college students and new college graduates is to accept the first job offer that comes their way. This is especially true in times of a tight job market. Do not make this costly mistake without some careful consideration! Realize that the time between when the offer is made and the time when you accept is a time for negotiation. Even if the job offer you receive is one that you consider your *dream* job, there may still be room for further negotiation. Following are strategies for evaluating a job offer, negotiating a job offer, dealing with multiple job offers, accepting an offer, and rejecting an offer.

Evaluating an Offer

Although you may feel that you know everything you need to about the job you are being offered and have asked all of the important questions in your interviews, now is the time to take a critical look at the position you are being offered. By now you have identified which factors of a job are most important to you, so you will want to make sure that you consider all of these key details. Besides the considerations of work–life balance already discussed, other common areas to examine in evaluating your offer include the base salary and performance bonuses; benefits such as medical, dental, life insurance, savings and retirement, profit sharing, and stock options; and other perks, including vacation time, personal days, opportunities for volunteering, and tuition reimbursement, to name a few. To help you evaluate your job offers, the *STUDIO* website accompanying this book provides a job offer checklist from collegegrad.com that you should fill out for each job offer you receive. This comprehensive list includes such topic areas as *general benefits*, *performance review schedule*,

BOX 10.2 Personal Questions to Ask in Evaluating a Job Offer

Personal questions to ask in evaluating a job offer:

- Will I like the job?
- Will I gain personal satisfaction in performing the job?
- Is the job something I am truly interested in?

- Is the job in line with my long-term career goals?
- Will I like the people I work with?
- Am I proud to represent the company?
- Will I have fun at work?
- Will I look forward to going to work at this company?

and *training*. It also includes a list of questions to ask your prospective employer. This checklist will allow you to critically evaluate each offer and can also prove helpful for comparing multiple job offers.

Once you have considered all of the working details of the job you are being offered, perhaps the most important questions to ask yourself are the ones listed in Box 10.2, which are concerned with your personal feelings and your core values.

Consider findings of a survey published in 2014 by the Conference Board (Cheng et al., 2014), a NYC-based nonprofit research firm, which reported that the majority of Americans are unhappy with their jobs. Three decades ago when the survey was first done, 61.1 percent of workers liked their jobs. Areas in which there was the least amount of satisfaction included promotion policies (for women) and company benefits, such as health insurance. The same survey showed that, although income levels did tend to increase satisfaction levels, even high-end earners' satisfaction levels have fallen over time. For example, only 41.4 percent of workers earning $50,000–$75,000 were happy with their jobs. The factors that made people more likely to be happy at work were "interest in work" and "people at work." Susan Adams (2014) reported about this survey for *Forbes* and highlighted that 47.8 percent of men say that they are satisfied with their work compared with 46.3 percent of women. Therefore, in addition to considering the specific responsibilities and the salary of the job, do not forget to evaluate your personal feelings concerning the position. No matter how good an offer may seem, it will not be worth much if it is a job in which you have no interest.

Another word of caution when evaluating job offers—do not make the mistake of letting others tell you what you *should* do. Of course you will want to consider others' opinions concerning your decision, especially those persons whom you respect, or those who also have a stake in your decision, such as a spouse and perhaps other family members. However, do not accept a job because someone else tells you to, or for reasons such as the status it may offer you in the eyes of your friends. Use the lists you have prepared, and remember that you are the best person to make the ultimate decision because you know yourself best.

Negotiating an Offer

Once you have critically evaluated all aspects of the job offer, it is now time to begin the negotiation process. For many college students and recent graduates, this is the most difficult part of the job search. However, do not make the mistake of accepting an offer without negotiation. Even if the job sounds "perfect," there may still be room for negotiation. In fact, most companies will expect you to do this. Remember, you will not receive any more than what you ask for. Although your goal is to secure the most you can, a company's goal is to hire you for the least they can.

Negotiating an offer does not always involve asking for more money. However, if you are not happy with the salary offer, this should be your first area of negotiation. In order to successfully negotiate a higher salary, you must research what you are worth. Almost all websites addressing career issues will offer a section of "typical" salaries for a particular job in a certain region of the country. A particularly useful site is salary.com, which offers a salary calculator (the "Salary Wizard") that lists typical entry-level positions and their average salaries. Some of the positions relating to fashion, retailing, and apparel merchandising include design assistant, technical designer, assistant buyer, store manager, district retail sales manager, and social media specialist. If you plan to ask for more money, you should use this information to justify your request. Letting the prospective employer know that you have researched this topic will lend far more credibility to your request than letting him or her think that you just invented a random number. A typical statement for presenting your request could be: "According to my research, the average salary for a _____ [e.g., assistant buyer] in the Midwest is between _____ and _____ [range of salary]. Given my experience and background, I believe that a fair salary for this position would be _____."

As previously mentioned, negotiating an offer does not always involve salary. In fact, as you begin evaluating your job offer and complete the list provided on the accompanying *STUDIO* website, you will no doubt identify numerous areas for negotiation. Some of these include benefits, vacation time, profit sharing, promised salary increases over time, training and education reimbursement, compensated travel and travel opportunities, and overtime. In evaluating each of these areas, if you find any aspects of the current offer that are not satisfactory, you should make note of what it would take to make each acceptable. Prepare to discuss these issues with your potential employer. In communicating your concerns, you need to keep the outlook for resolution positive. Collegegrad.com suggests the following dialogue for an offer that is unacceptable:

> I am still very interested in working with you and your company; however [never use the word 'but'], at this point I am not able to accept the offer for the following reason(s): [state your reasoning succinctly and what part or parts of the offer are lacking]. If you were able to _____ [give your proposed solution], I would gladly accept the position immediately. Are you able to help bring this about?

Be aware, however, that you should only use this negotiation tactic for offers that are truly unacceptable, and you should be prepared to walk away entirely if no compromise can be reached. Sometimes if the company sees you are ready to walk away, they may make you a better offer. On the other hand, they may tell you they have given you their best offer and withdraw the offer completely. In addition, if the company meets your request, you should be prepared to follow through and accept the offer.

If the previous approach seems uncomfortable to you, you may approach the negotiation in a slightly different way. Be brief and straightforward and say, "I have a concern with an aspect of the offer," then stop talking and wait to see what they say.

A last word of caution when considering the negotiation of an offer. Many positions in fashion and retail have set salaries for a particular job title with future raises based on performance. However, there may be a salary range, which gives you a little bit of negotiation space. Remember, too, that salary is not the only thing that is negotiable concerning your job offer. Perhaps you would be happy with an extra week of vacation. Or would you like your first performance review done earlier than what is typical for the company? Regardless of your priorities, be assured that you must make your needs known in order for them to be considered. To help you, Box 10.3 lists some common areas that are often negotiated when considering a job offer.

Multiple Job Offers

Although most students do not believe it when their job search begins, it is common for college students and recent graduates to receive multiple job offers. When this happens, the focus of the job search switches from finding a job to choosing the right one. Many of the tools you need to aid in your decisions are the ones we have previously discussed. For each job

BOX 10.3 Items to Negotiate in a Job Offer

Money or Money-Related

- Salary
- Initial, and subsequent, pay increases (the percentage and timing)
- Performance bonuses (percentage and timing)
- Tuition reimbursement (present if you are still in school at the time of the offer; future education)
- Stock options and profit sharing
- Benefits

- Vacation, overtime, and personal days
- Company car
- Travel expenses and reimbursement
- Relocation assistance

Nonmoney

- Technology and equipment provided
- Training/development
- Your title
- Performance review dates
- Telecommuting/working from home

you are offered, you should fill out the job offer checklist on the accompanying website. This will allow you to carefully evaluate the responsibilities of the job, the company itself (including the benefits package), and your projected level of job satisfaction. In reviewing your evaluations of each offer, you may be able to easily reach a decision.

In the case that you cannot reach a decision based on the evaluations you have already made, it may be helpful to do a side-by-side comparison of each position. On the left-hand side of a piece of paper, make a list of all the job factors that are most important to you. After completing the list, rank each factor in order of its importance to you. Across the top of the page, list each company from which you have an offer. Work through the list of factors and evaluate every job you are considering against that list. Which company provides the most benefits in relationship to your particular requirements?

Another strategy you can employ in evaluating your job offers is to simply list the advantages and disadvantages of each position. Look at the lists side by side. Which position offers the most advantages? Which position has more disadvantages? If, after employing these strategies, you are still unable to make a decision, you may just have to make a decision based on what *feels* best to you at the time. *Gut feelings*, or intuition, many times play an important role in decision making and will most often guide you to the right decision.

We also want to emphasize the value of going outside of your comfort zone when it comes to selecting a job located in an unfamiliar city or with workplace colleagues who present diverse perspectives that are unfamiliar to you. Hopefully you have embraced early work experiences and internships that have enabled you to try new geographic and social surroundings, but if not, be sure to recognize some of the fears that considering a job in an unfamiliar location presents. We urge new career professionals to take risks and accept challenges. These are steps you need to take to grow—and your courage to take on exciting, new experiences reflects positively on your professional profile.

One of the most common dilemmas that students have regarding multiple job offers is what to do if they receive a great job offer after already accepting another position. Unfortunately, there is no easy solution to handling this situation. In fact, the easiest solution to this problem is to avoid it. Making sure you have eliminated every other employer as a possibility before accepting any offer can do this. In fact, receiving a job offer from one company may prompt other employers to make a quicker decision concerning your hiring.

If you receive a job offer before hearing from another employer that you have interviewed with and are interested in, it is perfectly acceptable to tell the employer making the offer that you need more time before reaching a decision. Most employers realize that college students are interviewing with many companies and that entry-level employees want to consider all of their options before reaching a decision. Of course, some recruiters will still pressure you to make a decision right away. Remember, it is their job to get you to accept the company's offer! However, do not let them sway you into making a snap decision. Tell them that you need more time. You should then call all employers that you have interviewed with, or that you would like to interview with, and tell them of your job offer. For those companies with which you have interviewed, you might say something like this: "Ms. Jones, this is Sally Johnson. I interviewed with you last week for the _____ position you have available. I am very interested [or, *most* interested, if that is the case] in working for your company; however, I have received another job offer for which I need to make a decision. I do not want to make any decisions before weighing all of my options. When might I expect you to make a decision concerning my candidacy with your company?" Ideally, this will prompt the second employer to make a decision regarding an offer, especially if the company is interested in you.

If there are companies that you would like to interview with, you should call them and tell them that you currently have a job offer but would like to interview with them before making a decision. Again, this may prompt a quicker response on their part. Someone who is attractive to one company usually becomes more attractive to another. Having a job offer in hand definitely empowers you in communicating with other potential employers.

As mentioned previously, you should do everything you can to avoid the situation in which you have accepted a job offer and then receive another one that you find more attractive. In this case, you should never accept a job with Company A and then back out because Company B has given you a better offer. Once you make a decision, do not entertain any other options. This is a matter of professional ethics. Remember, in today's fast-paced and interconnected world, it is highly likely that at some point in your career you will encounter the people from Company A again, and they *will* remember that you did not honor a professional commitment with them. Remember, too, that may mean that you may never have another opportunity to work for them, and at some point in your career that may be highly regrettable.

Accepting an Offer

Once you have evaluated all offers and reached a decision, you should call the employer and verbally accept the offer. It is a good idea to repeat the offer back to the company to make sure you are both in agreement as to what you are accepting. You should also indicate that you will be expecting a written offer of the agreement. One word of caution: *Until you have a written agreement, you do not have an official job offer.* If you are working for another employer, or if you are waiting to hear from other potential employers, do nothing (e.g., resigning, withdrawing your name from consideration) until you have a signed, written agreement from your new employer. Verbal agreements can be withdrawn, and it is actually fairly common that they are, especially in tough economic conditions. Once you do receive a written offer, you will need to give your current employer sufficient notice (e.g., two weeks, minimum), and also notify others with whom you have interviewed that you are no longer available.

Once you have verbally accepted an offer, you will also want to prepare a brief acceptance letter to send to your new employer. Include a statement that you are accepting the offer for the specific position (e.g., assistant buyer) at the agreed-upon salary. You should also provide your start date. Close the letter by thanking the company for the opportunity, and mention that you are looking forward to becoming a productive member of its team. For ease of preparation, the *STUDIO* website (www.bloomsburycentral.com) provides you with an acceptance-letter template.

On a related note, it may be that you will not start your new job for several months, or even a full school year, after you have accepted a position. This situation usually occurs when college students complete successful internships during their undergraduate schooling, after which the company makes a permanent offer. If you find yourself in this situation, continue to keep in touch with the company until you begin working there full-time. Of course, if you will be working at the company part-time during the school year, this will happen automatically. However, if not, you can keep in touch via email, phone calls, or simply by dropping in to say hello once in a while. This is especially important in the merchandising and retailing field because people tend to move around and get promoted quickly, which means you may be working for an entirely new management team by the time you begin your permanent position. Therefore, keeping in touch is not just good PR on your part, but it will assure you that the new management knows you and, most importantly, knows about the offer you have been made. You may want to exercise some of the strategies presented in Box 8.5, "Reasons to Contact Future Work Experience Sites."

If you are relocating for your new job, it is never too early to start planning for your move. Although many companies will offer you help to assure a smooth process with the actual move, some new graduates find themselves somewhat homesick and at a loss as to what to do with themselves socially once they arrive in a new city. In that regard, Box 10.4 offers tips for a successful relocation strategy.

Rejecting an Offer

There are a variety of reasons for rejecting a job offer. Regardless of the reason, however, turning down a job is not easy for most job seekers. Some will even avoid this conversation by leaving voice mails after hours or sending emails, neither of which are acceptable. Rejecting an offer in a more professional manner leaves the door open for future opportunities with those employers.

A best-case scenario is that you are accepting a better offer with another company. In that case, you should call all other employers with whom you have interviewed, or sent résumés, to let them know of your decision. Your communication with the companies that you are eliminating, or whose offers you are rejecting, should be straightforward and honest. If you are turning down one company because you have received a better offer in terms of salary and other benefits, you should tell them that also. Depending on how badly the other company wants you, and how much flexibility they have, they may counteroffer.

It is perfectly acceptable to keep in contact with recruiters who represent companies that you have rejected, especially with the availability of LinkedIn and other social networking resources. That is, in fact, an excellent networking strategy. You never know when a particular

BOX 10.4 Tips for a Successful Relocation Strategy

- Contact a realtor. Work with a realtor while you are seeking housing, even if you plan to live in an apartment. A realtor can give you insights into the characteristics of various neighborhoods and help you discover a fit between your interests and your new neighborhood.

- Become active in professional organizations. This is a great way to meet people who have similar interests and values to yours, as well as a method of establishing professional and career growth.

- Join a faith-based organization. If you are inclined to seek a spiritual home, the networks that are available to you through churches, synagogues, mosques, and other faith-based organizations can create a support system separate from your work acquaintances. Many social opportunities that are consistent with your spiritual beliefs and values will be available to you through this organization.

- Volunteer. This is another great way to meet other people—and to do good work that has a positive impact on your new community. Opportunities ranging from Big Brothers/Big Sisters to the local humane society, homeless shelters, and Habitat for Humanity are choices from which you can select.

- Join a fitness club. Joining a fitness club or other exercise-oriented activity is another way to meet people, and has the added benefit of fitness and improved health. Exercise is a good way to reduce the stress that builds from a day at the office and maintain your stamina as you work hard in your new career.

- Explore a hobby. Whether you are already an avid scrap-booker or you have always wanted to learn how to ice skate, explore opportunities to develop and become (or stay) active in a hobby. Many towns and cities offer continuing education classes on a plethora of topics. It is important to develop your interests!

- Contact a local alumni association. University alumni associations are often located in larger cities across the United States and sometimes abroad. If you are an alumna/us of a social organization such as a fraternity or sorority, there is likely to be an alumni association for you to join in the vicinity.

company will be a perfect fit for you in the future. Many long-term professional relationships, in fact, have begun through an interview situation—with the job search candidate ultimately taking a position with another company. You never want to burn bridges. The professional contacts that you are making during the career search process may be able to offer opportunities that are a better fit for you a year or so down the road, but this will only happen if your initial interactions with these contact people resulted in relationships that remain mutually honest and cordial.

YOUR FIRST JOB

The impressions people form of you in the first few weeks of your new job may have everlasting effects on your long-term success. Therefore, it is critical that the image you create for yourself is positive. The way you talk, behave, communicate through emails and telephone, make decisions, dress, and portray yourself on social media are just a few of the areas in which your co-workers will immediately evaluate you. Knowing what to expect during the first day, and subsequent weeks, at a new job should help you put your best image forward.

What to Expect Your First Day on the Job

One of the things that may surprise you about the first day on the job is that you may find yourself bored. This is because much of the day may be filled with minor details such as being shown where you will work, how to find things that you will need (e.g., office supplies), and how to do certain tasks, most of which you may find unchallenging. You may also have to fill out numerous forms relating to your employment, health care, and liability. It is also common to be given an employee handbook to read or to spend the day viewing training videos. Even though the tasks you are completing may seem mundane to you, remember to keep a positive attitude and exhibit enthusiasm.

On your first day, and continuing for several weeks, you will probably have many questions that you need to have answered. In that regard, find out who you should ask when those questions do arise. For example, should you ask your immediate peers, or your supervisor? Who can answer the questions that you have? Because others will be busy doing their own tasks and may have minimal time to take away from their own responsibilities, it is important that you not repeatedly interrupt others. Although it is understandable that you will need answers to your questions, you do not want to be perceived as a pest. A good idea is to write your questions down in a notebook or use a note-taking feature on your phone or tablet so that if you must interrupt someone, you can ask several questions at once. (See Box 8.6 in Chapter 8.) Also, record your answers so that you can refer back to them. Do not expect to remember everything you are going to learn in the next few months.

It is also common to be confused on your first day at a new job. You will meet many new people with many different titles. Because you will want to remember names and faces, and how the people you meet fit into the company structure, it is a good idea to record that information in a notebook or on your phone for future reference. Collect business cards if feasible. If writing things down makes you feel uncomfortable, it is perfectly acceptable to ask the person showing you around if he or she minds if you take some notes as you go through the day. Most people will perceive this as a positive sign of your willingness to learn what you can as quickly as you can. Taking a student role the first few weeks on the job is something you should expect to do and will be a good transition for you, too.

Another important aspect of your first day will be learning about the rules at your new company. For example, find out what your normal working hours will be, including any breaks or lunch times. Regardless of what you see others doing, you should adhere to those rules, especially during your first few weeks. Every company has written and "unwritten" rules that you need to identify as quickly as possible. One of the best ways to do this is to watch other employees who are successful and model their behavior. These are also the individuals you may be able to ask for direction, as needed.

How to Succeed in the First Few Weeks

The stress of transitioning from the role of a college student to that of a young professional with a brand-new job can be somewhat overwhelming. Following are a few guidelines to follow that may help ease some of the anxiety that you are almost certain to feel.

- Identify a mentor. One of the best things you can do to assure your success is to identify a mentor within your new company. If you do not know anyone, you may ask the human resources office if there are people willing to serve in that capacity. Or, better yet, if you can find someone who is an alumnus from your college, you will more than likely have an immediate rapport with that person by virtue of your shared alma mater. If the human resources office at your new job cannot help you identify someone, many college career offices keep records of past graduates who want to serve as mentors to new hires within their particular company.

- Identify key players within the company. First, and as previously mentioned, one of the best things you can do during your first few weeks at a new job is to identify key players and model their behavior. This also includes understanding the chain of command and the importance of following that as you navigate your new responsibilities. Perhaps one of the worst career moves a new employee can make is going above an immediate supervisor or not following the proper chain of command, whether that move is intentional or not. At the same time, you should get to know the successful employees and make yourself known to them. Many times these are the people who will influence your career and who can also be instrumental in helping you transition successfully into your new position. The successful people in the company are the ones that you need to impress. Being visible and letting people know who you are will go a long way in establishing yourself as a potential star within the company.

- Avoid gossip and most office politics. Within any company, you will find a certain amount of office politics and gossip mills. Many recent graduates find this to be the most unexpected and difficult part of their new position. Many people at your new job will try to involve you in gossip or in "bashing" your new bosses. You must never participate in this type of behavior, even though it can be quite contagious. Show respect for all of those you work with, especially your boss, and avoid becoming involved in gossip or behavior that you may later regret. Also, remember that you can be cordial to others without joining in their unprofessional behavior. In fact, taking a stand against such behavior may encourage others to do the same. Note, however, that avoiding or ignoring the politics entirely is not your best course of action. Refer to Box 9.5 in Chapter 9, which offers advice on how to best deal with these situations.

- Dress professionally. Dress in the retailing field can vary considerably from one company to another (e.g., upscale department store versus discount retailing) and from one aspect of the industry to another (e.g., design industry versus buying industry). As a new employee, you should find out what your company's dress code is and adhere to it conservatively, at least for your first few weeks. Again, observe how a successful person in the company dresses if you are unsure of the appropriateness of your wardrobe. Today, many companies have adopted a business casual look; however, because of abuse by employees or perhaps just because of a lack of understanding of what "business casual" means, some companies are now rethinking those guidelines. You should also note that business casual does not generally include denim jeans. However, if your company does allow you to wear denim (for example, on "casual Fridays"), there are also guidelines you should follow if you choose to do so. As mentioned previously, you should always err on the side of being too conservative with your dress versus being perceived as unprofessional. There are many good wardrobe planning and professional dress resources on the market to help you as needed. You can also review Chapter 7, which discusses professional dress in terms of interviewing and Box 9.2 in Chapter 9, which addresses typical workplace rules for dress and appearance. These same principles apply to dressing for your first job. One last word of advice given to a class of our students by one of our former students: *Dress for the position you want and not the position you currently hold.*

- You cannot be everything to all people. No matter how hard you try, there will be some people in your new environment who will not like you. Expect this to happen and do not take it personally when it does. Others not liking you can happen for a variety of reasons, most of which have nothing to do with you as a person. For example, maybe you are stepping into a position that another employee wanted or that a friend of that employee lost. Some people do not like new employees simply because they are new. Regardless of the reason, if you find yourself in a situation in which another employee seems less than cooperative with you, ignore the problem if possible and continue to behave in a professional manner. It is not realistic to expect that everyone in a work environment will like each other. Even so, it is important to behave professionally and respect differences with others that will no doubt occur. Even if you are unable to resolve your conflicts with some, you will gain the respect of others by behaving professionally.

- Relax and take care of yourself. Most employees are too hard on themselves during the first few weeks of a new job. Putting yourself under such undue stress will not only result in your making more mistakes, but may also make you physically sick. Although you will want to do your best, do not forget that it is extremely important to take care of yourself at the same time. Your co-workers are human beings who will probably be forgiving of any minor mistakes that you are bound to make during your first few weeks. Mistakes are to be expected, and simply seeing you put your best effort forward to do the best job possible will impress your new co-workers. Therefore, do not try to do too much in the first few weeks, or you will find yourself completely stressed and burned out in a short amount of time.

Heather Holoubek, Senior Buyer of Prestige Skincare with Ulta Salon, Cosmetics & Fragrance, Inc., notes that when she entered the "real world" from college she found herself facing some challenging situations that she was not expecting. Box 10.5 contains her list of the top ten things she wants you to know about the real world. The list also summarizes many of the important points covered in this book.

BOX 10.5 Heather Holoubek's Top Ten List of Things to Know about the Real World

1. Never, ever sell yourself short. Even if you are asked to do something that you do not feel particularly confident about, figure out a way to do it. If you exude confidence and believe in yourself, others will also believe in you! Sometimes it is necessary to jump in feet first and take a chance.

2. You will do a lot of things that are not in your job description. As a new employee, you should be willing to take on any job that is asked of you. In the first few months on the job, you should say yes to almost all requests from your superiors. Although you want to protect yourself from being taken advantage of, you should have the attitude of being willing to do anything that is needed!

3. Find a trusted mentor. Your mentor should be someone within the company you join, and preferably in a position above yours. If you cannot identify someone within the same company, you should at least find someone in the same industry that you can turn to for advice. As you progress in your career, you should return the favor and become a mentor to someone else. Relationships with mentors can last a lifetime and will be among the most important professional relationships you have.

4. No job is perfect. At first the position you hold will sometimes be about what you learn in that position and where it can take you rather than about the actual position you are currently in. In other words, many entry-level positions are stepping stones to better things, but you

must be willing to learn everything you can and work hard.

5. Never forget where you came from. As you progress into management, you should always remember what it was like, or would be like, to be in positions below you. A great rule of thumb is, "Never ask others to do something that you are not willing to do yourself." Managers should lead by example, which often means doing the most mundane jobs alongside sales associates or other entry-level personnel. When others see that you are willing to do what is necessary for the good of the team, they are more likely to take the same attitude. In the long run, this makes a better work environment for everyone!

6. Set goals. One of the most effective tools you can use to aid in your development is to set goals and work toward achieving them. Once you have identified your goals, you should write them down. Generally, when you write down something, you are more likely to get it done. Remember that your goals can take various forms. They can be general or very specific, and can apply to your personal or professional life. They will also change as time goes by. However, the bottom line is that you need to set goals!

7. Always move "up" when making job changes. Never take a new position that is a step backward. Always move up when taking another position. Of course, this can mean many things, depending on who you are and where your priorities lie. Always ask yourself what you have to

gain by taking another position (e.g., better opportunities in the long run, more money, fewer hours, etc.).

8. Be your own advocate! Let people know what you are doing—do not assume they know. For many young professionals, this is one of the hardest things to do. However, it is one of the most important things you can do for your professional development and advancement. In the hectic pace of today's work world, some of your work may go unnoticed if you do not point it out. Also, keep documentation of your efforts—such a record will be particularly useful at review time. Remember, it's a good thing to pat yourself on the back when you have done a good job!

9. Hold onto your friends from each position you hold. The retail and merchandising field tends to be a very small industry, and you will no doubt encounter the same individuals throughout your career. Never "burn bridges"; instead, retain good relationships with former co-workers and supervisors. They will be a valuable network for you!

10. Remain professional at all times. No matter how pervasive gossip and office politics are in your work environment, you should avoid both. Although it may be difficult to remain neutral, especially when others are participating, you have nothing to gain by engaging in this conduct. It is especially important to never criticize your boss to others at work. If you have a problem with your boss, you should address it with him or her in a professional manner, rather than complaining to others. Over time, your professional behavior will earn you respect by all concerned. Remember, no matter how hard it may be, never gossip or become embroiled in office politics!

What If You Don't Like the Job?

Sometimes, no matter how efficient you have been in evaluating a new job, or how hard you have tried, you may find that your job is not living up to your expectations. Although you may ultimately decide that you should move on, this should not be your first course of action.

Before making any decisions, you should be sure that you have had time to adequately assess your job. If you have been at your job for fewer than six months, you probably do not yet have a realistic view of what to expect. If this is your first job after college, the stress or dissatisfaction that you are feeling may be due, in large part, to your transitioning into the different life role of a young professional. In other words, make sure that you are not blaming your new position for angst you may be feeling about other changes in your life. In that case, changing positions will not solve your problems.

However, if you do find yourself unhappy with your job, you will need to discuss your concerns with a mentor or your immediate supervisor.

Ask for an appointment to speak with this person in private and be prepared to specifically state your issues. Examples of items you may want to discuss include promises that are not being kept, the lack of challenges in your position, or any situations causing you undue stress. It is a good idea to prepare a list ahead of time so that you will have an outline of all of the major points you want to cover in your meeting. This list will help to keep the meeting focused, as there is sometimes a tendency for individuals to stray from their intended topics, especially if they are upset or disappointed about something. Having such a list will also let your supervisor or mentor know that you have put some thought into your concerns and that you are not just acting on a whim. After you have covered all of your points, try to come to a mutual agreement on specific courses of action to solve your problems. Then, schedule another meeting within a reasonable time frame to follow up on the proposed solutions. At your next meeting, you can evaluate how the proposed solutions are, or are not, working and revise the previous strategies as necessary. If, after several months, things have not changed, then you may have to consider other options.

Exploring Opportunities Beyond Your First Job

Although switching jobs after less than a year does not carry the same stigma it once did, you should still weigh your decision heavily before doing so. The ultimate decision you make may come down to asking yourself how important it is for you to honor your commitments and how much you feel you owe your employer.

Should You Stay or Should You Go?

According to Alan Goodman, chairman of the National Association of Colleges and Employers' Committee for Professional Conduct, if the company is delivering on its promises to you, it may be your ethical responsibility to stay. However, if it is not, and company representatives will not talk about it, then new hires have the right to look elsewhere. Table 10.1 provides some guidance on this topic.

If you find that you cannot get along with your boss, you may also have a valid reason for leaving a new job. However, be sure that you have made every effort to resolve your differences rather than simply quitting at the first sign of conflict. Sometimes, as mentioned previously, no matter what you do or how hard you try, there will be those with whom you cannot get along. If this person is your boss, it may be very difficult for you to be promoted regardless of your efforts and achievements.

TABLE 10.1

SHOULD YOU CHANGE JOBS OR STAY WHERE YOU ARE?

Remain with Your Current Employer If . . .	*Change Employers If . . .*
You like to think about your job on weekends and decide what you might do to perform it better.	You can hardly wait until 5 o'clock rolls around.
You'd like to do this kind of work, even if you didn't need the money.	You really don't have much in common with your fellow workers, customers, clients, or others with whom you deal.
Many of your interests are centered on your job.	You feel tired and irritable much of the time.
It's the kind of thing you do well, and you like the feeling of success that it provides.	It is almost impossible to lead the kind of life you want on your income and there's not much chance of improvement.
You like the feeling you get when something is completed.	The hours and kind of work interfere drastically with your preferred lifestyle.
Your colleagues are great and you enjoy the atmosphere.	Your employer isn't doing well and conditions may not get better.
What you do is identified so you have the feeling that you will be judged on your own merit.	The job stress and requirements adversely affect your self-concept.
You like the geographical area where you must live.	The work is boring and it is getting to you.
Promotional opportunities appear to be present.	There doesn't seem to be any job to which you might transfer.
You are proud, or at least not embarrassed, to tell friends where you work.	You have discussed your plans to leave with persons you respect.
Your position is compatible with your needs and values.	You have another job to go to.
Your work enables you to express your life purpose.	The work and organization are not congruent with your needs and values.
	You are unable to express your sense of purpose through your work.

Source: *Career Opportunities News*, P.O. Box 190, Garrett Park, MD 20896. Reprinted with permission of *Career Opportunities News.*

Before giving up entirely on the relationship, you should seek the advice of someone in the company whom you respect and can trust (e.g., your mentor). If you are having problems with your boss, chances are that others have had similar problems. If this is the case, others may have solutions that you have not considered. If, however, your repeated efforts to get along with your boss are fruitless, you may need to consider other options. Those may be with another company, or perhaps you would be happy if allowed to transfer to another area within the same company. The accompanying website (www.bloomsburycentral.com) for this book contains an interactive quiz to help you with such a decision.

In today's job market, another valid reason for switching jobs sooner than you may like is if you notice the company's financial rating becoming increasingly bleak. This may be evident in plunging stock values or massive layoffs, which, unfortunately, have become more commonplace these days. If you find yourself in this situation, it is a good idea to be proactive with your career. You should do everything to protect yourself, which means that it is perfectly acceptable to start looking for a new job. You do not want to wait until you are unemployed to start looking for another position. Remember the adage, "It's easier to find a job when you have a job!" In other words, you want to avoid the added stress that being unemployed brings to any job search.

Looking for Another Job While You Are Still Employed

Regardless of the reason, if you find yourself looking for another job while you are still employed, consider the following words of caution. One of the quickest ways to get fired or to be laid off from your current job prematurely is for your supervisor to find out that you looking for another job. Therefore, you should be as discreet as possible. Do *not* use the office equipment at your present job to type your résumé, copy your résumé, or communicate in any way with prospective employers. Invariably you will leave a copy of your résumé, or a cover letter, lying around (usually in the copy machine) for the wrong person to find.

On a related note, be very careful about who you tell that you are looking for another job, and continue to perform at your highest ability. Ideally, no one at your current job should know about your new job search. However, this may not be possible, especially if you need to use some of your present co-workers as references. In this case, tell only those select few and make sure that you can trust them to keep your secret. You may also need to let your prospective employers know that they should not call anyone at your current job other than those whose names you have provided to them. You can achieve this by mentioning in your cover letter and correspondence with them that you would like your application to remain confidential at this time.

Lastly, you will need to be somewhat creative in terms of taking phone calls and scheduling interview appointments with potential employers. List your cell phone number on your résumé and provide an outgoing voice mail message letting callers know either what time you will be available to answer the phone, or what time you will return their call. You will also need to schedule interviews before or after your current working hours or on your lunch break if that is convenient. Most prospective employers will respect the fact that you are currently working and will be flexible in scheduling around your commitments.

Resigning from Your Job

When the time comes for you to resign from your current job, you will need to do so in a professional manner. People tend to be mobile within the fashion and retail-merchandising fields, making it somewhat of a "small" world, especially if you stay within the same region of the country. You may think that you never want to work for your present company again, but chances are extremely good that you will encounter many of your current co-workers again. Although, like many people, you may dream of expressing every frustration and discontentment you have had with the company when you submit your resignation, the truth of the matter is that you should not do so. It is extremely important that you continue to exhibit professional behavior when resigning and "burn no bridges" when leaving a company.

As you will note by looking at the example and template provided on the *STUDIO* website (www.bloomsburyfashioncentral.com), a resignation letter need not be long or detailed, but rather should be short and to the point. It should simply state that you are giving your current employer notice of your resignation as of a specific effective date. Of course, you should give a minimum of two weeks' notice and be as considerate as possible concerning deadlines or projects for which you have prior commitments. The closing of the letter should be a general thank-you for the opportunities you have been given. Remember that this letter will probably become a part of your permanent record with the company, so you should say nothing negative in it that might damage your reputation. You never know when you might want to return to the company in a different capacity, or how the letter may be used when future employers request references.

Although most employers will appreciate your willingness to stay on the job and honor the resignation date you have provided them, do not be alarmed if your employer does not. At some companies it is policy to terminate an employee immediately upon his or her resignation. In these cases, you will probably be told to pack up your belongings and leave the premises at once. This practice is common, especially where employees are in charge of a large amount of inventory, privy to confidential company data, or when your new employer is a competitor. Be prepared for this to happen, and if you find yourself in this situation, continue to behave in a professional manner, remaining courteous and cooperative. Once you leave, you always have the option of calling your new employer to tell them you will be available to start earlier, providing that is what you would like to do. If not, enjoy the extra, unplanned days off to relax and regenerate before starting your new and exciting job!

In the event that your employer allows you to stay to work out your notice, use that time to perform your job at an exceptional level. Save any celebration for friends and family members. Although some of your co-workers may be happy for you, there will be others who will not be. During your last weeks on the job, and as in any work situation, you should continue to behave professionally and to do everything you can to help others transition into your position or responsibilities once you leave. Some examples of things you may offer to do include giving others updates on any projects you are currently involved with, and providing co-workers with pertinent information about company clients. Remain gracious and, before leaving, be sure to thank everyone for the opportunity of working with him or her. Your behavior during the last few weeks on a job speaks volumes about your work and professional ethics. Be sure to leave on a positive note.

MOVING THROUGH YOUR CAREER

Because this book is aimed at the new professional, we have chosen to concentrate on career advice for college students and entry-level professionals. However, we believe a few things are worthy of mention that will become more important as you move through your career. Specifically, we encourage you to work with a mentor, or mentors, and to value life-long learning.

Working with a Mentor

Throughout this book, we have mentioned the importance of identifying and working with a mentor. At all stages in your career and even in your personal life, working with someone who is more experienced than you in whatever field you are in can have a huge impact on your success. Over the past few years, increasing importance has been given to the role a mentor can play, especially for women, and we do not see that trend going away anytime soon. In fact, mentorship continues to grow in popularity, partly because of Sheryl Sandberg's best-selling book *Lean In* (2013). Note in the Careers Up Close 6.2 profile highlighting Molly Doyle and her daughter Katie Cawley the importance of mentoring and work–life balance in their successful careers.

As you advance in your career, you may also find yourself transitioning to the role of mentor to those who are less experienced. Take this opportunity, especially given that many mentors learn as much from their mentees as the mentees learn from them. Becoming a mentor is a win-win situation when people are matched properly. For example, mentors today often have their younger mentees teach them about social media and other tech applications that younger workers are generally more skilled at using. Because we have only skimmed the surface concerning mentoring in this book, we hope you will take time to learn more about the subject. There is an activity focused on mentoring on the STUDIO website (www.bloomsburyfashioncentral.com).

Lifelong Learning

One last topic for consideration before concluding this text: Although we have encouraged you to think through the career path you want to follow before embarking on your first job, we also encourage you to be flexible and realize that your career path will not be linear. As mentioned in Box 10.1, Dr. Laura McAndrew's research shows that many career paths resemble "lattices" rather than ladders. Also, as Collin Wood Perdew (profiled in Careers Up Close 10.1 of this chapter) suggests, you should always remain open to opportunities you hear about that interest you and take advantage of every opportunity you have to continue learning. Participating in lifelong learning will not only keep you relevant in the fast-paced job market, but it will also keep your mind sharp and help you to identify interests you may not know you have. As you progress through your career, acquiring other skills and interests will also make it easier for you to redefine yourself and your career when (not *if*) that time comes. Take every opportunity to participate in workshops offered at your place of employment, and when possible, volunteer to take a leadership role in planning those workshops if they are centered on a topic in which you are particularly competent. Although there seems to be no consensus on how many times people will change careers in their lifetime, it is generally agreed that change, whether it be career-related or simply job-related, is the one constant. Adding new skills to your résumé and into your portfolio will definitely serve you well when new opportunities present themselves.

CAREERS UP CLOSE 10.1
COLLIN WOOD PERDEW
Senior Manager for Retail Implementation
US Cellular HQ

Collin Wood Perdew was already taking advantage of every opportunity to build her résumé and skill set in fashion and business, even before she had any formal college education. Collin started working for The Limited as a teenager, beginning her journey onto the career path of retail merchandising.

Collin realized early on that her interest lay in the creative side of retail. She started gaining experience working for successful retailers such as Stein Mart®, Jo-Ann Fabrics, Burdines, and Robb & Stucky. Her desire to achieve led her to roles in visual merchandising and interior design, creating planograms and stage sets. Before she had completed her associate's degree in design, she had become the Visual Merchandiser–Flagship Store for the number one women's retailer in the United States: Chico's FAS, Inc.

Collin eventually combined her knowledge and experience to start her own consulting business called Driving Fore Profit, with a focus on visual merchandising geared to the golf industry. Her company branched out to include educational seminars for AGM, the PGA, and universities. This new area helped Collin to hone her verbal presentation skills.

Realizing that more formal education was important to her, both personally and professionally, she began researching college programs. When Collin and her husband relocated to Illinois, it gave her an opportunity to go back to school to complete her bachelor's degree in textiles, apparel, and merchandising. Having put her career on hold while pursuing her degree, Collin approached her education in the same professional manner that she had approached her career. She was able to bring her work experiences to the classroom, reached out to her professors to form positive relationships, and developed her leadership skills as the President of the Fashion Industries Organization on campus. Despite her extensive retail experience, she completed the executive internship program with Target Corporation. Her willingness to compile knowledge and experience with a new retailer only helped to enhance her résumé and career network.

Upon graduation, Collin accepted a position at Sears Holdings Management Corporation, where she was the Creative Manager for Store Environments and Design. This position was an excellent fit for Collin's experience in fashion and retail merchandising. This position allowed her to spearhead the design of all shop concepts in Sears stores, including the high-profile Kardashian Kollection. The position also required Collin to communicate and coordinate the store design among construction units, business units, and all levels of Sears leadership to ensure successful implementation and adherence to corporate design standards.

As Collin's journey progressed, she realized that a new direction would broaden her skill set. When the opportunity to apply for a position in the social media department arose within Sears, she expressed an interest. Collin was subsequently promoted to Social Media and Digital Design Strategy Manager, where she coordinated social media campaigns within the Sears promotional calendar. Realizing the importance of social media within the retail sector today, Collin knew the new skills she developed here, coupled with her prior visual design and entrepreneurial experience, would be invaluable to her skill set, regardless of the type of career opportunities she chose to pursue in the future. Currently she is Senior Manager of Retail Implementation Visual Design and Instore Merchandising for US Cellular Corporate Headquarters in Chicago, and she is considering applying to MBA programs.

Throughout her career, Collin has taken advantage of many opportunities to learn about every aspect of the fashion-retailing industry and recognized the importance of networking. She maintains an active social media presence and frequently connects with others who are part of her professional network.

Projects

1. By now you should have identified at least three positions that interest you. Using the Internet, look up the typical entry-level salaries for each. A particularly useful online tool for doing this is the Salary Wizard at www.collegegrad.com or one of the salary calculators found at www.quintcareers.com/salary-negotiation. Identify salaries for each of the positions in your job market and in a different job market that interests you. Report the following:

   a. The salaries in each job market, comparing and contrasting your findings

   b. What you think might account for the differences and similarities that you found

   c. Some other factors you would need to consider in deciding which is the best salary

2. Identify someone at your college, or another young professional, who has recently accepted a job offer. Interview that person about the factors that were most important in reaching an employment decision. If multiple offers were considered, what was (were) the deciding factor(s)? Compare your results with those of your classmates. Were you able to identify any areas not listed on the job evaluation checklist available on the *STUDIO* website? Do you agree with the factors the person used in making the decision?

3. Identify someone who has recently quit a job or changed careers. Interview him or her as to what factors led to the decision to depart. Were there any factors that could have kept this person at the position or in the career that he or she recently left? What is your reaction to the findings?

4. Identify someone who has accepted a job that he or she later regretted. Discuss with this person how the situation may have been avoided. What could have been done differently when evaluating the position initially? Also talk with this person about what was learned from the experience and what advice he or she may have for others.

5. Identify someone who has a mentor. Discuss with this person what qualities the mentor possesses that are most admired and what some of the most important things are that the mentor has taught him or her.

6. Identify someone who is a mentor. Discuss with this person what he or she likes about being a mentor and ask for advice regarding finding a mentor.

Questions for Discussion

1. What are the most important job factors to you in considering an offer? Explain your answers.

2. Do you think that salary is the most important factor to consider when evaluating a job offer? Why or why not?

3. What are some concerns you may have in terms of negotiating a job offer? What could you do to lessen your concerns?

4. Do you agree that you should never accept one job offer and then back out if a better offer comes your way? Defend your position.

5. Why is it important to prepare a strategy for evaluating a job offer?

6. What would be the most likely reason that you would reject a job offer?

7. What are some qualities you would like to see in a professional mentor?

8. Do you feel it is important to have a mentor at a new job? Why or why not?

9. What are some positive things you could do to make you stand out during the first few weeks at a new job?

10. What strategies could you use to cope with the stress of transitioning from being a college student to a young professional in your first career position?

11. What would you do if you found yourself in a job you did not like after a few months?

12. What are some legitimate reasons for leaving a job in a shorter time than normally expected?

13. Why is it important to not let co-workers know that you are looking for another job?

14. Why it is important not to "burn bridges" when resigning from your job? Identify three reasons.

STUDIO Activities

Visit the *Guide to Fashion Career Planning STUDIO* available at www
.bloomsburyfashioncentral.com. The key elements are:

1. Summary of Chapter 10 text
2. Leadership quiz
3. "Stay or Go" checklist
4. Job offer checklist
5. Sample acceptance letter template
6. Sample resignation letter template
7. Relocation Activity
8. Links to professional associations' websites

VIDEO: Approaching a Job Transition

References

Adams, S. (2014). Most Americans are unhappy at work. *Forbes*. Available online:
http://www.forbes.com/sites/susanadams/2014/06/20/most-americans-are
-unhappy-at-work/

Cheng, B., Kan, M., Gad, L., & Ray, R. L.(2014). Job satisfaction: 2014 edition.
The Conference Board. Available online: https://www.conference-board.org
/publications/publicationdetail.cfm?publicationid=2785

Clark, D. R. (August 17, 2015). Leadership styles. Available online: http://nwlink
.com/~donclark/leader/leadstl.html

Feitelberg, R. (June 4, 2015). Victoria Beckham talks fashion, family and fame at 92Y.
Available online: http://www.wwd.com/fashion-news/fashion-features/victoria
-beckham-92y-fern-mallis-10142335/

Ousborne, J. (n.d.) How to deal with office politics. *WetFeet*. Available online: http://
schools.wetfeet.com/advice-tools/on-the-job/how-to-deal-with-office-politics

Sandberg, S., & Scovell, N. (2013). *Lean in: Women, work, and the will to lead*. New
York: Knopf.

GLOSSARY

Academic research (Chapter 1): Careful study of a given subject, field, or problem, undertaken to discover facts or principles.

Advertising (Chapter 1): The activity of attracting public attention to a product or business, as by paid announcements in the print, broadcast, or electronic media.

Allocation Analyst (Chapter 1): The person who determines the amount and type of inventory that the company should make available to operate most efficiently and achieve financial goals. (see Planner).

American Marketing Association (Chapters 3, 9): Professional organization for people in the marketing profession.

Analytical ability (Chapter 2): Aptitude relating to analysis; having the skills to use analysis to solve a problem.

Analytical skills (Chapter 2): The ability to visualize, articulate, conceptualize, or solve both complex and uncomplicated problems by making decisions that are sensible given the available information.

Analytics (Chapter 1): The systematic computational analysis of data or statistics.

Apparel (Chapter 1): Clothing; merchandise that is worn on the body.

Area Manager (Chapter 1): A manager who is responsible for a company's work in a specific part of the country; can also refer to the manager of a particular section of a store or business.

Assertiveness (Chapter 2): The quality of being self-assured, confident, and able to act on what one thinks should be done.

Assessment (Chapter 4): An evaluation; the act of assessing; e.g., evaluating how a student did in a course or a program of study.

Assessment portfolio (Chapter 4): Portfolio that demonstrates growth and accomplishments over a period of time; commonly used in academia for program evaluation.

Assistant Buyer (Chapter 1): Entry-level position in the area of buying; assists with the process of placing and evaluating orders for merchandise under the direction of the buyer. Responsible for day-to-day communications with sales reps on behalf of the buyer.

Associate Buyer (Chapter 1): In some organizations, this is an entry-level position; for others, it is an intermediate position between assistant buyer and buyer. Assists with the process of placing and evaluating orders for goods, whether for stores, institutions, or other settings.

Assistant Store Manager (Chapter 1): The assistant store manager reports to the store manager and carries out duties in his/her absence. Typically, the assistant store manager is an entry-level, full-time, permanent position in a retail store that prepares successful incumbents to move into store management positions and beyond.

Atelier (Chapter 1): The workroom of a couture designer.

Attention to detail (Chapter 2): Thoroughness and accuracy when accomplishing a task through concern for all the areas involved.

Behavioral interview (Chapter 7): Situation in which job seekers are asked to relate stories and experiences about how they have handled challenges in the past.

Block format (letter) (Chapter 6): Letter-writing format that uses one-inch margins, with everything typed flush left and one-line spacing between each paragraph.

Blogging (Chapters 1, 5): Maintaining or adding new entries to a blog.

Brand (Chapter 3): A category of merchandising provided by a given manufacturer or company. The make, designated to a specific retailer or manufacturer, as indicated by a name, stamp, or trademark.

Brand Rep (Chapter 1): A wholesaler, or sales representative (sales rep), responsible for obtaining orders from retail stores for the manufacturing company. Sales reps generally work with store buyers to provide merchandise for the store's customers; sometimes referred to as *road reps* because they are assigned geographic territories and usually travel a great deal to visit clients.

Business letter (Chapter 7): A formal type of communication that is usually typed on white stationery paper. Business letters must be targeted to a specific individual or group, have a clear and concise purpose, be convincing, and usually end with a specific objective, like a meeting date.

Buyer/Buying (Chapter 1, 2): The buyer is typically the highest-ranking merchant, and is responsible for a staff of people; negotiates prices and details of delivery with manufacturers and suppliers of the store's merchandise. Also responsible for merchandise analysis, forecasting marketplace and consumer trends, and procuring merchandise.

Buying Office (Chapter 1): Also referred to as an RBO (resident buying office); usually located in wholesale markets such as New York City and provides all services to member retailers related to making appropriate purchasing decisions.

Career (Chapter 1): A series of jobs that have a focus in a certain professional realm and progress in a pattern of upward mobility over time.

Career fair (Chapter 5): An event/exposition for employers, recruiters, and schools to meet with prospective jobseekers.

Career lattice (Chapter 10): Enables employees to move in several different directions rather than just upward as with a career ladder.

Case study (Chapter 8): A process or record of research in which detailed consideration is given to the development of a particular person, group, or situation over a period of time. Also a scenario given to students in order to provide examples of business situations for study and analysis.

CEO (Chapter 1): Chief Executive Officer; usually refers to the highest position in a company or corporation. Generally responsible for providing the company's vision, forming alliances, and overseeing all senior-level management.

Chain of command (Chapter 10): In business, the levels of authority within a company from the top position, such as the CEO or owner, down to the employees on the frontline.

Chronological format résumé (Chapter 6): Résumé that is formatted in a way that lists job experiences from most recent to furthest in the past.

Code of ethics (Chapter 9): A set of rules, based on personal or company values, guiding the behavior of an individual or a group of people.

COO (Chapter 1): Chief Operating Officer; typically the executive responsible for overseeing daily operations of the business and achieving the company's vision.

Co-ops (Chapter 8): Formal arrangements that recognize the educational component of the work experience; completed by students to gain practical work experience in their field of study.

Color theory (Chapter 2): A body of practical guidance to color mixing and the visual and emotional effects of specific color combinations.

Company culture (Chapter 7): The beliefs and behaviors that determine how a company's employees and management interact and handle outside business transactions. Often, corporate culture is implied, not expressly defined, and develops organically over time from the cumulative traits of the people the company hires.

Computer-aided design (CAD) programs (Chapter 2): Allows product developers and designers to easily manipulate ideas electronically, making it a much more efficient way to design clothing than the old-school method of drawing on paper.

Consultant (Chapter 1): An employment pattern that involves a succession of short-term contracts and part-time work, focused on an area of specialization, rather than the more traditional model of a long-term single job (see Freelancer).

Consumer behavior (Chapter 2): The study of individuals, groups, or organizations and the processes they use to select, secure, use, and dispose of products, services, experiences, or ideas to satisfy needs along with the impacts that these processes have on the consumer and society.

Corporate designer (Chapter 1): The corporate designer coordinates the ideas of design assistants and trend specialists to refine and finalize the fashion products to be developed for a given season or line that are presented on behalf of the company (rather than an individual designer).

Couture (Chapter 1): Hand sewn garments; associated with a designer who represents a "house" or design company.

Cover letter (Chapter 6): Accompanies a job application along with the résumé; provides detailed information on why you are qualified for the job you are applying for. Effective cover letters explain the reasons for your interest in the specific organization and identify your most relevant skills or experiences.

Cross-cultural communication (Chapter 2): A field of study that looks at how people from differing cultural backgrounds communicate, in similar and different ways among themselves, and how they endeavor to communicate across cultures. Intercultural communication is a related field of study.

Curator (Chapter 1): A keeper or custodian of a museum or other collection.

Customer (Chapter 1): Typically the customer is the end purchaser or user of a product; a wholesaler, however, might have a buyer as a customer. The customer is the person or company who purchases a given product or service.

Dean's List (Chapter 6): A list of students recognized for academic achievement during a semester by the dean of the college they attend.

Demographics (Chapter 2): Statistical data of a population, such as age, income, education, etc.

Department (Chapter 1): A division of a large organization, such as a government, university, business, or shop, dealing with a specific subject, commodity, or area of activity.

Department manager (Chapter 1): An individual who is in charge of a certain group of tasks, or a certain subset of a company.

Department store (Chapter 1): A large store stocking many varieties of goods in different classifications; each area of the store represents a different classification of merchandise and has its own manager or supervisor.

Design assistant (Chapter 1): Assists the head designer with any tasks required while also learning the trade from that designer.

Designer (Chapter 1): A person who plans the form, look, or workings of something (e.g., a piece of clothing) before it is made or built, typically by drawing or draping it in detail.

Diplomacy (Chapter 3): The art or science of conducting negotiations; skill in managing negotiations and handling people.

Display (Chapter 1): To make a prominent exhibition of (something) in a place where it can be easily seen.

District Manager (Chapter 1): Person in charge of an entire region where multiple stores operate. Whichever branches of the company operate within the district are the District Manager's responsibility.

Diversity (Chapter 2): The state of being diverse; variety.

Employment agency (Chapter 5): An agency that finds employers or employees for those seeking them (see Headhunter).

Entrepreneurship (Chapter 1): The enterprise of establishing one's own business venture, as opposed to working for others.

Ethical behavior (Chapters 2, 3, 9): Characterized by honesty, fairness, and equity in interpersonal, professional, and academic relationships and in research and scholarly activities. Ethical behavior respects the dignity, diversity, and rights of individuals and of groups of people.

Ethical dilemma (Chapter 9): Situations in which there is a choice to be made between two options, neither of which resolves the situation in an ethically acceptable fashion.

Ethics (Chapters 2, 9): Moral principles that govern a person's or group's behavior.

Ethnicity (Chapter 2): A group of people who share a particular set of biological and social traits.

Excel® (Chapter 2): A spreadsheet application developed by Microsoft for Microsoft Windows, Mac OS X, and iOS. It features calculation, graphing tools, and pivot tables.

Facebook® (Chapter 3): An online social networking service headquartered in Menlo Park, California, that was launched on February 4, 2004, by Mark Zuckerberg with his Harvard College roommates.

Fair Labor Standards Act (Chapter 8): A United States law that sets out various labor regulations regarding interstate commerce employment, including minimum wages, requirements for overtime pay, and limitations on child labor.

Fashion (Chapter 1): A diverse and exciting industry and career choice, involving trends for consumption, typically related to apparel, accessories, and home furnishings, but also including virtually all consumed products. Fashion industry components include design, product development, manufacturing, sourcing, retail, public relations, magazines, social compliance, and education.

Fashion Director (Chapter 1): Oversees the entire process of trend identification and promotion. It is the responsibility of the fashion director to coordinate store presentation, advertising, catalogs, and website messages so that the company is effectively promoting its image and communicating a consistent fashion message.

Fashion group (Chapter 3): Non-profit professional organization for the fashion apparel, accessories, beauty, and home furnishing industries.

Fashion industry (Chapter 1): The complex of designers, product developers, stylists, manufactures, sales force members, retailers, and promotional professionals who conceive of and provide apparel, accessories, jewelry, personal care, and related products to consumers in the global marketplace.

Fashion wholesaler (Chapter 2): Generally the person or company who sells their merchandise to buyers/retailers.

Faux pas (Chapter 7): An embarrassing or tactless act or remark in a social situation.

Flexibility (Chapter 2): The ability to be easily modified; adaptable to a situation.

Foursquare (Chapter 3): A local search and discovery service mobile app which provides search results for its users.

Freelancer (Chapter 1): An employment pattern that involves a succession of short-term contracts and part-time work, focused on an area of specialization, rather than the more traditional model of a long-term single job (see Consultant).

Functional format résumé (Chapter 6): Primarily highlights abilities, such as hiring, managing, or coaching, rather than chronological work history, although work history is also included.

Front person (Chapter 2): The one who interacts with customers, clients, vendors, or manufacturers.

Group interview (Chapter 7): Interview done with two or more candidates at the same time.

Hashtag (Chapter 3): The pound sign (#) preceding a word or phrase on a specific topic made popular by Twitter.

Head hunter (Chapter 5): A person who identifies and approaches suitable candidates employed elsewhere to fill business positions (see Employment Agency).

Heading (letter) (Chapter 6): The address from which a letter is being sent (e.g., your address).

Historic preservation (Chapter 1): Activities that focus on preservation of historic artifacts; in the fashion realm, it is focused on preserving textiles and home furnishings of periods, with emphasis on retaining artifacts that depict specific prominent fashions and styles of the given period.

Human Resources (Chapter 1): The personnel of a business or organization, especially when regarded as a significant asset.

Infographics (Chapter 6): Visual presentation of statistics, commonly with charts or graphs and minimal text.

Inside address (Chapter 6): The address you are sending a letter to.

Instagram (Chapter 3): An online, mobile, photo-sharing, video-sharing, and social networking service that enables its users to share pictures and videos on a variety of social networking platforms, such as Facebook, Twitter, Tumblr, and Flickr.

Instructor (Chapter 1): A person who teaches; in a formal capacity, an instructor is paid to teach information about which s/he has expertise in a classroom setting (see Lecturer and Professor).

Interpersonal communication (Chapter 5): The process by which people exchange information, feelings, and meaning through verbal and non-verbal messages; it is face-to-face communication.

Interpersonal relationship (Chapter 2): A strong, deep, or close association or acquaintance between two or more people that may range in duration from brief to enduring. This association may be based on inference, love, solidarity, regular business interactions, or some other type of social commitment.

Lecturer (Chapter 1): A person who teaches; in a formal capacity, a lecturer is paid to teach information about which s/he has expertise in a classroom setting (see Instructor and Professor). A lecturer may act as an independent agent (see Consultant) to speak about topics of interest or about which s/he has experience and expertise.

Lifelong learning (Chapter 10): The "ongoing, voluntary, and self-motivated" pursuit of knowledge for either personal or professional reasons.

LinkedIn (Chapter 3): A business-oriented social networking service. Founded in December 2002 and launched on May 5, 2003, it is mainly used for professional networking.

Line: A collection of related product pieces from a manufacturer, such as a "clothing line."

Long-term goals (Chapter 2): Goals that take a long time to achieve.

Loyalty (Chapter 2): A strong feeling of support or allegiance.

MAGIC (Chapter 1): The trade show featuring men's, women's, junior's, and children's apparel, footwear, accessories, and manufacturing resources; held biannually (February and August) in Las Vegas.

Manager-in-Training (MIT) (Chapter 1): Refers to an entry-level position; usually the position before one becomes an assistant manager of a store or department.

Manufacturer Sales Representative (Chapter 1): A wholesaler, or sales representative (sales rep), is responsible for obtaining orders from retail stores for the manufacturing company. Sales reps generally work with store buyers to provide merchandise for the store's customers. Some manufacturer sales representatives are referred to as *road reps* because they are assigned geographic territories and usually travel a great deal to meet with heir clients.

Manufacturing (Chapter 1): Production; the act of making products on a large scale using machinery.

Marketing Coordinator (Chapter 1): Ensures that the retailers' advertising and promotion program is developed and implemented at the local, national, and international levels.

Market research (Chapter 1): The action or activity of gathering information about consumers' needs and preferences.

Market Week: A common time when buyers shop with wholesalers for the products to carry in their retail stores; usually in a particular marketplace such as NYC or LA.

Mentor (Chapter 10): A person or friend who guides a less experienced person by building trust and modeling positive behaviors.

Mentee (Chapter 10): A person who is advised, trained, or counseled by a mentor.

Merchandise Coordinator (Chapter 1): The person whose responsibility it is to present fashion goods and other consumer products through retail venues (including, but not limited to, stores, catalogs,

and online) in ways that reflect company and brand values. This might involve buying activities (securing the merchandise) or might be limited to display and promotional activities, depending on the company's job description (see Merchandiser).

Merchandiser (Chapter 1): The person whose responsibility it is to present fashion goods and other consumer products through retail venues (including, but not limited to, stores, catalogs, and online) in ways that reflect company and brand values. This might involve buying activities (securing the merchandise) or might be limited to display and promotional activities, depending on the company's job description (see Merchandise Coordinator).

Merchandising (Chapter 1): Also referred to as *merchandise planning*. Involves planning for the sales of merchandise and products through effective marketing and displays. The act of merchandising might involve buying activities (securing the merchandise) or might be limited to display and promotional activities, depending on the company's job description.

National Association of Colleges and Employers (NACE) (Chapter 2): Provides publications, professional development events, etc., to help career services and recruitment professionals achieve their goals. See http://www.nace.org/

National Retail Federation (NRF) (Chapter 1): The retail industry's largest advocacy organization, which advances the industry through professional seminars, trade conferences, publications, and educational activities. See https://nrf.com/

Negotiation (Chapter 2): A discussion aimed at reaching an agreement. Successful negotiations consider the interests of both parties and reach a mutually acceptable outcome, often involving compromise by one or both parties.

Networking (Chapter 3): The act of meeting people who can enhance your access to professional opportunities and people with whom you might work in the future. Networking also includes meeting people who can benefit from your knowledge and experiences.

Nontraditional piercing (Chapter 7): In US culture, body piercings in places other than women's ears. For example, nose, tongue, and nipple piercings, and also earrings for men.

Non-verbal messages (Chapter 7): Communication through sending and receiving wordless cues.

Typically body posture, hand gestures, and eye/facial expressions send non-verbal messages.

Office politics (Chapter 10): A work environment that involves struggles for power and tactics people take to get ahead; involves differences in opinions and decision making; can create hostile work environment among workers.

Online retailers (Chapter 1): Merchants who offer their goods for sale to consumers via the Internet.

Part-time college teacher (Chapter 1): A person who instructs college classes but is not a full-time employee of the educational institution. Typically, a practicing professional teaches on evenings or weekends in the area of his/her career.

PDF (Chapter 4): Portable document format; a format that allows viewing of a document, on a computer, in a standard fixed layout.

Performance review and evaluation portfolio (Chapter 3): A document that presents past goals and the evidence of tasks and accomplishments demonstrating how those goals were met. This document is typically used by the employee to reflect upon and present accomplishments and by the supervisor to assess the employee's performance.

Personal brand (Chapter 3): Identification of a persona associated with a person developed for the purpose of marketing oneself and advancing one's career. The personal-branding concept supports the idea that success comes from self-packaging.

Personal mission statement (Chapter 6): A declaration of one's values and goals presented in a way that documents a plan for work. This statement offers the opportunity to establish what is important and can serve as a guide when making decisions about career options and personal activities.

Pinterest (Chapter 3): A free website that requires registration to use. Users can upload, save, sort, and manage images—known as pins—and other media content (e.g., videos and images) through collections known as pinboards. Pinterest acts as a personalized media platform. Users can browse the content of others on the main page.

Planner (Chapter 1): A specially trained and experienced individual who possesses a unique combination of knowledge and analytical ability, as well as strong communication and presentation skills. The job of a planner involves making decisions about the merchandise that is distributed to each store (see Allocation Analyst).

Portfolio (Chapter 4): A document, displayed in a large binder or electronically, that shows evidence of work style and accomplishments. Often used by designers to show the range of work achieved as well as depicting the style of art, portfolios can also showcase work of merchants and stylists. Think of a portfolio as a "file cabinet" of items that "tell your story" as a professional. The careful precision demonstrated in compiling a portfolio presents valuable information to the observer about the creator's abilities.

Prioritize (Chapter 2): To designate or treat (something) as more important than other things.

Product design (Chapter 1): The process of creating a new item to be sold by a business to its customers. A very broad concept, it is essentially the efficient and effective generation and development of ideas through a process that leads to new merchandise. Design differs from development in the way a concept is generated, with designing being more original and innovative.

Product development (Chapter 1): The process of designing, creating, and marketing new products or services to benefit customers. Sometimes referred to as new product development, the discipline is focused on developing systematic methods for guiding all the processes involved in getting a new product to market. Development differs from design in the way that a new concept is generated, with development more of a conversation between the developer and the manufacturer with respect to specifications of the product, and design being more innovative in developing new concepts.

Professional (Chapters 1, 2, 3): A person competent or skilled in a particular activity, possessing key dispositions such as a body of knowledge, value for lifelong learning, commitment to one's company and industry, awareness and execution of professional communication, personal contribution to the field, and career advancement.

Professor (Chapter 1): A teacher of the highest rank in a college or university, with progressions from the entry-level Assistant Professor and the mid-level Associate Professor as intermediary career positions. The term *professor* is often used generically to denote a full-time college or university teacher in any of the aforementioned ranks.

Profit-sharing (Chapter 10): A system in which the people who work for a company receive a direct share of the profits.

Promotion (Chapter 1): Activity that supports or provides active encouragement for the furtherance of a cause, venture, or aim. In a career, a promotion indicates a step forward with greater compensation and greater responsibilities.

Protégé (Chapters 5, 8): Synonymous with *mentee*; a person who is advised, trained, or counseled by a mentor.

Public relations (Chapter 1): The professional maintenance of a favorable public image by a company or other organization or a famous person.

Quality Assurance Assistant (Chapter 1): Quality assurance personnel work, often in laboratory settings, to guarantee the quality of the goods their firms produce. Their responsibilities include verifying dimensions, color, weight, texture, strength, or other physical characteristics of their products.

QR (Quick Response) codes (Chapter 3): The square icons that are printed on many items, such as music posters, corporate advertisements, sales receipts, business cards, and résumés, for the purpose of being read by a mobile device app, which converts the message so that the desired website or PDF opens on the mobile device.

Recruiter (Chapter 7): An individual who works to fill job openings in businesses or organizations.

Regional Manager (Chapter 1): A career position that oversees stores and supervises store managers within a specified geographic region.

Reference page (Chapter 6): The last section of an essay or research paper that has been written in consultation with already published information. The reference page lists all publications that have been cited within the document.

Researcher (Chapter 1): Someone who conducts an organized and systematic investigation into a given topic, with the expected outcome to publish or otherwise disseminate the findings.

Résumé (Chapter 6): A brief account of a person's education, qualifications, and previous experience, typically sent with a job application.

Retailers (Chapter 1): Businesses that offer goods for sale to end-use consumers.

Retail chain (Chapter 2): An assortment of two or more stores that share a brand name and central management; these stores usually have standardized business methods and practices.

Retail management (Chapter 1): A career path that involves work within stores overseeing the merchandise assortment, operational activities, and supervision of employees.

Retail Sales Associate (Chapter 1): A store-based employee whose primary role is to interact with customers and provide service that incentivizes and results in sales.

Road rep (Chapter 1): Some manufacturer sales representatives are referred to as *road reps* because they are assigned geographic territories and usually travel a great deal to interact with their clients.

Salary Wizard® (Chapter 10): An interactive internet tool, available on www.salary.com, that enables searches for typical entry-level salary levels associated with specific career positions and geographic areas.

Sales rep (Chapter 1, 2): A wholesaler, or sales representative (sales rep), is responsible for obtaining orders from retail stores for the manufacturing company. Sales reps generally work with store buyers to provide merchandise for the store's customers. Some manufacturer sales representatives are referred to as *road reps* because they are assigned geographic territories and usually travel a great deal to their clients.

Salutation (Chapter 6): In a letter, the initial greeting; e.g., *Dear Sir.*

Selling (Chapter 1): The act of offering merchandise to consumers for purchase. Active selling involves working with customers, understanding their needs, and executing a persuasive and helpful interaction, resulting in a consumer purchase.

Short-term goals (Chapter 2): A list of anticipated accomplishments that are expected to be completed within about 1 year.

Showroom (Chapter 1): The wholesaler's selling space. Sometimes a market facility is rented at a seasonal marketplace; other times a permanent showroom is operated, often in an urban district where like products are geographically near to one another.

Showroom assistant (Chapter 1): An entry-level position based in a showroom. The role is to assist sales reps with daily business operations that occur in that space.

Snapchat (Chapter 3): A fun messaging application for sharing pictures and videos. You can take a photo or a video, add a caption or doodle, and send it to a contact or add it to your story to share with some or all of your contacts (friends). Friends can view snaps for up to ten seconds, and then they disappear from the viewing device.

Social Compliance Auditor (Chapter 1): The career position whose responsibilities include assessing the activities of a company (often a manufacturing company that is contracted by a brand-holding company) to ensure that practices are aligned with laws, contract terms, and industry standards (see Social Compliance Manager).

Social Compliance Manager (Chapter 1): The career position whose responsibilities include assessing the activities of a company (often a manufacturing company that is contracted by a brand-holding company) to ensure that practices are aligned with laws, contract terms, and industry standards. The manager may oversee a network of auditors (see Social Compliance Auditor).

Social media (Chapters 1, 3, 5): Websites and applications that enable users to create and share content or to participate in online networking activities.

Social Media Specialist (Chapter 1): The career position that is responsible for the consistent theme of the company's social media presentation and for monitoring and executing social media promotion, branding, and sales strategies.

Specialty store (Chapter 1): Retail businesses that focus on specific product categories, such as office supplies, men's or women's clothing, or floor coverings. The limited breadth of their product offering determines the categorization as a specialty store.

Stock broker (Chapter 9): A certified professional who buys and sells securities on a stock exchange on behalf of clients.

Stock options (Chapter 10): A benefit in the form of an option given by a company to an employee to buy stock in the company at a discount or at a stated fixed price.

Store Manager (Chapter 2): The person who is responsible for the day-to-day operations (or management) of a retail store and who supervises all of the employees of that store.

Store Owner (Chapter 1): A specific entrepreneurial role focused on financing and operating a retail 'brick and mortar' (store) venue.

Stylist (Chapter 1): Typically, a stylist is self-employed as a freelance agent who contracts work to dress talent (models and actors) in print, television, and motion picture industries. Some stylists work for corporations in which they oversee the visual presentation of advertising and display in print, television, and store venues.

Sumptuary regulations (Chapter 1): Rules governing the type of clothing that can be worn (often due to cultural or religious values; work dress codes are also an example).

Technical Designer (Chapter 1): The technical designer is the person who takes a designer's idea and translates it into the actual product. A primary responsibility in doing so is ensuring that the product can be manufactured efficiently and within a particular budget.

Toastmasters (Chapter 5): A professional organization that provides opportunities for its members to practice public speaking and refine their skills as speakers.

Trade publication (Chapter 5): Magazines and journals that are written for an audience of professionals within a given industry or field.

Transferable skills (Chapter 5): Skills that you have developed in one job, or life experience, that you can take to another job or life experience (e.g., decision making).

Trend (Chapter 1): A general direction in which something is developing or changing.

Tumblr (Chapter 3): A microblogging platform and social networking website founded by David Karp and owned by Yahoo! Inc. The service allows users to post multimedia and other content to a short-form blog.

Twitter (Chapter 3): An online social networking service that enables users to send and read short (140-character or less) messages called "tweets." Registered users can read and post tweets, but unregistered users can only read them.

Vendor (Chapter 2): A person who represents the company, or the company itself, who offers merchandise at the wholesale level to be purchased by a retailer. The vendor is the supplier of merchandise to the retailer.

Virtual interview (Chapter 7): An interview that occurs via web-based or other electronic means such as Google+ or Skype®. This format enables people to engage in interviews without physical travel.

Visual merchandising (Chapter 1): The activity and profession of developing floor plans and three-dimensional displays in order to maximize sales. Both goods and services can be displayed to highlight their features and benefits.

Wholesaler (Chapter 1, 2): An intermediary entity in the distribution channel who buys in bulk and sells to resellers rather than to consumers.

Women's Wear Daily (Chapter 5): A fashion-industry trade journal, widely known and referred to as WWD and sometimes called "the bible of fashion."

Work–family balance (Chapter 10): An equilibrium, measured differently by different people, between the conflicting demands of time and effort at work and at home (in one's personal life). Lack of work–family (or work–life) balance often generates specific issues (e.g., need for child care provided by employers, flexible work schedules, relationship stress) to resolve these opposing forces.

Work under pressure (Chapter 2): The stress or urgency of matters requiring attention, specifically when facing a firm deadline.

YouTube® (Chapter 3): A video-sharing website headquartered in San Bruno, California, that enables individuals, companies, and other organizations to post videos for public consumption.

INDEX

hobbies and career, 3, 34, 82, 167, 226, 291

Hobby Lobby (store), 157

Hochwater, Wayne, 262, 264

Holoubek, Heather, 295–6

honor societies, 152

honesty/integrity, 55–6, 72, 194; and ethics, 112, 247–69; in interviews, 194–8

Hootsuite, 86

hoovers.com (Web site), 121

Hosler, Olivia, 24–5

How Could You Do That? (Schlessinger), 261

Huhman, Heather, 77

human resources, 15, 75, 123

human rights and ethics, 248, 252–3

Hurd, Helen G., 69

Hurst, Jessica, 217

in-basket exercise, 50

In Her Makeup Bag (blog), 97

initiative, 42–3, 49–50, 53, 63, 108, 157, 196, 206, 217, 228, 231, 243

insider knowledge, 263

Instagram, 24, 34, 84, 87–9, 92, 97

in-store training, 7, 9, 227

instructor, 35; full time, 36; part time, 35. *See also* teacher

International Boutique Show, 8

Internet (Web sites), 2, 83–90; copyright, 113–14; on ethics, 271; for job search, 121; for portfolio, 104–10; on salary ranges, 285. *See also* electronic mail

internships, 211–13, 220; at AmericasMart, 225–6; appropriate, 224–5; best practices, 231–3; in buying, 222–3; compensation for, 230; contacts for, 234–7; contribution to the company, 231; duration of, 230; environment, 227–8; evaluating, 243; expectations for, 230–1; expenses in, 180; feedback, 242–3; goals, 230, 238–9; journal, 242; listed on resume, 159; making the most of, 239–41; mentor for, 237–8; in merchandising, 225, 231–3; multiple, 212, 221, 222–3; negotiation, 221; networking, 130; note taking in, 240, 242; and portfolio, 112; in product development, 218–20; resources

and information on, 233–4; in sales, 5, 78–80, 223; searching for, 130; Smithsonian, 30; stylist assistant, 35, 95–6; timeline, 214–16; tips and techniques, 213–14; value of, 230

interpersonal skills, 48. *See also* people skills

interviews, 137–8; appearance/attire for, 189–91; appropriate questions for, 193–4, 198; behavior, 191; common questions in, 191, 197; confidence in, 181, 186, 188; duration of, 204; establishing verbal contact prior to, 18–83; ethics for, 266; evaluation of, 204; follow-up, 205; honesty in, 194–5; money question in, 198–9; most frequent mistakes in, 189, 193; nonverbal behavior in, 191; and organizational culture, 254; and portfolio, 96, 101, 110, 208; practice, 127, 196; preparation for, 186–9, 196–7; questions for interviewer, 198–9; response to questions in, 191–3; scheduling of, 182–6; settings, 200–4; recorded practice, 186; situational, 261; telephone, 200; telephone etiquette for, 182–4; tests in, 189; tips for success in, 208; virtual, 201–2

Ipaye, Halimat (Hali), 36

JCPenney (retail company), 17–18, 23, 58, 222, 255, 258; Business Ethics Policy, 258

Jo Ann Fabrics (company), 154

job changes, 302; resignation, 301; while still employed, 300. *See also* career advancement

job fairs: *See* employer fairs; career fairs

job offers, 283–91; accepting, 289–90; evaluating, 283–5; multiple, 286–9; negotiation of, 285–6; rejecting, 290; relocation for, 57, 230, 292; and satisfaction, 293–7

job satisfaction, 284, 287; dissatisfaction, 143; with internship, 229, 239, 297

job search, 118–32; 135–6; 138, 226; assessment of, 138; college resources for, 122; Internet sites for, 121; for internships, 130; landing your perfect job; 175–6; myths about, 142–3; networking

for, 129–30, 135–6, 144–5; in newspapers, 131; proverbs about, 119–20; and relocation, 57, 262; resources for, 83–93; 121–33; responding to failure in, 137; in trade publications, 131; websites, 121. *See also* interviews

Jobvite, 83–4, 93, 121

journal keeping, 242. *See also* notebook

Journey Shoes (company), 88

Joynoelle (brand), 34, 80–2

Kansas City, 246

Kardashian Kollection (brand), 153

Kenner, Jane, 104

Kenya, 73

Ketch, Emily Ellerbrock, 57

Ketz, J. Edward, 268–9

Kikuyu, 73–4

King, MacKenzie, 16, 78, 224–5

Klaus, Peggy, 265

Klein, Hannah, 221

K-Mart (retailer), 153, 186

Kohl?s Department Stores, 2, 5, 21, 23, 49, 61, 255

Krueger, Brian, 128, 149

Lane Bryant (store), 17

leadership skills, 43; in interview, 144, 147; in portfolio, 73, 77

Lean In: Women, Work, and the Will to Lead (Sandberg), 303

Leave your mark: Land your dream job. Kill it in your career. Rock social media (Licht), 67, 82

Lescault, Ava, 84

letter writing, 167, 168–72, 173: acceptance letter, 289; components, 168–72; job rejection, 290; post-interview thank-you, 205; recommendation letter, 113; resignation letter, 301. *See also* cover letters

Licht, Aliza, 41, 67, 82, 93

lifelong learning, 71, 303

Lilly Pulitzer (brand), 27

Limited, The (retailer), 6, 14, 30, 58, 152, 177

LinkedIn, 11, 85–6, 90, 92–3, 98–9, 109, 114, 121, 127, 135–6, 140, 165, 175–6, 214, 235–6, 241, 290

Listening, 29, 46, 57

Living Ethics (Bugeja), 253